The *Essential* Practitioner's Handbook of Personal Construct Psychology

D1073579

The *Essential* Practitioner's Handbook of Personal Construct Psychology

Edited by

Fay Fransella
Centre for Personal Construct Psychology
and *University of Hertfordshire, UK*

JOHN WILEY & SONS, LTD

Copyright © 2005 John Wiley & Sons Ltd, The Atrium, Southern Gate, Chichester,
West Sussex PO19 8SQ, England

Telephone (+44) 1243 779777

Email (for orders and customer service enquiries): cs-books@wiley.co.uk
Visit our Home Page on www.wiley.com

All Rights Reserved. No part of this publication may be reproduced, stored in a retrieval system or
transmitted in any form or by any means, electronic, mechanical, photocopying, recording, scanning or
otherwise, except under the terms of the Copyright, Designs and Patents Act 1988 or under the terms
of a licence issued by the Copyright Licensing Agency Ltd, 90 Tottenham Court Road, London W1T
4LP, UK, without the permission in writing of the Publisher. Requests to the Publisher should be
addressed to the Permissions Department, John Wiley & Sons Ltd, The Atrium, Southern Gate,
Chichester, West Sussex PO19 8SQ, England, or emailed to permreq@wiley.co.uk, or faxed to
(+44) 1243 770620.

Designations used by companies to distinguish their products are often claimed as trademarks. All
brand names and product names used in this book are trade names, service marks, trademarks or
registered trademarks of their respective owners. The Publisher is not associated with any product or
vendor mentioned in this book.

This publication is designed to provide accurate and authoritative information in regard to the subject
matter covered. It is sold on the understanding that the Publisher is not engaged in rendering professional services. If professional advice or other expert assistance is required, the services of a competent professional should be sought.

Other Wiley Editorial Offices

John Wiley & Sons Inc., 111 River Street, Hoboken, NJ 07030, USA

Jossey-Bass, 989 Market Street, San Francisco, CA 94103-1741, USA

Wiley-VCH Verlag GmbH, Boschstr. 12, D-69469 Weinheim, Germany

John Wiley & Sons Australia Ltd, 33 Park Road, Milton, Queensland 4064, Australia

John Wiley & Sons (Asia) Pte Ltd, 2 Clementi Loop #02-01, Jin Xing Distripark, Singapore 129809

John Wiley & Sons Canada Ltd, 22 Worcester Road, Etobicoke, Ontario, Canada M9W 1L1

Wiley also publishes its books in a variety of electronic formats. Some content that appears in print
may not be available in electronic books.

Library of Congress Cataloging-in-Publication Data
The *essential* practitioner's handbook of personal construct psychology / edited by Fay Fransella.
        p.   cm.
Includes bibliographical references and index.
     ISBN 0-470-01323-0
  1. Personal construct theory.   I. Fransella, Fay.
     BF698.9.P47E87 2005
     150.19′8—dc22

                                                                    2004029113

British Library Cataloguing in Publication Data
A catalogue record for this book is available from the British Library

ISBN 0-470-01323-0 (pbk)

Typeset in 10/12pt Times by SNP Best-set Typesetter Ltd., Hong Kong

Contents

Section III: How Can PCP Help Us to Understand People or Help Them to Change?

About the Editor

Fay Fransella is Founder and Director of the Centre for Personal Construct Psychology, Emeritus Reader in Clinical Psychology, University of London and Visiting Professor in Personal Construct Psychology at the University of Hertfordshire, UK. She has written eleven books, eight of them specifically relating to personal construct psychology and published over one hundred and fifty journal papers and chapters.

She trained and worked as an Occupational Therapist for ten years before taking a degree in psychology and a postgraduate diploma in clinical psychology in 1962. It was during her first job as a lecturer at the Institute of Psychiatry, London that she was introduced to George Kelly's personal construct psychology. It was a revolutionary alternative to the dominant behaviourism of the time. She found the view that we are all free agents responsible for what we make of the events which continually confront us particularly liberating. Since that time she has carried out research, mainly into problems of stuttering and weight, together with teaching and writing within the framework of Kelly's ideas.

International Advisory Panel

Dr Sean Brophy, *Rainsford, 59 Beaumont Road, Dublin 9, Ireland. E-mail: seanbrophy@eircom. net*

Dr Trevor Butt, *School of Human & Health Sciences, University of Huddersfield, UK. E-mail: t.butt@hud.ac.uk*

Dr Nelarine Cornelius, *Brunel Business School, Brunel University, UK. E-mail: nelarine.cornelius@brunel.ac.uk*

Ms Jacqui Costigan, *Late of La Trobe University, Victoria, Australia.*

Dr Pam Denicolo, *School of Pharmacy, Graduate School for the Social Sciences, University of Reading, UK. E-mail: p.m.denicolo@reading.ac.uk*

Dr Guillem Feixas, *Department of Psychology, University of Barcelona, Spain. E-mail: Gfeixas@psi.ub.es*

Dr Devorah Kalekin-Fishman, *Faculty of Education, University of Haifa, Israel. E-mail: dkalekin@construct.haifa.ac.il*

Professor James Mancuso, *Emeritus Professor of Psychology, Department of Psychology, University of Albany SUNY, USA. E-mail: mancuso@capital.net*

Associate Professor Dusan Stojnov, *Psychology Department, Faculty of Philosophy, University of Belgrade, Serbia and Montenegro. E-mail: dstojnov@f.bg.ac.yu*

Professor Linda Viney, *Department of Psychology, Wollongong University, Australia. E-mail lviney@uow.edu.au*

Professor David Winter, *Department of Psychology, University of Hertfordshire, and Barnet, Enfield and Haringey Mental Health Trust, UK. E-mail: d.winter@herts.ac.uk*

List of Contributors

Professor Jack Adams-Webber, *Department of Psychology, Brock University, St Catharines, Ontario, Canada L2S 3A1. E-mail: jadams@spartan.ac.brocku.ca*

Scott A. Baldwin, *Department of Psychology, University of Memphis, Memphis, TN 38152, USA*

Don Bannister, *Deceased*

Associate Professor Richard C. Bell, *Department of Psychology, University of Melbourne, Victoria 3010, Australia. E-mail: rcb@unimelb.edu.au*

Dr Sean Brophy, *Rainsford, 59 Beaumont Road, Dublin 9, Ireland. E-mail: seanbrophy@eircom.net*

Dr Nelarine Cornelius, *Brunel Business School, Brunel University, Uxbridge Campus, Uxbridge, Middlesex UB8 3PH, UK. E-mail: nelarine. cornelius@brunel.ac.uk*

Ms Jacqui Costigan, *Late of La Trobe University, Victoria, Australia.*

Dr Malcolm C. Cross, *Department of Psychology, City University, Northampton Square, London EC1V 0HB, UK. E-mail: m.c.cross@city.ac.uk*

Dr Peter Cummins, *Consultant Clinical Psychologist, Head of Adult Psychological Services, Coventry Healthcare NHS Trust, Gulson Hospital, Gulson Road, Coventry CV1 2HR, UK. E-mail: pac52@btinternet.com*

Dr Pam Denicolo, *School of Pharmacy/Graduate School for the Social Sciences, White Knight Campus, University of Reading, Earley, Reading RG6 1HY, UK. E-mail: p.m.denicolo@reading.ac.uk*

Dr Julie M. Ellis, *School of Nursing and Midwifery, La Trobe University, PO Box 199, Bendigo 3552, Australia. E-mail: J.Ellis@latrobe.edu.au*

Professor Franz R. Epting, *Department of Psychology, University of Florida, PO Box 112250, Gainesville, FL 32611-2250, USA. E-mail: epting@ufl.edu*

Fay Fransella, *Professor of Personal Construct Psychology, University of Hertfordshire, c/o The Sail Loft, Mulberry Quay, Falmouth TR11 3HD, UK. E-mail: Ffransella@aol.com*

Dr Brian R. Gaines, *Centre for Person–Computer Studies, 3635 Ocean View, Cobble Hill, British Columbia, Canada V0R 1L1. E-mail: brian@repgrid.com*

Marco Gemignani, *Department of Psychology, University of Florida, PO Box 112250, Gainesville, FL 32611-2250, USA*

Professor Devi Jankowicz, *Graduate Business School, University of Luton, Putteridge Bury, Hitchin Road, Luton, Bedfordshire LU2 8LE, UK. E-mail: animas@ntlworld.com*

George A. Kelly, *Deceased*

Professor Robert A. Neimeyer, *Department of Psychology, University of Memphis, Memphis TN 38152, USA. E-mail: neimeyer@cc.memphis.edu*

Professor Maureen Pope, *Institute of Education, Faculty of Economic and Social Sciences, University of Reading, Bulmershe Court, Earley, Reading RG6 1HY, UK. E-mail: mjpope@waitrose.com*

John Porter, *Interactions Ltd, Foxglove, Blackberry Lane, Delgany, Co. Wicklow, Ireland. E-mail: john@interactions.ie*

Dr Harry Procter, *70 Staplegrove Road, Taunton, Somerset TA1 1DJ, UK. E-mail: harry@procterh.freeserve.co.uk*

Dr Tom Ravenette, *Meadway House, 20 Meadway, Epsom, Surrey KT19 8JZ, UK*

Nick Reed, *74 Kingsway, Petts Wood, Kent BR5 1PT, UK. E-mail: nick@grid-pcp.co.uk*

Adrian Robertson, *Programme Director, Cabinet Office Centre for Management and Policy Studies, Sunningdale Park, Larch Avenue, Ascot, Berkshire SL5 0QE, UK. E-mail: adrian.robertson@cabinet-office.x.gsi.gov.uk*

Dr David Savage, *Director of Applied Psychology, Physical Education & Sports Science Department, University College of Chester, Parkgate Road, Chester CH1 4BJ, UK. E-mail: D.Savage@chester.ac.uk*

Professor Kenneth W. Sewell, *Department of Psychology, Box 311280, University of North Texas, Denton TX 76203, USA. E-mail: sewellk@unt.edu*

Dr Mildred L.G. Shaw, *Centre for Person–Computer Studies, 3635 Ocean View, Cobble Hill, British Columbia, Canada V0R 1L1. E-mail: mildred@repgrid.com*

Associate Professor Beverly M. Walker, *Psychology Department, University of Wollongong, Northfields Avenue, Wollongong, NSW 2522, Australia. E-mail: beverly_walker@uow.edu.au*

Julie Watkinson, *School of Nursing & Midwifery, Flinders University, GPO box 2100, Adelaide, Australia 5001. E-mail: Julie.watkinson@flinders.edu.au*

Professor David Winter, *Department of Psychology, University of Hertfordshire, Hatfield Campus, College Lane, Hatfield, Hertfordshire AL10 9AB and Barnet, Enfield and Haringey Mental Health Trust, UK. E-mail: d.winter@herts.ac.uk*

Preface

Any use to which personal construct psychology is put is, by definition, based on personal construct theory. Therefore, John Wiley & Sons' suggestion that I might select chapters of interest to 'users' or 'practitioners' at first sight seemed impossible. But, as many at the sharp end of practical work know, a problem that looks intractable at first glance turns out to be soluble when examined in depth.

It became clear to me when looking through this present book's birthplace, the *International Handbook of Personal Construct Psychology*, that all accounts of practice in that book were embedded within their theoretical core. So, I made a rough selection of chapters that might be construed as being particularly informative for 'users' and called upon the opinion of all those on the International Advisory Panel which had been created for the *International Handbook*. What is contained in this *Essential* and shortened version of the original Handbook is the result of their enormously helpful comments and opinions.

The job of the Advisers was not over yet. It seemed to me that the chapters selected had to be ordered in some way that made some sense to readers. There was also something else. I have always been of the opinion that George Kelly's ideas were written for all those who were interested in extending their understanding of themselves and others. That, of course, includes psychologists but is not limited to them. It was important to have sections in the book that were not based on activities of psychologists such as 'clinical', 'educational' and so forth.

The result of all this activity is that the first section explains 'what it is all about'. Although there could not be a chapter wholly on personal construct theory, the three chapters have a theoretical focus and talk about George Kelly the person, put his theory in the context of practice, emphasise its stress on feelings, and give an example of how one theory can inform practice in the particular context of organizations.

The second section focuses on practice and methods. But, again, theory is everpresent. No one (least of all Richard Bell) can talk about repertory grids without mentioning the dichotomy corollary nor laddering without the organization corollary, nor psychotherapy without a wide variety of theoretical constructs.

The third section describes what has been done with the theory and is divided into two parts. It is perhaps not surprising that there are two chapters on counselling and psychotherapy. The second chapter may, at first glance, seem not to fit easily into a 'users' book. But nowadays one cannot talk about these topics without considering that vexed question 'evidence-based practice'—one should not do anything that has not been *proved* to be effective. While there are many who argue that such an approach is not a good idea, anyone wanting to use personal construct psychotherapy or counselling will need to be able to state where it stands in relation to its 'evidence base'. The basis for the division of this section into two parts is a rough distinction between those chapters basically talking about work with individuals or small groups of individuals and work with large groups of people such as in organizations.

The last section is small, just two chapters, both of which look ahead of the present time. One looks at how personal construct psychotherapy has evolved since 1955 and where it might continue to evolve in the future. The other looks at where future users of personal construct psychology might come from. Some are exploring new areas of application already while others are just taking glimpses of 'what might be'. One thing that users can be certain of, or as certain as anyone can be about anything, is that *we are all forms of motion*. It is where we are going to move to which is the intriguing question.

Acknowledgements

There are so many who have given invaluable support to me in the creation of this book. Shortening the original Handbook of forty-three chapters could not have been accomplished without the support and help of the International Panel of Advisers, as I have indicated in the Preface.

A particular problem, I found, was how to divide the chapters up in a way that made sense to readers. Sean Brophy provided me with an idea that enabled me to see how this might be done. Perhaps the poet in him enables him to see through the words that can trap us and thus provide us with new ways of looking at our stereotypes. I thank him for all his help and support.

Ruth Graham took over from Vivien Ward as Psychology Editor for this book. I thank her for her continuous support and 'rapid response' to all moans and groans from me. I also found myself in contact with Gillian Leslie, Publishing Editor, for the first time. Gillian never seemed to mind spending time dealing with my many questions and problems in completing this book. Perhaps I should go as far as thanking John Wiley & Sons for looking after its authors so well.

Essential to preparing this book for publication, there has been, once again, my husband. He unfailingly provides help, sympathy, and tolerance as I struggle to fit everything in time-wise. He never complained when my computer claimed time that I would otherwise have spent with him.

I also want to thank those whose chapters could not be included in this book because their contributions in the *International Handbook of Personal Construct Psychology* are largely or wholly theoretical. I thank the following authors not only for their original contributions but also for their unfailing support of the idea of having a shorter and user-focussed version that automatically excluded them.

There are three chapters on personal construct theory and philosophy in the *International Handbook*. These are: by Ganriele Chiari and Maria Laura Nuzzo covering Kelly's philosophy of constructive alternativism, Trevor Butt's chapter discussing those ideas and phenomenology while Bill Warren looks at the degree to which pragmatism and religious ideas may have influenced Kelly. Spencer McWilliams writes about belief, attachment and awareness, Jack Adams-Webber provides an overview of research in personal construct psychology, and David Winter takes a new look at so-called 'psychological disorders'. In the social area, Devorah Kalekin-Fishman gives the first ever detailed account of the relationship between sociology and personal construct psychology in her chapter 'Social relations in the modern world', Jörn Scheer's talks about cross-cultural construing and there are two chapters on politics, one by Don Bannister (taken from a talk he gave) and one by Dusan Stojnov. In an educational setting, James Mancuso looks at the evidence of how children develop personal constructs, Phillida Salmon describes how personal construct psychology can provide a framework for teachers to work with and Martin Fromm discusses his research into what students actually learn from a lecture or seminar— not always what teachers like to think they learn. Because personal construct theory is basically about individuals, three describe how the theory has influenced their lives and work—these individuals are Dorothy Rowe, Miller Mair and Rue Cromwell. I thank you all.

What Personal Construct Psychology Is All About

CHAPTER 1

George Alexander Kelly: The Man and his Theory

Fay Fransella
University of Hertfordshire, UK

and

Robert A. Neimeyer
University of Memphis, USA

> . . . thinking of the scientist and the thinking of the human subject should be considered to be governed by the same general laws. If the aim of science is usefully construed as prediction, why not try operating on the assumption that the aim of all human effort is prediction and see where this line of psychologizing leads us?
>
> (Kelly, 1955/1991, p. 605/Vol. 2, p. 35)

In 1955, two heavy volumes containing 1218 pages of *The Psychology of Personal Constructs* landed on the desks of psychologists. Kelly's 'brief introduction' in the previous chapter is, in relation to the two volumes, indeed brief. The reception of this revolutionary work was mixed. Jerome Bruner, among the most prestigious of the many reviewers, said:

> These excellent, original, and infuriatingly prolix two volumes easily nominate themselves for the distinction of being the single greatest contribution of the past decade to the theory of personality functioning. Professor Kelly has written a major work. (Bruner, 1956, p. 355)

We discuss some of the difficulties experienced by reviewers and subsequent readers later in this chapter. But, first, a word about the man who created this work.

The Essential Practitioner's Handbook of Personal Construct Psychology. Edited by F. Fransella.
© 2005 John Wiley & Sons, Ltd.

GEORGE A. KELLY, THE MAN

His Education

George Kelly was born on 28 April 1905 on a farm near Perth, Kansas, to Theodore Vincent Kelly and Elfleda Merriam Kelly. He died on 6 March 1967, when he was Professor of Behavioral Science at Brandeis University, Boston, USA. His father was a Presbyterian Minister who gave up his ministry to take up 'hard scrabble' farming in a time and place that imposed both poverty and rural isolation on the hard-working family. Kelly says of his mother that she was the daughter of a Nova Scotian captain of a sailing ship who was driven off the North Atlantic Trade routes by the arrival of steamships. He had then gone into the Caribbean trade, making his headquarters in Barbados where his mother had been born. It is interesting that the 'spirit of adventure' symbolized by this maternal grandfather, seems to have seeped into the spirit of Kelly's later psychological theorizing.

Kelly tells how his father set off in 1909 in a covered wagon to take up a claim in eastern Colorado, becoming one of the last homesteaders on the American frontier. But there was little water there to grow crops or raise livestock, so the family returned to the Kansas farm in 1913 after four hard years of struggle. During that time Kelly did not attend any school and was educated by his parents. In fact, as far as one can tell, George Kelly's formal education was virtually nil during the first dozen years of his life. The first substantial period of formal education he had was from late 1918 to 1921 in Wichita. At 16 he then went to the Friends' University academy in Wichita where he took college and academy courses. He often told people that he had never graduated from high school—something that clearly pleased him. He then completed his baccalaureate studies in 1926, majoring in physics and mathematics. It is at Friends' University that we find the first evidence of George Kelly the thinker, the writer, a person with social concerns. He was awarded first place in the Peace Oratorical Contest held at the University in 1924 for *The Sincere Motive*—on the subject of war (Kelly, 1924).

Kelly gave up the idea of a career in engineering to study for a masters degree in educational sociology at the University of Kansas. In 1927, with his masters thesis not completed, he went to Minneapolis and supported himself by teaching various classes for labour organizers, the American Bankers Association, and prospective American citizens. He then enrolled at the University of Minnesota in sociology and biometrics, but soon had to leave because it was discovered that he could not pay the fees. In the winter of 1927, he found a job teaching psychology and speech at Sheldon Junior College in Iowa. There he also coached drama, laying the groundwork for his novel use of enactment in psychotherapy, and there met his future wife, Gladys Thompson.

Kelly's moves around academe were not yet finished. He received an exchange fellowship to go to Edinburgh University in Scotland to study for a Bachelor of Education Degree, which he completed in 1930. There was one last task—to get a doctorate degree—which he finally accomplished at the University of Iowa under Carl Seashore in the Department of Psychology. His PhD, on the common factors in reading and speech disabilities, was awarded in 1931. In that year he married Gladys Thompson and began seeking his first real position. America was in the midst of the Great Depression, which was decimating the economy, making it hardly an auspicious moment to launch a promising career.

His Professional Years

After what can only be described as an unusual educational history, George Kelly's first employment was in 1931 at the Fort Hays Kansas State College, where he served for 12 years. Faced with a sea of human suffering aggravated by bank fore-closures and economic hardship, Kelly found little use for the physiological psy-chology that had initially fascinated him, and soon turned his attention to what he saw as being needed—the psychological evaluation of school-aged children and adults. It was here he started to make his distinctive contribution to psychology. He was instrumental in setting up a pioneering travelling clinic that toured western Kansas and offered a psychological diagnostic and remedial service to children of that area. It was staffed solely by George Kelly and his undergraduate and post-graduate students, eventually being funded directly by the financially strapped state legislature (Neimeyer & Jackson, 1997).

While at Fort Hays Kelly started to develop his thinking about psychological change, leading eventually to the psychology of personal constructs, his philosophy of constructive alternativism, and the basics of fixed role therapy (see Chapter 11, pp. 113–122). Informing all of these developments was the view that persons have created themselves and therefore can re-create themselves if they have the courage and imagination to do so. Finding himself largely alone in his efforts to help trou-bled students, he turned to Freud's ideas for inspiration. Although Kelly developed a respect for Freud's bold attempt to 'listen to the language of distress', he ultimately rejected the idea that offering correct therapist 'interpretations' of client experi-ences was the key to change. Instead, he began to realize that it was what the *clients* did with his interpretations that really mattered, and the only criterion for a useful therapist-offered conceptualization was that it should be relevant to the client's problem and carry novel implications for a possible solution (Kelly, 1969k).

It was early on in his time at Fort Hays that Kelly wrote his textbook *Under-standable Psychology* (unpublished and dated 1932). There is also a draft manu-script of a book with W.G. Warnock entitled *Inductive Trigonometry* (1935). Both his interests in comprehensive theorizing and mathematics are to be found in the unique structure of *The Psychology of Personal Constructs*.

In the late 1930s Kelly was put in charge of a flight-training programme at Fort Hays College and in 1943 was commissioned in the US Naval Reserve, where he conducted research on instrument panel design and other problems of applied and clinical psychology. Shortly after the end of World War II, Kelly was appointed Pro-fessor and Director of Clinical Psychology at Ohio State University. During his nine-teen years there he formalized his theory of personal constructs and its assessment tool, the repertory grid. Apart from his two massive volumes, he published little, but played a leading role in defining the emerging field of clinical psychology through leadership positions in the American Psychological Association. Kelly also extended his influence internationally, speaking at a number of universities around the world, and cultivating enduring contacts with such young European psychologists as Don

Bannister in the UK and Han Bonarius in the Netherlands. In 1965, the American Psychological Association bestowed on him its Award for Distinguished Contribution to the Science and Profession of Clinical Psychology.

Kelly left Ohio State University in 1965 to take up the Riklis Chair of Behavioral Science at Brandeis University, Boston, at the invitation of Abraham Maslow, the prominent humanistic psychologist.

He was a remarkable man. Not only did he become a distinguished academic in spite of a very unpromising education, but he also influenced the nature of psychology itself in ways we shall describe later. But first we offer a few words about the nature of this author of an unorthodox, grand vision of how each individual person gives personal meaning to life, others, and the world in general.

The Man Himself

To take a look at Kelly the man we can use an essential feature of his own theory—its reflexivity. Personal construct theory emphasizes that, in all our interactions, the same explanatory framework is equally applicable to both parties—to scientist and subject, therapist and client, husband and wife, and parent and child. Kelly did not emphasize this important feather in his theoretical cap, but many have done so since. For instance, see Bannister (2003, pp. 35–36) and Fransella (Chapter 4, pp. 43–44). To try to find out something about the author of personal construct theory, we can be reflexive and look at him through the eyes of his own theory.

It is clear that Kelly viewed his work with some ambivalence. On the one hand, Al Landfield, a student of Kelly, claimed, 'I knew beyond a shadow of a doubt that Kelly's hopes for the theory went way beyond ordinary ambition. His hopes went beyond himself, I believe' (Fransella, 1995). On the other hand, Kelly (1966b) said that only one of the five books he had written had been published and that might have been a mistake. This radical shifting of views can be related to the theoretical bipolarity of all construing. All construing is bipolar—all personal constructs have opposites. It was as if Kelly felt the pull of those opposites in his own life, to the point of both boldly announcing and then questioning his own life's work.

One major pull for Kelly was his great breadth of vision coupled with his equally great attention to detail. One can relate that also to the theory's *Creativity Cycle*. To create new ideas and new ways of relating to the world one cultivates a *loose*, wide-ranging view of events until a thought or feeling emerges that enables one to *tighten*, focus down upon that thought or feeling to see whether it really is a good idea or not. See Chapter 11, pp. 118–120, for more details of 'tight' versus 'loose' construing. Kelly's own tendency to shift from breadth of vision to attention to detail gave many problems to those who knew him—particularly his students. Al Landfield claimed:

> Kelly was a revolutionary in the guise of a very formal man. No students would
> be called by their first name until they had been awarded their doctorate. He
> was bound by many such rules. Then the revolutionary would take over and he
> would become the warm, excited, involved, creator of ideas. (Fransella, 1995)

Could it be that this ability or tendency to shift from the tight to the loose construer in any way was related to his possibly conflicting religious experiences? He received his early life and education largely from his Presbyterian Minister father and lived for some time in the Bible-belt of America. He then was exposed to the much looser religious culture in his adolescence and early adult life at a Quaker College and then at a Quaker university. See Weihs (2004) for a discussion of the possible influence of Quaker beliefs on Kelly's theory of personal constructs.

GEORGE A. KELLY: INFLUENCES ON HIS THEORY AND PHILOSOPHY

Influences from Psychology

Many of the influences on Kelly's thinking are discussed in other chapters in this book. The obvious negative influences he saw at the time he developed his theory were behaviourism and the psychodynamic approaches, although the former seemed to be especially objectionable to him. He saw both of these as denying us any right to make decisions and be in charge of our own lives. The behaviourism of Kelly's day made the person a passive respondent to environmental events—in Bannister's (1966b) ironic words, 'a ping pong ball with a memory'. Bannister (2003) provides a comparison between behaviourism and personal construct theory. On the other hand, early psychodynamic theorists made the person a passive respondent to internal unconscious forces. For Kelly, we are forms of motion and we propel ourselves—no one person or no one thing does it 'to' us. Thus, Kelly can be seen as the 'loyal opposition' to the dominant psychologies of his day, challenging them while maintaining a commitment to developing a more humane alternative.

Influences from Philosophy

In contrast to Kelly's rejection of most of established psychology, he drew more eagerly on cutting edge developments in the philosophy of his day. He frequently cited the pragmatist and religious thinker John Dewey as one of the main philosophers to influence him, a connection analyzed by Bill Warren (2003). Trevor Butt considers how Kelly's thinking may also have been influenced to some degree by phenomenology (2003). Beyond these two sources of philosophic inspiration, it is clear that Kelly drew on the linguistic philosophy of Alfred Korzybski in his ideas that 'constructs' are interpretations that say at least as much about their human users as they do about the 'realities' they purport to describe. Likewise, Kelly acknowledged the influence of Hans Vaihinger's (1924) philosophy of *'as if'* in his formulation of constructive alternativism, and the psychodrama of Jakob Moreno in shaping the make-believe, role-playing strategies that occupies an important place in personal construct therapy. Thus, although he was highly original, Kelly was situated within a broader set of intellectual developments in the early twentieth century, importing and systematizing these themes in the construction of a unique approach to psychology (Neimeyer & Stewart, 2000).

Influences from Physics and Mathematics

It has been suggested that Kelly's degree in physics and mathematics may have played a major role in the development of his theory and his method of measurement—the repertory grid (Fransella, 1983, 2000). Most strikingly, Kelly asked us to look at individuals 'as if' each of us were a scientist, each having a theory about what is currently happening to us, each making a prediction based on that theory and then each testing out that prediction by behaving. That is the basis of construing and, in that model, behaviour becomes the experiment rather than an end result. Personal construct theory takes the quantum mechanics view that none of us has neutral access to reality. Einstein's relativity theory, among other things, sees the world as an undivided whole in which all parts merge into one another. Kelly says: 'The universe . . . is integral. By that we mean it functions as a single unit with all its imaginable parts having an exact relationship to each other' (1955/1991, p. 7/Vol. 1, p. 5). Al Landfield tells how a physicist commented at one of his personal construct seminars that 'Kelly's theory can be seen as a good theory of physics' (Fransella, 1995).

As to mathematics, there is a branch called *mathematical constructivism*. These minority party mathematicians stand against the majority who take the *Platonic* stance which says that mathematical statements are there to be discovered, having an independent reality apart from the human mind. Mathematical constructivists on the other hand argue, along with Kelly (1954), that such 'ideas are not discovered, they are invented'. In addition to this general philosophic compatibility with developments in mathematical theory, Kelly commonly drew on his love of mathematical concepts and methods to conjure and measure some of the complexity of psychological space. He is reported by Hinkle as saying: 'Johann Herbart's work on education and particularly mathematical psychology influenced me. I think mathematics is the pure instance of construct functioning—the model of human behaviour' (1970, p. 91).

Other Influences

Because of its great scope and richness, personal construct psychology can be viewed as situated in a vast web of reciprocal influences with other important developments in twentieth-century thought, and indeed, with broader traditions of human understanding that span millennia. For example, Mair (1985) has argued persuasively that Kelly's theory represents a counterpoint to the religious ideology of his conservative Christian parents, in which he emphasizes the human potential to live boldly and unconventionally, by audacious experimentation rather than blind faith in authority (see also Warren, 2003, on personal construct theory and religion, pp. 387–394). Could that counterpoint be related to his later exposure to the Quaker religion during the latter part of his education? Existential themes of choice and agency clearly pervade the theory, as well as an ethic of advocating construing the outlooks of others as a precondition for meaningful role relationships on personal or cultural levels (see also Scheer, 2003). Deeper currents in Euro-American thought no doubt also shaped Kelly's thinking, such as his evident belief in human progress, and his fundamental individualism. But in a sense, Kelly's genius resided in the way he integrated these many streams of thought into a comprehensive, coherent, practical, and generative theory, one that is still being actively elaborated by psychologists and social theorists around the world. It is this final topic, the reception of Kelly's theory, to which we now turn.

DEVELOPMENT OF PERSONAL CONSTRUCT THEORY SINCE 1955

A consideration of the development of personal construct theory as a field since 1955 could yield a book in itself—indeed, it has done just that. Neimeyer (1985c) has drawn on models and methods devised in the sociology of science to depict the theory's social and intellectual emergence from the 'normal science' of its day. It first represented a radical departure in psychological theory, then moved through the evolution of small 'clusters' and larger 'networks' of like-minded researchers, to become the established and diversified 'specialty' that it is today. At each stage of its development, the theory encountered important challenges, such as the premature death of its founder, the need to develop international cohesiveness in the pre-internet era, the establishment of training centres inside and outside academia, and the creation of respected publication outlets for the work of group members. That such challenges were met successfully is evident in the range and vitality of chapters that make up this volume.

Here, however, we would like to focus on four particular issues: the abstract, 'value free', orientation of the theory; the ambivalent relationship between personal construct theory and cognitive perspectives; the difficulty in grasping the developmental implications of the theory; and the distinctive nature of its major methodologies.

FOUR ISSUES ARISING FROM PERSONAL CONSTRUCT THEORY

Its 'Value Free' Orientation

One of the remarkable features of personal construct theory—and one that no doubt contributes to the flexibility with which it has been applied to people and problems of all sorts—is its abstract, content-free orientation. Unlike many psychological theorists, Kelly did not propose a detailed list of human needs, motives, conflicts or ideals that presumably hold for all people, but instead focused on the general *processes* by which people made sense of, and navigated, the social world. This abstractness makes personal construct theory about as 'value free' as a theory of personality could aspire to be, and helps the clinician, psychological scientist and general observer of human events to 'step inside' the outlooks of those persons they seek to understand. Kelly enshrined a respect for individual and cultural differences in his basic theory, and advocated a *credulous*, rather than critical approach as the more enlightened way to either study human beings or attempt to promote their development across a range of settings. As Kelly (1955/1991, p. 608/Vol. 2, p. 37) noted:

> In the broadest sense we are restating here the philosophy of constructive alter-nativism. In a narrower sense we are describing the value system of the clinician [or psychologist more generally] as a kind of liberalism without paternalism. The clinician is not only tolerant of varying points of view . . . , but he is [also] willing to devote himself to the defence and facilitation of widely differing patterns of life. Diversity and multiple experimentation are to be encouraged.

Thus, decades before respect for diversity became the watchword in psychology and related disciplines, Kelly strove to draft a genuinely respectful psychology in which the active appreciation of alternative perspectives and ways of life was at the core.

Still, some have argued that personal construct theory is not truly value free; even celebrating and exploring diversity is, after all, a value. Clearly, Kelly did have his values, which he enshrined in his theory: risk-taking, adventure, creativity, and an unwillingness to settle for conventional answers to life's probing questions (Mair, 1985; Walker, 1992). In fact, it would not be too much to say that personal construct theory and like-minded constructivist perspectives even carry with them an ethical mandate, to 'try on for size' the initially alien or threatening perspectives of others, according them the same level of potential validity as one's own (Mair, 1989a; Neimeyer, 2002b). Ultimately, then, personal construct theory enjoins us to deal with the question of values by both recognizing the values implicit in our own core con-structs, and attempting, insofar as possible, to accord equal legitimacy to the value perspectives of those persons we seek to comprehend.

Personal Construct Theory and Cognition

One prominent psychologist who hailed George Kelly as the creator of the theo-retical model of cognitive or thought processes was one of his students, Walter Mischel. In a personal tribute to Kelly, Mischel (1980, p. 85) said:

> That George Kelly was a very deep, original, refreshing voice was always evident to all who knew him well. What has surprised me was not the brilliance with which he first spoke but the accuracy with which he anticipated the directions into which psychology would move two decades later.

A little later, Mischel (1980, p. 86) continues: 'Long before "cognitive psychology" existed, Kelly created a truly cognitive theory of personality, a theory in which how people construe is at the core.'

Although Mischel's tribute appropriately acknowledges the role of Kelly's think-ing in foreshadowing the enthusiasm for cognitive science and cognitive therapy that was so apparent in the second half of the twentieth century, many contempo-rary personal construct theorists take exception to their theory being closely aligned with cognitive perspectives. Certainly, Kelly took great pains to emphasize that his theory was at least as concerned with human passion and action as with thought, and at a fundamental level, he attempted to integrate all of these features of human functioning in his definition of the construct. In Chapter 2 (pp. 15–28), entitled 'The logic of passion', Don Bannister discusses the thought–feeling dichotomy.

The common tendency to assimilate personal construct theory into a cognitive framework ignores much in the theory—such as its novel treatment of emotions as signals of a sometimes threatening transition in our construing. In turn that reflects the priority of an ingrained cultural construct that contrasts thinking with feeling, as well as the role of historical accidents, such as the publication of the first three chapters of Kelly's basic theory as a convenient and widely read paperback, while the 'emotional' and 'action-oriented' parts of the theory were relegated to Kelly's two-volume *magnum opus* encountered by relatively few readers. The resulting selective reading of the theory has given it more of a cognitive cast than it deserves, with many of its radical implications for understanding human behaviour remaining to be developed. Gabriele Chiari and Maria Laura Nuzzo discuss the many philosophical differences between cognitive and personal construct psychologies in Chiari and Nuzzo (2003).

Levels of Awareness

One aspect of Kelly's theory that has not been emphasized so far, is the fact that his theory includes 'fresh interpretations of "the unconscious"'. Freud argued that some psychological energy had to be present to explain why people did what they did. He called it 'psychic energy'. Kelly said there is no need to create an energy system for human beings similar to that in physics. Human beings are not inert substances that need energy to move them. They are living matter and one crucial property of living matter is that it moves.

Having that as his starting point, Kelly then agreed with Freud that much of human construing takes place outside of consciousness. Instead of 'the unconscious' as the reservoir of psychic energy, he suggested the notion that there are *levels of awareness* with 'conscious' construing being at the highest level of awareness. At the lowest level is 'preverbal' construing. That consists of discriminations a baby and young child create to make sense of their experiences but they have no verbal labels attached to them. These preverbal constructs can account for much of our seemingly irrational reactions to events. As we develop over the years, we find verbal labels to attach to many of them and so are able to look at them in the cold light of day to see if they are still useful ways of looking at events. Much of counselling and psychotherapy is concerned with exactly that—finding verbal labels to attach to our preverbal construings. Thus, those who call personal construct theory a traditional 'cognitive' theory—meaning that it deals with only verbally or intellectually accessible thought processes—are taking no account of the majority of what Kelly calls construing. It is interesting to note that in this respect Kelly foreshadowed more contemporary cognitive theories, which now routinely recognize the limits of consciousness in grasping the 'metacognitive' basis of much of human functioning. Clearly, people 'know' much more than they can tell, in the sense that some of the bases on which we construe events in our lives can only be inferred, rather than directly reported. Much more will be said about the role of non-verbal construing, particularly relating to core parts of our systems of meaning, in the chapters that follow.

Human Development

A recurrent complaint is that Kelly did not talk about development—that is, from birth to adulthood. It has been argued (Fransella, 1995) that the omission was deliberate, in the sense that the whole theory of personal constructs is about development—human beings are seen as forms of motion, no matter what our age. There is a second reason for the omission. The theory rejects all attempts to put people into categories or boxes. It follows that Kelly was sceptical of the prescriptive age-and-stage models that characterized the developmental theories of his day, even those of theorists like Piaget who shared some of his constructivist leanings.

A close inspection of Kelly's work shows that he was hardly lacking in experience with children. He spent several years at Fort Hays working extensively with children, and used frequent examples of children to illustrate theoretical issues in his two volumes. Instead, Kelly, like Werner and more recent developmental theorists, preferred to view human 'becoming' as a highly individualized process of psychological development, in which both children and adults constantly extend, revise and reorganize the system of meaning/emotion/action schemes that they construct (Mascolo et al., 1997). However, his rather abstract approach to developmental issues could have contributed to the relative neglect of this aspect of his theory, leaving its application to the world of childhood in need of further development. What we do know about the psychological development of children can be seen in the chapters in the *International Handbook of Personal Construct Psychology* (2003) of Jack Adams-Webber on research (Chapter 5, pp. 51–58), Jim Mancuso on how children develop psychologically and in particular their sense of self (Chapter 27, pp. 275–282) and Tom Ravenette (in this book) on working with children and teachers when children are seen as having problems (Chapter 13, pp. 133–143).

Scientific Research

Kelly's influence here is profound. Although it is not claimed that he, alone, started the change in research methods, it can certainly be claimed that his thinking has played a part. He suggested that his philosophy of *constructive alternativism* was an approach to science that was an alternative to the scientific method favoured by psychology, for which he coined the term *accumulative fragmentalism*. Details of the differences are given in Chiari and Nuzzo (2003, Chapter 4).

Qualitative as Well as Quantitative Methods

Kelly's repertory grid technique represented a creative and flexible set of methods—much expanded by subsequent construct theorists—that allow qualitative data to be quantified. As described specifically by Richard Bell in Chapter 6 (pp. 67–76), the grid technique addresses a central goal in personal construct theory, namely, bringing to light the distinctive ways that individual human beings or groups organize and interpret some aspect of their experience. Kelly's unique contribution was to show how these data can be given arithmetical equivalents by placing them within a repertory grid matrix consisting of rows of personal constructs and columns of items to be construed by those constructs. Although grid methods have proved useful in even rather informal paper and pencil forms, countless researchers and practitioners have made use of the burgeoning number of sophisticated computer programs for eliciting, analysing and interpreting grid data.

Less widely recognized, but equally novel, were Kelly's contributions to qualitative assessment of personal construct systems. Indeed, methods like self-characterization, in which a person is invited to write a free-form description of him- or herself from a sympathetic third-person perspective, anticipated the present surge of interest in narrative concepts and methods in psychology. Kelly's characteristically detailed recommendations for analysing and using such material in psychotherapy are congruent with the current expansion of hermeneutic, constructivist and interpretive methods in the social sciences, recognizing the contribution of both words and numbers to psychology as a human science (see Chapter 8 (pp. 87–94) and Butt (2003, Chapter 38)). Many different ways of eliciting and making sense of personal constructs have been created since 1955. Some of these are described in Chapters 4 (pp. 41–56) and 5 (pp. 57–66). Greg Neimeyer also gives a useful account of many such measures (1993).

CODA

We have tried to provide some historical context for the chapters that follow, both in terms of Kelly's distinctive biography, and in terms of the subsequent development of his theory. Doing so is in keeping with Kelly's emphasis on reflexivity, which places the theorist firmly within the purview of his theory, as well as his focus on anticipation, on how construct systems evolve as they stretch to embrace the future. Personal construct theory has clearly evolved since its origins in Kelly's work, while nonetheless retaining its distinctive core commitments. As such, the theory represents not only a reflexive distillation of the themes of Kelly's life, but also a highly original anticipation of its extensions over the half-century that followed.

CHAPTER 2

The Logic of Passion*

Don Bannister

> If my 'anger' is rejected because I have no good 'reasons' or my 'argument' is dismissed because I lack 'feeling' then I accept that others experience me as segmented. I do not have to experience myself thus.

Psychologists strive for novelty while repeating the patterns of their culture. Thus, they have, in large measure, followed the lay tradition that man is to be viewed psychologically as a collection of poorly related parts. Psychology has been structured around concepts such as learning, motivation, memory, perception, sensation, personality and so forth, all of which clearly derive from common-sense language and each has been given autonomy as an *area of study*. Psychologists have invented little and contented themselves largely with refining notions which have a long and tangled intellectual history.

Perhaps the most unbreakable grip exercised by traditional thought over the formal discipline of psychology is manifest in the historic division of man into *thought and feeling*. The effect of this dichotomy has been to deny psychology any unity and produce what are essentially two psychologies: on the one hand, cognitive psychology with sub-psychologies such as memory, perception, thinking and reasoning; and, on the other hand, a psychology of emotion, ranging around such concepts as drive, motivation and libido.

So deeply ingrained in our culture is this division of man into his thinking and feeling aspects that it would have been surprising if psychology had, to any great extent, escaped it. It is grieving that it has barely thought to question it. We can observe this segmentation of man, both in terms of the way we analyse our personal experience and the ways in which our literature records it. As children we grow rapidly to accept the idea that we are, each of us, two persons—a thinker and a feeler. We learn to speak of our ideas as something distinct from our emotions, and we learn to speak of the two as often contrasted and competing.

So deep and continuous has this distinction been in our language, folklore and

---

*This work has been published previously in *New Perspectives in Personal Construct Theory* (1977) by Academic Press.

The Essential *Practitioner's Handbook of Personal Construct Psychology.* Edited by F. Fransella.
© 2005 John Wiley & Sons, Ltd.

philosophy, that literary comments on it achieve the status of platitudinous but inescapable truths. Such 'truths' often espouse the rival and crusading causes of thought and feeling. Thus the thought/feeling distinction can be seen, in Kelly's terminology, as a superordinate bipolar construct.

Treasured comments can be found which praise thinking and condemn feeling. 'All violent feelings . . . produce in us a falseness in all our impressions of external things, which I would generally characterise as the "pathetic fallacy"' (Ruskin). Then again there is the kind of pronouncement which, while favouring reason, seems sadly convinced that passion will conquer:

> The ruling passion, be it what it will,
> The ruling passion conquers reason still. (Pope)

Then there are those comments which are contemptuous of the thought aspect of the dichotomy:

> And thus the native hue of resolution
> Is sicklied o'er with the pale cast of thought. (Shakespeare)

or Keats' cry:

> Oh for a life of sensation rather than of thoughts.

The contrapuntal relationship between the concepts of feeling and thought are further explored in those treasured platitudes which counterpose the two: Pascal's

> The heart has its reasons, which reason knows nothing of.

or Walpole's

> This world is a comedy to those that think, a tragedy to those that feel.

Our language is replete with expressions of the dichotomy: rationality versus emotion, reason versus passion, feeling versus thinking, the brain versus the heart, cognition versus affection, faith versus argument, mind versus flesh. Whole subcultures, periods and groups have swung the pendulum to those credos that worship the rational man, he who fights the forces of blind instinct, prejudice, chaotic emotion and bestial passion. Conversely the pendulum has swung oft-times the other way, to the Romantic and the apotheosis of emotion as the authentic, sincere and soaring expression of the true nature of man, as opposed to the mercenary practices of intellectualizing cleverness and bloodless logic.

THE USES OF THE DICHOTOMY

If the construct thinking versus feeling has enjoyed such a long history and played so major a role in our ways of delineating ourselves and others, then clearly it must serve many purposes and serve them well. It must reflect and express aspects of experience which we need to express and reflect. Even a cursory consideration brings to light some of the purposes the distinction may serve.

- If I am willing to negotiate my position and entertain yours, then I may say 'I think that . . .' and proceed to a verbal accounting. If I am unwilling to negotiate my position and do not wish you to challenge it, then I may say 'I feel that . . .'.
- If I want to notify myself or you of some, *as yet*, publically unsupported suspicion I may say that 'I know that the evidence is in favour of the view (thought) that . . . nevertheless I have this feeling that . . .'.
- If I want to picture and represent to myself or to you *conflicts* I am experiencing I can say that 'while I *know* (think) that I ought to do that, I *feel* that I ought to do this . . .'.
- If I want to make some kind of sense out of, excuse, respond to the inexplicable behaviour of myself, my neighbour, lover, friend, I can believe that the puzzling actions are not for this or that *reason* but are caused by mood, passion, overwhelming fear, rage, desire.

Historically, each pole of the thinking versus feeling dichotomy has had its implications extensively developed so that we have arrived at an elaborate language of feeling and an elaborate language of thinking. We can make myriad subtle distinctions which stem from and support the basic idea of two occasionally interacting *personae* within each of us—a thinking man and a feeling man. Thus reason takes unto itself the subsets of memory, logic, the accurate and systematic observation of events: we can assess our thoughts as fulfilling the principles of the syllogism, the rules of linguistic definition, the fair weighing of evidence. Feeling has become feelings and we can work with the distinctions between sadness, resentment, exhilaration, tension, grief, triumph, anxiety—the pallet of passion enables us to portray the world and ourselves in many hues. Thus these developed subsystems concerning thinking and feeling are guides to action and movement so that we can *assemble arguments to influence* or *arouse feelings to attack*. Logicians can teach us strategies of thought while encounter group leaders broaden our resources for feeling. Lawyers can weigh evidence and poets evoke emotions (though be it noted that successful lawyers often plead poetically while great poets emote cogently).

THE LIMITATIONS OF THE CONSTRUCT

Kelly repeatedly made the point that a bipolar construct both liberates and restricts: it brings events within our grasp in one set of terms, while blinding us to other aspects of the same configuration of events.

Thus, in both the informal psychology of our culture and in formal academic psychology, the distinction between thought and feeling has often proved disintegrative and hindering. It is significant that it is precisely in those areas in which the distinction makes least sense that psychologists have spoken to least purpose. *Invention, humour, art, religion, meaning, infancy, love:* all seem areas of particular mystery to psychologists and it may be that they puzzle us because it makes no sense to see them as clearly 'cognitive' or clearly 'affective'. Nor does calling to the rescue that holy ghost of the psychological trinity 'conation' seem to help matters.

The separation of feeling from thought seems to have driven psychologists into a barren physiologizing in a vain attempt to give substance to the dichotomy. Thus there is a long tradition in psychology which seeks to deal with 'emotion' by translating it into a physiological language and redefining it so that it even has a geography (*vide* the 'pleasure' centre) or a transporting fluid (*vide* endocrine secretion). Psychologists never seem to have broken entirely free from the kind of concretism, of which even a man as sensitive as William James was guilty, in arguments such as the following (1884):

> And yet it is even now certain that of two things concerning the emotions, one must be true. Either separate special centres, affected to them alone, are their brain-seat, or else they correspond to processes occurring in the motor and sensory senses, already assigned, or in others like them but not yet mapped out.

Equally in their ponderings on the issue of 'thought', psychologists have been driven to that ultimate in hardening of the categories, the notion of the 'engram'—the notion that a thought is somehow more real if you think of it as the permanently altered state of living tissue.

The central limit set to our understanding by our adherence to the bipolarity of thought and feeling has been that it has prevented us from adequately elaborating the notion of a *person*. Psychologists came close to beginning their study of a person with the concept of 'personality' but again they failed because this was turned into a segment, a chapter heading, a branch of psychology. Either personality is psychology or it is not worth the study. Thus a person is not emotions or thoughts, not cognition or drive. To speak of a person is to invent a concept which points to the integrity and uniqueness of your experience and my experience and to the wholeness of your experience of me and my experience of you. The distinctions that such a construct encourages us to make are those of time, the past and the future person and the continuity between them; the distinction between person and object; the distinction between the ways in which the person is free and the ways in which he is determined. None of these distinctions gains, and all are obscured by the traditional dichotomy of thought and feeling. Consider the distinction between free with respect to and determined with respect to. The very notion of feeling has developed in such a way as to entail the idea of determinism. Thus we are *overwhelmed* by rage, *seized* by anger, *moved* by joy, *sunk* in grief. It is interesting to note here our failure to develop the idea of feeling in its active sense as meaning exploration, grasp, understanding, as in feeling the surface of a material, feeling our way towards (Mair, 1972). Equally, psychologists have followed that intellectual tradition which makes rational thought almost something which is a determining external reality. We must *follow* logic, we are not credited with *inventing* logic. Had we pondered the person rather than the two homunculi of thought and feeling we would have seen man as an active agent rather than the passive object of the environment or his own uncontrollable innards.

WHATEVER HAPPENED TO EMOTIONS?

It is a platitude in personal construct theory, but a very powerful platitude, that to elaborate one's own understanding of oneself and the world it is necessary not only to develop new constructs but to escape from some old constructs. Yet to abandon a construct is to abandon a part of oneself and this is a task not lightly undertaken. However, George Kelly addressed himself formally to just such a task. He lists at one point the constructs that do not appear in personal construct theory although they are hallowed by respect and use in traditional psychology.

> For example, the term learning so honourably embedded in most psychological tests, scarcely appears at all. That is wholly intentional; for we are throwing it overboard altogether. There is no ego, no emotion, no motivation, no reinforcement, no drive, no unconscious, no need.

Clearly, in constructing his theory, George Kelly had a right *not* to use the constructs of other theories, just as each of us has an inalienable right not to use the constructs of another person. However, when this is done, both professions and persons tend to accuse the doer of failing to deal with *the facts*. If I do not deign to categorize people in terms of their 'intelligence' then others may respond that I am ignoring the *fact* of intelligence (and thereby being *stupid*). In psychology this strategy most frequently takes the form of transmuting a concept into a 'variable' and then arguing that it is something that *must* be taken into account.

There can be no onus on any theory to duplicate the constructs of another. To do so would have the effect of making alternative theories simply co-equivalent sets of different jargons. If my public theory or my private construct system lacks certain constructions, then you may legitimately ask me with what constructions I intend to deal with the kinds of problems that you handle by using the constructions that I have abandoned. But if you do so it must be a serious enquiry designed to find out how I am handling aspects of my world, what meaning I am giving to them, what usefulness I find in the constructs I am using. It must not be simply an attempt to prove that there are culpable gaps in my system because it does not exactly duplicate yours. To make such an enquiry seriously is no easy undertaking for we all tend to long for familiarity, even in what is new. This is presumably the reason why some vegetarians strangely refer to some forms of vegetable as 'nut meat rissole'.

Kelly left the great traditional dichotomy of emotion versus thought out of construct theory and proposed an alternative way of dealing with the kinds of *issue* that are classically dealt with by the emotion versus feeling dichotomy.

Inevitably it was assumed that he had somehow retained the dichotomy but failed to elaborate one end of it, one pole of the construct. In this case the accusation was generally that he had failed to deal with 'emotion'. Thus, when the two volumes presenting the theory first appeared in 1955, Bruner (1956) reviewed them favourably. But inevitably he saw the theory as a 'cognitive' theory—i.e. one which does not deal with 'emotion'. He commented on what he saw as its limitations as a 'mentalistic' theory which failed to deal with issues of emotion. Carl Rogers (1956) went even farther by not only pointing to the same 'deficiency' but waxing much more angry and much more concerned about what he saw as a failure to deal with the passions of mankind.

For two decades construct theory has been expounded, discussed and used. One might imagine that by now psychologists would have stopped construing construct theory pre-emptively as 'nothing but a cognitive theory'. One might hope that they would recognize the novel and adventurous attempt to elaborate a theory of man which did not dichotomize him into a reasoning man and a feeling man. One might hope that, even if they felt that this integrative venture had failed, they would recognize the *deliberate* nature of the venture and understand that it was not simply that Kelly had failed to consider 'emotion'. But, for the most part, psychologists are not, in philosophical terms, Kellyian constructive alternativists—they are naïve realists and emotion is apparently a *real thing*, not a construct about the nature of man. Two decades after the presentation of the theory we have exactly equivalent condemnations offered to those propounded by Bruner and Rogers. Mackay (1975, p. 128) opens his critical appraisal of personal construct theory as follows.

> PCT has been widely criticised on the grounds that it is too mentalistic. The ideal rational man, as depicted by Kelly and Bannister, seems more like a counter-programmed robot than a human being who is capable of intense emotional experience.

Peck and Whitlow (1975, p. 92) comment similarly:

> Kelly's approach to emotion is deliberately psychological but in order to achieve this position he is forced to ignore a wealth of knowledge from the field of physiology; furthermore some of the definitions seem to fly in the face of common sense. Bannister and Mair (1968, p. 33) state that 'Within this scheme, "emotions" lose much of their mystery'; it can be argued that they also lose most of their meaning.

Virtually every textbook over the past two decades that has dealt with personal construct theory has unquestioningly classified it as a 'cognitive' theory. Kelly was, in many ways, a man of real patience but even he chafed at the persistent attempt to allot him to constructs whose range of convenience did not span his work.

He used to plan/fantasize a new book which he might write to re-present construct theory. Essentially the content and force of the theory and the nature of its argument would remain the same but it would be stylistically re-presented as 'personal construct theory—a theory of the human passions'. His dream was to complete the volume and let the people who saw construct theory as a cognitive theory wrestle with the new presentation. Had he completed such a work it seems likely that he would have been open to academic attack for failing entirely to understand the rational aspects of man, the nature of thinking and the degree to which behaviour is a function of cognitive processes. In summary, then, psychologists have failed to take seriously Kelly's attempt to dispense with the thinking–feeling dichotomy. He stated it as explicitly as may be. Thus (Kelly 1969a, p. 140):

> The reader may have noted that in talking about experience I have been careful not to use either of the terms, 'emotional' or 'affective'. I have been equally careful not to invoke the notion of 'cognition'. The classic distinction which separates these two constructs has, in the manner of most classic distinctions that once were useful, become a barrier to sensitive psychological inquiry. When one so divides the experience of man, it becomes difficult to make the most of the holistic aspirations that may infuse the science of psychology with new life, and

may replace the classicism now implicit even in the most 'behaviouristic' research.

ALTERNATIVE CONSTRUING

Kelly attempted to deal with the kind of issue normally handled under the rubric of 'emotion' by offering constructs which relate to *transition*. The underlying argument is that while a person's interpretation of himself and his world is probably constantly changing to some degree, there are times when his experience of varying validational fortunes make change or resistance to change a matter of major concern. At such times we try to nail down our psychological furniture to avoid change or we try to lunge forward in answer to some challenge or revelation by forcefully elaborating our experience. Or we may be tumbled into chaos because of over-rapid change or move into areas where we cannot fully make sense of our situation and its implications and our system must either change or the experience will become increasingly meaningless. It is at such times that our conventional language most often makes reference to feeling.

Kelly strove to maintain construct theory as an integrated overview of the nature of the person; to deal with all aspects of our experience within the same broad terms. Whether he succeeded or failed, the theory is thus essentially grandiose in that it attempts to deal with all aspects of human experience. Thereby it is in contrast with most psychological theories which are essentially theories of something. Conventionally, even broadly structured theoretical frameworks such as learning theory specifically acknowledge that there are areas of human experience and behaviour which are outside their range of convenience—learning theory is a theory of learning. Other theories are much more explicit and limited, being theories of memory, or theories of perception or theories of sensation, and so forth. Most relevant to this argument is that they may be theories of cognition or theories of emotion.

CONSTRUCTS RELATING TO TRANSITION

In naming his constructs relating to transition, Kelly adopted a curious strategy. He chose terms such as guilt, hostility, aggression, anxiety, all of which have a traditional lay and formal psychological meanings and then redefined them in construct theory terms. In each case the new definition is cousin to the traditional definition but the differences are such as to cause some confusion on first inspection. Kelly was never explicit as to why he adopted this strategy rather than create entirely new names for these constructs. However, one suspects that he did little without malice aforethought, and one possibility is that he was trying to draw attention to the *difference* between his preferred definition and the standard one, by using the same term. The suspicion is strengthened when we examine the nature of the difference. In every case it seems that what Kelly is pointing to is the meaning of the situation for *the person* to whom the adjective is applied, as contrasted with the meaning of the situation for those of us who are confronted *by the person* to whom we apply the adjective. Thus standard ways of using terms such as *hostile* are such that the emnity, attack and hatred of the person is seen as directed towards us, almost as if they were traits of the person, almost as if they were unreasoning hatreds. True, we may enquire for what reason a particular person is hostile, but the term hostile itself does not carry with it any kind of causal explanation. In construct theory *hostility* is defined as 'the continued effort to extort validational evidence in favour of a type of social prediction which has already been recognised as a failure'. Essentially Kelly is pointing, in this definition, to the situation as it exists *for the person* who is being hostile. For such a person some part of his theoretical structure for making sense out of the world is threatened, some central belief is wavering and, because he cannot face imminent chaos, he attempts to bully the evidence in such a way that it will 'substantiate' the threatened theory. Similarly, the traditional definitions of *aggression* give it a meaning very much like the meaning we attach to the term hostility, whereas Kelly defines it as the polar opposite of hostility thereby seeking to draw our attention to the nature of aggression from the aggressor's point of view as distinct from its discomfort for those of us who confront it. Thus, *aggression*, as defined in construct theory terms is 'the active elaboration of one's perceptual field'. Aggression is the hallmark of a person who is being adventurous and experimental, who is beginning to make more and more sense out of a wider and wider range of experience and who is leaping into further experience to capitalize on the sense he is making. Truly it can be very unpleasant for us to face aggression of this sort because we may not always wish to be part of the other person's experiment, to be the means whereby he enlarges his understanding.

Kelly's definitions try to make us recognize that we can only understand the persons from within, in terms of the 'why' from their point of view. This places construct theory in sharp contrast to trait psychology which sees the person as *caused* from within or stimulus response psychology which sees him *as caused* from without. Kelly (1969l, p. 273) makes this point in the following words:

> If we are to have a psychology of man's experiences, we must anchor our basic concepts in that personal experience, not in the experiences he causes others to have or which he appears to seek to cause others to have. Thus if we wish to use a concept of hostility at all, we have to ask, what is the experiential nature of hostility from the standpoint of the person who has it. Only by answering this question in some sensible way will we arrive at a concept which makes pure psychological sense, rather than sociological or moral sense, merely.

A few of Kelly's constructs relating to transition are briefly examined in order to give some impression of the way in which the theory handles the issue of 'feeling'.

ANXIETY

Kelly defines anxiety as 'the awareness that the events with which one is confronted lie mostly outside the range of convenience of one's construct system'. Thus, anxiety is not seen as a kind of psychological ginger pop fizzing around in the system or physiologized into a chemical process or left vague as referring to an uncertain general state of the person. It is given a specific meaning in construct theory terms—it directs our attention to the range of convenience of a person's construct system in relation to the situation which he confronts. Anxiety is our awareness that something has gone bump in the night. The 'bump' is within the range of convenience of our construct system in that we can identify it as a 'bump' but the implications of the bump lie mostly outside the range of convenience of our construct system. What do things that go bump in the night do next? What can be done about them? A common objection to this definition of anxiety arises from the fact the people often claim to be very familiar with precisely those things which make them anxious. Thus students honestly claim to be familiar with examinations yet feel extremely anxious about them. But here we have to look at the exact meaning of the phrase 'lie *mostly* outside the range of convenience of one's construct system'. Certainly, as far as examinations are concerned, aspects of them are well within the range of convenience of the student's construct system. He is familiar with the whole business of answering two from section A and not more than one from section B, he is at home with problems of time allotment between questions, he is familiar with all those standard demands to 'compare and contrast', 'discuss', 'write brief notes on'. He may be a positive authority on strategies for revising, guessing likely questions, marking systems and so forth. Yet it is likely that there will be a whole series of questions relating to an examination, the answers to which lie in very misty areas. What will I think of myself if I fail this examination? What will other people think of me if I fail this examination? What will the long-term effect be if I fail this examination? It may be these, and a whole range of related questions, which run beyond the range of convenience of the construction system of a particular person facing a particular examination.

Not only is the definition cogent but, since it is part of a systematic theory, it relates in turn to yet further constructs within the theory. Thus, if we consider ways in which we handle our anxieties, we can observe at least two kinds of strategy which are defineable within the construct theory. We may handle our anxieties by becoming aggressive—that is, we actively explore the area that is confronting us to the point at which we can bring it within the range of convenience of our construct system. In Kelly's terms this would involve *dilation*—this occurs when a person broadens his perceptual field and seeks to reorganize it on a more comprehensive level. In contrast we can withdraw from the area altogether. This involves *constriction*—a narrowing of the perceptual field.

HOSTILITY

Kelly's definition of hostility, that it is 'the continued effort to extort validational evidence in favour of a type of social prediction which has already been recognized as a failure', can be exemplified by referring back to Kelly's root metaphor, his invitation to consider the proposition that 'all men are scientists'. We can recognize the plight of the scientist who has made a considerable personal and professional investment in his theory, but who is faced by mounting piles of contradictory evidence. He may well recognize the failure of his *predictions* in an immediate sense, i.e. that what he has predicted in a particular experiment has not happened. What he may be unable to recognize and accept is the overall implication that a series of such mis-predictions negates his total theory. His investment may be too great, his lack of an *alternative* theory too oppressive and he may proceed to cook the books, torment his experimental subjects and bully his co-scientists in a desperate attempt to maintain a dying theory. All of us have experienced this situation personally. Clearly hostility is not simply 'a bad thing'. Sometimes we cannot afford readily to abandon a belief. If the belief is central to our way of viewing ourselves and others and if we have no alternative interpretation available to us, then it may be better to maintain that belief, for a while, by extorting validational evidence, rather than abandon the belief and plunge into chaos. At crucial times the alternative to hostility may be psychosis.

This kind of definition has practical implications for the ways in which we can make change possible. It suggests that we must facilitate change not by assaulting each other's central beliefs but by helping each other to construct alternatives, beginning with areas of peripheral contradiction. Thus, we may gradually replace a central belief without the need for hostility.

We can recognize hostility readily when we witness someone destroying his relationship with someone else in order to 'prove' that he is independent. We see it in the teacher who has growing doubts of his own cleverness and therefore begins to bully his students into stupidity so that his superiority as a teacher is demonstrated. It can manifest itself with most brutal clarity in the behaviour of the person who has to physically beat his psychological opponent to his knees in order to prove that he is 'best'.

The whole conception of the nature of change and resistance to change implied in the idea of hostility recalls the traditional philosopher's model which compares the problem of life to the problem of rebuilding a ship while at sea. If we have to rebuild our ship while sailing it we obviously do not begin by stripping out the keel. We use the strategy of removing one plank at a time and rapidly replacing it so that, given good fortune, we may eventually sail in an entirely new ship. This kind of conception is particularly important in areas of deliberately undertaken change, such as psychotherapy, education, religious and political conversion. We must remember that those whom we seek to change—and it may be ourselves that we seek to change—must *maintain* their lives while change continues.

AGGRESSION

As has already been noted, Kelly defines aggression as 'the active of elaboration of one's perceptual field'. Thus, aggression is perhaps the centrally triumphant experience for a person. The aggressive poet is one who sees ways of transmuting more of his experience into verse, the aggressive peasant is the one who is grasping ways of making his fields grow more. Aggression is our willingness to risk in order to find out, our passion for truth given embodiment in action. Aggression is the flourishing love affair, the child learning to walk, the conjurer with a new trick.

Again, each construct within the theory links into the total structure. Linked to the idea of aggression is Kelly's notion of 'commitment'. Morris (1977) makes the point that commitment in construct theory terms, is not a static posture, a clinging to the security of a set position. It means the converse: commitment is to the *frontiers* of one's construct system, a willingness to risk elaboration into what is, at the moment of risk, the unknown.

Kelly discusses at length the nature of the strategies whereby we give force to our aggression and particularly the idea of tightening and loosening. When a construct is used tightly, it leads to unvarying predictions, its relationship to other constructs is fixed: when a construct is used loosely it leads to varying predictions while retaining its identity, its relationships to other constructs is tentative. Loosening is that phase in our inventive cycle when we step back to gain a wider perspective, when we take liberties with the logic of our construct system in such a way that we can examine new possibilities. Loosening is whimsy, humour, creativity, dreaming, a bold extension of argument. Yet to *remain* loose is to deny oneself the opportunity of testing reality, of embodying one's dreams in informative and informed action. Loosening must run into tightening, into operational definition, into concrete forms. When we tighten we give our ideas a form definite enough to yield up the yeas and nays of actual events so that armed with new evidence we can begin again to loosen and re-examine the meaning of what we have concretely found. In relation to the traditional thinking–feeling dichotomy, we can raise here two questions. If you consider your own experience of moving from tight to loose and back again to tight, do you regard this experience as best designated by the notion of 'feeling' or best designated by the notion of 'thinking' or is it not adequately designated by the construct at all? Equally, it is significant that if we look at the nature of areas such as 'problem solving' in Kellyian terms, then we are immediately enmeshed in precisely those constructs related to transition, such as tightening and loosening, which Kelly offered as his way into 'emotion'. We are not safely in the area of 'cognitive' psychology as presented in standard textbooks.

GUILT

Guilt is a significant concept, both in theoretical psychology and in social argument, because, at best, it fits awkwardly into the boxes of 'feeling' and 'thinking'. Thus, we often speak of guilt as a tremendously intense and disturbing feeling. At the same time we '*find* ourselves guilty', we argue for or against our guilt, our guilt is presented as a cognitive conclusion.

Kelly defines guilt as 'the awareness of dislodgement of self from one's core role structure'. Core constructs are those which govern a person's maintenance processes, they are those constructs in terms of which identity is established, the self is pictured and understood. Your core role structure is what you understand yourself to be. For Kelly, self is an element which must be construed as must any other element. Equally, therefore, its unfolding must be anticipated like any other element. You may find yourself doing things that you would not have expected to find yourself doing had you been the sort of person you thought you were. Indeed you are fortunate if this is not part of your experience. If you find yourself, in terms of those constructs/themes around which your behaviour is centred, behaving as 'not yourself', then you will experience guilt. The guilt is experienced not because one has defied and upset social taboos but because you have misread yourself.

Again, this is a construct about transition. Unbeknown to yourself you have changed and guilt comes when you experience your own behaviour as reflecting the change and thereby contradicting that 'self' which is now part of history and no longer valid as a contemporary guide. Kelly talks about guilt in relation to sin (1969c).*

WORDS AND CONSTRUCTS

The foregoing sketch was designed merely to indicate the directions which Kelly took in proposing an alternative to the superordinate construct of 'thinking–feeling'.

The question remains: Why has construct theory been so persistently seen as 'cognitive'? The answer may lie partly in an unrecognized tenet of the theory and partly in the way in which the theory has been received.

A central contention of construct theory is that constructs are not verbal labels. A construct is the actual discrimination a person makes within the elements of his experience. For a given person a particular discrimination may or may not have a verbal label, it may be partly or obscurely labelled with only one pole indicated or it may have been a discrimination which was evolved in infancy before verbal labels became part of operating strategies. Perhaps, because in *discussing* our own and other peoples constructions we have, by the nature of our act, to label them, we too often forget this definitive assertion within construct theory. Thus constructs are most often regarded as verbal labels and thereby denied 'emotional' meaning. For it has been a prime characteristic of the way in which the concept of emotion has developed that it should denote those aspects of our experience which are well nigh impossible to verbalize. *Ergo*, by a kind of chop logic, construct theory has been seen as 'not dealing with' emotions because it is seen as dealing with words.

Construct theory has been received rather than used. It has been given a modest place in textbooks but it has had only a limited experimental and applied career and this largely in the form of expansions in the use of repertory grid technique. It may be that our failure to argue about *experience* using construct theory has impoverished the theory (for theories live and grow by use) in what it has to say about those aspects about experience conventionally dealt with under the rubric of 'emotion'. If this is true, then it is only when we seriously undertake explorations of our own and other people's experience and behaviour in terms of constructs like guilt, aggression, anxiety, hostility, that we will begin to understand their meaning and their content. Until then, construct theory will appear impoverished by contrast with the richness of lay language as a way of talking about 'emotional' aspects of experience or the evolved usefulness of, say, psychoanalytic language as a way of delineating interpersonal drama.

THE NOTION OF PERSONAL TEST

The crucial and continuing test of any psychological theory is that it should challenge and illuminate the life of the individual from the individual's viewpoint. Traditionally, psychologists have used the construct *objective–subjective* to deny the validity of personal evaluation of psychological theories. It is not only admissible but most appropriate that psychological theories should be examined in the light of

---

*Inserted by the editor.

personal experience. The reflexivity argument—the notion that psychological theories should account, among other things, for their own construction—has two sides to it. The *nature* of an argument should not, of itself, deny its truth. An argument should be valid for the person by whom it is proposed.

The first demand is rarely made by audiences of and for psychologists. Granted, if a speaker were to say, 'I have proved beyond any possibility of doubt, by carefully controlled experiment, that in no circumstances can a human being utter a sentence of more than four words', we might sense some intrinsic invalidity. Yet we listen solemnly and frequently to psychologists who give us *reasons* for believing that man's behaviour is entirely a matter of *causes* and we rarely protest.

The corollary of the contention that the statement must fit the speaker, is the speaker's demand that the statement must fit him. Personal validity is a necessary basis for consensual validity. Otherwise the speaker is lying.

In terms of personal test, I experienced the need for Kelly's integration/abandonment of the feeling/thinking dichotomy long before he presented the personal construct theory or I read of it.

As an adolescent I accepted the distinction and duly thought of myself as a container for two homuncoli—a feeling man and a thinking man. Yet even while I accepted the distinction as reflecting inescapable reality, I found that it served me poorly. The legend seemed to have it that two *personae* were at war within me. If it were not for the harsh discipline of my intellect then, so it seemed, I could have enjoyed a much more intense freedom for and through my feelings. If it were not for the distorting and prejudicial effect of my emotions, then my thoughts would have been so much clearer, more finely formed and truthful. Given this kind of bipolarity I was to choose and re-choose between the demands of reason and the dictates of passion and whichever choice I made seemed somehow to diminish me. I was to be a more miserable lover because I was a better logician, a more muddled philosopher because I was a more sensitive man. In one area after another I was to be intellectual Roundhead or libidinous Cavalier. The choice seemed inescapable.

My then solution for this dilemma was either to alternate or to seek some middle position which made me a compromised representative of both. This seemed less damaging than to take up everlasting residence at one pole or other of the dichotomy but at best I felt/thought it to be a mean and confusing compromise.

Kelly, by offering notions such as tightening and loosening and above all by proposing the notion of constructs in transition solved for me an ancient problem. I could, in the vision of personal change and resistance to change, account for the intensity of my experience while accepting that the 'me' that changed or resisted change was a whole person and not a pair of warring dwarfs. And the 'me' that commented on myself I could see as reflexive and superordinate but still entailed in all levels of me.

I no longer see myself as the victim of my 'emotion'. My 'emotions' may torment me but I accept them as an integral part of me, as entailed in all that I have 'thought'. I now accept that in my 'emotions' lie the beginnings, endings and forms of my 'thoughts' and it is to what I have 'thought' that I 'feelingly' respond.

Nor can others so easily use the schism to confuse and condemn me. If my 'anger' is rejected because I have no good 'reasons', or my 'argument' is dismissed because I lack 'feeling', then I accept that others experience me as segmented. I do not have to experience myself thus.

CONCLUSION

The idea of thought and feeling as the two great modes of human experience relates to and bedevils a number of superordinate debates.

A popular vision of Art versus Science is because it aligns them along this dimension, thus denying the enormous complexity of structure which underlies poetry or music or painting and the intensely personal commitment which informs scientific endeavour. Equally, such a contrasting leads us away from an exploration of the nature of *invention* which is at the heart of both. The blinkering effect of such a contrasting of Art and Science manifests itself through our cultural inheritance and produces a myopia in our educational system so that 'artists' are kept ignorant of the creative possibilities of hypothesis while 'scientists' are encouraged to see themselves as routine clerks to nature.

The male versus female roles which are the root *personae* of society, pivot most often on some version of the belief that man is 'by nature' rational and woman emotional. There is no way of calculating how many lives have been constrained, if not crippled, by the attempt to live to such specifications but we can observe the liberating effect of a refusal to bow to the doctrine of the insensitive man and the fearful woman. In work, in relationships, in the very legal arrangements we live by, the thought–feeling dichotomy has been pedestal to man–woman, beginning with the tearful but charming little girl and the tough, capable little boy and elaborating into the adult who cannot find ways of sexually differentiating himself/herself that are not bounded by the poles of this construct.

Even the time line along which we live has been dominated by the exclusivity of thought and feeling so that we seem condemned to move from the enthusiasm and passion of *youth* to the wisdom and calmness of *age*. The range of our choice of style, cause, engagement is arbitrarily limited by what we are socially taught is appropriate to young and old respectively, and what we are taught derives much of its content from what are seen as the irreconcilable claims of passion and reason. A psychological theory cannot be simply a specification of what humanity is. Because it is self-reflecting it must be a tool that people use in going about the business of being persons.

A psychological theory cannot be a simple representation of a state of affairs—it must be a challenge, a liberating vision, a way of reaching out. If it is not these things then it will be a justification for a personal and social status quo, a form of retreat, a prison.

Most psychological theories have not sought to challenge the picture of people as segmented into thought and feeling. Indeed they have not even seen it *as a picture*, they have taken it as 'real' and worked within the boundaries thereby set. Kelly was truly adventurous in abandoning the construct and offering alternative ways of interpreting experience. The alternative he offered, the construct of 'change', is open to criticism, it is an invitation which we are free to refuse. The least sensible or gracious response to his invitation is not to see that it was being made, and to categorize Kelly as a man who did not understand 'emotion' and who thereby constructed a merely 'cognitive' theory.

CHAPTER 3

The Power of a Good Theory

Sean Brophy
Dublin, Ireland

Fay Fransella
University of Hertfordshire, UK

and

Nick Reed
Petts Wood, Kent, UK

Theories are the thinking of men who seek freedom amid swirling events.
(Kelly, 1955/1991, p. 22/ Vol. 1, p. 16)

WHAT IS A THEORY?

Some choose to work within a theoretical framework—most often belonging to someone other than themselves—while others choose to rely on their own knowledge and experience. So, first, a few words on what is meant by the word 'theory'. A theory is a way of binding facts together so that they mean more than any individual fact itself. A theory consists of a formalized set of ideas which may ultimately explain much that was not even thought of at the time the theory was constructed. It is a place to go when in doubt. It informs future action. It is a framework within which certain deductions can be made and outcomes anticipated. A theory therefore needs to be as complex or as simple as its subject matter. Personal construct theory has to be as complex as we see ourselves as being. Theories are also, of course, expendable and designed to be tested to the limit. But as long as they continue to prove useful and fertile, they survive.

There is a certain resistance to theories within psychology. It is the belief of some that theories limit one's thinking; that they act like a pair of blinkers. But to those who work within the psychology of personal constructs, a theory is liberating and exciting. The theory allows one to be creative while, at the same time, setting limits on that creativity. It stops one going wild. The very flexibility of Kelly's psychology has led to a wide range of interventions being conducted in the life of

The Essential *Practitioner's Handbook of Personal Construct Psychology.* Edited by F. Fransella.
© 2005 John Wiley & Sons, Ltd.

organizations. The following should be viewed as examples of how personal construct theory can be applied within a single work context, be that a hospital, a school, a police force, a bank or a multinational organization. Within that single work context the personal construct theoretical framework can range from work with large groups to single individuals.

One central premise must be stated from the outset. As with all other contexts in which this psychology is being found useful, *it is the construing of the groups or individuals that matters and not that of experts or consultants.* That means that no ideas, hopes or fears are imposed. The only language of importance is that of the groups that make up the organization. In that way ideas and attitudes, which no one had guessed had existed, are given a chance to emerge.

WORK AT A LARGE GROUP LEVEL

Personal construct theory and repertory grid methods have been used to specify cultural and people/relationship issues within the group. These studies have often been carried out to provide the baseline for designing and implementing change programmes. An important feature of this work is that the information yielded is couched in the language of the target groups and the data can be used to sign the way forward.

The theory and its underlying philosophy lead personal construct interventionists to carry out their work from the point of view that it is the person or client organization that has the answers to the issues confronting them. The approach provides the context within which those answers may be surfaced. No 'truths' are imposed on personnel. The only 'truths' are to be found within the organization itself. These group 'truths' may take the form of what Kelly called 'super-patterns', as discussed by Robertson (Chapter 19).

There is one guiding principle that comes from personal construct theory. That is, one respects the integrity of the individuals with whom one works. In practice, that means that one never asks a person to change until one has at least a glimpse into that person's ways of viewing the world, and so has an idea of what that change might mean to them. That should apply as much to change programmes within organizations as it does in individual psychotherapy. However, when working with large groups of people, that principle must be violated. All that can be done is to ensure that one gains as much knowledge as possible about the current views of the target group before embarking on a programme that is asking them to change those views.

The Diagnostic Research Method

The Centre for Personal Construct Psychology in the United Kingdom played a role in developing ways of exploring the construing of groups within an organization (Fransella, 1988). The diagnostic research method it developed consists of linking personal construct qualitative interviewing methods with its quantitative tool—the repertory grid—to produce statistical data.

It has been said that this is 'nomothetic', focusing as it does on the construing of groups rather on the individual as Kelly envisioned. But Fransella argues that the approach is 'idiographic', in the sense that all the personal constructs are elicited from the group of people in question, and that the common constructs included in the final repertory grid have been derived from those individual interviews and not from work with thousands of workers and then imposed on participants. After all, the *Commonality Corollary* states that the more we share a given culture, the more our ways of construing will be similar. It is supposed that groups in organizations share such a culture. Kelly's own discussion of the idiographic–nomothetic debate can be found in Fransella, Bell and Bannister (2004, pp. 164–165).

The diagnostic research method was originally designed for the British Airways initiative *Putting People First* in the early 1980s. British Airways was concerned to find out what staff in various divisions of the company thought and felt about their work, the company, their passengers, their management and so forth. The results from twenty groups—ranging from different types of engineer to catering and information technology personnel—provided profiles of how people in the specified groups felt about the roles they were required to play, which could then inform the retraining programme. Hinkle's (1965) *resistance-to-change* grid was used to measure the relative importance of the constructs used in the grids (see Chapter 9, pp. 105–106).

A case study document of the Marketing Council (Galsworthy, 1997) describes the Centre's diagnostic research in some detail, and says of cabin crew:

> Sociability was identified as the dominant factor and that which caused the most problems. Staff would approach passengers in a friendly, social manner, but if the passenger for whatever reason did not respond in kind, they were classed as a 'bad' passenger and treated differently from then on.

The results clearly showed that cabin crew did not want to be like that. Instead they wanted to *meet the needs of individuals* and to *be professional*. Since that was how BA's Chairman and Chief Executive wanted them to be, the only retraining that was needed was for cabin crew to be given permission to behave as they felt right.

The report goes on to say that the Centre's research plus some market research on passenger attitudes 'set the direction for the first of British Airways' staff communication and motivation programmes, under the umbrella of "Putting the Customer First—if we don't, someone else will"'.

Apart from informing change programmes and identifying why some groups may resist change, the diagnostic research method can be used to study intergroup conflict, identify potential problems when two organizations merge, find out whether all levels of personnel agree on the meaning of a mission statement, and it can also help to address such difficult problems as bullying.

Bullying

Bullying has been described as endemic in British organizations whether in the public, private or voluntary sectors (Ishmael, 1999). However, the term 'bullying' is one of such imprecise meaning that carrying out research into the problem is often of little value. Standardized questionnaires, which either ask simply about 'bullying' or impose the researcher's construing of the meaning of 'bullying', can only provide limited and, possibly even misleading, data. Public, private and voluntary organizations all have different cultures. In addition, organizations in different sectors—industrial concerns, insurance companies, armed and public services, to name but a few—will all have their own 'definitions' of bullying. In a white collar office, the term 'bullying' may include something which is construed as innocent larking around in a Royal Marine Commando barracks.

Thus, the first task an organization committed to eradicating bullying has to address is how it is going to define 'bullying' behaviour, so that it identifies behaviours that are truly meaningful to those whom it concerns. If researchers impose their own definition, they are likely to get it wrong. One way of approaching the problem is to design a specially modified version of the diagnostic research method described above. The organization can then find out:

- the behaviours that people who work in the organization construe as 'bullying'
- the incidence of bullying in the organization
- who is bullying whom
- the effects of bullying behaviours on those who are bullied (for example, stress, anxiety, depression)
- the effect that bullying is likely to have on the organization (for example, in terms of absenteeism, low quality of work and staff turnover).

Further analysis of the repertory grid data can then be used to:

(a) inform the drafting of a detailed disciplinary code;
(b) inform the design of training programmes/workshops to reduce the incidence of bullying in the company;
(c) assist in the assessment of the financial costs of bullying behaviours to the organization, for example, in relation to reduced quality of work, absenteeism and staff turnover;
(d) enable the company to comply better with the various statutory provisions that exist in relation to bullying behaviours.

Knowledge Management

Knowledge management has proved to be of great interest to organizations in recent years and personal construct psychology offers both a theoretical and methodological approach (Reed, 2000). An early unpublished paper of Kelly's, entitled 'Knowledge: Discovery or Invention' (*c.* 1954), shows that knowledge and personal construct theory are intimately linked. He says:

> Man has a tendency to be mystified by his knowledge, even when it is his own. He is likely to think of it, not so much as a product of his own venturesome efforts, but as something that happens to him, like the wind and the rain. . . . It is terribly hard for most of us to be convinced that knowledge is something that we can and often do create for ourselves.

The aim of what has come to be called 'knowledge management' is to make explicit the knowledge that exists in an organization. In a sense, that is essentially what the personal construct diagnostic research method of focused interview and repertory grid administration and analysis does. Jankowicz (2001) has described this as the surfacing of tacit knowledge. Another way of eliciting or surfacing implicit knowledge is by the computer study of 'expert systems', as described in Chapter 8.

ORGANIZATION STRUCTURE

Structure is an arrangement of roles used in organizations to focus power, responsibility and accountability. Usually when complaints are made about one or another structural feature, the underlying cause is a problem of power or lack of it. Personal construct psychology can be used to make explicit the construing of personnel about a problem inherent in a particular structure. That may be about inadequate decentralization of decision making, overly long lines of communication, inadequate personal discretion and autonomy. Moreover, when allied to a personal construct understanding of resistance to change in those centres of power under threat, the process of change can be rendered less painful and traumatic for those concerned (see Chapter 9, pp. 102–106, for a discussion of resistance to change).

WORKING WITH SPECIFIC GROUPS

Management Processes

Management processes such as meeting schedules, reporting formats and various policy guidelines for action can be rationalized. Personal construct research focusing on a range of management processes as elements in a repertory grid can highlight areas of dissatisfaction and malfunctioning. Feedback of the results of this research can lead to changes that allow organization members to function more effectively with their time more optimally focused on the core mission, such as service to clients as opposed to meeting internal bureaucratic needs that are often wasteful of effort.

Functional Processes

The possibilities here are many. The examples below offer a mere hint of the range of applications of personal construct psychology.

Planning

One possibility is to identify several planning scenarios as elements. For example, Enter Industry 'A', Exit Industry 'B', Take Over Business 'C', Merge With Business 'D' and so on. These can be construed by representative groups of different layers of management. Further, they can be rated in terms of the probability of their occurrence and attractiveness to the respondents. The results are a best guess of the future by the groups, allowing a planning team to pursue, from an evidential point of view, the hypothesis set out by the respondents.

Marketing

The construing of customers' needs for products and services and perceptions of those products currently on offer from an organization and its competitors can be elicited. Another use is for a group of product designers to construe their level of innovation as perceived by their major stakeholders—for instance, the sales personnel in an organization.

Customer Service

Customer service values espoused for a particular brand can be transformed into bipolar constructs in conversation with service personnel. They could then be asked to rate themselves as service providers 'now' and as they 'would like to be', say, in three months' time. Other elements rated could be 'my unit or department', 'my organization', 'how I think the customer sees me' and so on. The resultant analysis can form the basis for removal of factors that inhibit good service, training to provide good service and promotional programmes to highlight service features to customers.

Team Development

This can be based on generic aspects of intact groups. For example, Brophy (2002) has suggested that this can be based on the ideas of Schein (1985). Clear goals, roles and processes for dealing with the world outside the group and with relationships inside the group can be the focus. Initially each member of the group is asked to elaborate their understanding of their responsibilities and the expectations of critical stakeholders to their role. These statements are then tested in a plenary session with all team members to clarify understanding of and negotiation of changes to their responsibilities and expectations of each other. The facilitator can then elicit their construing of a range of elements consisting of the network of stakeholders external and internal to the group who are making demands on them, in terms of processes to deal with these demands. The resultant set of constructs can be arrayed on a repertory grid and rated by individuals on elements such as 'How I see my team now' and 'How I see my team in six months' time'. The ratings are pooled anonymously and displayed to allow for a group discussion. In the discussion the pattern of ratings can be examined on each construct in turn to search for the meaning behind the clustering or otherwise of ratings. Laddering and pyramiding questions (see Chapter 4, pp. 48–54) can be used to deepen their collective under-standing of why the ratings are as they are and how they can be illustrated in terms of observable behaviours. The scope for, and desirability of, change on various con-structs can be examined and ideas elicited for practical experimentation by indi-viduals or through negotiation by stakeholders. A very early report on team building is that of Tony Armstrong and Colin Eden in 1979, in which they demonstrate the usefulness of using both implications and repertory grids (see Chapter 6, pp. 67–76, for repertory grids and Chapter 9, p. 99, for implications grids).

Goal Setting

An example here would be to elicit a group's constructs of the demands made on them by a network of stakeholders by treating the group as an 'Open System' (Beckhard & Harris, 1977). Members are then invited to indicate how they are meeting those demands at present. That discussion is followed by a collective construing of trends likely to impact on the life of the group in such elements as economics, technology, politics, demography and the behaviour of consumers, competitors and new entrants into the group's markets. This analysis allows for a construing by the group of demands from stakeholders in, say, five years' time, followed by a debate on how to meet those demands. Options can be tested using some form of grid and their ranking in terms of effectiveness and viability using resistance-to-change grids. That final process allows the team to select goals and related action plans over the time period in question.

Training

An example could be training in leadership skills. One could take a generic list of the attributes of a good leader in the particular context of a business unit. Constructs elicited from these can be arrayed on a repertory grid. Clients on a training course rate themselves on a number of elements and the ratings are pooled anonymously to reveal a pattern for the group. Individuals can then see the degree to which they share experiences with their colleagues. Each client is then helped to find insights from the ratings and to consider actions whereby they could act on their own initiative through experimentation to reach the desired ratings over the time period agreed.

WORK WITH INDIVIDUALS

Coaching and Counselling

Coaching and counselling are at opposite ends of a spectrum of interventions with individuals in work contexts that might be described as 'Opportunistic' through coaching and 'Distress' through counselling.

Opportunistic Coaching

This is designed to improve their efficiency as managers. One way to do this is to help individuals to turn their desired management competencies, like 'Communicating well' into a series of dichotomous constructs in a repertory grid. They would be asked to rate themselves on two elements, 'Me in my job now' and 'Me in my job as I'd like to be, say, in six months' time'. Through a process of laddering and pyramiding coachees are helped to understand their own construing. They can then carry out experiments to test a desired view of themselves and are helped to reflect on the results.

Distress Coaching

An individual could, for example, be counselled to adapt to changes in his or her life, perhaps to help the individual to cope with the loss of a particular job through demotion or a failure to be promoted. In these contexts the counsellor helps the individual to reconstrue the events in question. The aim is to help clients to regain a sense of control and autonomy in their lives, through new interpretations, alternative perspectives and careful experimentation.

Improving Interpersonal Relationships

One example would be to meet two individuals who had a poor relationship separately, prior to a team-building exercise. That would allow them to express their feelings privately in the first instance. One could then elicit constructs to do with each client's expectations from the other and, reciprocally, their notion of what the other expects of him or her. These expectations are then converted into dichotomous constructs in conversation with each client to reveal what they wish to achieve and to avoid. The couple are then brought together against the background of ground rules for a fair process like, for example, separating the person from the problem, focusing on interests rather than positions and no monopolies on the truth or of being hurt (Fisher & Ury, 1991). The constructs based upon expectations of each other can then be checked with the two persons for clarity of understanding, and acceptance of the various terms can be negotiated. This can take up several sessions and the process can be helped by inviting the individuals to work on the relationship separate from the substantive issues that divide them. Fisher and Brown (1989) have evolved a series of principles for what they call an 'unconditionally constructive strategy' for collaboration. These principles can also be converted into dichotomous constructs by the participants to reveal what they want and what they wish to avoid. Further, they can be helped to consider the implications of adopting the principles and of accepting each other's expectations as valid within the relationship. Later sessions can be focused on reviewing their experiences.

Mentoring

The word 'mentoring' is a very abstract term which is used to describe a range of ways to help people in work and other settings. The most familiar concepts of the mentor are:

(a) the older, wiser person taking on the less experienced member of staff as a 'protégé', or
(b) the mentor as expert in a particular type of work, who tutors the novice such as the trainee psychotherapist and her supervisor, or
(c) the mentor who is a trainer, facilitating the training of an individual or group.

However, the concept of mentoring under which personal construct mentoring most usefully fits is the 'Developmental Alliance' (Hay, 1995). Hay describes such an alliance as:

> a relationship between equals in which one or more of those involved is enabled to: increase awareness, identify alternatives and initiate action (and) to develop themselves. (p. 3)

In personal construct terms, mentoring can be subsumed under such a concept as regards the *purpose* of the mentoring relationship. But the skills and methods used in personal construct mentoring can also be applied to the other types of mentoring.

Skills are those involved in any constructive intervention (see Chapter 4, pp. 41–45 for details). For instance, the mentor adopts a 'credulous attitude', he or she tries to see the world as the mentee sees it and accepts as 'true' what the person says. Often, the mentee will be asked to write a character sketch of herself in either her present role or in some other significant role that is relevant to her circumstances. She may to asked to complete a repertory grid, perhaps concerning her relationship with others in the organization. Very likely, the link between how she construes her situation will be explored in relation to her core personal values and beliefs using the technique of laddering—usually essential if a real understanding of the person is to be achieved (see Chapter 4, pp. 48–53). When appropriate, an action plan can be devised.

More concrete and precise ways of dealing with a situation can be established through the use of pyramiding (see Chapter 4, p. 54). The end result is that the action plan and its implementation will relate precisely to that particular mentee based specifically on the information that she and her mentor have elicited using personal construct methods. The relationship and the product of the 'developmental alliance' will be truly personal in every sense.

SUMMARY

We believe that having a theory to work within is important. Its main importance when working within organizations lies in allowing the practitioner to relate understanding gained at different levels and in different contexts within the same frame of reference. There can be studies of culture, of selection, or of interdepartmental conflict, all of which are couched in the same language and use the same methods of enquiry. Under the direction of George O'Connor, the Irish Airports Authority set about applying a personal construct model to every aspect of its work that involves people. Apart from being seen as a valuable philosophy to permeate an organizational culture, a single theoretical model also provides a framework for creative thinking and action and offers a guiding hand to practice. Kelly puts it thus:

> A theory may be considered as a way of binding together a multitude of facts so that one may comprehend them all at once. . . . But this is not all. A theory provides a basis for an active approach to life, not merely a comfortable armchair from which to contemplate its vicissitudes with detached complaisance. Mankind need not be a throng of stony-faced spectators witnessing the pageant of creation. Men can play active roles in the shaping of events.
>
> (Kelly, 1955/1991, p. 18/Vol. 1, p. 13)

What Are Some of PCP's Techniques?

CHAPTER 4

Some Skills and Tools For Personal Construct Users

Fay Fransella
University of Hertfordshire, UK

> It would, in my opinion, be a serious mistake for psychologists who hope to raise man from the position of an unwitting subject in an experiment to a posture of greater dignity, to abandon technology. The spirit of man is not enlarged by withholding his tools. . . . A man without instruments may look dignified enough to those who do not stand in his shoes, but he most certainly will be incapable of making the most of his potentialities.
>
> (Kelly, 1969a, p. 143)

This chapter has two main sections. There are skills that all personal construct practitioners need to acquire in order to carry out any intervention with a client, be it in psychotherapy and counselling or in coming to understand a child having trouble at school. There are also many tools that are available to personal construct practitioners to assist them in eliciting information about how a client construes his or her personal world. Skills and some tools are combined into one chapter because they overlap considerably—the skills are nearly all required by those who want to use the tools.

SOME NECESSARY SKILLS

The Ability to Subsume Another's Construing

An essential skill required of the personal construct practitioner is the ability to subsume the construing system of the client. That is basically the ability to see the world through the client's eyes. Kelly talks about this mainly in relation to psychotherapy and counselling. In that context the practitioner needs to subsume the

The Essential *Practitioner's Handbook of Personal Construct Psychology.* Edited by F. Fransella.
© 2005 John Wiley & Sons, Ltd.

client's construing under Kelly's *professional constructs*. These are such things as *tight* versus *loose* construing, as described in Chapter 1 (pp. 118–120) and defined in Appendix 1. Kelly puts it like this: 'since all clients have their own personal systems my system should be *a system of approach* by means of which I can quickly come to understand and subsume the widely varying systems which my clients can be expected to present' (Kelly, 1955/1991, p. 595/Vol. 2, p. 28).

Apart from the therapy and counselling situation, the ability to subsume the client's construing system is essential for anyone who is a personal construct practitioner. Subsuming is a basic part of Kelly's idea of role relationships expressed in the Sociality Corollary. He makes the point that subsuming another's ways of looking at things need not be reciprocal:

> . . . while one person may play a role in a social process involving the other person, through subsuming a version of that other person's way of seeing things, the understanding need not be reciprocated. (Kelly, 1955/1991, p. 98/Vol. 1, p. 69)

It is useful to note that subsuming a person's construing is not the same as 'empathizing'. Empathy usually implies not only entering the other person's world but experiencing how the other person is feeling about that world. Subsuming involves seeing the world through another's eyes—and even experiencing some of the feelings involved—but also maintaining a sense of oneself as being separate from the other. Only in that way can one gain a personal understanding of that person and play a role in relation to that person.

Suspending Personal Values

There is a second component involved in understanding the construing of another—suspending. In actual fact, Kelly does not discuss suspension in relation to subsuming, but sees it in relation to memory and forgetting. Over the years of discovering the value of subsuming a client's construing, it became very apparent that the personal construct interviewer has to suspend his or her own values. If one does not, the other's construing is filtered through the interviewer's values. The only way to see the world as someone else sees it is to have no values through which it is filtered. The skill of suspending one's own values in order to truly listen to another is not an easy one to acquire, as many students of personal construct psychology have found.

Listening Credulously

The idea of listening credulously is mentioned many times in this volume as being one of the requirements of a skilled personal construct practitioner. It is sometimes believed that it applies to any and all work that a personal construct practitioner undertakes with another person. But that is to misunderstand what Kelly meant. He describes it like this:

> ... the personal-construct psychologist observes a person's own abstractions of behaviour. . . . He starts by taking what he sees and hears at face value. He even takes at face value what he sees and hears about his subject's constructs. In psychotherapy this is commonly called 'acceptance' of the client. . . . Our term . . . is *the credulous attitude*. (Kelly, 1955/1991, p. 174/Vol. 1, p. 121)

What Kelly was proposing is that the personal construct practitioner is always trying to subsume the client's construing and this does not mean 'going along with how the client sees things'. 'Acceptance does not mean seeking mere commonality of ideas between clinician and client, it means seeking a way of *subsuming* the construct system of the client. One must retain his integrity in order to be of help to the client' (Kelly, 1955/1991, p. 374/Vol. 1, p. 277).

Once some understanding of a person's construing has been achieved, any programme to help the person reconstrue may well involve the practitioner in acting so as to invalidate some construing of the client. But that is always done in the context of attempting to 'hear' and 'see' how the client is construing that invalidation. The trap that needs to be avoided is to think that 'acceptance' is the end of the process. It is only the beginning. While even obvious lies are accepted at being meaningful and important to the client, at some later stage those lies may become the focus of the counselling if it is thought that would help the client reconstrue themselves and life.

Reflexivity

One final skill that is essential for anyone wanting to apply personal construct psychology in a professional capacity—or in daily life if they wish—is *reflexivity*. Don Bannister discusses this at some length and shows how reflexivity is central to all Kelly's thinking (2003, Chapter 3, pp. 35–37). To emphasize its importance, below is a description that Don Bannister gave to a group of American psychologists of how the ability to be reflexive discourages psychologists from diminishing their concepts of themselves and those they study. He said:

> ... At a joke level psychologists may argue that a particular psychoanalyst is writing a particular paper in order to sublimate his sex instinct, or we may toy with the notion that a book by some learning theorist is evidence that the said learning theorist was suffering from a build-up of reactive inhibition. But in our more solemn moments we seem to prefer the paradoxical view that psychologists are explainers, predictors, and experimenters, whereas the organism, God bless him, is a very different kettle of fish. . . . The delight and instruction which many of us find in George Kelly's Personal Construct Theory derives in no small measure from the fact that it is an explicitly reflexive theory. There may be no onus on the chemist when he writes his papers on the nature of acids and alkalis to account in terms of his acid–alkali distinction for his behaviour in writing a journal paper. But psychologists are in no such fortunate position.
> Turning this issue of reflexivity the other way around, I am reminded of a recurrent theme in certain types of science fiction story. The master-chemist has finally produced a bubbling green slime in his test tubes, the potential of which is great but the properties of which are mysterious. He sits alone in his

laboratory, test tube in hand, brooding about what to do with the bubbling green slime. Then in slowly dawns on him that the bubbling green slime is sitting alone in the test tube brooding about what to do with him. This special nightmare of the chemist is the permanent work-a-day world of the psychologist—the bubbling green slime is always wondering what to do with you.

(Bannister, 1966a, pp. 21–22)

Personal Characteristics of Psychotherapists and Counsellors

Four vital skills that a personal construct practitioner has to acquire have already been mentioned. These are being able to subsume a client's construing of the world (as far as that is humanly possible), suspending his or her own values, being able to listen credulously, and being able to apply the theory to one's own construing processes.

Apart from those, Kelly suggests that psychotherapists and counsellors should have four other skills.

Creativity

Kelly argues that every client will present new challenges which will mean that the therapist has to devise methods and construe in ways not used before.

> Creativity implies that one can construe elements as being alike and different in ways which are not logically deduced or, as yet, literally defined. Creation is therefore an act of daring, an act of daring through which the creator abandons those literal defenses behind which he might hide if his act is questioned or its results proven invalid. The psychotherapist who dares not try anything he cannot verbally defend is likely to be sterile in a psychotherapeutic relationship.
> (Kelly, 1955/1991, pp. 600–601/Vol. 2, p. 32)

Skill in Observation

In order to be alert and sensitive to a wide range of client responses, clinicians need to have a well-elaborated construing system of their own coupled with a variety of experiences. For instance, it is necessary to be able to decide when it is important to ask for a medical opinion about a client—perhaps the client's current confusion is the result of a developing brain tumour.

Clear Construction of the Psychotherapeutic/Counselling Role

In the reflexive manner that permeates personal construct psychology, the clinician has to be able to recognize when he or she is threatening or making the client anxious. In subsuming the client's construing system, the therapist and counsellor are able to maintain enough distance from the distresses of the client not to be overwhelmed by them. They have to be able to cease that role when they return home.

Verbal Skill

Kelly also says the therapist and counsellor need to be verbally skilled. That is not so much about vocabulary but about being able to get to the meaning that often lies behind the words.

SOME 'TOOLS OF THE TRADE'

Kelly created two 'tools of the trade', one being the repertory grid (see Chapter 6, pp. 67–76) and the other the self-characterization (see Chapter 5, pp. 59–60). Here we are concerned with 'how do you do it?' Richard Bell gives an extensive overview of many aspects of repertory grid methodology in Chapter 6, so the following is an example for those who want to explore the methodology by designing a ratings grid themselves.

Repertory Grids

First of all, a grid is nothing more than a blank matrix. The job of the designer is to fill it in with 'element' labels at the top of each column, 'construct labels' on either side of each row and ratings in each of the cells showing how the person construed each element in relation to each construct.

Richard Bell, in Chapter 6, describes ways in which the elements can be chosen and constructs elicited. As he says, the choice of elements is crucial and relates totally to the purpose of the grid. Choice of elements is centrally determined by asking the question 'What am I trying to find out by using this grid?' Having decided on the purpose—for example, why people choose specific makes of toothpaste—the elements must then cover the broad spectrum of toothpaste available. They must also be within the range of convenience of the constructs being used. It is no use, having elicited constructs from different toothpastes, adding an element 'my favourite jewel', as that is unlikely to be within the range of convenience of such constructs as *has a peppermint taste*. One of the best examples of a range of convenience problem comes from Brown's review of the *Semantic Differential* when he asked 'is a boulder sweet or sour?' (1958).

Most grids are designed to find out how a person construes people or events in their lives. If you wanted to find out whether people taking part in a course you are running have the same views about their organization, then the elements would be about their work and their organization, such as:

'my manager', 'my job now', 'my organization', 'the best manager I can think of', 'how my organization will be in 3 years' time', 'how customers see my organization', 'how I would like my job to be', and 'my organization 3 years ago'.

These elements include the essential 'ideal' element. That element acts as an anchor against which all other elements and constructs can be compared. If that ideal does not have mostly very positive ratings, then something is going wrong from the client's point of view—perhaps he or she just does not want to complete the

	My manager	My job now	My organization	Best manager I know	My organization in 3 years	As customers see my organization	How would like job to be	My organization 3 years ago	
Constructive	5	3	7	1	5	7	1	7	Mundane
Disorganized	6	2	2	6	4	1	6	1	Organized
Listens	4	6	5	1	6	6	1	2	Doesn't hear
No clear view	4	5	4	6	4	3	7	5	Takes strategic view

Figure 4.1   Ratings grid

grid and is answering randomly. Those elements enable one to see how the organization is perceived in the present as compared with the past and the future, how immediate authority is perceived and how the recipients of the service or product provided are perceived. The constructs elicited were:

Constructive vs. *mundane; disorganized* vs. *organized; doesn't hear* vs. *listens; has no clear view* vs. *takes a strategic view; easy-going* vs. *rigid; in tune with things* vs. *discordant; communicates well* vs. *communicates badly.*

A grid form into which ratings can be inserted is shown in Figure 4.1.

Ratings can be elicited from your client by having each element written on a small card and spread out on the table in front of the client. It is sometimes useful to have the scale range indicated. If you use a 7-point scale—which is most common—then it would be shown as '1 ... 7'. That applies whether or not the evaluatively more positive pole of the construct is on the left- or right-hand side of the card. In fact, it is important to have some positive poles on the left-hand side of the grid and some on the right. Most computer programs will sort out the constructs so that all the positive poles are on the same side (see Appendix 3 for details of some programs).

To elicit the ratings, the client is asked to look at the first element and then at the first construct and decide, first of all, whether 'my manager' is best described as being *constructive* (ratings 1, 2 or 3), or as being more *mundane* (ratings 5, 6 or 7). In the example, the person said 'my manager' was slightly on the *mundane* side, giving that cell a '5'. The client then gives ratings for all the elements on construct 1, *constructive* versus *mundane*.

Different Types of Grids

Many grids have been created along these lines. For instance, Ryle and Lunghi (1970) found it useful to have constructs elicited in terms of relationships. The *dyad grid* uses elements such as 'you in relation to your priest' and 'your priest in relation to you'; 'you in relation to your mother' and 'your mother in relation to you'. The task for the client is something like 'are there any ways in which your relationship with your priest is similar to or differs from your mother's relationship with you?'

Then there is Bob Neimeyer's *biographical grid*. For this, the client identifies significant events or stages in his or her life (Neimeyer, 1985b). The client can then be asked to construe these events indicating, as usual, how any two of them may be alike and thereby different from the third, or simply being asked to describe the events.

The *exchange grid* (Mendoza, 1985) has been used in many contexts, especially where team building is involved. Members of a group or couple complete their own personal grids, A's, then one or others complete the A grids 'as if' they were the other person and produce the B grid. Comparisons of the A with the relevant B grid can be very informative. Like most procedures in a personal construct context, these grids need to be carefully handled because the comparisons may well cause people to feel personally threatened or to become anxious.

One type of grid has been found useful in relation to decision-making issues. Shaw and McKnight (1981) suggest that once a grid on, say, the construing of cars, has been completed with a 1 to 5 rating scale, with 5 being the most favourable rating, constructs in the grid are changed so that all favourable poles of constructs are on the left-hand side of the grid. Naturally, in a grid about cars, the elements are different types of car. The ratings are simply added down each column to give an overall rating for each car. One step further measures the relative importance of each car. Each construct is assigned a number from 1 to 10, with 10 being given to the most important construct. The rating for each element on each construct is multiplied by the assigned number indicating construct importance. Those numbers are then added up to show precisely the relative importance of each car.

Dunn and his colleagues (1986) describe the 'policy grid' they designed to study 'frames of reference towards criminal justice information policies in a large urban municipality'. In fact, as Richard Bell says, it is the very versatility of this type of repertory grid that is both its attraction and its challenge. Denicolo suggests that there is too much reliance on the grid (Chapter 5) (see also Neimeyer, 1985a).

Such grids are basically determined by their elements. If one uses situations for a person to construe—such as someone who stutters—then one has a 'situations' grid. If different countries serve as elements, then one has perhaps a 'cultures' grid. Sometimes a particular grid is developed so as to become an assessment tool in its own right. Such a grid is the one developed by Bob Neimeyer on the construing of death (see Neimeyer & Epting, 1992).

The Death Threat Index

Bob Neimeyer describes his long and fruitful line of research deriving from personal construct theory. It examines the degree to which people are aware of imminent, comprehensive change in their core role structure when asked to reflect on their own mortality. The original, repertory grid-based measure of this concept, the Threat Index (Krieger et al., 1974), required eliciting a sample of death-relevant constructs (for example, *painful* versus *painless*, *meaningful* versus *meaningless*) from the respondent through a comparison of situations involving death, such as 'a tornado kills three children in an elementary school', 'your grandmother dies in her sleep'. The person then rated the elements 'self', 'preferred self' and (personal) 'death' on these constructs. The number of *splits* in which both self-elements were aligned with one construct pole, and death with its contrast, served as the index of the subjective threat that would be entailed in construing the death of self as a personal reality. The Threat Index was streamlined into a standardized measure using frequently occurring constructs and its validity and reliability documented in dozens of studies, making it the best established measure in the entire literature on death attitudes (Neimeyer, 1994).

The availability of a solid measure of death threat made possible numerous applications to such topics as the death threat experienced by suicide intervention workers (Neimeyer & Dingemans, 1980), the link between death anxiety and the completion of one's existential goals (Neimeyer & Chapman, 1980), and the personal anxieties about death experienced by gay and bisexual men living in the shadow of the AIDS epidemic (Bivens et al., 1994). Later research has expanded this focus to include the threat and discomfort of counsellors working with clients presenting with either death-related problems, such as grief or AIDS, or with non-death-related problems, such as marital discord or physical handicap (Kirchberg et al., 1998). As hypothesized, counsellors reported greater discomfort in responding to the death than non-death situations—a response that proved to be mediated by the personal death fears of the counsellor. Moreover, the least empathic responses were provided by counsellors who construed death in fatalistic terms on the Threat Index, suggesting that working with death and loss can prove especially challenging for those counsellors whose personal constructions of death leave them vulnerable to such work.

Further details of repertory grid theory and methods can be found in the forthcoming second edition of the *Manual for Repertory Grid Technique* (Fransella, Bell & Bannister, 2004).

Laddering

It is difficult to decide whether laddering is a skill or a tool. It is really both. A very complex skill to learn and one of the most useful tools to have come from personal construct psychology. It is primarily used to elicit superordinate, more value-laden constructs from individuals. It is sometimes very useful to put one or two of these into a person's grid. When Denny Hinkle first described this procedure (1965), he did not call it laddering. It seems likely that Bannister and Mair (1968) coined that name.

Hinkle called it 'the hierarchical technique for eliciting the superordinate constructs of the preferred self hierarchy'. His theory of construct implications is described in Chapter 9 (pp. 98–99). Here the focus is on the method.

Ever since Hinkle described the procedure, people have argued about how it should be carried out, its usefulness and its validity—does it 'really' elicit superordinate personal constructs? The method he described is clear enough. You ask the person to say which pole of a construct he would prefer to describe himself and then ask why he prefers that pole rather than the other. 'What are the advantages of this side in contrast to the disadvantages of that side, as you see it?' One of Hinkle's people preferred to be *reserved* rather than *emotional*, because being *reserved* implied being *relaxed* while *emotional* implied being *nervous*. Thus, *relaxed* versus *nervous* is the first laddered superordinate construct. Hinkle then says that you ask the question 'why does the person prefer to be *relaxed* rather than *nervous*?' That is repeated until the person can produce no more constructs. These instructions are very general when one starts to try to ladder someone, so it is not surprising that there are differences of opinion about how one should do that.

Since I was one of the first to use the technique in research and therapy (Fransella, 1970), and have taught it to many hundreds of people over more than 35 years, I shall here write in the first person and present the way I use it.

To me, laddering is a complex skill and not a simple interviewing technique. The snag is that it looks simple. But it first of all requires the use of the three skills already mentioned—the ability to be a credulous listener, to suspend one's own value system and, thereby, to be able to subsume the client's construing. It is in the process of laddering that one gets nearest to that experience of being almost a part of the other person. Larry Leitner talks of this as 'distance' between two people (2003, Chapter 25, p. 263). That can happen because one of the most important aspects of laddering is to be able to concentrate 100% on what the client is trying to say. Very often clients find it increasingly difficult to put their more superordinate constructs into words and it is important to glimpse what it is they are struggling to convey. Not, I hasten to add, so that one should help with the words, but rather to gain an understanding of the meaning that lies behind the words.

I think it useful to see laddering as a structured interview. It is structured in that one needs to ensure that the person does not stray away from the current ladder. If the person appears to be straying, one can simply ask 'is that the same thing we have been talking about before on this ladder?' It is structured also in the sense that the interviewer is definitely in charge and the client is not free to roam at will. It is definitely, in my view, not some free association exercise. I also think it very important to keep the person self-focused. 'Why is it important *for you* to be ... ?' Otherwise one can just get generalizations.

The first decision to be made is which construct to start the ladder on. A client may have provided perhaps ten personal constructs from one of the elicitation procedures (many of these are described in Chapter 6 as well as in Chapter 5. If you are doing research, then you will have worked out a formula, such as choosing the first, third and fifth elicited personal construct. If it is in the context of helping a person reconstrue, then I use three criteria: the two or at the most three constructs to be laddered should be relatively subordinate, should look different from each other, and look as if they are likely to develop my understanding of the client's construed world. The relative subordinacy of constructs is, of course, a very evaluative choice. What is subordinate to me may well be superordinate to my client. But I will have learned a fair bit about the client from conversations and from the elicitation procedure. So, I do not go for such constructs as *respected, helpful* or *likeable* as they are fairly superordinate to me already, but I might choose instead constructs such as *studious, talkative* or *easy-going*.

An example of a ladder comes from my work with those who stutter. We were starting to ladder from constructs elicited for this person's 'non-stutterer' grid and

I selected the construct *nice personality* versus *disinterested in other people*. His preference was for being a *nice personality*.

Q. What are the advantages for you of being a nice personality?
A. People enjoy being with you.
Q. Whereas those who are *disinterested in other people*?
A. Are not enjoyable to be with.
Q. Why is it important, for you, that people enjoy being with you?
A. They are likely to open up to you—you get to understand them.
Q. Whereas? (*Here one can indicate by gesture that you are looking for the opposite.*)
A. They remain a closed book.
Q. That is very interesting. I'm just wondering why you like people to open up to you?
A. Because it shows people are relaxed with you and trust you and respect you.
Q. Whereas, if they remain a closed book?
A. You never get to know them—people rarely open up to stutterers.

So, we ended up on the non-preferred pole, where the person actually lives. That example raises one of the questions most often asked. '*How do you know when to stop?*' I stopped there for two reasons. One was that I think it is not always useful to go beyond superordinates to do with trust and respect. The other was that he had come out with an idea that he had never thought of before. His stutter was indeed very bad and he could see just what he was missing by being as he was. There could be little doubt that this revelation was disturbing to him and any further exploration would have been counter-productive for him.

Another common question is '*Do you always ask for an opposite?*' My answer here is 'it depends'. It depends on how the interview is going. If it is running smoothly and the client clearly understands what he is supposed to be doing, I may only ask for an opposite at every second or third rung. If the process is rather laboured, I find it good to ask for opposites more often. As in this case, it is not necessary to use words to elicit the opposites; a hand movement with the word 'whereas . . . ?' will suffice.

One of my personal rules when teaching laddering is that one should never ladder on the non-preferred pole of a construct. That pole nearly always has negative connotations and I feel I have little idea where it might ladder to. It is also likely to be a very depressing experience. People quite often give their replies in relation to the non-preferred pole, as in the example. There is no problem with that. But if the laddering is to continue, I think one should return to the preferred side of the construct.

Another question concerns '*What does one do if a person replies with more than one construct?*' In the example, the client gave three constructs at the end, so that did not matter. If that happened on a ladder that was to be continued, I would ask the person which best described the importance or the advantages of *people opening up to you*. One last point about the example, more words were spoken than appear in that text. But not a great many more. For me, conversation to do with the construing interferes with concentration and can easily turn into part of a therapy or counselling session. Of course, there is nothing wrong in using laddering in that way, but if it is being used as a short-cut to getting as much insight into the world of the client as possible in the shortest space of time, then general conversation should be kept to a minimum.

This second, shorter example comes from teaching laddering to a group of people. I think it serves a useful theoretical purpose if one starts at a very subordinate level. If one can get a ladder to 'work' from, say, shoes, one can point out that, indeed, construing takes place at different levels as stated in the *Organization Corollary*. How people construe shoes may do well as the starting point of a ladder, but I recommend that you do not choose to ladder constructs to do with hair. Both men and women have a great deal invested in how they wear their hair and—once tried, never again!

If students are sitting around a table, I have found it useful to have coloured folders on the table from which they can choose when they arrive. For the laddering they can be asked if anyone went for a particular colour. You ask for a volunteer from those who made a definite choice and then try to ladder the colour construct.

Q. You chose the green folder. What is the opposite, for you, of green?
A. Well, there are some I definitely would not choose—let me say *grey*.
Q. OK. So you prefer a green folder to a grey one. Why is that? What is special about the green one?
A. The green one is *bright*.
Q. Whereas the grey one is . . . ?
A. It's dull.
Q. Would it be right to say you prefer *bright* things in general to dull things? (*An attempt has to be made at some point to move it away from the specific starting point.*)
A. Oh, yes!
Q. So, in general, what is it about *bright* things that make you prefer them to *dull* things?
A. They make me feel good.
Q. Yes, I can see that. But what is it about *bright* things that makes you feel good?
A. Well, that's not easy. It's something to do with sparkling. It's like a bright star that beckons you. It reminds you that the world is full of wonderful things to be discovered.
Q. Whereas *dull* things . . . ?
A. Make you feel enclosed, trapped, what you have is all you'll get.
Q. So, I think I understand about the bright star, but just to be certain, can you say what it is that is so good about the bright star and everything?
A. You know you are alive.

When people talk about *being alive*, or say *that is what one is on earth for* or *one must do what one can for others*, I am prepared to say that is the top of the ladder. The other point I would make about that example is my not accepting the answer 'it makes me feel good'. People often respond with that or such things as 'makes me happy' and these are, of course, personal constructs. However, they are not helpful on most occasions. Most of us want to feel alive and to be happy. I like to ask the additional question to find out what the ingredient is that leads to one feeling alive or happy. That usually gets the ladder on the move again.

One final common issue concerns what is seen as the client giving an answer that looks very much more subordinate than superordinate. The ladder seems to have stopped going up and to have started coming down again. The most usual reason is that the client cannot find an answer that goes to a more abstract level of construing and, since an answer is required, they give an answer that is familiar to them.

But that is not always the case. For instance, Butt (1995) talks of snakes and ladders and gives an account of his client going from *relaxed—tense* to *able to be myself with others—put up a front*, then to *assert myself—give in to others* the preference to being about to assert herself was that she could *deal with my mother* and the reason why she preferred that was because *mother makes me feel so guilty*. One point to make is that Butt says the construct *able to be myself with others* versus *put up a front* clearly has a wider range of convenience than *deal with my mother*. It may well have a wider range of convenience, but Hinkle was talking about networks of implications. These are not necessarily the same. What is implied by *deal with my mother*? The fact that it is linked to feelings of guilt means she is aware that she is constantly being dislodged from her core role. That may suggest some quite superordinate construing involved in not being able/willing to deal with her mother. Could it not be that, for the present, the whole world for this lady centres around her mother and the guilt she is made to feel about her? Its range of convenience is narrow, but range of implication is vast. Being able to be herself with others is much less important, has many fewer implications, compared with dealing with mother.

Whether or not that is a valid point to make in the specific case of Butt's client, there is no doubt that sometimes clients do give a reply that sounds like something that has gone before or to be more subordinate. If that seems to be happening, it is important to check, repeat the question and to indicate you would like the client to think about the answer again. If the same response is given, then it is clear that the client either does not want to continue the exercise or has really reached the 'top' of her ladder. Perhaps she is not used to the intellectual exercise of trying to find words for some feelings or ideas that she has never put into words before. In the end, the client must always have the last word. Perhaps, as is often the case, the construct with which the laddering has started is, itself, at an already very superordinate level. So the person really struggles to provide answers but just cannot do so because there is nothing higher up the ladder—she must come down again or feel she has failed in the task.

Costigan and colleagues (2000) discuss their use of laddering in relation to how psychiatric nurses construe their changing role, and provide a very useful commentary on its general use. They also emphasize the care that must be taken with laddering. When teaching people about laddering, I never fail to say that it is not a party game. It can, indeed, be quite psychologically damaging to some people who become faced with an aspect of their own construing that they did not know was there. They now 'see' a previously unknown aspect of their construing and find that knowledge most disturbing. It is therefore always important to keep a keen eye on the person you are laddering and to stop at the first sign of unease. If the laddering is taking place in a counselling context, then it will be up to the counsellor to decide whether it is useful to continue with the process or not.

Bob Neimeyer (1993) has described a useful variation of Hinkle's laddering which he calls *dialectical laddering*. It is of use when a client finds it impossible to say which pole of a personal construct is preferred. Both poles have negative implications. In his example Suzy said she had difficulty trusting anyone, but both *trusting* and *distrusting* had disadvantages. He then asked 'What would be the implication for you of being *trusting*?' She replied *burdening others* with its opposite *being controlled*. That then led to *not relaxed* and *relax control completely*. All other constructs were similarly undesirable at both poles. He then went back to *controlled* versus *burdening others* and asked her to try and find some way of bringing them together—an alternative that would create a synthesis. She came up with *realistic trust*. That questioning was repeated for *not relaxed* versus *relax control completely* and the synthesis was *relax control to some extent*. And so the process continued until all the constructs had been dealt with in this way. Neimeyer says that, of course, this cognitive exercise is not a 'cure' in itself, but that Suzy found the process genuinely therapeutic and they continued to explore the implications of this major reconstruction of her world.

Support for Hinkle's Ideas

As a direct test of Hinkle's work, I checked to see whether the laddered constructs for my group of stutterers (Fransella, 1972) had more implications than the previously elicited constructs. They consistently did. Eric Button (1980) also found that superordinate, laddered constructs had more implications than subordinate ones with a group of anorexic women.

Neimeyer and colleagues (2001) carried out a validity study of Hinkle's hypothesis that laddered constructs are more important than non-laddered constructs, and so the procedure provides a measure of hierarchical structure. The authors interviewed 103 university students and carried out laddering with each one. Their findings supported Hinkle's hypothesis that laddered constructs are more important than subordinate ones. In addition, their results confirmed what most practitioners know, and Hinkle also found—that laddered constructs take more time to put into words than do more subordinate constructs. One other measure Neimeyer and his colleagues took was the 'meaning' of the constructs. They found that significantly more superordinate constructs fell into the *Existential* category than subordinate ones and that more subordinate constructs than superordinate ones fell into the *Specific Interests* and *Relational* categories. Thus, as one would expect, superordinate constructs were found to be more value-laden than the more subordinate ones.

Summary on Laddering

Several people have provided lists of do's and don't's for laddering. For instance, advice is given on the Internet at http://www.EnquireWithin.co.nz/busChap3.htm, but my own view is that the only way to learn laddering is by practising it. I have given indications above of what I find useful, but it is such a personal skill that each person who masters it will have developed his or her own style and will have a personal list of things to do and not to do.

Pyramiding

Al Landfield described a way of moving downwards to more concrete or subordinate constructs which he called *pyramiding* (1971). Most practitioners and clients find this considerably easier to work with than laddering.

The client is asked to think of a person they know and to select one characteristic of that person and then proceed along these lines: 'He is kindly.' 'How would you describe a person who is not kindly?' 'He is unkind.' 'What sort of person is a kindly person?' 'He would take care of someone if they were in trouble.' 'What sort of person is an unkindly person?' 'He walks on the other side of the street.' The procedure continues in this way asking about one pole of the construct and then its opposite.

Once that pyramid has been created, Landfield suggests that further questioning might be along the lines of asking how the client would know, say, that a person was kindly. The client might reply, 'He has a kindly smile.' Once one gets to that level, one is into behaviours. That can be extremely useful when designing behavioural experiments that a client might conduct between therapy sessions. Or, sometimes it is useful to know more precisely what a particular superordinate construct actually means. Then one can start directly with the 'how do you know that someone is (for example) *trustworthy*'?

The ABC Model

In 1977, Finn Tschudi, in collaboration with Sigrid Sandsburg, wrote a chapter on 'Loaded and honest questions' in which he described the ABC Model. He suggested that Kelly's definition of 'disorder' as representing 'any structure which appears to fail to accomplish its purpose' was too flexible. The authors preferred to use 'symptom' and 'symptomatic behaviour'. Thus, symptomatic behaviour becomes any behaviour 'which obliquely gets at the issues which are important for the person'.

A typical form of construct network consisting of three constructs—which they label A, B and C—helps to locate the important issues that are obliquely related to the symptom. A central feature of this model is the question: 'What keeps the person from moving?' There must be some advantage to remaining as, say, a smoker, when the person explicitly says she wants to give up smoking.

The method goes like this. The person says she wants to change from, for example, being a smoker to being a non-smoker. That forms the first step in the method. The second step is to ask the person to state the advantages of being a non-smoker and the disadvantages of being a smoker. Now, the C level looks for the double-bind or 'implicative dilemma', as described by Hinkle (1965). Such implicative dilemmas result in preventing the person from moving from the undesired position to the desired position. For example, it might go like this:

A. The statement of desire to change
    A1: Being a smoker   A2: Being a non-smoker

B. The disadvantages of A1 and the advantages of A2
    B1: 1. It makes a lot of dirt   B2: 1. Everything is much cleaner
           2. It ruins your health   2. It is much healthier

C. The disadvantages of the desired state A2 and the advantages of the present state A1

C2: 1. It gives me something to do with my hands	C1: 1. Feel ill at ease in company
2. You are more popular	2. People who don't smoke are not popular

That procedure is useful in many contexts other than the clinical one. In the work context as 'I want to be more assertive'. In the marital context as 'I want to listen to my husband more'.

Nick Reed and I have modified the ABC Model so that it can be used for decision making, calling it 'Quandary Resolution'. By just putting forward two possible ways of moving forward, looking at the disadvantages and disadvantages of both as above, the desirability of one over the other often emerges very quickly.

As with laddering, the ABC Model needs to come with a health warning. It can show to clients the advantages of remaining as they are before they are psychologically ready to deal with that revelation. Again, it should not be viewed as a party game.

The Core Process Interview

In this interview, described by Helen Jones (1993), clients have the opportunity to look at how their lives have progressed and at the choices they have made that have affected their lives. It focuses on the good rather than the bad experiences. She describes it as consisting of the following seven parts.

1. *My life till now*: The client is asked to think back over his or her life and to divide it into four natural divisions of time in relation to age—and then to say what those age 'chunks' are. These might be '0–11', '11–16', and so on.
2. *Reminiscences*: The client is now asked to think of two occasions in each period when he or she felt really wonderful about life. As far as possible, the replies are written down verbatim.
3. *Unique qualities*: What were the special qualities about that time?
4. *Other happy times*: The client is now asked to describe seven other occasions in which his or her life felt really good. That is followed by a request that the client think of another occasion when he or she felt as good or happy as that time. There is then a request for two memories from each of the other time 'chunks'.
5. *Review*: The client is then passed the notes that have been made and asked to highlight passages that seem particularly important in terms of fulfilment. Looking at these highlights, the client is asked to 'highlight the phrases that best complete the sentence "For me to be fulfilled ..."'. A statement is sought from the highlighted passages.
6. *Fulfilment*: That is the statement that has emerged from the previous stage.
7. *Simple truths*: Jones says: 'It is always a lovely feeling to write down these simple things; they always ring true for the individual concerned. It is a powerful experience' (Jones, 1993, p. 20).

Jones uses this procedure after completing a resistance to change grid (see Chapter 9, p. 106 and Fransella, Bell & Bannister, 2004) and finds that the fulfilment statement closely reflects the relative importance of the values that emerge from the grid.

Viney Content Analysis Scales

These are standardized scales designed to tap into a variety of psychological states, especially positive and negative emotions. Computer-supported versions of all of these Australian scales have been developed. These scales include: the Cognitive Anxiety Scale, the Origin and Pawn Scales, the Sociality Scales, the Positive Affect Scale and the Content Analysis Scales of Psychosocial Maturity. Their psychometric qualities are impressive. Linda Viney and her colleagues have provided a scoring manual for the *Content Analysis Scales of Psychosocial Maturity (CASPM)* (1995b), and one of a number of chapters describing these scales is Viney (1993). Some of these scales are also discussed in Chapter 12, pp. 123–132.

The Self-image Profile

This is a standardized tool (Butler, 2001) that compares how children rate themselves on a 6-point scale compared with their rating of how they would like to be. The discrepancy between the two is seen as a way of assessing children's self-esteem. The 25 items in the Self-Image Profile were selected from the 12 most frequently elicited positive self-descriptions and the 12 most frequently elicited negative descriptions provided by large groups who were asked to describe three ways in which they think about themselves. The self-description scales contain only one pole of each construct.

The Profile can be changed to contain a child's own personal constructs. It then, of course, becomes a form of repertory grid. Some examples of the uses of the Self-Image Profile can be found in Butler and Green (1998).

SUMMARY

The skills described are requirements for any personal construct practitioner. Some are quite straightforward and others, such as suspending one's values, require considerable experience to achieve. The same applies to many of the so-called 'tools'.

Many of the 'tools' ask the interviewees to explore their construing that has, up until that point, not been available to them consciously. The construing is present, but words have to be found to explain their meaning to someone else.

CHAPTER 5

A Range of Elicitation Methods to Suit Client and Purpose

Pam Denicolo

University of Reading, UK

> I am suggesting that the avoidance of subjectivity is not the way to get down to hard realities. Subjective thinking is, rather, an essential step in the process the scientist must follow in grasping the nature of the universe ... science tends to make its progress by entertaining propositions which appear initially to be preposterous.
>
> (Kelly, 1969d, p. 150)

This handbook is replete with examples of how the key instrument of personal construct psychology, the repertory grid, has been used in its traditional form, and in imaginative variations of it, to explore personal construing (see Chapter 6, pp. 67–76). Indeed, the repertory grid is probably the most frequently encountered technique used to serve this purpose, and is often the first one met by novices to the field, so much so that personal construct psychology and the repertory grid are sometimes viewed as synonymous. However, there are other techniques that have been used by personal construct psychologists to good effect.

While these techniques are based on the kind of questioning that underpins repertory grid elicitation, they each have a benefit to offer to particular client groups or to suit different situations experienced by practitioners and researchers. Despite Kelly's suggestion in relation to the self-characterization that if you want to know something about a person, then ask him and he may tell you, the mode of asking using any technique certainly has an effect on the answers received. Establishing rapport and a common purpose, with agreement about how far and with whom the information will be shared, are fundamental to all personal construct dialogues. The actual technique used should then be selected from the plethora designed to suit different clients and contexts.

Some examples are provided in this chapter to demonstrate the range available as alternatives, or additions, to grids to illuminate the uniqueness and complexity of

The Essential *Practitioner's Handbook of Personal Construct Psychology.* Edited by F. Fransella.
© 2005 John Wiley & Sons, Ltd.

the perceived world of the person. As a prelude, though, some theoretical considerations underpinning the development of these techniques are reviewed.

LOOSENING PERCEIVED CONSTRAINTS

Kelly was critical of over-reliance on psychometric methods. He emphasized that knowing that there was a correlational link between two variables did not help him to decide what approach should be taken with an individual client. He also questioned the utility of research that used approaches that did not lead to emancipation for the participants. He suggested that there should be more emphasis in psychology on studying the individual; hence his creation of, first, the Repertory Test for eliciting personal constructs, and then the repertory grid with its method of statistical analysis for those who wanted to 'get beyond the words'. That basic stance is also a fundamental tenet adopted by qualitative/interpretative researchers today.

In the process of encouraging participants or clients to reveal personal meaning, to articulate tacit knowledge, personal construct psychologists have used a variety of techniques in an attempt to embody the spirit of Kelly's writing and the challenge it presents to its users. He encouraged us to look at his theory and suggestions for practice *as if* they might be useful ways of looking at things, discarding aspects that do not prove useful. Thus we are specifically invited to engage in theoretical extension, elaboration and reformation to inform our practice by extending our horizons.

Practitioners using personal construct psychology are no less prone to perceiving artificial constraints on their horizons than are their clients. Those for whom an allegiance to 'qualitative' practice is an important construct may eschew without further consideration methods that are highly numerical or require statistical manipulation of the data since they are perceived as fitting a 'quantitative' approach. As previously described by Pope and Denicolo (1986) at the height of the qualitative/quantitative debate, novice researchers have found some comfort in the traditional formulation of ratings grids because they appear to pose less threat within the, then prevailing, quantitative tradition in psychology. This was perhaps a sensible resolution to their paradigm dilemma at a time when short papers were favoured for publication in journals since 'a grid is worth a thousand words'.

In such cases the difficulty inherent in the use of the terms 'qualitative' and 'quantitative' to describe *approaches* to research becomes apparent. Those terms are more appropriately used to describe *data*. Thus, those subscribing to an interpretativist/constructivist approach, with a focus on meaning exploration, may use tools and techniques that produce either qualitative or quantitative data. Indeed, they may use a range of such techniques, some more structured and numerical than others, in order to build a mosaic of meaning, each technique contributing a small tile or 'tessera' to the picture. As Kelly demonstrated, numbers need not be anathema to constructivists, nor yet should they become an obsession.

Bannister recognized that the grid had encouraged many psychologists to value the central tenets of personal construct theory. Nevertheless he raised a caveat about unwarranted concern with the statistical analysis of the resulting data, saying that the:

> grid method is a Frankenstein's monster which has rushed away on a statistical and experimental rampage of its own, leaving construct theory neglected, stranded high and dry, far behind. (Bannister, 1985, p. xii)

In this he was urging a greater emphasis on understanding meaning through construct elicitation and the raw grid data than on the statistical analysis *per se*.

Rather than neglect the essentially idiographic nature of constructivist data collection, practitioners should consider the purpose of the activity engaged in, their own skills and the inclinations of the clients to express their meaning in a preferred form, if they are to be responsive to situations they encounter. The techniques described below are useful for different purposes and provide some possibilities from which to select a form most conducive to the aptitudes of the joint explorers of meaning systems. They all produce a mass of rich but unstructured data that requires skill in making it manageable by the identification of key themes, categories and patterns that are meaningful to all engaged in the task. Nevertheless, although insightful interpretation of such complex verbal data is demanding, it can be rewarding if the elicitation process has been one that the client/participant finds helpful in the articulation of their embedded meanings.

ALTERNATIVE TECHNIQUES

It is fitting to begin with Kelly's qualitative method of assessment, ground-breaking in its time, and to follow this with techniques selected from a range devised subsequently.

Self-characterization Sketches

Because of shyness, or concern for implications, some requests for information about self produce rather self-conscious, sanitized responses. Kelly's original version of the self-characterization sketch has much to commend it for occasions when the goal is inducing self-understanding as a prelude to considering change. The procedure involves asking the person to write a character sketch of himself or herself, as if a principal character in a play, from the perspective of a friend who knows the person very *intimately* and who is *sympathetic*. It should be written in the third person, beginning something like: 'name (e.g. Joe/Joanne) is . . .'. The phrasing of this request:

- permits people some latitude to use their own constructions of self;
- emphasizes that it is structure rather than detail that is important;
- allows them to make themselves plausible from an outsider's perspective;
- indicates that something more than a superficial description of appearance is required;
- frees them from feeling threatened into providing either an incriminating description or a litany of what they 'ought' to be like.

Such sketches are replete with constructs, the emergent poles at least, not only about how people view themselves but how they perceive the worlds that they inhabit.

While these can then be explored further, perhaps using laddering, pyramiding or ABC techniques (see Chapter 4, pp. 41–56), analysis of the sequence and linking of ideas, the organization of them, shifts in emphasis, the emergence of themes and the repetition of them, all provide evidence of personal viewpoints. Kelly suggests that the first sentence may be productively viewed as if it were a key statement about the person's view of self. Similarly, he suggests that the last sentence is a good indicator of where the person considers he or she is going. What is excluded is also relevant. In characterizing oneself, it is likely that important features will be included that distinguish self from others. Thus, if mode of dress has little significance to a person, then it is unlikely to be mentioned. Trevor Butt (2003, Chapter 38) writes further about the 'credulous approach' advocated for the analysis of such sketches and their value at the beginning of a phenomenological inquiry (see also Chapter 4, pp. 48–55).

The self-characterization has been productively used with novice professionals describing themselves in the professional role. For example, 'Josh as a nurse is primarily concerned with helping patients . . .'. Such a sketch enables the practice supervisor or mentor to appreciate areas of concern or confidence, while the novice is alerted to current priorities, and sometimes to those being ignored—sketches can act as springboards to considering alternative self-constructions. When self-characterization sketches are elicited at intervals and compared, development can be demonstrated, as with Fransella's (1981) client who used the self-characterization as a means of helping himself to reconstrue over time.

Bow-ties

Procter has had extensive experience in both personal construct psychology and family therapy work which has resulted in innovative assessment and intervention techniques. One of these involves the 'bow-tie' principle (Procter, 1987, see also his discussion of family therapy, Chapter 17.2, p. 178), named from the pattern formed when constructs and resultant behaviour are elicited from each member of a couple or larger group. The behaviour of the individuals in relation to the perceived constructs of the other may serve to reinforce the actual constructs of the other, leading to the continuance of their own behaviour. A form of 'zigzagging' questioning of the individuals about how they construe themselves, what they think the other thinks of them and how they consequently behave in response, demonstrates the pervasive and pernicious feedback loops in operation as each person tests out his own hypotheses about the other and has them apparently confirmed.

For instance, a manager may perceive herself as a democratic leader, delegating tasks and encouraging her employee to make decisions about them. She is disappointed in her employee. She perceives him as lazy, unable to take responsibility, so she refuses to continue to give guidance. She produces more tasks for him that require self-organizing behaviour and independent decision-making. In contrast, the employee perceives himself as hard-working, his job as responding to the manager's needs. He is frustrated by 'unclear' tasks. He spends time on strategies to explore actual requirements before starting on the task. The vicious cycle continues, sometimes exacerbated by other members of the team. Some colleagues reinforce the manager's view by complaining about the employee's continuous questions and his apparent inability to get on with the task. Others reinforce the employee's view-point by commenting informally on the vagueness of the manager's direction.

It is only by uncovering and recognizing these self-fulfilling prophecies that construing can be challenged and reconsidered to end this destructive cycle.

The Lying Game

Bright (1985) considered the general philosophy of lying as a human activity and how it might be used within a personal construct framework to help people to shift away from the constraints of troubled construing towards recognition of potential change. Acknowledging Kelly's principle that you cannot fully understand what people are saying until you gain some notion of what, for them, is the opposite, Bright devised a game based on lying—a game because there is no real intention to deceive.

The technique is particularly useful when people, perhaps enmeshed in describing how they feel, have difficulty in expressing the contrast poles of constructs. These lies can be especially informative when explored further for their implications, heightening awareness of 'truth'.

Respondents are asked to write down lies about themselves within a chosen parameter, for example, myself as a worker or a parent. When an individual is unable to produce any more relevant lies, two columns are added to the side of the page in which to insert the respondent's replies (Y or N) to these questions:

1. Would you like this lie to be true?
2. Would you like other people to believe this lie?

This produces the following potential patterns of response for each lie: NN, YY, YN, NY

- An NN response indicates complete rejection of the lie, with no wish for change.
- A YY response indicates a wish for change at a high level of awareness—a good start.
- A YN response indicates a wish for the lie to be true but not for others to believe it—perhaps a wish for change that would be unpopular with significant others.
- An NY response indicates a concern for image presentation rather than a desire for change—a potent source for skilled exploration.

The game format is relaxing so that people can more readily produce lies about themselves, the fun element ameliorating the sense of being tested sometimes experienced with grids. The next methods use other means to achieve a similar aim.

Illuminative Incident Analysis

Cortazzi and Roote (1975) developed this technique as a means of investigating the thoughts and feelings of members of teams. Though team development can be encouraged by a frank interchange of ideas and feelings about incidents that have happened while the team have been working together, the emotion connected with

Figure 5.1   Tightrope walker—an example of a drawing used for illuminative analysis

certain incidents often blocks verbal discourse. Words can also hide reality whereas feelings, as every art therapist knows, are more accurately portrayed in drawings. The drawings encourage all team members to confront their own feelings about the incident and allow, by comparisons between drawings, each one to come to an understanding of the other's perspective. Thus drawings are a conduit from the non-verbal to the verbal. A new member of a research team produced the drawing shown in Figure 5.1. He portrays himself as blindfolded, setting out across a tightrope. Though it is firmly tied to his previous experience, the end-point is shrouded in mist while the rope itself is fraught with obstacles. He clings to a trusty pole—current knowledge—to keep himself steady.

The researcher was relieved to find that he was not alone in experiencing trepidation, and that more experienced colleagues would be willing to lead the way.

Analysis of such drawings requires the combined efforts of the listener and the producer of the drawing to interpret the nuances encapsulated in the lines, to tease out their full significance. In other words, the drawing in its production provides the first step in expressing ideas and feelings and then acts as a catalyst to the verbal commentary.

No artistic prowess is required because it is the simple, unrefined nature of the line drawing that allows it to capture the essence of meaning. The illuminative value of simple drawings is further demonstrated by Tom Ravenette who uses drawing to elicit the meanings of specific situations with children (see Chapter 13, pp. 40–41). The use of illuminative incident analysis is demonstrated further in the next technique.

Interview about Instances

Osborne and Gilbert (1980) used this technique to explore students' views of the world in relation to scientific concepts. They generated a series of cards, each showing a stick figure (for example, a golfer) engaged in an activity (hitting a ball with a club) that represents the scientific concept being explored (in this case, both force and energy). The cards were used as a stimulus to conversation about the concept. From analysis of the conversation the alternative, but coherent, understandings that students have about the concepts were demonstrated. These frequently diverged from scientists' views. Awareness of such alternative frameworks by a teacher is important in helping the students to move from a layperson's understanding towards that of experts in the field. See Chapter 18 for coverage of the role of pupils', students' and teachers' construing in the learning process. For further information see Chapters 29, 31 and 32 in the *International Handbook of Personal Construct Psychology* (2003).

Such uncomplicated drawings encourage a focus on the action depicted, so this method can be readily adapted for use in a variety of situations in which understanding process is the focus. Similarly the next technique uses a simple drawing technique to explore the influence of the past on the present.

Snakes and Rivers

Contradictory as it may seem, the anticipatory power of constructs lies in the past. In order to come to an understanding of the present we need to compare and contrast it with experiences we have had previously and use these to predict the future. The success of our predictions will depend on our selecting appropriate and relevant constructs and being willing to contemplate adapting them to fit current circumstance or amending a network of constructs to meet new situations.

Thus biography has an important influence on the constructs we bring to bear on any situation in which we find ourselves. The ones that predominate are likely to be those that have served us well in what appear to have been similar circumstances in the past. Since much of life is hectic, encouraging action rather than reflection, we are often unaware of the constructs guiding that action and from whence, in our pasts, these are derived. This means that, although well established, some of our personal constructs may now be redundant or even counter-productive. However, unless we become consciously aware of them and attach words to them, they cannot be challenged, and they remain influential in how we relate to events.

Denicolo and Pope (2001) devised 'career snakes' for exploring the useful and redundant constructs held by professionals about their development in their roles, and later used them to research commonly held productive and limiting constructs within professions. Similar to the Salmon Line (see Salmon, 2003, pp. 315–318), the rationale for the technique drew on a recognition that constructs evolve over time and are particularly influenced by formative experiences. Only by reflecting on their origins can the opportunity be provided for contemplating alternatives and breaking free from biography.

Participants draw up in private a representation of their working lives in the form of a winding snake, each turn of its body depicting a personal experience that influenced the direction that their career took. These turns are annotated briefly (Figure 5.2), forming the bases for later discussion and elaboration with the researcher, about their significance as formative experiences both for career decisions and for their personal style as practitioners.

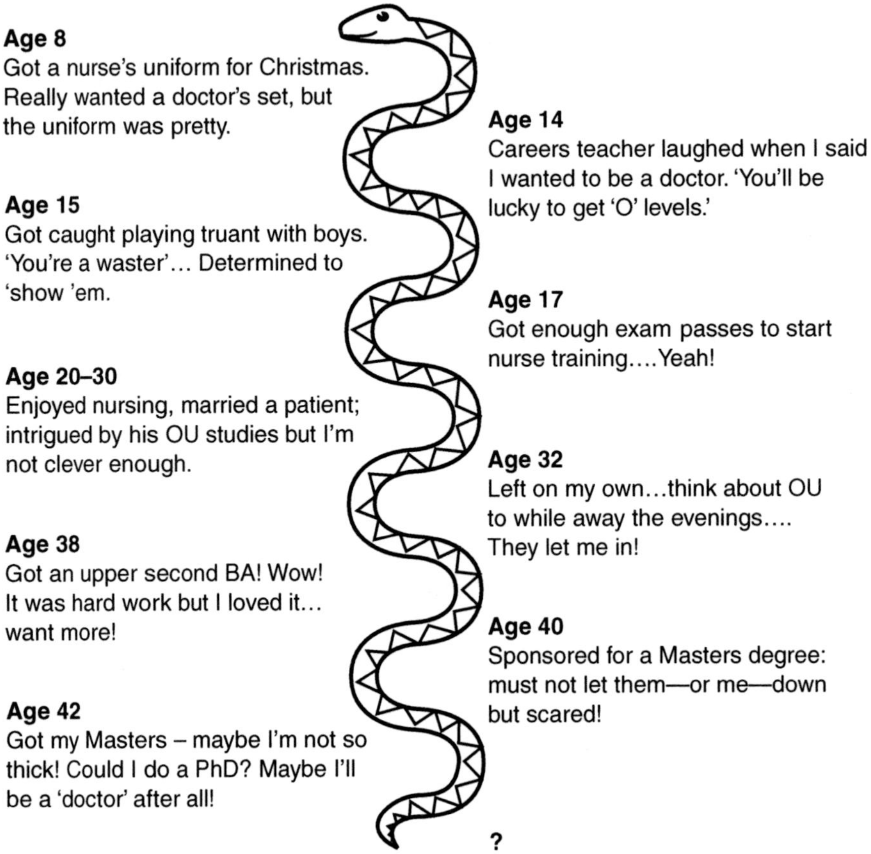

Age 8
Got a nurse's uniform for Christmas.
Really wanted a doctor's set, but
the uniform was pretty.

Age 14
Careers teacher laughed when I said
I wanted to be a doctor. 'You'll be
lucky to get 'O' levels.'

Age 15
Got caught playing truant with boys.
'You're a waster'... Determined to
'show 'em.

Age 17
Got enough exam passes to start
nurse training....Yeah!

Age 20–30
Enjoyed nursing, married a patient;
intrigued by his OU studies but I'm
not clever enough.

Age 32
Left on my own...think about OU
to while away the evenings....
They let me in!

Age 38
Got an upper second BA! Wow!
It was hard work but I loved it...
want more!

Age 40
Sponsored for a Masters degree:
must not let them—or me—down
but scared!

Age 42
Got my Masters – maybe I'm not so
thick! Could I do a PhD? Maybe I'll
be a 'doctor' after all!

?

Figure 5.2   A career snake

The subsequent discussion generally requires little input from the researcher, other than interest, as participants interrogate themselves about reasons for isolating a particular incident, how it was influential and perhaps still is. They often report feeling empowered by the experience. Many researchers now using the technique to explore the influence of previous experience on current practice prefer the title 'rivers of experience' in deference to those who dislike snakes! The 'river maps' encourage participants to discuss other topographical features of their lives, high points, rapids and calm sections, demonstrating yet again the power of metaphor (Mair, 1988) in eliciting and elucidating constructs.

Metaphors are often found in everyday speech to provide the connecting threads between constructs and their personal meaning, as well as being graphically evocative.

Metaphors and Artefacts

Some writers contend that all language is metaphorical. Lakoff and Johnson (1980) illustrated how metaphors pervade our lives not only as descriptors of people, events and objects but also in governing and orientating action. A salient example provided is the terms in which argument is described in Western languages—to be won, using ammunition and counter-attack, for instance. Examining documents and records of people's descriptions of their worlds for the *metaphors they live by* can be a rich resource for understanding the meaning they attribute to them.

Similarly, asking people to provide a metaphor to describe themselves, or a situation, can provide a conduit to their pervasive constructs. For those who are less adept at using figurative language forms, or reticent about personal disclosure, a less invasive alternative is to ask them to identify an artefact that represents something they think or feel about themselves or their role. The artefact may be a picture, photograph or an object such as a treasured ornament or favourite tool.

CONCLUSION

The examples of techniques described above represent only a selection of those available. Several can be used together, or in conjunction with grids, to explore meaning more fully. These innovative techniques reinforce Kelly's point that we are only restricted in developing our construing by the limits of our imagination.

CHAPTER 6

The Repertory Grid Technique

Richard C. Bell

University of Melbourne, Australia

> ... But we can look beyond words. We can study contexts. For example, does the client use the word 'affectionate' only when talking about persons of the opposite sex? ... The answers to such questions ... may give us an understanding of the interweaving of the client's terminology and provide us with an understanding of his outlook which no dictionary could offer.
>
> (Kelly, 1955/1991, p. 267/Vol. 1, p. 189)

WHAT IS A REPERTORY GRID?

The repertory grid is probably the most widely known aspect of the work of George Kelly. Originally called the 'role construct repertory test' it soon became known as the 'repertory grid'. The repertory grid is not simply a technique that is independent of personal construct theory (Bell, 1988). Kelly's Fundamental Postulate says that *a person's processes are psychologically channelized by the ways in which he anticipates events*. That underpins the repertory grid. The *ways* are the constructs of a repertory grid, and the *events* are the elements. The technique of the repertory grid thus involves defining a set of elements, eliciting a set of constructs that distinguish among these elements, and relating elements to constructs.

SOME HISTORY

Following Kelly's original publication of the technique in 1955, the repertory grid attracted only limited and sporadic attention in the following decade (see Bonarius, 1965, for a review of research up to that time). The turning point came with research by Don Bannister into the thought processes of schizophrenics in Britain in the early 1960s (see Chapter 9, pp. 95–97). The grid test of schizophrenic thought disorder, subsequently published with Fay Fransella (1967), drew attention to the technique. Although this variant did not eventually succeed as a practical clinical tool, the general use of the grid *per se* became more widely known in Britain due to the availability of a 'scoring service' provided by Patrick Slater at the Institute of Psychiatry. Slater (1976) reports that by 1973 the service was processing 10,000 grids per year. The grid was less generally adopted in North America.

In the next decade, the grid was seen as dominating published research in personal construct theory (Neimeyer, 1985c). However, a recent count of references to 'Repertory Grid' or 'Rep Test' in the database, PsycINFO, shows that publication peaked in the late 1980s and has subsequently declined.

REPERTORY GRID DATA

A repertory grid may contain both qualitative and quantitative data. The identity of the elements and the nature of the constructs may provide qualitative information while the relationships between the constructs and elements may be interpreted as quantitative data. However, the information in a grid clearly depends on only the elements and constructs that have been included.

Choosing Elements

In standard grid elicitation procedures, elements are determined first, and constructs elicited from distinctions made among these elements. Therefore the choice of elements is crucial, yet oddly enough has been little studied. Most studies have followed the Kellyian process of defining the sample of elements by giving the respondent 'role titles' (such as 'rejected teacher' or 'ethical person') as a basis for choosing elements. The effect of this has only been empirically studied in a limited fashion. Mitsos (1958) compared 'acquaintances' as elements elicited by role title with those simply selected from a list, finding the role title approach showed greater consistency over time. Williams (1971) and McFayden and Foulds (1972) both varied the Bannister and Fransella (1967) grid test of schizophrenic thought disorder by comparing the standard supplied photograph form with an 'elicited persons' form, and both found that when familiar persons were used as elements, greater intensity and consistency indices were found. Adams-Webber (1997) used both real and 'nonsense' elements in one of his many studies into the ratio of assignment to positive or negatively valued poles, finding differences in the ratios of assignment to poles. These studies thus confirmed that the choice of elements does, indeed, affect the nature of grid data.

Supporting evidence comes from Bell et al. (2002) who examined the sources of variation (in an *analysis of variance* sense) in grid data collected in a variety of ways and found that elements usually accounted for about four times as much variance as did constructs. Clearly the 'element choice' aspect of the grid is important and needs further research work.

Two process-oriented variants have been proposed. Keen and Bell (1981) described a procedure where constructs and elements were elicited alternately. Bell (1990a, p. 28) reported a small study where the Keen and Bell procedure did not produce any advantages (from a construct perspective) over traditional triadic construct elicitation. Shaw and Thomas (1978) described an interactive process, where the respondent was invited to supply a new element that would distinguish between constructs that were similar (in terms of having a high matching score). While the impact of these different procedures has not been closely examined, they perhaps point to an opportunity for more process-oriented research with the technique.

Eliciting Constructs

Perhaps the most basic concern for the use of *personal* constructs in a repertory grid is the issue of whether they should be elicited from the respondent or supplied by the person administering the grid. From a purely Kellyian perspective, the technique would seem to demand that the constructs be elicited from the person, since they are *personal* constructs. However, much research (and, as indicated above, research is a major user of repertory grids) demands aggregated data, and data cannot be aggregated without commonality. The theory provides for this in the Commonality Corollary that states: *to the extent that one person employs a construction of experience which is similar to that employed by another, his processes are psychologically similar to those of the other person.* This is an issue of some practical importance since the use of grids in organizational research is often concerned with the construing of groups rather than individuals, as shown for example by Fransella (1988; see also Chapter 3, pp. 30–31).

A tradition of research has focused on whether supplied and elicited constructs produce similar results. Adams-Webber (1970) reviewed studies such as this and concluded that although people preferred to use their own constructs, it made no difference when summary measures of grids were calculated. More recently the same author (Adams-Webber, 1998) found that when a person had to make inferences about another, those based on constructs elicited from the other were significantly more accurate than were those based on supplied ones. The issue of supplied versus elicited constructs would thus seem to depend on the context in which the grid is being used.

If, however, we adopt the elicitation perspective, we are confronted by a further set of issues. Kelly originally listed six triadic methods, the most influential being what he termed the 'minimum context' form. In that form the respondent is presented with sets of three elements (triads) and for each set is asked to specify some important way in which two of the elements are alike (the emergent pole of the construct) and thereby different (the contrast pole of the construct) from the third. This bipolar elicitation of constructs accorded with Kelly's Dichotomy Corollary. Some of Kelly's original variants on this involve use of a constant element (the self) or the sequential changing of the triad, an element at a time. Other approaches include pairs (two-element) elicitation of constructs, sometimes referred to as dyadic elicitation (for example, Caputi & Reddy, 1999; Epting, et al., 1993), although that terminology can be confused with the use of dyads as elements (for example, Ryle & Lunghi, 1970; Butt et al., 1997b). Comparisons by Caputi and Reddy (1999) and Hagans and colleagues (2000) suggest that different results are obtained under different construct elicitation procedures. Another technique for eliciting superordinate constructs was devised by Hinkle (1965) and is popularly known as 'laddering' (see Chapter 4, pp. 48–53).

Another important concern is whether the elements chosen ensure that the respondent's universe of constructs is appropriately sampled. Unlike the element situation where stratified sampling can be used through role titles, construct elicitation can use no such stratification (since the stratifying characteristic would be an imposed or supplied superordinate construct). The only way to ensure a representative sampling is through an appropriate sampling design. Bell (1990a, p. 27–28) has outlined the difficulties in achieving this when the grid contains more than seven elements. For example, in Kelly's original grid with 32 constructs elicited from 24 elements, almost 70% of possible pairs of elements were not considered. A recent example of the use of an appropriate design can be found in the grids of Leach and colleagues (2001).

Relating Elements to Constructs

In a number of practical situations, the focus of the technique is on the nature of the constructs elicited and these are used as qualitative data, sometimes as the starting point for other investigations such as 'laddering'. However, in other settings (for example, most research settings) there is an interest in relating elements to constructs. There are two related aspects to this: how the data are collected, and the scaling of the relationship. A choice exists on how data are collected for relating elements to constructs. Do we take each construct in turn and relate all the elements to it, or do we take each element in turn and consider its relationships to the set of constructs? Does it make a difference?

The issue of how elements are related to constructs has received more attention. Kelly's original grid allowed for three dispositions of elements with respect to a construct. The element could be set at one pole, or the other pole, or could be designated as not being related to the construct (theoretically, lying outside the 'range of convenience' of the construct). This last option, while theoretically attractive, posed problems for some subsequent analyses of grid data, and has consequently not been widely used. One of the earliest alternatives to the original method was to rank elements on each construct. This is discussed in some detail by Fransella and Bannister (1977, pp. 30–39) as, prior to the wide availability of computers, manual or calculator-based analysis of grid data was required, and ranks provide some simplicity in this. Of course, ranks impose a distribution of elements along a construct and restrict the free allocation of elements. Rankings were more popular in Great Britain while 13-point ratings were promulgated by Landfield (1971, 1977) in North America. This variant used a +6 to 0 to –6 rating basis. Recent research elsewhere (Krosnick, 1999, p. 544) has shown that the signing of numbers as positive or negative can influence construing. Simple ratings (such as 1 to 7) have been more generally used with the advent of computers. Computer programs (and websites) that can be used for the elicitation of repertory grids are listed in Appendix 3 in this volume.

ANALYSING THE DATA OF REPERTORY GRIDS

The compact appearance of a tabular representation of a completed repertory grid can be misleading with respect to the amount of data contained. For instance, if elements and more particularly constructs, have been elicited then these provide information to the enquirer. Landfield (1971) devised a coding system for the content of constructs of North Americans, which has not perhaps received the attention it deserves, while recently another such system has been proposed by Feixas and colleagues (2002) based on the constructs of Spanish subjects.

Attention has rather focused on the quantitative data in the grid, which can also be substantial. Sixteen elements rated on 16 constructs requires 256 judgements of a respondent, more than many personality inventories. Grid data can be analysed at the univariate, bivariate and multivariate levels to answer different kinds of questions about the psychological processes represented in the grid. An example of this kind of comprehensive evaluation can be found in Bell (2000b).

Indices

Where a ratings form of the grid is used, simple statistics can provide information about constructs and elements. Standard deviations will show how elements are distributed between the construct poles, while skewness measures will show lopsidedness (termed maldistribution by Fransella and Bannister (1977, pp. 83–84)). Landfield and Cannell (1988) developed a similar (but idiosyncratic) measure of the tendency to use extreme ratings (that is, locating elements at one pole or the other) in a grid called 'New Ord'. Interestingly, it was assumed by Landfield (1977) to be a measure of superordinacy of a construct. Chiari and colleagues (1990) have similarly argued, from a theoretical perspective, that superordinate constructs will be lopsided.

The basic building block for examining the structure of a grid is the relationship between pairs of constructs. Such relationships between constructs are usually measured by correlations or other measures of association, such as city-block distances (see Shaw, 1980, pp. 158–160). For relationships between elements, distances should be used (Mackay, 1992). As previously mentioned, in some computer interactive elicitation these indices are computed during the elicitation to provide the respondent with an opportunity of adding an element to increase the distinction between constructs or a construct to increase the discrimination between elements.

There has been a long tradition of summarizing indices of association, particularly among constructs, where it is known as 'cognitive simplicity-complexity' (Adams-Webber, 2003, Chapter 5). Bieri's (1955) original index was a simple sum of matchings of element allocation to constructs, consequently the values the index could take depended on the size of the grid and the kind of rating adopted. Other measures include Fransella and Bannister's (1977) 'intensity' (the sum of squared rank correlations multiplied by 100), Landfield and Schmittdiel's (1983) functionally-independent-construct 'FIC' index, the percentage of variance accounted for by the first principal component of construct intercorrelations (suggested by several authors) and Bell and Keen's (1981) use of intraclass correlations. While these measures tend to agree with one another (see Epting et al., 1992; Feixas et al., 1992), Bieri's index has attracted some criticism (e.g. Applegate et al., 1991), as has Landfield's FIC index (Soldz & Soldz, 1989).

Element indices have been less widely investigated and confined to grids where the 'self' appears as an element. One of the most robust indices is that attached to the allocation of self and other figures to positive and negative poles of constructs. Adams-Webber (1990) summarizes much of this work, although it has continued since, which produces some striking constants with respect to the proportions of total positive construals, positive construals of self, and like-self judgements. Of course, since these are constants they are of little use in considering relationships with other variables, but they have been used as the basis for conjectures about the possible mental models for such judgements (see Adams-Webber, 1990, for an outline of the possibilities).

The other kind of index associated with elements has been the notion of discrepancy between them. First noted by Jones (1961), with respect to 'self' figures as elements (such as 'me now', 'me in six months', 'actual self', 'ideal self'), the notion was used in clinical research by Makhlouf-Norris and others (for example, Makhlouf-Norris & Jones, 1971). These are usually calculated as distances. However the possible distances that can be calculated will depend on the rating scale used in the grid. Norris and Makhlouf-Norris (1976) wished to identify abnormally close or distant figures, so used random data in grids to provide a 'baseline' reference. Slater (1977) devised an expected distance which could be used to rescale individual distances so that they were comparable. Hartmann (1992) showed that Slater's correction did not take into account the number of constructs considered, and suggested a correction. A subsequent empirical evaluation (Schoeneich & Klapp, 1998) supported this change.

Representations

Summary indices such as those above play a large role in the use of the repertory grid in research. In individual contexts, such as professional settings, the demands can be different and a more 'qualitative' picture of the relationships among constructs and elements is often desirable. Such a picture can be obtained through quantitative modelling. The two traditional approaches to representing these relationships have been principal component analysis and cluster analysis. The former is the older tradition. Kelly, himself, outlined an approximate method of representing relationships among constructs, while Levy and Dugan (1956) showed how conventional principal component analysis could be used to show the structure of relationships among constructs.

The major advance was provided by Patrick Slater (1964), who showed that a related technique (singular-value-decomposition) could be used to provide an analysis that gave a simultaneous representation of constructs and elements. Slater referred to this as 'principal components', which led to confusion among those familiar with the traditional principal component approaches to factor analysis. More recently, correspondence analysis, or the similar technique, biplot (both also related to singular-value-decomposition) have also been used to provide joint construct-element spatial representations of repertory grid data. Multidimensional unfolding (a variant of multidimensional scaling) can also be used to provide a joint construct-element spatial representation of repertory grid. Leach and colleagues (2001) provide examples of representations of a repertory grid with these different approaches. Yet another approach which represents hierarchical structures among constructs (in line with Kelly's Organization Corollary) has been demonstrated by Sewell and colleagues (1996).

Cluster analysis has been popular, particularly in the United Kingdom, since Shaw and Thomas (1978) introduced the program 'Focus' that ran on early Apple computers. Most clustering that is relevant to repertory grid data is hierarchical clustering. Such clustering differs from principal components in that there are many criteria for the formation of a cluster (while there are only minor differences in principal component algorithms), and cluster analysis solutions can look very different from one another. Another difference is that, apart from one exception (Leach, 1981), cluster analysis is carried out separately on elements and constructs, although they might be visually represented by a computer program simultaneously as clusterings on the rows and columns of the grid matrix.

How well our representation of constructs or elements corresponds to the original grid data cannot always be determined. For example, while we can estimate the construct correlations from the construct factor solution and compare these with the original construct correlations, we cannot reconstruct the element data from such an analysis (it has been 'lost' in the calculation of construct correlations) and thus we cannot compare our construct factor analysis with the original grid data. In some kinds of analyses, such as correspondence analysis or singular-value-decomposition analysis (for example, Slater's INGRID) we can, however, measure the discrepancy between the grid generated from our representation and the original grid. Curiously this seems to be rarely done.

Most of the above representations of repertory grid data are based on association or distances. However the theory does not consider this kind of relationship between constructs, rather, through the Organization Corollary, hierarchical or super- and subordinate relationships are posited between constructs (see Bell, 1988). Such relationships are essentially asymmetric (unlike distances or correlations) and need to be modelled in different ways. Shaw and Gaines (1981) introduced such an approach using conditional probability as an asymmetric measure of association.

Computer software for analysing repertory grid software is listed in Appendix 3 to this volume, although standard statistical packages can also be used. Bell (1994) has produced a document showing how SPSS can be used to carry out a wide range of analyses, while Leach and colleagues (2001) have shown how SYSTAT might similarly be used.

MULTIPLE REPERTORY GRIDS

As indicated above, research often involves the use of repertory grids collected over a number of respondents and/or a number of occasions. Where each of these multiple grids is unique with respect to both elements and constructs, the only way in which the data can be aggregated across the grids is via the summary indices reviewed above. However, these summary indices have the disadvantage of suppressing the detail of the repertory grids. The alternative is to restrict either elements or constructs (or both) to be common across grids. Commonality of elements can be less of a problem when the elements are some common external event (such as types of tea, or aspects of lectures) but may be more of a problem when elements are less defined (a close friend). This issue has not been studied in detail. Commonality of constructs is possible (the theory has a corollary defining this) and Bell (2000a) has suggested a way in which the degree of commonality may be assessed.

If there is commonality of an aspect of multiple grids, then this may enter into the design of the study, either as a repeated-measures variable for significance testing or as a facet to be represented in spatial representation. Examples of such spatial representations (through individual differences multidimensional scaling or unfolding) has been described by Leach and colleagues (2001). If both elements and constructs are common, then the further possibility of three-mode factor analysis as a way of representing the data becomes possible. Kroonenberg (1985) provides an example of this.

Analysis of multiple repertory grids can usually be carried out through the standard statistical packages referred to above. At present there are few grid-specific programs for multiple grid data (see Appendix 3).

OTHER TYPES OF GRID

Repertory grids are not the only kind of grid associated with personal construct theory. Another kind of grid which is based on constructs is the implication grid devised by Hinkle (1965). A modification of that was used by Fransella (1972) in a study of people who stutter (see Chapter 9, pp. 98–101). Caputi and colleagues (1990) reviewed the methods of analysing Hinkle's data and presented a relational model that was advantageous in allowing the fit of the model to be assessed and a simultaneous estimation of all hierarchical relationships in the data. Kelly also devised a situation–resource grid (now often called a dependency grid) in which 'elements' are resources and 'constructs' are situations (see Chapter 7, pp. 77–86). While these grids can be analysed as ordinary grid data there is often an additional concern for the ways in which resources are allocated to situations. Walker and colleagues (1988), and Bell (2001), have devised indices (available in GRIDSTAT; Bell, 1998) which indicate the extent to which resources may be dispersed across situations and vice versa.

PSYCHOMETRIC ISSUES

The variety of ways of carrying out the repertory grid technique preclude an overarching conclusion about the reliability or validity of the technique. As an example, G. Neimeyer and Hagans (2002) varied four aspects of the repertory grid technique and found up to three-way interactions (between number of elements used in elicitation, wording of elicitation and rating direction) affecting Landfield's index of functionally independent constructs. Further, not all aspects of traditional test theory have the same meaning for repertory grid data (Bell, 1990b). Nevertheless some reviewers have adopted a traditional perspective (Jackson & Paunonen, 1981, p. 519; Neimeyer, 1985c, p. 153) and have suggested that the technique is faulty in psychometric terms. Such reviews have tended to ignore the evidence to the contrary. In a work that has often been overlooked, Bannister and Mair (1968) reviewed a substantial amount of research which show test–retest correlations of around 0.80 for construct choice, element choice and grid rating. Subsequent studies have confirmed these conclusions. For example, Lohaus (1986) found average test–retest reliabilities of 0.88 when subjects could choose their own rating schemes, and both Feixas and colleagues (1992) and Caputi and Keynes (2001) found substantial retest reliability (up to 0.90) for a number of grid measures.

Validity issues have been less commonly addressed in a measurement context although more widely carried out with respect to the theory of personal constructs (for example, Fransella & Bannister, 1967). However in a grid-measurement context, Dempsey and Neimeyer (1995) found convergence of repertory grids and implications grids with respect to the assessment of construct structure. In a more specific examination of grid indices, Applegate and colleagues (1991) reported a lack of convergent validity for Bieri's index of cognitive complexity, while Walker and colleagues (1988) demonstrated the validity of an index of dispersion of dependency derived from dependency grids. There are many more indices, however, for which evidence of validity or reliability is not available. Research with the technique continues, much of which is now reported in the *Journal of Constructivist Psychology*. For example, a special issue (April–June 2002) is centred on the work of Greg Neimeyer (2002).

CONCLUSIONS

The repertory grid technique has been the most widely known and widely used aspect of George Kelly's personal construct theory. Why is this? There are many reasons: it is a measurement device that has a solid conceptual basis for its structure; it provides a succinct representation of the way a person construes his world or some aspect of it; it is flexible in allowing for both individualized and normative kinds of assessment; it can be applied in an almost limitless range of contexts; and it can be used to provide many different kinds of information. While there have been concerns about a preoccupation with this technique (for example, Neimeyer, 1985c) and, as indicated in this chapter, some issues that need further examination, there is no other technique as general and as flexible as the repertory grid.

More details on the practical use of repertory grids can be found in the second edition of the *Manual for Repertory Grid Technique* by Fransella, Bell and Bannister (2004), and Jankowicz (2003) provides greater detail on repertory grid design and administration.

CHAPTER 7

Making Sense of Dependency

Beverly M. Walker

University of Wollongong, Australia

Now, may I invite you to look at psychology in a new way, more particularly at counseling in a new way, and especially at interpersonal dependency. This is not an attempt to proselyte. You may continue to be as loyal as ever you like to whatever you believe to be true of the psychotherapeutic process in general, and of dependency in particular. This is, instead, a proposal to explore the implications of a new viewpoint, even to the extent of experimenting with it actively.

Now, let me see if I can shake the kaleidoscope for you. Watch closely. See what happens.

(Kelly, 1966a)

Kelly makes an important distinction between the ways in which we depend on others. Not surprisingly, the kind of construing involved is central. This chapter will explore this distinction, outline an associated methodology and use case studies to demonstrate contrasting examples, locating this distinction within broader theoretical issues.

PATTERNS OF CONSTRUING

In presenting a way of understanding our dependence on others, Kelly (1969g) feels it important to consider the overall pattern. Do we concentrate our dependencies, so that those we depend on are each expected to provide the satisfaction of all our needs? Or do we view our support network and needs in more differentiated ways, so that some resources meet some, while others satisfy different needs. The first of these patterns he terms *undispersed*, the second *dispersed*, dependency. He regards undispersed dependency as a less useful way of taking care of needs. Its problematic nature stems, not from a link with unhappiness, nor with pathology as traditionally defined, but rather the vulnerability of the person when change occurs.

The Essential *Practitioner's Handbook of Personal Construct Psychology.* Edited by F. Fransella.
© 2005 John Wiley & Sons, Ltd.

To explore these patterns, Kelly presents an instrument he called the 'Situation Resources Test' (Kelly, 1955/1991, pp. 312–317/Vol. 1, pp. 233–237), now known as a 'Dependency' grid. The grid indicates the perceived relationship between possible resources the person can call upon and a sample of problem situations. Respondents select resources from their current and past networks. In the original version, they think of a time when a particular problem occurred and indicate with crosses for which problems they would have been able to go to each resource in turn. The participants are asked to make a decision *as if* the resource had been available when the problem happened. Walker et al. (1988) propose a statistical means of assessing dependency dispersion. That Dispersion of Dependency Index has now been applied in a variety of contexts (Walker, 1997), and a worked example can be found in Fransella, Bell and Bannister (2004). Kelly's method has been further adapted to create two forms of dependency grids, the original termed a 'Being Helped' grid, and an adapted version, showing whom the respondent helps with particular problems, called a 'Helping' grid.

The initially curious thing about these grids is that they do not appear to contain personal constructs. In contrast with a repertory grid, which looks at the relationships between elements and constructs (see Chapter 6, pp. 67–76), dependency grids explore the relationships between two sorts of elements: resources and problems. The construing is implicit in the grid, reflected in the patterns of crosses and blanks. Construct poles can be made explicit by asking respondents questions such as why they went to the particular people for each problem in turn, with this questioning supplemented by obtaining opposites as well as laddering.

In exploring the importance of dispersion of dependency Kelly takes a developmental perspective. He rejects the commonly held position that children are more dependent than adults, suggesting that in some senses the reverse is true. He proposes instead that the important feature of dependence in childhood is that it is concentrated, so that immediate family members meet all the young child's needs. As the child matures the pattern of depending becomes more differentiated, so that ultimately the mature adult is maintained within a dispersed dependency network, although some adults retain the relatively undispersed pattern. Increasing dispersion is closely tied to our developing capacities and willingness to understand how others view the world, what Kelly termed 'sociality', since we need to balance our demands on others with their preparedness to give.

In terms of the construing involved with increased dispersion of dependency, it is not just that more discriminations are made between resources, problems and needs, but the nature of the construing changes as well. Kelly considers that constructs could be distinguished in terms of the extent to which they can apply to new contexts and events. 'Permeable' is the term he gave to those that could, 'impermeable' to those that could not. The former is associated with increased dispersion, the latter with undispersed dependency.

Another way of differentiating construing is in terms of its relationships to other constructs. Pre-emptive construing makes sense of the element in one, and only one, way, so that, for example, mother is 'just the person who looks after me', and hence is not seen in any other way. By contrast, constellatory construing means that once one dimension is applied to an element, a whole complex of other construct poles also apply. This happens with stereotyping, so that, for example, once an individual's gender is known, they may be construed as having many other additional characteristics. However, propositional construing entails no implications for how the construing relates to other constructs, neither involving its isolation nor the enlisting of a constellation of others. Kelly associated propositionality with dispersed dependency.

One way of looking at Kelly's proposals about these different ways of construing is to see them as a developmental progression. Impermeable, pre-emptive and constellatory construing would tend to be more common in childhood and, with maturity, replaced increasingly by permeable and propositional construing. To understand why some forms of construing are preferable to others it is useful to look at how they are applied in practice. The examples that follow, illustrating differing dispersion, clarify this issue.

TYPES OF DEPENDENCY

An Example of Dispersed Dependency

Karen, aged 18, explained that her parents were divorced and she lived with her mother and sister, but did not get on with her parents. Her Being Helped grid is shown in Table 7.1.

In the interview based on the grid, her most widely applied construct was *close relationship–not close relationship*, a distinction verbalized by many people, though varying in meaning. For Karen closeness concerned talking in an involved way (not superficially) and being understood. That construct was linked to whether the problems were serious and involved or merely required superficial help.

She distinguished people who listen and try not to sway her, as opposed to people, like her parents, who simply tell her what to do. The former gave an honest opinion and cared about how she felt. The latter were more concerned with what she had done, not her feelings. Of her parents she said: 'We're really different in values, have completely different ideas. Lots of these problems have to do with my parents. They cause them.'

While she felt she gained her security from her grandparents, sister and boyfriend, she had reservations about the help that her grandparents could give her in some areas as they were a bit old fashioned. Further, they were the sort of people whom she did not like to worry.

People *who take your mind off it cheer you up, make you forget about problems*, such as her teacher, were the supports she required for certain situations, such as when she felt lonely and needed to be more cheerful. By contrast, for other problems she wanted to be persuaded to think about better things (as when she was discouraged about the future) and so she would go to level-headed people, like her cousin. They were perceived as *older people, more grown-up, people who are still coping in their future*. By this she meant that they were coping at ages that still lie ahead for her.

Thus, from Karen's Being Helped grid were elicited a variety of elaborated clusters of predominantly propositional constructs, linking groups of people with groups of situations. Furthermore underlying these intersections of people and problems were constructs to do with the kinds of help required, including superficial talk,

Table 7.1　Karen's Being Helped grid

Problems	Self	Mum	Dad	Nan	Pop	Sister	Boyfriend	Female friend	Boss	Minister	Neighbour	Doctor	Adviser	Teacher	Cousin
With vocation	X	X	X				X	X						X	X
With opposite sex	X	X	X	X	X	X	X	X						X	X
Were unlucky	X	X	X	X	X	X	X	X	X		X		X	X	X
With finances	X	X	X	X	X		X								X
With illness	X	X	X	X	X		X				X	X		X	X
Made serious mistake	X	X	X	X	X	X	X	X	X		X		X	X	X
With failure	X	X	X	X	X	X	X	X	X		X		X	X	X
Were lonely	X	X	X	X	X	X	X	X	X		X			X	X
Discouraged with future	X			X	X	X	X	X		X	X			X	X
Felt better off dead	X			X	X	X	X	X			X				X
Were misunderstood	X		X	X	X	X	X	X			X				X
Were angry	X		X	X	X	X	X	X			X		X	X	X
Hurt someone	X	X		X	X	X	X	X			X				X
Were ashamed	X	X	X	X	X	X	X	X			X				X
Were frightened	X			X	X	X	X								
Behaved childishly	X			X	X	X	X	X					X		X
Were jealous	X	X	X	X	X	X	X	X							
Were confused	X					X	X	X							
With parents	X			X	X	X	X	X			X		X	X	X
With sister	X	X	X	X	X	X	X	X			X		X	X	X
With boyfriend	X	X	X	X	X	X	X	X			X			X	X

having a yak, cheering her up, providing material assistance, helping her to forget about problems, persuading her to think more positively. Indeed, one cannot help but agree with her that, as far as her future is concerned, she will indeed cope effectively.

Examples of Undispersed Dependency

Kam's Grids

Kam's Being Helped grid (Table 7.2) is illustrative of an undispersed pattern of dependency. Kam was the same age as Karen and had come to Australia five years ago as a refugee from Vietnam. He had no difficulties in understanding the task, also completing a Helping grid which is not shown here.

Two major sets of constructs emerged from both grids. The first concerned the priest and counsellor, the professionals. These were people *who give advice in my interest* as opposed to *people who tell me what to do, irrespective of my likes*. Professionals know a lot, are smart, are objective and understand human behaviours while the others express opinions rather than facts. With regard to the helping grid, professionals can handle things on their own, whereas non-professionals must canvass others' opinions. It was to the professionals that Kam takes problems that were major.

The second set of personal constructs differentiated people relative to Kam's age. He found it easy to talk with older people about personal things, but not younger ones. Paralleling this for the helping grid, he felt that older people would not come to a younger person like him if they were puzzled or confused. Further there were friends, *who tell everything*, in contrast to *those who are either younger or older*.

What is evident about these overarching discriminations is that they were what Kelly termed 'constellatory construing'. Once you know people are either professional or not, younger or older, all sorts of things follow on. People are either professionals who understand facts about human behaviours and to whom one can go for advice, or they are non-professionals who express mere opinion; they are either older than he or they may be younger and, if so, the appropriate interaction is proscribed by this comparison. Compared to Karen, the rigidity of the construing is apparent. With regard to his best friend of the same age, Kam would go to him for the problems indicated, not for advice, but merely to let him know. When asked 'why?' he explained 'because I think I can do it myself or go to someone who knows better, the professionals'. Unlike Karen he did not feel he personally could cope with whatever occurred. There are problems that he had control over and those that were more major, that he could not control, but nevertheless could solve by seeking professional advice.

Allen's Grids

A great deal of biographical information about Allen emerged in the process of the construct elicitation interview. He was 33 years old, worked at the Water Board and had finally fulfilled his ambition to come to university. He described his family of

Table 7.2   Kam's Being Helped grid

Problems	Self	Mother	Father	Male friend	Priest	Counsellor	Teacher	Young friend F	Young friend M	Female friend
With vocation						X				
With opposite sex	X				X	X				
Were unlucky	X				X	X				
With finances		X	X		X	X				
With illness		X	X		X	X				
When gullible					X	X	X			
Made serious mistake	X					X				
With failure	X				X	X				
Were lonely	X	X	X	X	X	X				
Discouraged with future	X	X	X	X	X	X				
Felt better off dead					X	X				
Were misunderstood		X	X	X	X	X		X	X	X
Were angry					X	X				
Hurt someone	X				X	X				
Were ashamed					X	X				
Were frightened	X				X	X				
Behaved childishly					X	X				
Were jealous					X	X				
Were confused	X				X	X				
With parents					X	X				
With sister					X	X				

origin, his parents and two sisters, as 'very close'. He was divorced, had remarried three years previously and his current wife had two married brothers, whom he saw a lot of on weekends. He and his wife were very close, 'talk over everything with each other', but regrettably were unable to have children.

Beginning construct elicitation with the Helping grid, Allen had a great deal of difficulty in operating in an 'as if' mode. To questions of 'Why could these people rather than those people come to you for this problem?' his answer focused on the fact that they *had* come to him previously. He gave reasons for this behaviour that focused on specific biographical details of their life or his.

As soon as this pattern became apparent, that he had responded in terms of who *had* come to him for help, not who *could*, this was pointed out. He understood the distinction clearly but when given the opportunity to make modifications, was unable to do so. He could make few predictions apart from those based on previous specific instances of help seeking. Similarly, he responded to the Being Helped grid (Table 7.3) in terms of to whom he had gone in those situations. The exception occurred with his wife: 'we're very close. We discuss things and not let them build up', 'we discuss everything we do'. Allen appeared to be highly motivated to be interviewed about his grids, having taken time off work to do so, and having discussed his responses to the grids at length with his wife. He was trying to make sense of what he observed on completion of them, particularly his differing response to his family of origin compared to his in-laws.

His constructs were isolated, rarely integrated into clusters, unlike the previous examples. Occasional exceptions occurred. In elaborating his relationships within his family he stated some of the subordinate constructs such as: 'I am the eldest. I have gone to uni. I haven't lived close to the family, so I've always been the odd one out, and the family turn to me because of this.'

Considering the construing of both grids together, the major construct he used was *close–not close*. Close people were either *part of the family, people I grew up with, have known a long time* and/or *have shared the same experience*. Such construct poles would not readily apply to new acquaintances, what Kelly termed 'impermeable'. You can not, after all, have new people you grew up with. While you can gain new members of the family, it is clear from Allen's puzzlement about the difference in the way he treated his own family of origin compared to his wife's, that the latter had not become close from his perspective. However this was not totally the case since Rass, his male friend, had become 'like part of the family', though some problems were too personal for a new friend. Further, work and non-work problems, work and non-work relationships, were kept totally separate.

His construing about himself, and indeed problems themselves, seemed more elaborated than those about others. The theme of wanting to work things out himself was one he emphasized, describing himself as 'a bit of a loner'. He distinguished problems that were a personal challenge from those that were not, as well as problems he preferred to work out himself, as opposed to those that he would discuss with others. There were also the things you hide from others, such as when he was gullible or ashamed. Looking at the other's perspective was quite important as a theme about himself. If he got angry he would cool down quickly by seeing the other's viewpoint. 'If in a situation, I'd quickly look at their perspective. This gives my wife the poohs.'

Table 7.3 Allen's Being Helped grid

Problems	Self	Mum	Dad	Sister 1	Sister 2	Wife	Male friend	Boss	Neighbour M	Neighbour F	In-laws	Female friend	Friend—Rass
With vocation	X					X		X					
With opposite sex	X	X	X			X						X	
Were unlucky	X					X	X					X	
With finances	X					X	X						
With illness	X	X	X	X	X	X							
When gullible	X	X	X			X							
Made serious mistake	X	X	X			X		X					
With failure	X	X	X			X		X	X	X			
Were lonely	X	X	X			X			X	X			
Discouraged with future	X	X	X			X		X					
Were angry	X					X							
Hurt someone	X					X							
Were ashamed	X					X							
Were frightened	X					X	X	X					
Behaved childishly	X					X							
Were confused	X	X	X			X		X					
With parents	X			X		X							
With sisters	X	X	X			X							X
With spouse	X					X							

TYPES OF CONSTRUING AND DEPENDENCY

What are the implications of these highly contrasting examples of dependency dispersion? The problem with lack of dispersion of dependency is that it leaves the person vulnerable to change. Commonly this involves a few resources meeting the host of varied needs that we all have. If those resources die, move or become exasperated at the demands from the undispersed person and withdraw their availability, then the undispersed are left high and dry. They may desperately search for someone else to replace the missing helper(s), or may be unable to substitute someone else without substantial reconstrual.

Integral to these patterns of depending, Kelly argues, is the link with certain sorts of discriminations. Clearly the dispersed pattern is accompanied by a rich, varied, multifaceted construing system, as Karen's example demonstrates. By contrast Kam and Allen show a more restricted range of constructs about resources as well as problems. But it was not just the number and complexity of construing that differentiated the patterns. The *kinds* of constructs were also important.

A striking characteristic of Allen's construing was its impermeability, that is its inability to encompass new situations. Allen based his sense-making on what had already occurred, which is a limited basis for construing the novel. The people he regarded as close were largely either family or people whom he had grown up with, both categories that are resistant to inclusion of new resources. By contrast Kam had a less vulnerable system, with constellatory construing being the predominant emphasis. Professionals had a variety of characteristics that differentiated them from non-professionals, seemingly without exception. Further patterns of helping depended on the age of the helper or the helped, not on characteristics self-evidently relating to helping behaviour. Elsewhere I have given an example of a further type of construing that has been linked to undispersed dependency; pre-emptive construing (Walker, 1993), which involves viewing the element concerned unidimensionally, in one and only one way, so that mum may be viewed as 'just the person who looks after me'.

Contrast these ways of construing to those used by Karen. She used what Kelly called 'propositional' construing, one 'which carries no implications regarding the other realm memberships of its elements'. Karen's construing did not mean a whole cluster of constructs were invoked once one feature of the element was known (constellatory construing), nor was the way elements were viewed restricted to one perspective (pre-emption). The system Karen used was one that could apply to new resources or problems she met, unlike impermeable construing. It was a flexible, adaptable system that could accommodate new challenges and contexts.

Of course impermeability, pre-emption and constellatory construing are not just confined to dependency construing but could be linked to more general developmental processes. But a further useful way of looking at them is as examples of what we have called 'nonvalidation' (Walker et al., 2000).

TYPES OF CONSTRUING AND EXPERIMENTATION

Kelly's assumption is that people have the *potential* to become like scientists in that their ways of seeing the world, like the scientist's hypotheses, are successively tested out and revised or retained depending on the outcome of that experimentation (Walker, 1992). However, all of us at times do not put our construing to effective test, illustrating 'nonvalidation'. Walker (2002) details a number of examples of nonvalidation. But the kinds of construing associated with undispersed dependency are further illustrations.

If we construe close people as *those we have grown up with*, an impermeable construction, then we never effectively test this out as we cannot become close to those with whom we did not grow up. This is very different from linking close people to *people who will listen* or *people who will not judge you*, since these are ways of behaving that one explores, tries people out on, conducts experiments with, in order to evaluate who does or does not fit the bill.

Analogously, if we associate a constellation of constructs with a characteristic of the person, such as their age, gender or race, then we have no need to test out the applicability of that constellation to any one individual. Further, frequently in such stereotyped thinking, the associated construing justifies avoiding the stereotyped individuals, thus bypassing any challenge to the view of those involved. Similarly, for example, if we can only talk with older people about our problems, then we never find out that a younger person might be as effective as a helper. The experiment is not conducted. Finally, with regard to pre-emption, if someone is 'nothing but' a particular characteristic, then it is only *that* aspect of behaviour that is of interest, and other features are ignored as the focus of experimentation.

SUMMARY

Kelly has pointed to an interesting distinction between extremes of patterns of dependence on others. Kelly presented his account developmentally, detailing ways of construing that are related to increasing dispersion. These include taking into account others' ways of making sense of things, as well as a greater differentiation between potential resources, problems and needs. Additionally there is the increasing reliance on the kinds of discriminations that can be applied to new eventualities, as well as tested out effectively to assess their continued viability. The practical implications of viewing dependency in this way are far-reaching as the kaleidoscope metaphor in the opening quote to this chapter suggests.

CHAPTER 8

Expertise and Expert Systems: Emulating Psychological Processes

Mildred L.G. Shaw

Centre for Person–Computer Studies, BC, Canada

and

Brian R. Gaines

Centre for Person–Computer Studies, BC, Canada

There once was a passionate dame
Who wanted some things made plain,
So she punched up the cards,
Filled tape by the yards,
But—somehow—*it just wasn't the same!*

(Kelly, 1963, p. 229)

The role of personal construct psychology in computer research and applications concerned with the development of 'expert systems' and their beginnings in 'artificial intelligence' and 'cognitive science' are covered in this chapter. Research on expert systems led to the identification of the 'knowledge acquisition bottleneck', that it was generally extremely difficult to make overt the presumed knowledge of human experts in order to program it for computers.

The history and reasons for the adoption of repertory grid methodologies and tools to overcome the knowledge acquisition bottleneck are described. Then a more fundamental analysis is made of why expert systems to date have had only limited success, and the merits of a personal construct approach to emulating human expertise in greater depth than has been achieved with existing cognitive science models are presented.

In conclusion, it is noted that the techniques developed to emulate human expertise are essentially ones for modeling and emulating *any* person's psychological processes, not just those of people valued by others as 'experts'. PCP-based expert

The Essential *Practitioner's Handbook of Personal Construct Psychology.* Edited by F. Fransella.
© 2005 John Wiley & Sons, Ltd.

systems methods and technology have wide relevance, for example, in clinical and educational research and applications.

RESEARCH ON PROGRAMMING COMPUTERS TO THINK

The arrival of the first commercial digital computers in the 1950s led to widespread interest in the potential applications of computing. The use of the term 'giant brains' became common in the press although it was clear that the precise, logical operations of computers had little in common with the human brain. However, interest in simulating human thought processes was common among the early computer pioneers. Alan Turing, a brilliant Cambridge logician who had helped to develop computers to break enemy message encryption during World War II, wrote a paper on 'Computing machinery and intelligence' for the journal *Mind* in which he considers the question 'Can machines think?' (Turing, 1950). He answers it in behavioural terms, proposing what has come to be known as the 'Turing test', that if a person communicating with the computer and with another person through the same medium (such as communicating teleprinters) cannot distinguish them correctly, then the machine, for all practical purposes, can be said to think.

Research on programming computers to think became widespread. McCarthy and colleagues (1955) proposed to the Rockefeller Foundation that it fund a study of *artificial intelligence* (see also Jack Adams-Webber on this topic in Chapter 17.5, pp. 189–192) to be carried out during the summer of 1956 at Dartmouth College, Hanover in the USA. The year of this proposal also saw the publication of Kelly's seminal work on personal construct psychology but, as discussed in the following section, the pioneers of artificial intelligence and cognitive science never became aware of this work. The next decade was also the era of the development of 'computer science' as a new field of study when computers were very expensive, and university and funding agency budgets were hard-pressed to supply the demand for computer facilities. In Britain the competition between those wishing to undertake research in computer science and in artificial intelligence was so intense that the UK Science Research Council commissioned Sir James Lighthill to report on the state of the art in 'machine intelligence'. His report (Lighthill, 1973) was damning about both the achievements and the prospects for such research and had a strong negative influence worldwide on funding for research to program computers to think (Fleck, 1982).

Embattled AI researchers focused on specific goals to develop programs that emulated human expert performance in fields of obvious practical value such as mineral exploration and medical diagnosis, and in the mid-1970s announced a number of breakthroughs in what came to be called 'expert systems' (Michie, 1979). The first successful expert systems were DENDRAL (Feigenbaum et al., 1971) for reconstructing molecular structures from mass spectrometer data and MYCIN (Shortliffe, 1976) for diagnosing microbial infections from medical data. The systems were programmed as collections of 'production rules' that expressed a relationship between a premise and a conclusion such that if the conditions of the premise were satisfied then those of the conclusion could be drawn. For example, a rule from MYCIN is:

If: (1) the infection is primary-bacteremia, and

     (2) the site of the culture is one of the sterile sites, and

     (3) the suspected portal of entry of the organism is the gastro-intestinal tract,

then: there is suggestive evidence (0.7) that the identity of the organism is bacteroides.

Such rules are obtained from specialists in microbial infections and their application to particular data is fairly simple data processing. The rules are validated through their application to many cases and revised when they fail to give the correct diagnosis. MYCIN was designed to interact with a clinician in order to make a diagnosis and suggest therapy for a particular patient with a suspected microbial infection. It first gathers data about the patient and then uses this to make inferences about the infections and their treatment.

The success of the early expert systems attracted industrial and research attention, and a major industry developed in the early 1980s. The research objectives were then defined by one of the commercial AI pioneers, Hayes-Roth (1984), in a workshop on 'AI Applications for Business' in May 1983. He enumerated some situations appropriate to expert systems, such as: the organization requires more skilled people than it can recruit or retain; job excellence requires a scope of knowledge exceeding reasonable demands on human training and continuing education.

As a modern example of the success of expert systems technology, the April and July 2000 issues of *InTech Magazine* published by the Instrumentation, Systems and Automation Society have a two-part paper from Eli Lilly on the use of an expert system in its fermentation plant (Alford et al., 2000). The evaluation in 2000 corresponds well to Hayes-Roth's predictions in 1983. Within a few weeks, the expert was satisfied that the expert system reliably came to the same conclusions he would have by looking at the same data. The expert system then took over this part of the expert's job, freeing up 40 hours a month of his time for other work.

THE KNOWLEDGE ACQUISITION BOTTLENECK

Expert systems appeared at first to be a major validation of the possibility of digital computers being able to emulate human thinking, and there is continuing evidence of some successful applications. However, the industry has not grown to the extent predicted, largely because programming such systems has been very much more difficult than expected. Feigenbaum (1980), one of the pioneers of expert systems, termed this the 'knowledge acquisition bottleneck'. Hayes-Roth and co-workers (1983) in their book *Building Expert Systems* noted that, since the programmer has far less knowledge of the domain than the expert, communication problems impede the process of transferring expertise into a computer program. The vocabulary initially used by the expert to talk about the domain with a novice is often inadequate for problem-solving; so that the programmer and the expert must work together to extend and refine it. One of the most difficult aspects of the programmer's task is helping the expert to structure the specialist knowledge, to identify and formalize the expert's concepts.

From a personal construct perspective, the task of the expert system programmer is to reconstruct the conceptual and operational framework that an expert in a domain uses to solve problems in that domain, noting that the terminology used may be highly idiosyncratic, that is, personal to the expert. However, the expert is, by definition, someone who is effective at problem-solving in the domain and, hence, her or his knowledge is valid in some practical sense. The expert's knowledge has been acquired by some mix of processes, such as trial and error, mimicking others, reflection on personal experience, reading text written by other experts, conversations with others, and so on. That corresponds to Kelly's notion of an individual as a *personal scientist* (Shaw, 1980) about which he asks:

> Might not the individual man, each in his own personal way, assume more of the stature of a scientist, ever seeking to predict and control the course of events with which he is involved? Would he not have his theories, test his hypotheses, and weigh his experimental evidence? (Kelly, 1955/1991, p. 5/Vol. 1, pp. 4–5)

Kelly merges the notions of prediction and control into the unitary notion of *anticipation* and hence his Fundamental Postulate: 'a person's processes are psychologically channelized by the ways in which he anticipates events'.

Thus, from a personal construct perspective, the task of the expert system programmer is to model the personal construct system of the expert in operational form as a computer program such that the program is able to anticipate events in the same way as the expert. It was suggested in the early years of expert systems (Gaines & Shaw, 1980) that new methods for rule extraction made Kelly's repertory grid a suitable tool for eliciting knowledge from experts. Existing computer programs for interactive elicitation of repertory grids were rapidly modified to support knowledge acquisition for expert systems (Shaw & Gaines, 1983; Boose, 1984). The approach proved successful in industrial applications (Boose, 1986), and a framework based on personal construct psychology became accepted as the foundation for developing knowledge acquisition techniques and tools (Ford et al., 1993; Gaines & Shaw, 1993).

A PERSONAL CONSTRUCT ALTERNATIVE TO RULE-BASED COGNITIVE MODELS

While repertory grids were widely used as knowledge acquisition tools in the 1980s and 1990s, expert systems themselves failed to achieve as much as had been expected, and a large-scale artificial intelligence industry did not materialize. Various writers have speculated on the reasons for that failure, the deepest analysis being that of Dreyfus and Dreyfus (1986). They see the problem as a manifestation of Wittgenstein's (1953) argument that the notion of human behaviour following a rule is paradoxical because, as he showed, by a suitable interpretation every course of action could be made to accord with the rule.

The pioneers of cognitive science had modelled the human mind as a repository of so-called 'production rules' (Anderson, 1983) and the designers of expert systems had followed this model in their 'knowledge representation' schemes. Dreyfus and Dreyfus argue that such representation is a major weakness and that systems based on it could never fully emulate human expert behaviour. In the AI literature,

Clancey (1989) has criticized approaches to expert system development based on the assumption that expertise can be captured in overt knowledge, and has noted that all processes of behaving, including speech, problem-solving and physical skills, are generated on the spot, not by mechanical application of scripts or rules previously stored in the brain. He argues that knowledge is a capacity to behave adaptively within an environment; it cannot be reduced to representations of behaviour or the environment.

Repertory grid-based knowledge acquisition tools had of necessity delivered knowledge in the form of rules so that it could be utilized by existing expert system knowledge representation tools. However, the analysis leading to the rules is not part of the construction process and may be regarded as an artefact of the need to use rule-based expert systems technology. Kelly developed personal construct psychology from a perspective that was consistent with that of Wittgenstein, and did not introduce rules in his psychological model. For him construing was all that was necessary to account for human behaviour, and anticipation was a by-product of construction. That is, construction intrinsically supported anticipatory processes without the storage of anticipatory 'rules' but, at a particular stage in the construction of experience, these anticipations might have a regularity that an observer could ascribe to 'rules of behaviour'. This corresponds to anticipations being 'supervenient' on constructions, to use a technical term from the philosophy of mind (Kim, 1993). However, as the person construed more experience, then the anticipations might change and the observer could construe this in terms of the person 'learning new rules'. Kelly also emphasized time and again that personal construct psychology does not need a notion of 'learning' on the part of the person or personal scientist. Construction alone was sufficient to account for the person's mental processes and behaviour, and it could also account for the models being produced by observers or psychologists. The Wittgenstein paradox presents no problems to personal construct psychologists because there is no assumption that human behaviour is rule-governed.

It is unfortunate that the development of cognitive science in the mid-1950s became dominated by those whose background was in mathematical logic. Kelly published his major work on personal construct psychology in 1955, and it could easily have become adopted as the foundation for what became called 'cognitive science' and provided foundations for artificial intelligence and expert systems. In the few years until his death in 1967 he made a number of presentations to wider audiences that might have triggered recognition of the far-ranging implications of his work. In April 1961 he presented personal construct psychology to Luria and other members of the Moscow Psychological Society in Moscow as 'a mathematical approach to psychology' (Kelly, 1969f) paralleling the development of mathematical psychology in the USA by Miller, Mosteller and others (Hirst, 1988). In June 1962 he was an invited commentator at a conference on 'the computer simulation of personality' held at Princeton University and stated:

> In this connection I would like to make a plug for the psychology of personal constructs. Not only is it a system built upon the notion that scientists and human beings, alike, approach truth by erecting simulation devices—called constructs— but is a theory deliberately formulated in a language system which is based on binary elements and which does not accept the so-called subject–predicate error of the Indo-European language system. (Kelly, 1963, p. 228)

However, Kelly's work was not recognized in the 1950s by computer and cognitive scientists.

PERSONAL CONSTRUCT PSYCHOLOGY AS A FOUNDATION FOR MODELLING HUMAN EXPERTISE

The models of human thought processes derived from personal construct psychology and from mathematical logic can be contrasted through a simple example. Suppose a child has three constellations of experience:

> child is well-behaved; mother is attentive; mother smiles;
> child is naughty; mother is attentive; mother frowns;
> child is passive; mother is inattentive.

A machine-learning program might derive the rules:

> child is well-behaved **implies** mother smiles;
> child is naughty **implies** mother frowns;
> child is passive **implies** mother is inattentive;
> child is well-behaved or naughty **implies** mother is attentive.

So that a child who is well-behaved might infer that her mother will smile, but how does the child know when she is well-behaved?

A personal construct model would be that the child construes her three sets of experience in terms of the constructs: *well-behaved* versus *naughty*, *attentive* versus *inattentive* and *smiles* versus *frowns*. Supervenient on the construing of the three constellations of experience are *all* the compatible anticipations, that is, those above plus:

> mother smiles **implies** child is well-behaved;
> mother frowns **implies** child is naughty;
> plus others.

These reverse implications will be used to give meaning to the construct *well-behaved–naughty* in novel situations. To act to make the mother smile the child will choose situations where the child is well-behaved and the mother smiles. If the child wants the mother's attention then the child may choose situations where the child is naughty, the mother frowns but also pays attention to the child. There are no 'rules of behaviour' but there is the choice of situations in a rather more flexible way than would be entailed through sets of rules. In addition there is an increasing repertoire of behaviour as the child construes new situations in terms of her behaviour and the mother's smile or frown. One might say the child is 'learning' but there is no specific mechanism for learning, only for construction. One might say that the mother's smile 'reinforces' good behaviour but there is no reinforcement, only construction and choice. Kelly's view is that construction provides a complete account of human behaviour and can also model the constructs of different schools of psychology.

Now apply that model to human expertise. It models the expert as a construing agent not as a 'knowledge base' of rules. The model automatically updates as more experience is construed, that is, as the expert system attempts to solve more problems. The experience can be used in a variety of ways to solve problems and to give meaning to new situations, for example, the availability of a new drug or treatment. 'Knowledge acquisition' is intrinsic to personal construct-based expert systems and does not need to be treated as a separate phase. Expert knowledge can be transferred to the system not only through exemplary problem-solving but also by commenting on the system's problem-solving and by choosing problems for the system which are at the limits of the system's current capabilities. That is, experts can make their behaviour available to be mimicked and can also act as coaches commenting on performance and setting tasks, all major strategies in supporting human development.

An example of repertory grid-based expert system development and application tool is WebGrid, which is freely available on the World Wide Web (http://repgrid.com/WebGrid/). To use WebGrid an expert enters exemplary situations and, once some have been entered, can enter test cases to see how the system performs (Gaines & Shaw, 1997). If the system is incorrect, the expert can change the result and enter the corrected test case as an additional example until the system is generally correct. The system retains only the repertory grid of constructions as its knowledge base. WebGrid can produce sets of rules at any stage that characterize and explain its model of expertise at that stage, but these are not stored, just produced on request, and are truly supervenient on the expert's construction.

CONCLUSIONS

Expert systems were recognized as a breakthrough in artificial intelligence, in programming computers to emulate human thinking. However, they were based on a form of cognitive science that took mathematical logic as its foundations and was not well suited to modelling the full richness of human behaviour. Personal construct psychology developed over the same time period but was not recognized by those working on artificial intelligence and cognitive science as a complete psychological system providing more effective foundations for cognitive science and expert systems. Repertory grid elicitation *was* recognized as a valuable knowledge acquisition technique with which to develop rules for expert systems, but the knowledge transferred in the form of rules was static and brittle, and did not lead to the systems being open to experience. It would be timely to adopt personal construct psychology as the foundations of cognitive science and use it to build expert systems that fully emulated the capabilities of human experts, not only to solve problems but also to be effective in dealing with new problems as they arise.

As a final comment, it is noteworthy that while the expert system community has focused on emulating the capabilities of those with expertise of value to industry, the technology developed is useful for modeling the psychological processes of any person. Kelly noted that all people may be construed as 'scientists' in their processes of modeling their worlds and validating those models. Similarly, we construe everyone as 'experts' in being themselves and living their lives in their own way, whether or not the capabilities involved in doing this are singled out as being of special value by others. In therapy or in education, for example, emulation of the person in the computer may provide a *cognitive mirror* (Shaw, 1980) in which an individual can view their psychological processes and come to understand them better. If there are problems arising from these processes, the increased understanding may help the individual to develop alternative constructions to address them. One by-product of research on the application of personal construct psychology to expert system development is that it has advanced our capabilities to model and emulate a person's psychological processes in a way that may be useful to that person. The motivation for the research may have been to emulate the expertise of value to industry, but the outcomes have far wider significance.

ACKNOWLEDGEMENTS

Financial assistance for this work has been made available by the Natural Sciences and Engineering Research Council of Canada.

URLs

WebGrid can be accessed at *http://repgrid.com/WebGrid/*
Related papers on WebGrid can be accessed through *http://repgrid.com/reports/*

CHAPTER 9

From Theory to Research to Change

Fay Fransella

University of Hertfordshire, UK

> Instead of being a problem of threatening proportions, requiring the utmost explanation and control to keep man out of trouble, behaviour presents itself as man's principal instrument of inquiry. Without it his questions are academic and he gets nowhere. When it is prescribed for him he runs around in dogmatic circles. But when he uses it boldly to ask questions, a flood of unexpected answers rises to tax his utmost capacity to understand.
>
> (Kelly, 1970, p. 260)

Bannister and Fransella (1986) argued that one of the prime effects of carrying out research within a specific theoretical framework is that the theory decides the questions that are to be asked; that it not only provides the research with a language and a methodology but should also indicate what issues are fundamental. The tie-up between a theory and the questions that one asks is obvious enough. Not only does theory generate issues for experimental investigation, it also provides ideas for designing ways in which individuals may be helped to reconstrue. In particular, work within the framework of the psychology of personal constructs does not see 'normal' and 'abnormal' as two psychologies, but as merely different ways of construing described in the same terms. The following examples illustrate the tie-up between theory, research and practice.

DISORDER OF THOUGHT PROCESSES

Bannister's Theory

It was Don Bannister's theorizing and research work on the nature of the type of disordered thought processes seen in those diagnosed as suffering from schizophrenia that alerted the academic world in the United Kingdom to George Kelly's theory and repertory grid method. Bannister argued that it was excessive loosening

The Essential Practitioner's Handbook of Personal Construct Psychology. Edited by F. Fransella.
© 2005 John Wiley & Sons, Ltd.

of the thought process that produced language that is, in the experience of the listener, incomprehensible. In personal construct theory terms, one can ask whether it is a private language or just a very weak language. Many groups use subsystems of constructs that are incomprehensible to most of us. Mathematicians debating the deeper mysteries of their subject may be incomprehensible, but we would not judge them to be thought-disordered. We accept that they are probably saying something very meaningful and that it is we who lack the specialist construct subsystem to enable us to understand them. The shortcoming is ours not theirs. The same with painting. The loosely construed paintings of schizophrenic people used to be likened to the work of abstract artists. But it was pointed out that abstract artists differ in that they can tighten up their construing when it is time to go home and those with 'schizophrenia' cannot.

The Research Programme

Bannister's theory was tested in series of experiments using repertory grids (Bannister, 1960; Bannister et al., 1971; McPherson et al., 1973). They all found that thought-disordered schizophrenics do, indeed, suffer from a gross loosening of construing. That is, the mathematical relationships between the constructs were very low and the pattern of relationships between the constructs was unstable over time. In contrast, grids repeatedly given to other groups showed significantly closer relationships between constructs and the pattern of these relationships remained relatively consistent over time.

However, his early work with Phillida Salmon showed that such thought-disordered people are not equally perplexed by every aspect of the world in which they live. The greatest difference between them and other so-called 'normal' groups lay in the discrepancy between 'object' and 'people' construing. The thought-disordered group were only a little worse than 'normal' groups in their construing of objects, but they were vastly less structured and consistent in their construing on psychological dimensions. That suggested that schizophrenic thought disorder may not occur throughout their whole construing system, but may be particularly related to *interpersonal* construing (Bannister & Salmon, 1966).

Bannister argued that if it is interpersonal construing that has been specifically affected in thought disorder, then any theory about it being the result of brain disorder has to postulate an unlikely bug or 'schizococcus' that bites 'person-thinking' but not 'object-thinking' brain cells.

The Origins of Thought Process Disorder

Personal construct psychology places great stress on process and change. Thus, any research on thought disorder or any other problems, very rapidly forces the researcher to face the question of how do people come to have that problem. It is not enough to give an account of the condition as it stands.

Bannister's initial hypothesis about what causes thought disorder was that it is the ultimate result of the experience of *serial invalidation*. He argued that thought-disordered schizophrenics have been driven to loosen their construing *beyond the point* at which there are enough workable lines of implication between their constructs for them to re-tighten their system. By loosening our construing we place ourselves in the position of neither being right or wrong in our predictions. Loosening and tightening are not of themselves pathological reactions, but are normal reactions to varying validational fortunes.

To test his hypothesis Bannister conducted experiments in which so-called 'normal' people were 'serially invalidated' (Bannister, 1963, 1965). The experiments showed that successively telling people they were *right* did, indeed, cause them to tighten their construing. However, those who were successively told that they were wrong, did not loosen the interrelationships between their constructs immediately, but responded markedly with another strategy—they changed the *pattern* of inter-relationships. Thus, on one occasion a person might have a high positive correlation (say, 0.70) between *kind* and *sincere* then, on a later grid, these two constructs might be highly negatively correlated (say, −0.90). That wild swinging of the pattern of relationships between constructs seemed to be an initial and marked reaction to invalidation. However, in a final experiment it was shown that if only one cluster of constructs at a time, rather than a whole subsystem, was invalidated, then loosening did take place.

Bannister's ideas and research sparked a vast amount of activity among researchers, some producing results supporting his hypotheses, some against. Included in that research activity was the development of the standardized *Grid Test of Schizophrenic Thought Disorder* (Bannister & Fransella, 1967). The aim was to provide an aid to a reconstruction programme to help such people to become 'thought-ordered'. But it was destined to become only an aid to diagnosis.

The Resulting Therapy Research Programme

Although Bannister's research was an artificial and laboratory model of the process of serial invalidation, he felt that the experiments did suggest that thought-disordered people may have been wrong too often. That raised the question of how thought-disordered schizophrenics could again achieve 'ordered' thinking.

He suggested that a reduction of thought disorder might take place as a result of serial *validation* (having one's expectations confirmed). The programme he designed began with a very extensive search of each individual's construct system for dealing with people. The aim was to find some residual structure; some group of still semi-clustered constructs that would serve as a starting point for an elaboration of the whole system.

The thought-disordered schizophrenic people were encouraged to think about/relate to others and start having expectations about them. They were then encouraged to experiment with their environment in order that they could test out the implications of their construing. This research (Bannister et al., 1975) produced no startling 'cure' for thought disorder, but it did suggest that a 'journey back' may be possible, long and arduous though that journey would be.

THE CONSTRUING OF STUTTERING

As this is about my own theorizing and research, I will talk about it personally. Don Bannister's research in the 1960s made me realize that personal construct theory was a powerful way of trying to give meaning to the behaviour of some people that otherwise seemed incomprehensible. My particular interest in the mid-1960s was those who stutter. Why did they not stop doing something that obviously caused them so much unhappiness? There is no body of evidence to suggest that people stutter because of some brain malfunction. Like him, I turned to theory to provide an explanation for the continuance of stuttered speech in those who had been labelled 'a stutterer' from an early age.

A Personal Construct Theory of Stuttering

Kelly's model is of the *personal construer.* Those who stutter construe. They, like everyone else, have developed subsystems of constructs throughout their lives, through which to view the universe of events that confront them and enable them to predict and hence have some control over the course of these events.

Our personal construct systems make us both free and prisoners. We are free in that we can change our construing of events in the light of the results of our predictions. But we are trapped by that same construing system. We have choice, but we can only choose between the dichotomous constructs that make up our system; we cannot view the world along totally new construct dimensions at will. I was struck by Hinkle's (1965) rewording of the Choice Corollary:

> a person always chooses in that direction which he anticipates will increase the total meaning and significance of his life. Stated in the defensive form, a person chooses so as to avoid the anxiety of chaos and the despair of absolute certainty.
>
> (p. 21)

Eventually I came to theorize that *a person stutters because it is in this way that he or she can anticipate the greatest number of events: it is by behaving in this way that life is most meaningful to him or her.* Someone who stutters cannot change because none of us willingly walks the plank and so drops off into an unknown, unpredictable world. In the world of fluency there lie many unknown hazards for someone who stutters and a vastly decreased ability to predict these pitfalls.

People who stutter know all about being 'a stutterer'. They know the variety of ways in which a person is likely to react to their way of speaking, and know what their reactions will be to the listener's reactions. But they are unable to interpret the subtler forms of communication such as eye contacts, hand gestures and general body movements which usually accompany speaking for the fluent person. I argued that one of their problems is that they do not try to see the situation through the eyes of the listener. There is no role relationship as described in the Sociality Corollary. No attempt is made to see things through the listener's eyes, only an interpretation of the listener's behaviour.

The Resulting Therapy Research Programme

My reasons for carrying out this research were two-fold. One was purely theoretical, a wish to show that behaviour is directly linked to construing—as personal construct theory suggests. The other was to test whether personal construct theory could
be of use in gaining insight into another human problem that is also very resistant
to change. That, in turn, might lead to an approach to helping sufferers find a path
to fluency. The research was *not* designed to test the efficacy of personal construct
therapy.

The research was based on Hinkle's (1965) rewording of the Choice Corollary,
which states: 'A person chooses for himself that alternative in a dichotomized construct through which he anticipates the greater possibility for extension and definition of his system'. My principal research tool was a modified form of his
Implications Grid. There are no elements to be construed in the Impgrid, constructs
are compared with constructs. My simplified modification of Hinkle's grid was to
take one pole of a person's constructs at a time and ask that person to look at all
their other constructs—laid out on the table before them. The question asked was,
for example, 'if all you know about a person is that they are *thrifty*, are there any
other characteristics among those on the table here that you would *expect* a *thrifty*
person to be?'

Twenty people who, starting in 1966, were successively referred to me for treatment of their stutter, completed two such *bipolar impgrids*—one with constructs
elicited from 'me as a stutterer' and the other from 'me as a fluent speaker'. These
were repeated at intervals during the therapy. On each of those occasions, measures
were also taken of severity of stuttering and self-characterizations were written.

The precise prediction was that, as fluency increased, the implications of being a
fluent speaker would increase—it would become a more meaningful way of being.

Reconstruing from Stuttering to Fluency

As with all forms of therapy, the method stems from the theory about the problem.
If it is argued that people continue to stutter because that is the most meaningful
way for them to behave, then the therapy will be directed to making fluency a more
meaningful way to behave. Until that has increased meaning, the person who
stutters will not experiment with being a fluent person. The same applies to anyone
with a long-standing problem—to people who have a problem with weight, as is
described later in this chapter, to those who smoke (Mair, 1970) or who drink to
excess (Hoy, 1973). All ways of behaving that a person has adopted over many years
becomes part of their 'self' construing. The problem such people have 'is not a
symptom but a way of life' (Fransella, 1970).

The main therapeutic method used was what Kelly described as 'controlled
elaboration'. That is described fully in Fransella (1972) and in Chapter 11 (pp.
116–117). In this case, any occasion in which the client had experienced fluency was
focused on. 'What did it feel like?' 'How did the other person react to your fluency?'
But the crucial question was, 'Did you predict you would be fluent?' If the person
said they did 'know' they would be fluent, they soon came to realize that it was they

themselves who were responsible for the fluency and that it was not something that just 'came upon me'. It was their own construing that resulted in their response of stuttering or fluency.

At the end of the two-year programme, the results supported both my aims. Behaviour and construing were shown to be inseparable. The degree of increase in fluency was highly related to the number of implications people had for being a fluent speaker. The more meaningful a fluent speaker was being, the more fluent the person had become. Apart from that, there was also a decrease in meaningfulness of being a stutterer as fluency increased. Personal construct theory states that we do not have to give up one set of ideas before embarking on the elaboration of another. It is reasonable then to suppose that as one subsystem of construing becomes more meaningful and is seen to have increased predictive capacity, the other subsystem will eventually start to 'shrivel up'. Apart from that, it was shown that the personal construct theory of stuttering had led to a treatment programme that produced positive results.

Therapeutic Constraints

The very precise nature of my hypotheses meant that only work based on personal construct theory could be used to help the client reconstrue. But it seemed likely that using some speech modification technique would speed up the development of 'spontaneous fluency', and thus make reconstruing easier. Margaret Evesham and I (1985) investigated that hypothesis. One group of stutterers had fluency training in 'prolonged speech' and the other group had that training plus personal construct work. Measures were made of disfluencies and all forty-eight participants completed grids and self characterizations.

People in both groups experienced a decrease in their disfluencies, but the technique group showed more improvement. Although a seemingly disappointing result, it was of particular interest that the relapse rate for the personal construct group was significantly lower than for the technique group. That would, of course, be predicted from personal construct theory. Those in the personal construct group were actually changing how they saw themselves as a person. Once that happens, a person is less likely to go back to the beginning, although there may be sporadic relapses. Those who simply learn a technique for changing their behaviour, may or may not reconstrue themselves as a person.

Over the 30 years since that original research work, considerable use has been made of the personal construct approach by speech and language therapists in the United Kingdom (Stewart & Birdsall, 2001) but, as DiLollo and colleagues (2001) have pointed out, its application to the treatment of stuttering in the United States has been almost non-existent. These latter authors suggest that one of the reasons for that is the requirement of specialist training and the complexity of the assessment methods. While agreeing that some knowledge and experience of personal construct theory is necessary for any practitioner, the assessment methods are not a requirement of the reconstruction programme. I used the bipolar impgrids to test specific hypotheses and not as an integral part of the therapy.

DiLollo and colleagues recommend the use of *narrative therapy* (see Chapter 22,

p. 237). The framework outlined by White and Epston (1990) and cited by DiLollo and colleagues, is not far removed from that of the personal construct approach. For instance, they suggest that there is a need to talk about the relationship between the person and the problem; find out how the person is able to predict that they are about to stutter; and that there should be a focus on fluency. Manning (2004) has also pointed to the lack of interest in the personal construct approach to stuttering in the United States. He aims to rectify this situation!

A PROBLEM OF WEIGHT

Like stuttering, disorders of weight are notoriously resistant to change—particularly that described as anorexia nervosa, a potentially life-threatening disorder in which the extreme pursuit of thinness and avoidance of fatness dominates a person's life. Eric Button has spent many years trying to understand why these people, commonly young women, look as if they want to starve themselves to death (see Button, 1993, for full coverage of his work). His starting point was my work on stuttering.

His general hypothesis was that resistance to weight gain was related to the meaning of being a normal weight. The results from his first piece of research gave some support to that hypothesis and also showed that a greater degree of meaningfulness of being at a normal weight was associated with better weight maintenance following discharge from hospital. That is, relapse rates were lower.

A second study had one particularly striking finding, contrary to what one might expect. The young women construed 'me at my thinnest' in very negative terms compared to their ideal self. However, the picture was complex. For example, one person generally construed being normal weight as preferable to being thin, but in one crucial respect there was a snag. For her, being normal weight meant being *conspicuous*, which was the last thing she wanted, she would like to have been virtually invisible.

In addition to such findings about the *content* of their construing, later research demonstrated the importance of *structural* aspects of construing. These young women, compared with both healthy individuals and those suffering from bulimia nervosa (those who binge-eat, typically followed by vomiting), showed more limited and rigid forms of construing of people. Button's central theme now is that it is this limitation in how they construe people which leads them to take refuge in the more predictable and controllable world of just focusing on food, eating and weight.

Therapeutic Implications

Button now argues, in line with Fransella's approach, that therapeutic efforts should focus on developing 'person construing' rather than on weight. He comments that:

> Sadly, some thirty years after my original research, I am less optimistic about the possibilities of change in many of these individuals whose styles of construing can prove highly repetitive and resistant. My goal, however, is to help them find and be themselves in their own terms, in spite of their limitations and with or without their anorectic way of life. (Personal communication)

The above examples and many other psychological problems are characterized by the sufferers finding it very difficult to change and being subject to relapse. Why can we not become what we want to become? Why do people, who seem to be making good progress, in their own terms or those of others, suddenly stop that progress and sometimes even 'take a step backwards'?

RESISTING CHANGE?

Resistance to change for both psychoanalysts and cognitive-behaviour therapists involves some notion of failure on the part of the client. The personal construct practitioner strongly disagrees with that view. How can a client fail? If the client is seen as failing so must be the therapist, since they are struggling together on the same problem. If the client demonstrates that he or she is not seeing the problem as the therapist does, some reconstruing—on the part of the therapist—is required. As Kelly put it:

> The client who exasperates the therapist by his failure to deal with what the therapist wants him to, or by his refusal to see things the way the therapist so clearly sees them is not necessarily warding off the therapist as a person; more likely he is demonstrating the fact that his construct system does not subsume what the therapist thinks it should. (Kelly, 1955/1991, p. 1101/Vol. 2, p. 379)

The Choice Corollary leads us to think that the essence of living is to grow and develop, to extend and/or define our construing of the world—and therefore to change. Taking that view, clients are not *resisting* change, they are *choosing* not to change. They choose to *persist* in their present behaviour (Fransella, 1993).

WHY CHOOSE NOT TO CHANGE?

Although this chapter focuses primarily on the process of reconstruction for those seeking professional help, it is important to remember that Kelly's ideas are relevant to us all, whether or not we have a serious problem with which we need help. We all experience times when we choose not to change. These times can be looked at in terms of structure of a person's construing system and also in terms of transitions.

When the Problem is Part of the Core Role

For many people, their complaint is part of their core role and the alternative way of being has some serious negative aspect to it. That applies to both those who stutter and those with anorexia nervosa already described.

But choosing not to change is not an uncommon experience. For instance, many current change programmes require people, say, middle managers, to become *caring managers* rather than *directive*. These managers will resist change if that change requires them to become something they, at a core level, think is not *them*. In one organization this resulted in an alarming number failing their assessment at the end of a lengthy change programme. Through individual interviews involving elicitation and laddering of personal constructs, it was found that to be *caring*, for some, was the equivalent of being a *bad manager*, quite unacceptable. Once a problem such as this has been put into words, it can be discussed. In this case, many of these middle managers said that they were prepared to 'give it a go'. The majority passed at the assessment centre the second time round. They always had the skills to pass, but their understanding of their role did not allow them to. It is important to state that their jobs were not at risk.

Tight versus Loose Construing

It is often found that those who had tight construing subsystems of themselves change less than those who construe their world more loosely, for example, Fransella (1972) with those who stutter, Button (1980) with those suffering from anorexia nervosa and Sheehan (1985) with those who are depressed. That is easy to understand. If we are fairly certain how things are, we may realize, at some level of awareness, that one or two seemingly simple changes could have serious reverberations throughout the system. We choose not to change.

When there is Nowhere to Go

People who have stuttered for as long as they can remember have no alternative but to value the *status quo*. To suddenly find themselves fluent would plunge them into a world in which they can predict very little when speaking with other adult people. They cannot change until being fluent is meaningful to them. It is the same for anyone who has behaved in a certain way for a very long time.

When the Alternative is an Ideal

For many of those with long-standing problems such as stuttering, obesity, alcoholism or smoking, the alternative to being a stutterer, obese, an alcoholic or a smoker is to be 'an ideal'. They cry 'if only'. 'If only I were not someone who stutters I would be a great orator.' 'If only I were not an alcoholic I would be a powerful businessman.' 'If only I were not obese I would be one of the most successful fashion models.' Most of us cannot live an ideal.

THE EXPERIENCE OF NOT WANTING TO CHANGE

Having looked at reasons why a person chooses not to change how they see themselves and their problem 'just like that', the experience of such choice can be looked at in terms of 'transitions'.

Threat

A major reason for maintaining the psychological status quo is the awareness that, if change takes place, it will result in a comprehensive change in one's core construing. Luke spelled it out like this:

> I have a confession to make. I sort of feel that in the past I should have taken a
> more active interest in getting rid of my stammer. . . . I feel I'm capable of think-
> ing about the situation and trying to work out some new ideas—in general help
> you along as much as possible—I've been a bit on the lazy side. . . . I could easily
> sit down and think about my stammer, but when it came to the time, then I didn't
> feel like it and I think that this could well be the fact that probably somewhere,
> subconsciously, I didn't want to get rid of it because it was—you know—just this
> sort of thing. That there was something in the fluent world that I was afraid of.
>   (Fransella, 1972, p. 195)

He had definitely become aware of the imminent possibility of comprehensive
change in his core construing. He was correct in asking for more time to reconstrue.

Hostility

One of the most often experienced ways of making sure that no more change occurs
is by being hostile. As Kelly points out, hostility is often construed by the therapist
as 'resistance'.

> If the client is hostile he may, indeed, be making a whipping boy out of the ther-
> apist; but even this, we feel, is more profitably seen as an effort to retrieve some
> bad bets on which the client wagered more than he could afford. If the therapist
> has no more enlightened construction of what is going on than to insist that the
> client 'is being stubborn', it would seem that the therapist is hostile too.
>   (Kelly, 1955/1991, p. 1101/Vol. 2, p. 379)

Clients are extremely creative in the ways they find to convince the therapist that
there has really not been any improvement. Relapse can readily be seen as one
hostile strategy. Just to complete the theoretical picture, Kelly suggests that, where
there seems to be hostility, one should look for the guilt (Kelly, 19691).

Guilt

That is felt when the client actually glimpses, for instance, that new 'fluent self' or
that 'normal weight self'. They become aware that they have gone too far in their
psychological change and, for however short a time, have been dislodged from that
treasured core role.

It seems likely that some fairly radical core role reconstruing has to take place
before a person is able to judge whether what was so desirable to begin with is really
so desirable after all. What looked so wonderful when it was unelaborated and its
implications unknown may look very threatening in the cold light of reconstrual.
Evidence has to be extorted to show that, whatever change there is in the offing, it
is unimportant. That hostility prevents the person having to face the *guilt* of not
being the person they always thought they were. Kelly felt that *guilt* can be so
serious that he said:

> Since guilt, as we have defined it, represents dislodgement from one's core role
> structure, we could scarcely expect guilt not to be related to 'physical' health.

> Strictly within the psychological realm one might transpose the Biblical saying,
> 'The wages of sin is death' into 'The wages of guilt is death'. It is genuinely 'dif-
> ficult to sustain life in the fact of guilt'. Some people do not even try.
>
> (Kelly, 1955/1991, p. 909/Vol. 2, 246)

RELAPSE

Everything that has been said about choosing to resist change is relevant to our
understanding of why people relapse. The speed of change is too fast. Reconstruing keeps sending shock waves up to those core role areas and signals imminent
change in the system itself. Something has to be done about it. What better than to
go back a few steps to where it may be more uncomfortable but at least it is home.

But personal construct theory leads one to view relapses during therapy as useful.
They provide the person with a breathing space. Time to work out what all the
change they have experienced actually means. What is useful and what is still too
threatening to contemplate? As has been said before, such construing does not go
on 'in one's head'. It takes place below the level of conscious awareness. Relapsing
provides the client and therapist with much needed space to back-track and attach
more words to the underlying construing that is causing painful threat or guilt.

THEORY AND MEASUREMENT OF RESISTANCE TO CHANGE

Denny Hinkle (1965) outlined a theory of personal construing that he called a
'theory of construct implications' and described how that theory led to an understanding of change in construing. To test his theory he described the 'hierarchical
technique for eliciting the superordinate constructs of the preferred self hierarchy',
which has subsequently been called laddering, created the 'implications grid' and
also a way of measuring resistance to change. Basically, he was suggesting that
the meaning of a personal construct is provided by that construct's relationship
to other constructs. Thus, the meaning of each personal construct is to be found in
the poles of those other constructs that it implies plus those that are implied by
it. So each personal construct has a range of both superordinate and subordinate
implications.

His theory of construct implications led to his arguing that the range of implication of a construct could be used as a measure of the meaningfulness of that construct. He set about testing a number of hypotheses in his research. He theorized
that the relative resistance to change of personal constructs would be related to how
superordinate they are for an individual:

> ... the relative resistance to slot change of personal constructs will be directly
> related to the superordinate range of implications of those constructs. This is
> based on the principle of maximizing the total implicativeness of the system and
> the notion that the anticipated degree of threat will be a direct function of the
> number of implications involved in the change. (Hinkle, 1965, p. 28)

Another hypothesis was that:

> Constructs functioning at a higher level of superordination in a hierarchical context will show a greater relative resistance to slot change than constructs function at a low level. (Hinkle, 1965, p. 29)

Hinkle's research supported his hypotheses. He found also that the degree to which personal constructs are resistant to change is related to whether they are superordinate (laddered) constructs or are subordinate (elicited). The more superordinate personal constructs are, the more likely they are to resist any change.

Measuring Resistance to Change

His resistance to change grid is quite simple if somewhat laborious. Each personal construct, written on a card, is paired with all other constructs. The person is first asked to state which pole of each construct they would prefer to describe themselves, and these preferred poles are underlined. A form of questioning that has been found easy to use is: 'tomorrow morning you are going to wake up and find that you have changed on one of these two constructs. In this case, you will have changed from being *glamorous* to being *plain* or from being *thoughtful* to being *impetuous*. Which would you find it most difficult to change on?' The number of the construct on which the person indicates it would be most difficult to change is noted. The scoring is simply the sum for each construct on which it has been nominated as resisting the change. (See Fransella, Bell & Bannister, 2004, for details.)

Another way of getting an indication of how resistant to change personal constructs are is simply to ask the person to rank their elicited and laddered personal constructs from most important to them to least important.

SUMMARY

Personal construct theory can lead to new ways of looking at old problems. Different people have taken different aspects of the theory as their starting point. Thus, for instance, Don Bannister focused on loosening of construing as the basis of his theory of the type of disordered thinking found in some of those diagnosed as suffering from schizophrenia, and I found it was the Choice Corollary that led me to a new way of thinking about the problem of stuttering. The resulting theories not only lend themselves to testing but also lead to new approaches to helping the sufferers.

That same theory can then be used to explain why some people find it so difficult to 'give up' their problem. If the person feels that change resulting from the therapy is too fast, he or she may well *choose* to stop changing or even to go back a few steps. The therapist may well see the former as resistance and the latter as relapse. But the reflexive nature of personal construct theory enables the therapist to look at his or her own construing to find out what is going on.

How Can PCP Help Us to Understand People or Help Them to Change?

Part 1: Working With the Individual or Individuals in Small Groups

CHAPTER 10

Is Treatment a Good Idea?*

George A. Kelly

'Is treatment a good idea?' When one poses such a question to an audience like this—an audience dedicated to the mission of treating patients—he opens himself immediately to one of three charges: Perhaps he has nothing more to offer than the traditional answer and everyone hopes he will sit down as soon as he has said what he has to say. If not that, he must be a die-hard hereditarian who doesn't think crazy people can be helped and who is optimistic enough to think that his pessimism will be listened to. Or, perhaps, he is merely employing a speech-maker's sensationalism in order to get folks to listen to what otherwise is going to be a very dull talk.

Now let me say at the outset that I do not want to be placed into any of these categories. What I have posed is an honest question that I believe is worth examining carefully. Moreover, to show my good faith and make it clear that I am not merely dangling a question in front of you in order to make you keep your eyes open, let me say at the outset that my answer to this question is going to be 'No'. 'No, treatment is not a good idea.'

Now, will you examine, along with me, the notion of treatment itself—what it means—what it implies about the nature of man—and, in addition, some of the serious mistakes the idea of treatment has led us to make. I am inviting you to do this because I am convinced that a re-examination of the concept of treatment will have a salutary effect on what we all do as professional people.

First of all, I would like to say that, along with most of you, I still think it is good for people who are sick to get well. In addition, I still think there are things each of us can do to help them to get well. And I think some of those things are already being done here and there—not as often as they should be, perhaps, and maybe only in the out-of-the-way corners of hospitals and clinics, but still they are being done. Sometimes they are done by professional or administrative intent, and sometimes, you all would agree, in spite of it.

During the past century the notions of modern science have been extended to the realm of human behaviour. One of those notions is that everything that happens

---

*Address to a Conference on Treatment, 1958: US Veterans Administration Hospital, Sheridan, Wyoming.

The Essential *Practitioner's Handbook of Personal Construct Psychology*. Edited by F. Fransella.
© 2005 John Wiley & Sons, Ltd.

can be explained in terms of what preceded it. More particularly, this means that if we know everything that is going on today we can put it together and tell exactly what will happen tomorrow. Of course, in the down-to-earth practical sense, it is impossible to know absolutely everything that is going on today. Besides, as some scientists have recently argued, even if today's events are known, their consequences can be predicted only probabilistically. But here I am not concerned with either of these two interesting reservations on scientific reasoning. What I am concerned about is the effect such reasoning has on the human enterprise, particularly when the human enterprise begins to involve itself with the alteration of human behaviour.

Most psychologists, when they try to think scientifically about human behaviour, boil it down to two notions—something that goes on independently of the person, usually outside his skin, and something he does which is attributable to that outside event. The former the psychologist calls a 'stimulus' and the latter—once he had invoked the notion of 'stimulus'—the psychologist has no choice but to call a 'response'.

This little solipsistic invention of 'stimulus and response' underlies the major portion of psychology's scientific efforts to figure out what people are up to. While these efforts have by no means proved futile, the reasoning upon which they are based forces a strong bias on what men try to do for each other. If a person's behaviour is faulty, change the stimulus—change the stimulus, for are not his responses attributable to events which preceded them? Once we start to think this way the net result is inevitably to focus our attention upon the treatment rather than upon the person who is in trouble, as if something inherent in the treatment itself carries the seeds that will sprout into behaviour.

Let us approach treatment from another angle. Suppose, instead of abstracting the constructs of 'stimulus' and 'response', we talk about persons in 'dynamic' terms. In psychiatric circles this is supposed to be good and if you are wise you will always be careful to use such language in the presence of properly educated people, unless you happen to be one of those poor benighted creatures known as a 'state hospital' psychiatrist. It has for some time been a matter of interest to me why it is that people who can afford to pay private fees always have 'dynamics', while those who can't have 'diagnoses'. I have observed also that the more fees you can afford to pay the more dynamics you are likely to have. But, then, this is not what I came here to talk about.

Dynamic interpretations explain human behaviour in terms of such notions as motives, needs, and incentives, or, if you have invested in the Freudian lexicon, in terms of such artistic inventions as oedipal strivings, hostility, libidinal cathexes, etc. While, as a model of human thought, this is more primitive than the stimulus–response—in fact, if the truth is to be known, even more primitive than Aristotelian thinking—it does provide certain advantages over its competitors. For example, the dynamic model envisions the determinants of human behaviour as residing within the person, a more helpful way of looking at the matter if you hope to see him accomplish anything.

Treatment, under the aegis of dynamic thinking, becomes a matter of uncovering psychological forces and mechanisms, of venting pent-up impulses, of supporting some self-critical evaluations and undermining others, and various other interventions in the turmoil of the person's psyche. But still, even under this system of thought, the determinants of behaviour, while now residing within the person, are abstracted from him as extra-personal entities and not altogether his own doings. Treatment continues to be undertaken as something imposed from without—something done to juggle the patient's dynamics. The person is still a 'patient' with all the inert passivity that that unfortunate term has implied throughout its long history.

May I approach my thesis from still another angle. Mankind has a long history of intolerance and brutality. Over the centuries this history has been unfolding itself alongside an equally impressive story of expanding humanitarianism. For a long time it has been firmly believed that when a person went off his rocker he should first be given loving admonishment, and if that did not work he should be punished good.

In the meantime, medical science had made great progress in treating illness. Naturally enough it occurred to some physicians like Pinel that it might be better to treat certain kinds of misbehaviour as if they were symptoms of illness rather than outcroppings of devilment. This way of thinking has led to the employment of far more humane methods of dealing with certain people. Incidentally, it has served to create an enormous paradox in our system of social thought; some people get solicitous treatment for their misbehaviour while others, judged to be ineligible, get punishment measured out to them. Thus we try to live under two quite different and quite incompatible psychological systems for explaining human behaviour and for deciding what we ought to do about misbehaviour.

Treatment, of course, seems to hold more promise than punishment. It seems more civilized to say that a person is acted upon by forces over which he has no control and that therefore the corrective measures must likewise be provided by an external agency. By this line of reasoning any person who finds that he has done something he should not, is constrained to start looking for someone who will treat him, and while he is waiting for the doctor to come he may apply a little first aid, such as figuring out how it happened that his mother—the witch—made him into the kind of a person he turned out to be. He won't get far with this on his own, of course, because it requires some pretty time-consuming rationalization, and some kind of treatment, at least in the big cities nowadays, is not likely to be long in arriving.

Now what has all this to do with the topic of this symposium: 'Therapeutic Roles in Patient Treatment'? As you have probably already guessed, I am for assigning the most important role to the patient himself—only, I would prefer not to call him a 'patient'. This means developing a kind of psychology that is not especially popular these days, a psychology that envisions human behaviour as something initiated by the person who does the behaving. As I see it, such a psychology would have to abandon such notions as 'stimulus' and 'response' as well as a lot of psychodynamic constructs that imply that the determinants of human behaviour are independent operants within the psyche. Personally, I would just plain throw them all out, but I would be willing to settle for a compromise if psychodynamic concepts were used differently.

Something else follows from this line of thought. From our present vantage point in the course of human thinking it now seems to be a historical misfortune that psychological problems were ever placed in the medical context of illness. The twenti-eth-century institution which has emerged as 'the hospital' is so conceived, orga-nized, and committed that it represents altogether too much that is unwholesome for the troubled mind. The societal features which enlightened mankind seeks to reform—a rigid class structure stratifying both for staff and patients, listlessness, futility, anonymity, loss of family and community relationships, irrational authori-tarianism, regimentation, economic helplessness, endless waiting to 'be treated' *for something to happen*[1] and passive conformity to 'treatment programs' *what the straw boss says is 'good for you'*[1] to mention only a few.

Most of what I have said thus far will seem negative and destructive. If treatment is such an inappropriate idea what then, one may well ask, are the roles that are to be played by those who want to help? Certainly one thing becomes clear about such roles: they are to be played out as person-in-relation-to-person roles rather than as specialist-in-relation-to-illness roles. The primary question to answer about a staff member is: what do disturbed persons do with him? His area and degree of com-petence, when the chips are down, are operationally defined not so much by his edu-cation and list of former job incumbencies as by the practical uses to which he is put by those who need his help.

Mankind's approaches to its psychological problems are in for some drastic revi-sion. The notion of treatment, derived as it is from our fumbling efforts to apply notions of scientific determinism to human troubles, misplaces the emphasis on the various external roles to be played. But restoration of the wholesome life is some-thing done by the person whose life it is. His, then, is the principal role, and any system of psychological thought which envisions other roles as more important than his will serve only to stagnate mankind's efforts and turn out, for somebody to take care of, a generation of helpless creatures who seek 'treatment' every time they slip up, rather than doing something about it themselves.

---

[1] The words were struck out by George Kelly and those in italics written in the document by hand in their place.

CHAPTER 11

An Audacious Adventure: Personal Construct Counselling and Psychotherapy

Franz R. Epting
University of Florida, USA

Marco Gemignani
University of Florida, USA

and

Malcolm C. Cross
City University, London, UK

Psychotherapy should make one feel that he has come alive.
(Kelly, 1980, p. 29)

The project of helping others to undertake profound changes in their lives is the central mission of personal construct psychology. It is undertaken within a very special relationship with someone who helps open up space for personal development and understanding. Perhaps the best way to view what has gone wrong is to envision the person as having become stuck or trapped. In the everyday course of events, one would be getting on with life and not need professional assistance. As a matter of course there would be an opening up of new possibilities for either expanding one's interests or refining existing projects or both. Something, however, has come up which has impeded growth, despirited or disoriented the person and has resulted in some degree of helplessness and hopelessness. In these circumstances, personal construct psychotherapy or counselling offers hope and helps the person to feel alive again. Feeling alive means much more than just getting out of the bog. It means getting on with the most creative aspects of what life might hold.

The Essential Practitioner's Handbook of Personal Construct Psychology. Edited by F. Fransella.
© 2005 John Wiley & Sons, Ltd.

For the person in difficulty, the world has become solidified in such a way that there are no acceptable choices. There is at least boredom that often escalates to fear, dread or anxiety or the person escapes into fantasy. The central mission of the personal construct professional is to invite the person to see the world as pliable and as having the ability to offer up more possibilities than were seen on first inspection. For Kelly insists that one need not paint oneself into a corner. There are always choices and often choices that will offer relief and possibly an escape from some of the more dreadful aspects of the problem; if not escape, then more interesting corners in which to get stuck or choices that offer some level of human dignity while dealing with tragedy. It is often the case that the person has bought into some restricting social constructions of herself or her world so readily offered up by friends or injected into consciousness through the general social surround. She then takes these constructions to be real and sees no possibilities for viable change.[1] In order to explore just how soft this hard 'reality' might be, Kelly suggests casting our verbs in an invitational mood rather than in the usual indicative, conditional, subjunctive, or imperative moods, '. . . a verb could be cast in the form which would suggest to the listener that a certain novel interpretation of an object might be entertained' (see also McWilliams, 2003, pp. 79–80). Such a restatement could leave 'both the speaker and the listener, not with a conclusion on their hands, but in a posture of expectancy' (Kelly, 1969d, p. 149). Following the lead of Hans Vaihinger (1924) in his philosophy of 'as if', Kelly is suggesting, in a pragmatic vein, that we abandon a slavish devotion to reality and start entertaining alternative constructions.

Cast in the invitational mood, the ultimate aim of personal construct psychotherapy is to enable the person to pursue full cycles of experience which consist of anticipation, investment, encounter, confirmation and disconfirmation, and terminate in constructive revision. By completing full cycles of experience a person is able to 'rise above what he thinks he knows and so often then to do better than he knows how' (Kelly, 1977, p. 11). In this way the person is able to transcend the obvious. In approaching any significant issue the person is invited to take an active stance in anticipating what might be possible. This is followed by an invitation to make a personal investment in what is anticipated; letting the anticipations matter in a personal way rather than remaining detached from them. The invitation is to go to a level of involvement where the person has to cope with circumstances on an embodied-primitive-emotional-preverbal level as well as in an articulate manner using words. Then is added the further invitation to truly encounter these life circumstances. That means making a commitment to be fully self-involved in the moment as well as affirmatively anticipate what self-implications these events might have; thereby entering into possibilities for self-alteration and/or situation redefinition. Then comes the courage to face the confirmation or disconfirmation of what has been intimately anticipated at the outset; recognizing the fact that disconfirmation might hold the more exciting possibilities for further growth. Finally there is the invitation to constructive revision whereby the person is asked to receive the full impact of the experience in full cycle and undertake profound life changes. In

---

[1] Gender balance, in personal pronouns, is attempted by using both forms, intermittently, throughout the chapter.

short, at the end of the cycle both the client and therapist are changed by the enterprise, for this is truly a reflexive approach to psychotherapy.

CONSIDERATION OF OTHER APPROACHES

Before presenting the structure and process of personal construct psychotherapy, it might be most helpful to locate personal construct psychology itself in relation to the major theoretical classifications of cognitive-behavioural, psychodynamic and humanistic theories.

Cognitive-Behavioural Therapies

On the surface of things, it might appear that personal construct theory and cognitive-behaviourism are very similar, both being cast on a conceptual-cognitive level. However, there are substantial differences between them. These are spelled out in Chiari and Nuzzo (2003, Chapter 4, pp. 41–49).

Psychodynamic Theories of Freud and Others

Comparing psychodynamic and personal construct theories, one does find common interest in the interior meaning of events. However, for the psychodynamic theorist, a person's words have to undergo a content-specific and theory-based unique interpretation in order to be understood. In contrast, the personal construct theorist views the nature of this unique interpretation as resting entirely with the client. While the psychodynamic approach relies on an essentially thermodynamic model, in which energy and instincts represent the basis of motivation, personal construct theorists do not rely on such deterministic explanations for understanding others. In personal construct theory, personal and social constructions replace the absolute and universal causes used in the psychodynamic approach. Personal construct theory also highlights the process of knowledge creation and optimal functioning in contrast to the psychodynamic approach that stresses psychopathology and universal conceptualizations of human behaviour formulated as a 'treatment'. As a consequence, in therapy the 'psychoanalyst must become a kind of crossword puzzle solver' (Warren, 1990, p. 454) while personal construct therapists and counsellors rely on how the client personally and socially construes the world.

Humanistic Psychotherapies

Here the picture shifts to seeing many more similarities than differences. Leitner and Epting (2001) have reviewed concepts such as levels of awareness, dignity, optimal functioning and so forth, showing that there are substantive similarities between the two positions. One important difference is that personal construct theory opposes the notion of an essential human nature and argues for the importance of invention over discovery in trying to discern the most telling aspects of a person (Butt et al., 1997a; Kelly, *c.* 1954). We are seen as constructing or inventing ourselves rather than finding our essential natures. For this reason personal construct psychology is very sceptical of the notion that there are human potentials patiently waiting to be discovered. Along the same lines, the notion of self-discovery or the idea of a true self is not espoused. In fact, personal construct theorists are always trying to get the concept of self out of the way. Self-consistency and being true to a real self are seen as the very things getting in the way of a person's trying out new ways of being and behaving. In terms of style, the personal construct therapist and counsellor are much more active than, for instance, a Rogerian would be (Raskin & Rogers, 1989). There are many more personal experiments to be run and direct lines of inquiry to be made into personal meanings than one would expect in a Rogerian approach.

THE THERAPEUTIC ENTERPRISE

In the normal course of events the therapeutic enterprise starts by focusing on the client's immediate concerns or problems. That does not mean that we want the client to stop voicing complaints and simply conform to existing conditions, nor does it mean that the problem is viewed in purely personal terms independent of the meanings the client has unwittingly accepted from the social surround. Instead the intention is for the client to come to the widest possible understanding of his or her situation in such a way that some change can take place in the direction of either undertaking personal change or mobilizing the courage needed to change social conditions or both.

Controlled Elaboration

Nevertheless, the place to start is in the present moment so that an elaboration of the complaint can take place. The aim of the elaboration is to enable the client to place the problems along a time-line, to be able to see them as temporary rather than permanent and then to see them as responsive to reconstruing, the passage of time and varying conditions.

That is all undertaken in what Kelly calls a *controlled elaboration* of the complaint and even leaves room for confrontation when carefully planned. The therapist or counsellor is responsible for bringing up obviously omitted topics and is also responsible for dealing with the client's possible anxious or angry reaction to them. The counsellor does not just toss out new material simply to see if the client will react strongly. Confrontation is undertaken only when the counsellor has a good idea, ahead of time, of how the client will construe the material. Throughout the therapy, the counsellor or therapist must engage in *differential predictions*. These are guide-posts marking danger areas which include notations on the counsellor's ability to predict what the client will say next in such a way that clearly differentiates the choices the client is making in developing the interview material.

All this planning in psychotherapy must be balanced with periods of spontaneity.

It is important for an effective therapist or counsellor to go beyond what he or she can precisely verbalize. It is a mistake to think of the personal construct therapist as someone who completely maps out and completely knows the personal construing system of the client and then carefully says just the right (premeditated) thing. In Kelly's terms: 'The psychotherapist who dares not try anything he cannot verbally defend is likely to be sterile in a psychotherapeutic relationship' (Kelly, 1955/1991, p. 601/Vol. 2, p. 32). In addition, the effective therapist has the ability to be playful and creative and has the courage to be selectively self-disclosing (Epting, 1984; Epting & Suchman, 1999). See Chapter 4 (pp. 41–45) for an outline of some of the other skills that Kelly thought a personal construct psychotherapist and counsellor should have.

Transitive Diagnosis

Before any therapy is too far along, however, a *transitive diagnosis* is offered. The term 'diagnosis' might be better stated as a transitive understanding (Raskin & Epting, 1995). It is the planning stage of, and a mapping out of, the terrain using the professional constructs provided in personal construct theory. Personal construct diagnosis and these professional constructs are discussed more fully in Winter (2003, Chapter 19, pp. 201–209). Transitive diagnosis might also include notes to consider techniques borrowed from other theories. As Kelly (1980, p. 35) says, at the technique level:

> Personal construct psychotherapy does not limit itself to any pet psychothera-
> peutic technique. More than any other theory it calls for an orchestration of
> many techniques according to the therapist's awareness of the variety and nature
> of the psychological processes by which man works towards his ends.

After spending time elaborating the complaint using an accepting and supportive attitude, it is very important to move to the elaboration of the person or personal construing system. In fact, this is the central task of the psychotherapist. It gives a broader context for understanding the complaint in relation to other areas of the client's life. It also serves the purpose of broadening the therapeutic relationship; a relationship made by a broadly defined problem-centred attitude in which the client and therapist are seen as co-investigators working on the client's issues. It takes the focus off the client and places it on to the task at hand. The focus is on finding a way for the client to move forward. It makes the client's issues the problem and not the client's way of being. It also reduces the dependency in the relationship and what others might call the transference. In fact, the personal construct approach to counselling and therapy sees transference as a potentially useful aspect of therapy and not something that gets in the way. Transference is the process whereby clients use their construing of how to handle another person and then transfers that, unchanged, to the therapist. One of the aims would be to help the client transfer only selected qualities and use them as tentative constructions. It gives clients a way of understanding themselves better.

Another way of elaborating the personal construct system is to use structured and partially structured psychological tests including the rep-test (see Chapter 6).

Of equal importance is the use of self-elaboration procedures such as self-characterization where the person is asked to write out a description of himself as if a character in a play (see Chapter 5, pp. 59–60, and Butt, 2003, Chapter 38, pp. 384–386).
If that is too much for the client to manage, more structured questions might be
used, such as 'Who are you?', 'What kind of person are you?', What kind of child
were you?', or 'What kind of person do you expect to become?' (Kelly, 1955/1991,
pp. 986–987/Vol. 2, pp. 299–304). Following that may be the elaboration of the *life-
role* structure where the person starts to envisage changing over the years instead
of in daily cycles. That may include what clients expect from therapy in conjunction
with all this projected change.

At that point primary importance is given to invoking a progressive confrontation with alternatives in living where the client is asked 'What kind of action does
this call for?', 'What could you have done?', 'What else could you have done?', and
'Having done that, what comes next?' (Kelly, 1955/1991, p. 993/Vol. 2, p. 304) Even
further, a controlled elaboration through *prescribed activities* is often called for. In
cognitive-behaviour therapy this is often called 'homework' but the emphasis in personal construct therapy is on exploring the meaning of the task rather than being
concerned with its corrective nature as such. Clients are invited to engage in social,
recreational or occupation activities to test out sets of understanding they are just
beginning to grasp. 'Not all elaboration need be limited to verbalization in the
therapy room. Some of the most important elaborations take place outside, and
some of them are expressed only incidentally in words' (Kelly, 1955/1991, p. 994/
Vol. 2, p. 304). After all, this approach to therapy is as much about action as it is
about a verbalized way of knowing. It all might be extended further into play activities and creative production. In that way the person can begin to explore uncertain
and vaguely grasped aspects of themselves and their world which cannot be
explored in the more reality-based kinds of prescribed activities.

Tight and Loose Construing

One of the most important professional dimensions used in personal construct psychotherapy concerns the loosening versus the tightening of constructs. Much of the
work in personal construct psychotherapy can be seen as helping clients to weave
back and forth between loosening and tightening. Loose constructions are those
notions of the world which vary in their meanings, whereas tight constructions are
those which offer definite statements of structure and in which meaning can be
clearly specified. Kelly describes creativity as a cycle involving the weaving back
and forth between loose and tight constructs. That is a cycle that starts with loose
conceptions which allow wonderful new insights. It is followed by a gradual tightening in such a way that some definite statement can be made or some act can be
performed.

One of the most important areas for therapeutic gain, using this dimension, is the
work done with the reporting of dreams. Dreams are the most loosened constructions that can be verbalized. The potential for gaining knowledge through loosening can offer insight into concealed reservoirs of experience. Of primary interest is
the meaning which emerges out of loose construction as the dream is recalled. It is
very important not to offer any type of interpretation in the early stages of report-

ing because a type of tightening may start to take place which could conceal the productive material contained in the loosened construction. Of special interest are *milepost dreams* which are ones that are profound in their implications. In these dreams the main themes of the client's life occur and should not be interpreted as they stand on their own. They offer the client the opportunity to grasp the monumental movement which is about to take place in therapy. Another special category of dream is the *preverbal dream*. These dreams are vague and filled with visual imagery, have little or no conversation, and are slow to unfold in the telling, seeming as much imagined as dreamt. Here the therapist is more active, helping the client to activate his or her creative imagination in order to allow some meaning to emerge either verbalized or as a felt sense.

Often the most intense and exciting aspect of personal construct counselling and therapy comes when client and therapist are ready to undertake techniques designed to invite the client to experiment with new ideas and new behaviours. It is the point when the client is ready to undertake constructive revision with all the profound implications this will involve. The constructs to be revised are often core constructs; ones on which the person's identity rests and ones on which the person relies to maintain life itself. In using interpretations as an aid in this process, it is important to remember that it is the therapist's role to suggest things but it is the client who really does the interpreting. The important task for the therapist is to gauge the client's readiness for constructive revision. Resistance to an interpretation is not seen as something used to thwart the therapist's design but rather is seen as either a protective reaction in the face of anxiety or an attempt to point to other important directions neglected thus far (see also Chapter 9, pp. 95–106). When the client manifests anxiety and/or guilt when anticipating constructive revision, they are viewed as useful, not obstructive. Anxiety is the awareness that there is not yet sufficient structure provided in the interview for the client to take steps into the unknown. Therefore, the anxiety needs to be managed by the client through gaining more structure in order to ensure safety and make it possible to see the exciting aspects of anxiety in the face of new exploration. Guilt, on the other hand, is the awareness that core aspects of her identity have been shaken and work needs to be undertaken so that an emerging new identity can take place.

The central technique used for constructive revision is experimentation in which, initially, the therapist serves as the main validator of the new constructions. Experimentation may take the form of role playing in the therapy room. That can then be extended to new life-roles in relatively safe outside situations. Much careful preparation has to be undertaken before extensive outside experimentation begins. The client is given permission and is encouraged to enter into limited situations where something new will be expected of him. He is invited to set up specific expectations and to make both negative and positive predictions of what will happen to him. In addition, the client is invited to interpret the outlooks of others in the situation and to find evidence for his interpretation. If the client cannot manage it on his own, he is invited to act 'as if' he had the kind of support and encouragement that would give him the self-confidence needed to be in a given situation. Obstacles to this experimentation include both hostility and threat among other reactions. The hostile person tries to extort validation for his present system rather than experiment with it. This is because he feels backed into a corner; therefore additional time must be spent in making him feel comfortable before further experimentation can be undertaken. The threatened client, on the other hand, sees the experimentation as having far too many long-term implications and much time needs to be spent in trying to limit these implications as least long enough for him to actually get into the new situation.

Fixed Role Therapy

The final aspect of a therapeutic enterprise might be the use of fixed role therapy. If personal construct therapy is like rebuilding a ship under full sail one plank (construct) at a time—ripping up one or several planks at a time and slapping new ones in before too much water sinks the vessel—then fixed role therapy is like jumping ship for a brief period of time (Bannister, 1975). It is a way for the client to experience, briefly, being in the world in a different way. This is done not to 'fix' the person by having her adopt a new way of being, but to simply offer her an opportunity to experience herself and her world in a new way in order to demonstrate that change is possible and offer an opportunity to find out what new things might or might not fit (Epting & Nazario, 1987).

In the classical form, fixed role therapy begins by having the client write a brief characterization sketch describing herself. The therapist then prepares an enactment sketch based on the self-characterization and presents it to the client. Complete with a new name for the client, this sketch is a brief account of another person who is somewhat similar to the client but has one or two features that are quite different. The new features represent what the therapist thinks might be some growth opportunities for the client. After the presentation, the client and therapist modify it until the client is satisfied that enacting the new role is possible and even offers some fascination. Starting with role plays in the therapy room, the client is then invited to carry the new role out into the world. The amount of risk is calculated as each new outside situation is suggested and close contact is maintained with the therapist for support and reassurance. After about two weeks the experiment is ended and the client is invited to examine what has happened with an eye on selecting some aspects of the new role that she will start to make her own.

There have been many modifications of this procedure. It is most frequently used in a mini-fixed role form where the client is invited to take on just one new characteristic for a one- or two-day trial. In fact there might be several mini-fixed roles being carried out simultaneously. Brophy and Epting (1996) have even found good use of this procedure in a mentoring programme for a large corporation where the goal was to invite middle management executives to reinvent themselves.

IN A NUTSHELL

It is our hope that this chapter has provided the reader with something of the spirit of personal construct counselling and psychotherapy. We have tried to include most of the basic components of the therapy as outlined in Kelly's original work, but have taken the liberty of including some lines of thinking which have grown directly from the original formulation. Perhaps this chapter will serve as a reference point as readers consider the directions taken in related positions. Most of all it is our wish that the spirit of openness and sense of inquiry, so pervasive in the theory, comes across. Above all Kelly valued questions over conclusions. 'There is something exciting about a question, even one you have no reasonable expectation of answering. But a final conclusion, why that is like the stroke of doom: after it—nothing, just nothing at all!' (Kelly 1969k, p. 52).

CHAPTER 12

The Evidence Base for Personal Construct Psychotherapy

David Winter

University of Hertfordshire and *Barnet, Enfield and Haringey Mental Health Trust, UK*

> It is quite possible and thoroughly reasonable for a personal construct approach to psychology to lend itself to the requirements of empirical science. Indeed, if the notion of science is taken seriously as refinement of the psychology of man, something like the psychology of personal constructs is a natural consequence. Moreover, such a notion extends from the experimental laboratory to that special kind of laboratory we call the therapy room.
>
> (Kelly, 1959a, p. 54)

Clinical practice is increasingly required to have a demonstrable evidence base, or to be 'empirically validated' by research findings. In the USA, systems of managed health care and insurance companies generally require evidence of the efficacy of a particular therapeutic approach before agreeing to fund it, and may prescribe what form, and how many sessions, of therapy a client should receive. Although in Europe clinicians are currently allowed a little more freedom than this (Strauss & Kachele, 1998), the same trends are apparent. For example, a review of policy on psychological therapies by the British Department of Health states that:

> ... it is unacceptable ... to continue to provide therapies which decline to subject themselves to research evaluation. Practitioners and researchers alike must accept the challenge of evidence-based practice, one result of which is that treatments which are shown to be ineffective are discontinued.
>
> (Parry & Richardson, 1996, p. 43)

The British Department of Health also commissioned a review of psychotherapy research findings, entitled *What Works for Whom?* (Roth & Fonagy, 1996), to assist health care purchasers to decide on the appropriate mix of therapies for their populations.

The Essential Practitioner's Handbook of Personal Construct Psychology. Edited by F. Fransella.
© 2005 John Wiley & Sons, Ltd.

It is of considerable concern that the first edition of *What Works for Whom?* made no mention of personal construct psychotherapy, since its readers may conclude that this form of therapy works for no one and, if they are health care purchasers, that it should not be funded. However, publication of the second edition of this book, for which I was asked to provide the authors with evidence for the effectiveness of personal construct psychotherapy, is expected early in 2005. Although this still does not 'officially' designate personal construct psychotherapy as a therapy that works for someone, it does at least acknowledge that the absence of reports of evidence for this form of therapy in the book might reflect the authors' 'selection bias rather than a real absence of evidence'.

Despite the dangers noted above, there has been some resistance by personal construct psychotherapists themselves to carrying out empirical research on their therapies because it has been viewed as incompatible with the constructivist and humanistic assumptions which underlie them (Bohart et al., 1998; Botella, 2000). Specifically, it has been suggested that such therapies will be 'empirically violated' by the apparent emphases of empirical research on knowable realities, treatment manuals, treatments targeted for specific disorders, and natural science methodology. While many constructivists have some sympathy with these arguments, it could be contended that failure to enter the arena of evidence-based practice and empirical validation in effect displays a refusal to present our therapeutic approach to health care purchasers, policy makers, and probably most potential clients, in terms which are likely to be understood by them (Winter, 2000). The result of this could be that personal construct psychotherapy will be faced with extinction and that clients will increasingly be denied access to therapeutic approaches such as this, which are not based on the mechanistic assumptions (that is, viewing people as operating like machines) of those therapies which have more readily embraced the notion of empirical validation.

THE EVIDENCE

Fortunately, however, not all personal construct psychotherapy researchers have eschewed empirical research, and as a result there is a growing evidence base for this form of therapy.

Personal Construct Theory

Kelly's theory has generated a considerable amount of research, much of it employing repertory grid technique (see Adams-Webber, 2003, Chapter 5, pp. 51–58). Some of the research findings, for instance, that superordinate constructs are more resistant to change than are subordinate constructs (Hinkle, 1965) and that invalidation may lead to particular changes in an individual's construing system (Lawlor & Cochran, 1981), are of clear relevance to, and provide indirect evidence for, the approach adopted by personal construct psychotherapists.

Personal Construct Formulations

A review of the extensive clinical research literature derived from the theory has been provided by Winter (1992). This includes evidence supporting the formulation of particular disorders in terms of certain features of the client's construing system. It therefore provides an empirical foundation for therapeutic approaches based on such formulations (see Winter, 2003, Chapter 26, pp. 265–274, for details). Also included in that review is evidence of changes in construing accompanying positive outcome in a wide range of different forms of therapy; of features of construing which predict response to particular therapies; and of aspects of construing related to the therapeutic process. For example, a particularly influential early study was Landfield's (1971) demonstration that the more similar the constructs used by client and therapist, but the less similar the structure of their construing systems, the more improvement the client experienced. Although many of these studies have investigated therapeutic approaches other than personal construct psychotherapy, their findings indicate the value of conceptualizing therapeutic process and outcome in personal construct terms.

The Personal Construct Psychotherapy Process

The literature contains numerous single case reports of personal construct psychotherapy (for example, Neimeyer & Neimeyer, 1987; Winter, 1992), but there are relatively few empirical studies of the therapeutic process in this form of therapy.

Individual Therapy

Viney (1994) provided some evidence of similarities between personal construct and client-centred therapy, which differed from rational-emotive therapy, in how therapists responded to expression of 'distressed emotion' by the client. In the former approaches, there was more therapist acknowledgement of the client's distress, tending to lead to further expressions of distress, whereas in the latter the client's negative emotions tended to be viewed as manifestations of irrationality. However, the conclusions that can be drawn from this study are limited by the fact that, in each therapeutic approach, transcripts of the sessions of only one therapist were examined.

A study involving a larger number of therapists was conducted by Winter and Watson (1999). They demonstrated that personal construct psychotherapy differs significantly from rationalist cognitive therapy in terms of various aspects of therapist and client behaviour in therapy sessions and therapist perceptions of the therapeutic relationship. Analysis of transcripts of therapy sessions indicated that personal construct psychotherapists used less directive responses, but more interpretation, confrontation and exploration, and showed less negative attitudes to clients, than cognitive therapists. On a questionnaire measure of conditions that facilitate therapeutic change, personal construct psychotherapists showed more positive feelings for their clients but were less likely to assume that they understood their clients' views of the world. In the therapy transcripts, their clients showed greater participation and more complex levels of 'processing' of their experiences. A more facilitative therapeutic process was observed in personal construct psychotherapy for those clients who construed less tightly and were more concerned with their inner worlds, while the reverse was true in cognitive therapy. Finally, leading exponents of the two forms of therapy, Fay Fransella and Windy Dryden, were able to differentiate between the transcripts of the therapies without knowledge of the group to which they belonged. This study is of importance, among other things, in demonstrating that descriptions of personal construct psychotherapy as a cognitive therapy are erroneous.

Group Therapy

There has also been some investigation of the process of personal construct group psychotherapy. Winter (1997) demonstrated that the interventions which personal construct psychotherapists anticipate that they would make in groups differ significantly from those of group analysts, making less reference to the therapist's view of the underlying meaning of group events. In a particular type of personal construct psychotherapy group, an interpersonal transaction group (see Chapter 22, pp. 241–242), Harter and Neimeyer (1995) found that incest survivors saw the groups as involving less conflict than did those attending 'process groups', which focused upon group interactions. Agoraphobic clients in personal construct interpersonal transaction groups have been found to perceive the group as characterized by greater smoothness, less avoidance, and more experiences of self-understanding than did clients receiving therapy offering just support in an interpersonal transaction group format (Winter et al., 1999, 2005).

Self-understanding has also been identified as a therapeutic factor, as have increased identification with others, acceptance, instillation of hope, and self-disclosure, by survivors of breast cancer attending personal construct psychotherapy groups (Lane & Viney, 2001b). In interpersonal transaction groups with adolescents, group members have been found to experience increasing levels of belonging to, and understanding and acceptance by, the group, as well as greater self-understanding and acceptance (Truneckova & Viney, 2001). Their group leaders evaluated the members as increasingly experiencing validation and understanding from, and trust by, others in the group; as questioning more their construing; as experimenting with new behaviours inside and outside the group; and as increasing self-validation and self-regard by a process of understanding similarities and differences between group members. Qualitative analysis of reports from some of these groups, conducted with school-based adolescents, identified four main themes of group sessions, concerned with trust, closeness to others, sexuality and power (Viney et al., 1997). Recent research with clients with a diagnosis of borderline personality disorder has also indicated that they perceive interpersonal transaction group sessions in a distinctive fashion, as compared to dialectical behaviour therapy group sessions, although the particular differences identified between the approaches are not entirely consistent with research on other client groups (Winter et al., 2003).

An Alternative to Empirical Validation

In considering the process and outcome of the experiential form of personal construct psychotherapy (see Leitner & Thomas, 2003), Humphreys and colleagues (2001) adopt an interesting alternative approach to the demand for empirical validation. They argue that, since the essential ingredients of the process of this therapy have obtained previous empirical support, as components of forms of treatment which have been empirically validated, it can be claimed that experiential personal construct psychotherapy has already received empirical validation. The ingredients concerned include aspects of the therapeutic alliance and of the role relationship between therapist and client, the client being an active change agent, the need for empathy, and an emphasis on process rather than content. However, there is no empirical evidence to date that these ingredients do indeed characterize experiential personal construct psychotherapy, although studies such as that by Winter and Watson (1999) might provide some support for this argument.

Characteristics of Personal Construct Psychotherapists

Of some relevance to the process of personal construct psychotherapy is the question of whether practitioners of this form of therapy differ from those of other approaches. Winter and colleagues (2001) found that personal construct psychotherapists were more inner-directed and less rationalist (for example, tending not to accept that there is a knowable external reality) in their philosophical beliefs than were cognitive-behaviour therapists. They also differed in the latter respect from hypnotherapists and neuro-linguistic psychotherapists. In addition, there were differences in the content of the constructs used by therapists of different orientations in construing therapeutic approaches, with personal construct psychotherapists being particularly characterized by the use of constructs concerning personal meaning. The therapists in this study tended to differentiate cognitive-behaviour from humanistic therapies, and to place personal construct psychotherapy at the humanistic end of this dimension.

The Outcome of Personal Construct Psychotherapy

As in the literature on therapeutic process, there is a large number of single case studies of the outcome of personal construct psychotherapy. In addition, there is a growing body of group studies providing empirical evidence of therapeutic outcome. These have been reviewed by Winter (1992) and also by Viney (1998), who reports that the effect sizes (indices of degree of improvement) in studies of personal construct psychotherapy are comparable to those in studies of cognitive-behaviour therapy and psychodynamic psychotherapy. A meta-analysis of these studies by Viney et al. (2005) provided evidence of a more favourable outcome for personal construct psychotherapy than for other therapies at post-treatment assessment, and for personal construct psychotherapy as compared to no treatment both at post-treatment and at follow-up assessments. For ease of comparison with literature on other therapies, conventional psychiatric diagnostic categories will be used below in grouping these studies, although it should be noted that many personal construct psychotherapists would not employ such a classification, preferring to make a 'transitive diagnosis' with the constructs devised by Kelly for this purpose.

A few studies have examined the outcome of personal construct psychotherapy of clients within the spectrum of *neurotic disorders*. For example, Watson and Winter

(1997, 2005), comparing personal construct, cognitive-behaviour and psychodynamic therapies in a British National Health Service setting, found significant improvement on several measures in personal construct psychotherapy, with a degree of improvement equivalent to that in cognitive-behaviour therapy. Also investigating a heterogeneous sample of psychiatric outpatients, Morris (1977) found in an uncontrolled study—that is, one which did not include a comparison group of, for example, untreated clients—that during personal construct group psychotherapy the repertory grids of five of the eight group members became similar to grids which their therapists considered to reflect an ideal outcome.

There has been some research on the outcome of personal construct psychotherapy with particular anxiety disorders. Some studies used therapies described as variants of, or incorporating, Kelly's fixed-role therapy (see Chapter 11, p. 120). Karst and Trexler (1970) found this to be somewhat more effective than rational-emotive therapy in the treatment of *public speaking anxiety,* and Lira and colleagues (1975) found that it was more effective with people who were *phobic of snakes* than exposure to a videotape of a model handling a snake, or one of a snake alone, or no treatment. Beail and Parker (1991), in another uncontrolled study, demonstrated reductions in *social anxiety* and *social phobia* during group fixed role therapy for clients presenting with these complaints. Winter and colleagues (1999, 2005) demonstrated greater improvement in *agoraphobic* clients during a treatment that combined personal construct psychotherapy in an interpersonal transaction group format and exposure to anxiety-provoking situations than while they were on the waiting list. However, the evidence that personal construct psychotherapy was any more effective than therapy offering support provided in a similar format was more equivocal.

In an uncontrolled study of individual personal construct psychotherapy for *depression*, Sheehan (1985) demonstrated reductions in clients' depression and in the negativity of their self-construing, coupled with an increase in their capacity to tolerate logical inconsistency in construing. While she also found the two former types of change in a previous study of pharmacological therapy for depression, the change on the measure of logical inconsistency was specific to personal construct psychotherapy. Also investigating the treatment of depression, Neimeyer and colleagues (1985) found greater improvement on measures of depressive symptoms, suicidal ideas and self-construing in clients receiving group cognitive therapy incorporating personal construct interventions than in clients on the waiting list. Winter and colleagues (2000) have also provided evidence of more positive outcomes on measures of depression and feelings of hopelessness, and on repertory grid measures of construing in clients presenting with *deliberate self-harm* who received a personal construct psychotherapy intervention than in those receiving 'normal clinical practice'.

An uncontrolled study of *people who stutter* by Fransella (1972) indicated significant improvement in their speech following individual personal construct psychotherapy, such improvement being highly correlated with increase in the meaningfulness to them of being a fluent speaker. In a subsequent study of a group treatment approach combining personal construct therapy and speech techniques, Evesham and Fransella (1985) found that while clients receiving this treatment showed less improvement at post-treatment assessment than those whose treatment only involved speech techniques, there was a predicted significantly lower relapse rate after eighteen months in the group containing the personal construct psychotherapy component (see Chapter 9, pp. 98–101).

In an uncontrolled study of an interpersonal transaction group (see Chapter 22, pp. 241–242) for clients with *eating disorders*, Button (1987) observed a decrease in extreme views of the self and other people, an increase in self-esteem, and a reduction in perceived dissimilarity to others. Similar changes have been found by Coish (1990) in therapy groups for bulimic clients which drew upon personal construct theory. Group members also improved more than waiting list controls on measures of bulimia, depression, self-esteem, assertiveness and body image (Wertheim et al., 1988).

Bannister and colleagues (1975) compared their 'serial validation therapy' (see Chapter 9, pp. 95–97), which attempted to validate *thought disordered schizophrenics'* predictions about their world, with a 'total push regime'. They report a 'not proven' verdict, although there were more within-group changes indicative of improvement in the former condition.

Studying interpersonal transaction groups for *problem drinkers*, Landfield (1979) found that only one of twenty clients was still drinking at six-month follow-up, and that various positive changes were apparent in clients' grids, whereas there were no significant changes in the grids of a control group of students who underwent a four-session interpersonal transaction group experience.

Two uncontrolled studies have provided some evidence of the effectiveness of personal construct group treatment programs for clients with problems involving poor control of anger. Horley and Francoeur (2003) found that *men who had abused family members* showed an increase in self-esteem following such a program, which also included a psychoeducational component. Pekkola and Cummins (2005) also provided evidence that clients with *anger problems* attending their program showed a reduction in scores on a measure of anger expression to levels more typical of the normal population, and in their general level of mental health problems.

Various studies have evaluated personal construct group therapy for disturbed *adolescents*. Jackson (1992) found that adolescents attending a group focusing on construing of the self and others made more significant gains on various measures than did a control group. Viney and colleagues reported greater improvement in juvenile offenders and non-offending adolescents attending personal construct and psychodynamic groups than in adolescents receiving no group work, the personal construct group being particularly effective in reducing immature modes of psychosocial functioning and anger directed at others, and the psychodynamic group more effective in increasing mature levels of psychosocial functioning and reducing depression (Viney & Henry, 2002). Truneckova and Viney (1997, 2001, 2005) provided indications that personal construct group work for adolescents with problems in an interpersonal transaction group format was associated with progressive attainment of the goals of therapy, greater use of abstract and interpersonal constructs, and less disruptive behaviour. Finally, Sewell and Ovaert (1997), in an uncontrolled study, found that incarcerated, conduct-disordered adolescents with symptoms of *post-traumatic stress disorder* showed a decrease in these symptoms and more permeable self-constructions following group therapy including personal construct and narrative components. Although there has been no published research on the effectiveness of personal construct psychotherapy with younger children, Lofenvosse and

Viney (1999) evaluated personal construct groups for *mothers of children with special needs*, finding no significant difference in degree of improvement in life satisfaction between mothers attending groups and those on the waiting list. Given the very low number of participants in their study, this finding is not unexpected.

Viney and colleagues (1989) carried out a randomized-controlled trial of personal construct psychotherapy for *elderly people* with psychological problems, finding evidence of reductions in anxiety, depression and indirectly expressed anger in the treated group. This group also reported fewer physical symptoms after therapy than did the control group but made more visits to health professionals, these decreasing at follow-up (Viney, 1986). In a controlled study of a personal construct-oriented group incorporating autobiographical writing for elderly people who had experienced losses, Botella and Feixas (1992–93) found evidence of reconstruction during the group.

Several investigations of personal construct counselling and psychotherapy in the general medical setting have been conducted by Viney and her colleagues. With *medical inpatients*, they found evidence of differences in the effects of counselling programmes that focused on different types of feelings (Viney et al., 1985d); greater improvement on measures of negative emotions in the counselled group than in a group having no counselling (Viney et al., 1985a); and quicker physical recovery (Viney et al., 1985b) and lower health care costs (Viney et al., 1985c) in the former group. Lane and Viney (2001a, 2005) have also demonstrated a greater decrease in depression and anxiety, and a greater increase in hope, in *breast cancer survivors* during personal construct group psychotherapy than in a waiting list control condition. Foster and Viney (2005) provided some evidence of a long-term reduction in cognitive anxiety and helplessness in women attending *menopause workshops* run on personal construct lines, such changes not being evident in women not attending the workshops. Finally, Viney and colleagues (1995a), in an uncontrolled study, have provided evidence of reduction in anxiety in *AIDS caregivers* following personal construct counselling. In another randomized controlled study of people with physical problems, in this case chronic musculo-skeletal pain, those who attended a personal construct group were found to have reconstructed some of their life patterns (Steen & Hauli, 2001). One year after the intervention they showed significant pain reduction, greater ability to cope with pain, and reduced health care consumption as compared to clients receiving 'treatment as usual' (Haugli et al., 2001).

Alexander and colleagues (1989) have found interpersonal transaction groups for *women who had been sexually abused as children* to be comparable to less structured 'process groups' in their effectiveness in reducing depression and alleviating distress, relative to change while on the waiting list for therapy. However, there was greater enhancement of social adjustment in the process groups.

CONCLUSIONS

There is a growing body of evidence indicating that:

- psychological disorders are characterized by particular features of construing;
- effective psychological therapy is associated with reconstruing;

- the process of personal construct psychotherapy is distinctive, and contrasts in practice with that in rationalist cognitive therapy;
- personal construct psychotherapy is effective, in an individual or group format, with a range of client groups;
- the degree of improvement in this form of therapy is similar to that in other therapies.

Personal construct practitioners are urged to continue to take up the challenge of evaluating their therapeutic and counselling practice. They might usefully adopt a 'methodological pluralism' in which the constructivist approach to research advocated by Botella (2000) is combined with the use of methods, such as standard outcome measures, which may be more meaningful to a wider audience. Among the priorities for further research should be studies of personal construct psychotherapy with larger sample sizes, and investigations of its outcome with couples, families and young children.

CHAPTER 13

Constructive Intervention with Children when Presented as Problems

Tom Ravenette

Meadway House, Epsom, UK

> ... no psychologist, I think, is all that he might be until he has undertaken to join the child's most audacious venture beyond the frontiers of social conventions and to share its most unexpected outcomes.
>
> (Kelly, 1969h, p. 8)

The first part of this chapter is largely theoretical and the second part is pragmatic. The two are connected through their relevance to action. The context needs to be recognized as not academic, not research, not teaching, not therapeutic and not counselling. It is that of a school psychological service within which the task has been to intervene in schools when teachers have been sufficiently worried about children to seek outside help. More specifically such intervention will have been limited, probably, to one visit to a school with a follow-up some time later. It is a matter of some moment that Kelly was involved in a comparable task when operating a travelling service to schools some 20 years previously in Kansas and it will be seen that his observations arising from the experience have been a major influence behind the practice described in this chapter.

THEORY

In the practitioner's view the task is to make sense of the 'problems' as they are presented and to respond, if possible, in such a way as to 'make a difference'. Although personal construct theory works very effectively at the individual level there are two areas in which it is relatively weak. The first of these is concerned with interaction and communication and the second with child development.

Just as I was fortunate in coming across Kelly's theory, in like manner I acquired

The Essential *Practitioner's Handbook of Personal Construct Psychology.* Edited by F. Fransella.
© 2005 John Wiley & Sons, Ltd.

The Pragmatics of Human Communication (Watzlawick et al., 1967). That text is directed specifically at human interaction and communication. Part of their message is that the human needs to 'seek for contexts and sequences in the stream of events'. The authors make a link with personal construct theory when they say:

> A similar concept is at the basis of Kelly's monumental 'Psychology of Personal Constructs' although (he) does not consider the question of levels and presents his theory almost exclusively in terms of intrapsychic, not interactional, psychology. (p. 263)

More importantly, their analysis of the communication process is highly relevant both for understanding the nature of, and the basis for, a teacher's complaint about a child. As the complaint arises from pupil–teacher interaction, it therefore has implications for action. Every communication has three components. The first is its 'content' which may be verbal or non-verbal, for example, tone of voice, a look, a movement. The second is a communication of 'how I see you' and 'how I see myself'—that is, an implicit statement of 'relationship'. This clearly will be a reflection, in personal construct terms, of 'self constructs'. The third is 'context', that is, the circumstances in which the interaction is taking place. At a very simple level the communication between teacher and pupil in terms of 'content' and 'relationship' needs to be appropriate to the 'context', that is, what is appropriate in the playground may be completely inappropriate in the classroom.

There are also three forms of response in relation to each or any of the three components. The first is simply to 'confirm', to validate. The second is to 'reject', to invalidate. The third is to 'disconfirm', to ignore, to act as though the statement did not exist.

Communication between individuals usually happens naturally, easily and harmoniously. By contrast, problem situations may well be tantamount to disordered communications, especially around the 'sense of self'. Perhaps the most disturbing instance is reflected in the statement: 'While rejection amounts to the message "You are wrong", disconfirmation says in effect "You do not exist"' (Watzlawick et al., 1967, p. 85). How much of a child's disturbing behaviour is an assertion that 'I *do* exist'?

The second alternative theoretical framework is that of Piaget who, through observation and experiment, developed an encompassing theoretical system of the individual from infancy to late adolescence. Kelly, by contrast, saw children through the eyes of his theory but gave little guidance on the actual interviewing of them. Flavell, however, in his *The Developmental Psychology of Jean Piaget* (1963) is able to forge a link:

> Every act of intelligence, however rudimentary and concrete, presupposes an interpretation of something in reality, that is an assimilation of that something to some kind of meaning in the subject's cognitive organization. To use a happy phrase of Kelly's (1955), to adapt intellectually to reality is to *construe* that reality, and to construe it in terms of some enduring *construct* within oneself. Piaget's epistemological position is essentially the same on this point, requiring only the substitution of *assimilate* for *construe* and *structure* or *organization* for *construct*. (Flavell, 1963, p. 48)

As the links between Kelly and Piaget have been comprehensively described elsewhere, such as in Mancuso and Hunter (1985a, 1985b) and Soffer (1993), I shall not elaborate further.

PRACTICE

Who has What Problem?

Kelly eventually recognized that the complaint about a child which led to a referral arose from the teacher's construction of the child's behaviour. Different teachers may indeed vary in the extent to which they see the same child as a problem. It is worth a thought that, on occasion, a child's 'problem behaviour' may be indeed a solution, albeit inadequate, to some underlying issue in relation to that specific teacher.

This needs to be taken forward. When a child presents 'difficulties' to a teacher there may well be grumbles in the staff room and, perhaps, some invalidation of the teacher's peripheral 'self-constructs'. By contrast, 'problems' which lead to a referral may represent challenges to a teacher's 'professional core constructs'. These latter problems can be seen as four-fold:

1. This child's behaviour/failings is a challenge to my professional understanding.
2. Whatever I do with this child makes no difference. My professional competence is at stake.
3. In my view this child has 'special needs' and it is not my job to deal with such children.
4. This child is a 'problem' but I have been able to cope. I don't want the next teacher to blame me for not referring.

The importance of this analysis lies in the fact that the referral of a child represents double problems, problems separately to both teacher and child. An investigation of the child should hopefully lead to some understanding of his or her putative underlying problem and, sharing that with the teacher, should lead to an enlargement and simultaneous validation of the teacher's professional 'sense of self'.

The aim of an interview with the child is not specifically to investigate the validity of teacher's complaint since that is his or her construction of events. In fact the first part of the intervention needs to be a preliminary discussion at the school in order to find out what the complaint is all about. That means going beyond obvious generalities to a more precise statement of the troubling happenings.

THE INTERVIEW

Language in the Interview

The myth of the two-faced Janus provides a suitable metaphor for the nature of language. Language, at one and the same time points in contrasting directions. In one it points to 'commonality', to commonly accepted or dictionary meanings. In the other it points to 'individuality', to that which is personal and experientially based. Whereas in ordinary discourse we can get by with an assumption of 'commonality', the acceptance of such an assumption between interviewer and interviewee may lead to serious misunderstandings.

It is a part of the function of language in the interview to go beyond assumed 'commonalities' of meanings by seeking their 'individuality' aspects and this is done through the elaborative exploration of 'obvious' answers. In this way new 'commonalities' or shared meanings may be developed between interviewer and interviewee. This argument is reflected in the style and structure of the interview.

Structure

The first part of the interview with the child involves getting his or her view of 'what it is all about'. Children have not asked for an interview so why has he or she been taken out of class to see this strange person? They seldom know, hence 'your teacher is worried about you, do you know why'? 'I'm not learning', 'I don't behave myself', 'I don't get on with other children', 'I don't get on well with teacher' and so forth. It is useful then to say, 'I like to explore with children how they see themselves and their world. In that way they can sometimes then understand themselves better and in the outcome that can help teachers to understand them better too.'

The second part of the interview involves the exploration with the child of his or her ways of making sense of 'themselves and their circumstances'. Since this exploration needs to be methodical it involves using a range of interviewing techniques. It is important not to rely on words alone but also to use pictures and a child's drawings in order to elicit matters which are not so easily verbalized. This may then suggest underlying issues which make the child and the behaviour potentially more understandable.

The third part of the interview will be 'reconstructive'. It will attempt to create, out of the substance of the preceding part of the interview, alternative views of the 'child's sense of self and circumstances'. That can be communicated to the child, not as a prescription, but merely as a different way of seeing things, as an extension of potential awareness. Occasionally, in the light of this alternative view, a child may indeed be invited to experiment, for a limited time only, with some change of habitual behaviour.

A caution surrounds the use of the motivational 'Why?' When adults ask the question of a child it is usually perceived in a threatening or accusative way, implying that the child is somehow 'in the wrong' or 'ought to know'. And if the child says 'Don't know' is he or she then guilty of prevarication? The use of 'Why?', therefore, is usually ambiguous and is not necessarily motivational. How much less threatening it is to ask quite simply 'How come?' The interview with the child, however, is not the end of the matter. The teacher's problem, given shape by the 'complaint', will be considered later.

Once we are in the business of asking questions in the interview, my observations on the Janus nature of language require that we become circumspect in accepting answers at their face value. At the back of the interviewer's mind the following further elaborative explorations have been found helpful as ways for clarifying meanings and arriving at understanding.

1. *What, at the same time, is being denied.* This is in line with Kelly's bipolarity principle and is fertile in illuminating meaningfully the original statement,

in yielding more content and at the same time giving hints of underlying contrasts.

2. *What the statement further implies.* That gives some clue as to the underlying 'construct system' within which the original statement was given.
3. *The context within which the statement makes sense.* That follows from my earlier references to communication and interaction.
4. *The experiential grounds on which it is based.* 'How come?' will reveal something of the circumstances within which the statements were appropriate.
5. *The importance of the statement to the interviewee.* Whether or not it is important may reflect aspects of the child's attitude to the interview and interviewer. 'How come?' again is an invitation for elaborating the response.
6. *What's good and bad about what's 'good' and 'bad'?* That is an aphoristic version of Tschudi's (1977) 'ABC' model of questioning and invites a balanced evaluation of contrasting poles of a personal construct (Chapter 4, pp. 54–55).

A RANGE OF TECHNIQUES

As I see it, the purposes of all techniques in the interview are two-fold. The obvious purpose is the elicitation of information, of facts, of incidents and so forth, from and about the child. The more profound purpose, however, is to commit the child to seek for those answers which, within his or her own experiential reality, will be held at a lower level of awareness. The great power of the elaborative enquiry is to bring to light hidden aspects of that reality. In particular, together with the search for contrasts, it opens up the possibility to the child of an alternative 'sense of self', a 'self' whose behaviour might just cease to be a cause for concern. The techniques which I present below should be read in the light of these observations. They are just some of those methods that have proved effective in eliciting children's construing. With the first five techniques the elaborative questioning is along the lines described in the previous section.

Who are You?

This extended version of Bugental's (1964) technique asks for three responses to each of the questions: 'Who are you?', 'What sort of person would you say that you are?' and 'What sort of person would other persons say that you are?' (listing family members and others). A fully elaborated version is given in detail in Ravenette (1997, 1999).

How would you Describe . . . ?

Four persons, two of whom are friends, one who is admired and one who is disliked are specified. Again three responses are required. This is not necessarily 'construct eliciting' but, if the material is needed for subsequent use in a 'grid' procedure, contrasts may be sought.

The Trouble with Most Mothers (Fathers, Brothers and so Forth) Is?

Kelly (1955/1991, p. 994/Vol. 2, p. 303) cites this technique and acknowledges his debt to Mahrer who devised it.

Personal Troubles

This is a direct enquiry and not to be confused with 'A drawing and its opposite', which is described below. A sheet of paper is divided into six boxes and the child is asked to draw in five of them situations in which he or she would be troubled or upset. The child is then asked what is happening and his or her responses are amplified along the lines previously described. The sixth space is reserved for a contrasting situation which is similarly elaborated.

Perception of Troubles in Schools

The child is presented with eight drawings of situations which might occur in or around school and is invited to say what is happening in just three of them. These were drawn at my request by Arthur Jordan, then a trainee, to whom I acknowledge a debt. They have been used widely and are reproduced in *Educational Psychology Casework* (Beaver, 1996).

Family Interaction Matrix

This is a technique of a completely different order and can be used with a family of four members and upwards. The child is asked to say for each member of the family, which members he or she finds 'more easy' and 'less easy' to get on well with. The number chosen to fit each category of response is varied according to the size of the family but it is an essential feature of the design that, by implication, at least one member will be judged as neither 'more' nor 'less easy to get on with'. The matrix which arises from this procedure is then easily analysed in terms of family interactions. A worked example appears in Ravenette (1999, pp. 184–185).

Portrait Galley and Self-description Grid

We are indebted indeed to Kelly for grids, but the usual practice is to use them for looking outwards to the world of people or situations in order to arrive at a person's underlying construct system. With the self-description grid, however, the aim is somewhat different. Can the child, using a grid format, give an indication of how different people will see him, how they form clusters of validators and how he views himself. One version is given in Ravenette (1999, p. 192). The version here is less formal in style and format thereby increasing the boy's involvement in the whole process. Figure 13.1 shows an actual grid which was developed in an interview together with a verbal analysis of its linkages.

M	7	1	6	2	3	4	5
F	7	1	6	3	2	3	5
Br	6	7	1	2	3	5	4
Si	7	6	1	2	5	3	4
Bo	1	7	2	6	3	5	4
Te	7	1	4	2	6	3	5
S$_1$	7	1	6	2	5	3	4
R$_2$	1	7	2	5	3	6	4

Figure 13.1 R's portrait gallery and self-description grid

The boy in question (R) was a 12-year-old attending daily at a residential school for 'disturbing' pupils. His life had been one of constant moves in and out of children's homes. The current 'cause for complaint' was that although he got on very well with staff, he manipulated the other pupils so that they bullied him. I do not report the whole interview but the analysis of the grid data will be seen to illuminate the matter.

As can be seen, oval shapes representing faces are drawn along the top of the grid. The child then fills them in to create portraits which illustrate the descriptive language given previously in the interview, writing the descriptions underneath each. In this example the first four attributes were provided by the boy, while the other three were hypothetical, derived from the interview, and inserted for their potential relevance. It is a matter of significance that in the outcome those three received 'neutral' rankings! Along the side of the grid are written the names of members of the family: mother (M), father (F), brother (Br), sister (Si), teachers (Te), boys (Bo) and Self (S$_1$). R$_2$ is when he is a 'cause for trouble'.

The instruction then is: 'If I were to ask your mother, which of these would she say was most like you, which would it be? Put a 1 under that face. And which would she say was least like you? Put a 7. Which now would she say was most like you? Put a 2. And least like you? Put a 6, and so forth. Use the same process for each person in turn. When the child has completed this for 'Self ', he or she is asked to repeat the process for that version of self when 'in trouble' ('R$_2$').

A McQuitty Cluster Analysis (Ravenette, 1968) indicates that, in the boy's eyes:

Parents, teachers and Self form a cluster agreeing that he is *Polite* and *Intelligent* and denying that he *Doesn't care* and is *Naughty*.

Brother and sister agree that he is *Polite* and *Naughty* and deny that he is *Intelligent* and *Doesn't care.*

Boys and R₂ agree that he is *Naughty* and *Doesn't care* and deny that he is *Intelligent, Kind* and *Polite.*

In the light of the description above, this analysis seems to confirm that R identifies himself with the adult world view of him. At the same time, however, arising from his behaviour with his peer group, he creates for himself, in their eyes, the antithesis of that adult view. His siblings partly share the parental and partly the peer group view of him.

A Drawing and its Opposite

This technique is written up fully in Ravenette (1997, 1999) and is important in contributing material for the third stage of the interview. It involves the drawing, in the centre of a sheet of paper, of a three-inch-long line, bent over at an angle of about 45 degrees for a further half inch. The child is then invited to turn the line into a picture (not just an object). When that is finished, and only then, the child is asked to draw a picture which is an opposite. To achieve that aim the child will have to re-examine the first picture, and attribute a meaning to it, in order to draw the second picture. It may then be possible to derive from the child's account of the two drawings the unverbalized expression of an underlying bipolar 'construct'. More importantly, however, since each pair of opposites is held together by some underlying theme, the elucidation of that theme may have important implications both for understanding and for change. As a final part of the interview with R (above), he produced the two drawings shown in Figure 13.2.

Just as the analysis of the self-description grid data called for comment, so do these drawings. When I asked R for a contrast to the first drawing he was puzzled and then said 'Ah, I've got it!' and drew a repeat of the first but without the car. He said that it represented looking at the other side of the road. I reminded him that the interview had been concerned with looking at opposites and tentatively offered the following hypothesis, based on the manifest presence–absence of the car and its potential relevance to his 'sense of self'. Unless R can be like a big limo, bright and able (from his 'self-description'), he is afraid he might be like nothing. Perhaps he needs to put something there (in the lower drawing) 'that can grow'. He then drew in the diminutive matchstick figure!

Mutual Story-telling

This technique is one way of implementing the reconstructive stage of the interview. It is derived from Gardner (1971) but is modified to fit in with a personal construct style of interview. The child is invited to choose one picture from a set for which he or she can make up a story. The pictures I use come from a set of 30 postcards of 'Naïve Paintings' (Magna Books, 1993). The interviewer's task is not to 'interpret' but to make up a story in exchange, one which will honour the child's story but will

Figure 13.2 R's elaboration of a line and its opposite

be an alternative, drawing also on salient themes from the preceding interview. Like all stories, it will be fictional but one in which the child is offered a different view of things. It can be ignored, accepted or used to generate yet other views. Truth and theoretical correctness are not at issue, just the possibility of alternatives. The technique calls on the interviewer's recollection of what has arisen in the interview and his or her imagination and creativity. The very writing down of the exchange story is a great help to the creative and imaginative process since it gives time to select an appropriate continuation of theme.

A RETURN TO THE BEGINNING

In my opening paragraphs I have said that the matters to be discussed arose within a context where teachers referred children who were presenting as 'problems' but that, following Kelly, it was possible to see that their 'problems' arose from their constructions of events. Although the child may indeed have problems they would probably be on a different dimension. The body of the text has been concerned with the practice of intervention, directed primarily at the child, but with the aim also of helping to resolve the teacher's dilemmas. The child may, indeed, change, arising from personal 'reconstructions' in the interview; nonetheless, completeness demands a return to teachers.

Essentially the issue is one of a resolution of the teacher's 'problem' signalled by the original referral. The approach may best be seen in two dimensions. On the one hand, because the referral is a reflection of 'interaction and communications' involving child and teacher, change may be looked for in any or all of the 'content', 'relationship' and 'context' aspects of the interchanges. Exceptionally, the last of these may well involve action under the rubric of 'Special needs'. On the other hand, action to bring about change may best be seen within a personal construct framework—that is, arising out of the teacher's 'construct system'.

Firstly, there needs to be illumination, thereby leading to a 'reconstruing' by the teacher of the child and the situation. Sharing the information arising from the interview with a child can achieve that. Two cases illustrate the effect of that strategy; in each case teacher (or head teacher, or head of year) action was taken in the light of the discussion following the interview. An infant school head teacher handled a child's incomprehensible backwardness by taking him into her own special reading group (changing the teaching context) and, importantly, inviting the mother to 'stand back' from the child's learning (changing the relationships). The boy quickly made progress. A 'head of year' teacher resolved the problems around a troublesome 13-year-old boy by asking him to look after a new admission, a boy described as 'wet', to the school (changing the relationships and 'sense of self'). That also proved effective. In each case the teacher was able to reshape the children's actions from his or her own resources. All I had done was to shed new light.

Secondly, there can be a deliberate experimenting. Despite an interview with a primary school boy, neither his teacher nor I could throw light on 'the complaint'. I asked her to stand back from the boy as much as possible for the next four weeks (change of role and relationship) when perhaps we might understand better. I agreed a time and a date to meet again. The teacher was waiting at the door and said 'There's no problem, I saw a different boy'. She had had a trainee teacher with her and, therefore, was able to stand back and observe. Did she see a 'different' boy or the same boy 'differently'? No matter, there had ceased to be a problem.

Thirdly, and more rarely, there can also be a profound exploration of a teacher's understanding. My interview with this particular primary school boy was unrewarding except for recognizing an attitude in the boy of 'don't get too near'. After sharing this with the teacher I took my courage in both hands and asked what, deep down, it was that made her a teacher (personal exploration). She said how hard that question was and then 'I suppose it is that I care'. She then saw that the problem in relation to the boy was her sense that he was invalidating a 'core' sense of herself. When I enquired some time later she said that the boy was no longer a problem, it was 'just a reading difficulty'.

EPILOGUE

In an earlier formulation of approaches to promoting change, I gave a fourth channel. The channel goes back into antiquity and is recognized in the various fables and stories associated with all religions. It is simply the telling of a story. In fact I described earlier the 'mutual story-telling' technique as a way of ending an interview with a child. Likewise, when I relate my interview to the teacher, I am also telling a story albeit an alternative to the one he or she has long been holding.

In following the same train of thought, has the writing of this chapter been yet a further example of telling a story?

CHAPTER 14

How Can We Understand One Another if We Don't Speak the Same Language?

Devi Jankowicz

University of Luton, UK

> For any bold venture into human understanding leaves the wreckage of sacred ideas in its wake.
>
> (Kelly, 1996, p. 39)

TWO TRANSLATORS

More than ten years ago, a businessman trading into the post-command economies of Central and Eastern Europe described his experiences of those early days of radical transformation—the first year that followed the dismantling of the Berlin Wall and the reintroduction of the market economy. Asked for his single most useful recommendation to anyone engaging in the same activity, his advice (McNeill, 1991) was simple but profound. The activity depends crucially on translation between English and the foreign language in question; and his suggestion was to use two translators rather than one, the purpose of the second translator being to check on the success of the first.

Apart from businessmen and managers, a second type of West European was operating in Central and Eastern Europe in those days. Academics were seeking to transmit ideas about the market economy to academics and managers in the post-command economies, as part of a vast programme of development efforts which continues to this day. As they went about their job of communicating ideas, techniques, and principles of capitalist enterprise and its management, neither academics nor business people appreciated the soundness of McNeill's advice. That is a reassessment which came later. At the time their material, apparently competently translated, was being met with incomprehension ranging from simple misunderstanding to sheer disbelief. Those reactions were usually masked, to varying degrees, with the conventional politeness which the host extends to a visitor.

The Essential *Practitioner's Handbook of Personal Construct Psychology.* Edited by F. Fransella.
© 2005 John Wiley & Sons, Ltd.

It appears that there were two interrelated problems, the first to do with technique and the second with concepts and values. First, translators who should have known better were struggling with an unfamiliar vocabulary and providing crass and misleading translations—for instance, translating the word 'account' as 'record of financial holdings in a bank', where 'financial report' had been intended. The problem here (and actually, it was an infrequent one) is that the translator lacked the subject-matter experience to recognize, from context, the appropriate *dictionary equivalent* term, and hence failed to realize that financial reports rather than bank accounts were intended by the speaker.

The second problem was more serious and much more frequent. It had little to do with dictionary equivalence and familiarity or otherwise with subject matter or context, and everything to do with the structure of the languages involved. It appeared that there were no direct equivalents for many of the ideas, current in English-speaking capitalist economies, in the Central and Eastern European languages, because there had been no directly equivalent experiences in the countries concerned. To do business, to engage in management, had been to do something different than in the West, and the language reflected that. Rather than a matter of *dictionary* equivalence, the issue was one of '*construing* equivalence', to coin an adjectival term.

Tokens and Rules

Perhaps the Westerners should not have been as surprised as they were. After all, if one is to offer Western know-how, the assumption is that that particular form of know-how is absent in Central and Eastern Europe, so the concepts on offer will not map easily onto those that are in place. Language, as a medium of communication, is going to be problematic in translation. And the real surprise comes from the second, and some would say more important, function of any language. As well as being a medium of *communication*, it is a medium of *representation*. It is a system of tokens and rules for encoding (representing, recording, reporting) experience in a particular culture. If the nature and range of experiences in that culture differs from another, so will the language. The vocabulary will be different, and so some words will be missing, and will not translate. The structure of the language, the rules by which phenomena are noticed and placed in relationship to each other, will also differ. Different cultures notice different things standing out as meaningful figures against the background of the phenomenal flow. Since meaning is a matter of associations and relationships between ideas, different cultures will give different meanings to events. Another way of saying this is that experience in one culture does not match experience in another. What are recognized as distinct, nameable events in one culture may be regarded differently, or even be unnoticed, in another. As a system which encodes those events, the language of each of the two cultures will therefore slice up the phenomenal flow differently. When one language is translated into another, there may be nothing that can be transferred. Meaning evaporates in the attempt at translation.

No Word for Manager

There is no word for 'manager' in Polish (Jankowicz, 1994), or in the related Slavonic languages, because there was no activity quite like 'management' as the Western business person understands it. There are parallel terms and corresponding terms, but they correspond to the local reality and not to the reality of the West. There is '*Zarządca*' (a noun linked to the verb '*Zarządzać*', to rule or govern); there is '*Kierownik*' (the corresponding verb is '*Kierować*', to steer); and there is '*Dyrektor*', which looks similar to 'Director' but is not confined to members of a Board. All of these terms overlap with part of the meaning of 'manager'; that is, they represent one or two of the associations to 'manager' without covering them all. The result is that none of the Polish words covers the manager's *role* as it exists in the market economy, and the new business culture emerging in Poland has had to invent a new word, '*Menedżer*', to represent the role when it became known and enacted in the post-command economy.

'So what?' you might ask. The translator can surely work a little harder. Instead of establishing a single dictionary equivalence, he or she has to establish several, and regard the resulting blend of meanings as the meaning of 'manager' to a Pole. That is one way in which the meaning of a local usage can be appreciated by a foreigner. Unfortunately, establishing an extended dictionary equivalence in this way is not sufficient. Each of the Polish words carries different associations to the English word 'manage', and so they mean something different. In English, 'managing' associates with directing, organizing, administering, just about succeeding at something, handling, gaining control and using it, coping, bringing about consent. The two networks of associations, one English and one Polish, do not overlap, and the result is two rather different structures of meaning. This has practical consequences.

For example, in English, the way in which one engages in one or more of the activities associated with 'managing' is unspecified. The management style one might adopt is entirely open, and academics may spend time in researching the most appropriate style for the manager to adopt contingent on the situation. In contrast, for Polish managers 'ruling'/'governing' is something one does fairly authoritatively to someone who is, *de jure* or *de facto*, subordinate to one as a superior, and kept in that position thereby. 'Steering' is a matter of setting out a specific and single course and actively correcting the slightest deviation from it. There is no question of a variety of possible styles.

Indeed, there is a sense in which the concept of 'management style' does not exist, for there is just one way of being a manager. One does what one does directively as superior to subordinate, and that's that. Suddenly, the world of enterprise looks a little different. Without a concept of 'management style' Western notions of industrial participation do not transfer straightforwardly. The idea of varying one's approach to leadership depending on the experience and competence of a particular employee needs to be explained as something that is not, in fact, removed from effective management but is, in contrast, an intimate part of it. A variety of ways of conferring agency (representing, or delegating, or mandating, or contracting) become possible, and the conduct of business, directly or on behalf of someone else, takes on a different range of possible flavours. That is not to say that these options do not exist in the Polish culture. Rather, it is to say that they are structured differently with respect to each other. Their meanings differ—in other words, they are construed differently—because that particular part of experience has been partitioned differently by the language that represents it.

LANGUAGE AS A SYSTEM FOR REPRESENTING EXPERIENCE

Perhaps the most useful way of addressing these unfamiliar difficulties is to see them as an extreme form of the familiar; as international variants of local issues with which we are familiar within our own, single nation state. Kelly's Individuality Corollary, 'People differ from each other in their construction of events', is relevant within our own local culture. We are not carbon copies of each other because we develop different ways of making sense of events—and we develop different ways of making sense of events because our personal explanations of those events are systematically validated or invalidated in a particular way in the light of our personal experiences of those events.

We discover, among the ways in which we are similar to other people, that there are common words and grammatical rules with which to do the encoding, and we find ourselves sharing a common language with which to represent, and share, that varied experience. The language acts as a unifying force, which offers shared ways of making sense of experience. Localized discourses reflect localized subcultures within single organizations. One thinks of technical acronyms, 'war stories', ceremonies and symbols which give identity to those subunits while dividing them from each other (Young, 1989). Technical and professional argots reflect the shared meanings that are found to be useful forms of construing by people within one craft or profession as distinct from another, but within a single national culture (Wright, 1974).

When we generalize these processes across national boundaries, we see how the differing experiences of Western states and their Central and Eastern European counterparts led to different ways of construing. Different ways of recognizing and allocating meaning to business phenomena developed, together with different symbols and language rules in which to represent them. Perhaps we can add a new corollary to Kelly's eleven: 'To the extent that people within a single culture encode experience similarly among themselves but differently from people across different cultures, their language will be different, and this will have practical consequences'.

Varied Teaching Concepts

This poses problems when we seek to teach the Western way of management. Not only because the concept of management differs, but also because the concept of teaching varies! In Polish, Russian, and the related Slavonic languages, 'teaching' and 'learning' share a common root. 'Teaching' is '*Uczyć*' and 'learning' is '*Uczyć się*'. Now, '*Się*' is a reflexive term, which conjures up associations of learning as a relatively passive experience. It is as if, in English, we were to use the word 'is-taughtsing' instead of the word 'learning'. The teacher teaches; the learner 'is-taughtses', a term which carries associations of subordination, the main initiative in the endeavour lying with the teacher. And indeed, there is a Polish cultural preference for learning through *ex-Cathedra* professorial pronouncement. Writing an authoritative presentation of Western-style management education which emphasized the great importance of active learning methods in MBA programmes, the Polish authors (Sulejewicz, 1994), searching for an alternative to the word 'student' to apply to the mature, post-experience senior managers taking part, chose the word '*Słuchacz*', 'listener', rather than the equally valid Polish word '*Uczestnik*', the dictionary equivalent of our English term 'participant'.

And so, an activity construed differently (management) is taught to people who construe the encounter by which this happens (teaching and learning) differently. It is obvious that we are no longer dealing solely with political differences, Marxist or capitalist, which have existed for a half-century, but with cultural, historical and institutional differences, as encoded by distinct languages, which have existed for a half-millennium!

Take that simple word 'capitalism'. Kelly (1962) gives an account of the varied meanings associated with the word 'capitalist' among Georgian speakers in the Caucasus. Historically, it was the local princeling who had the means to engage in trade and business activity; this, however, was also the person who, as absolute ruler, exercised *droits de seigneur* when a villager married, and had the right to decide on the amount, if any, of schooling which the villagers' children received. One can see how these associations, involving some rather fundamental values of life and existence, would have informed the meaning of 'capitalist' in Georgian culture over the centuries, while providing a background of meaning into which the communist stance towards capitalist economics might fit compatibly (but as recent froth on a centuries-old brew), resulting in a specifically Georgian variant of the command economy.

UNDERSTANDING THE OTHER PERSON'S EXPERIENCE

Understanding one another as the first step towards effective knowledge transfer about how a market economy should be run is only a little to do with a search for dictionary equivalence, and much more to do with similarity of construing at a much deeper, cultural level. But how might one arrive at this understanding? How can one do business effectively in a different culture, and how might we teach about the market economy with sufficient understanding of each other? Teaching and learning, however construed, are collaborative processes.

In suggesting we use one translator to check the success of another, McNeill was advocating an exercise in sociality. The role relationship of 'doing business across cultural boundaries' is enhanced to the extent that each participant is enabled to construe the other's construing. Using one's own constructs to characterize the other's constructs requires one to elicit, and then to understand, the other's constructs, as far as possible *using* the other person's constructs—the other's personal meanings for the terms in question—rather than one's own.

When translating, one can use general and specialist dictionaries (business and etymological dictionaries; dictionaries of popular usage and of terms with foreign origins) and, through translation and back-translation, get a good feeling for the web of associations which give a particular term its meaning. Jankowicz (1994) used dictionary techniques to show that the absence of an equivalent term for 'marketing' in Polish meant that local construing emphasizes operational issues relating to bargaining and selling, with the result that there was no concept of marketing as a strategic discipline. The meanings associated with 'accounting' were encoded in words of similar scope and cultural origin to the English terms and were thereby, for all practical purposes, similar to English. 'Training' carried associations which made the Western distinction between teaching strategy and learning strategy problematic.

One can go further than vocabulary, and utilize the grammar, metaphor and style of the language in question. Gutt (2000) lists a variety of stylistic clues to meaning (forms of semantic representation, syntactic and phonetic properties of utterances), and Jankowicz (1999) shows how metaphors (live and 'dead') and idiom add to vocabulary and grammar in encoding experience and hence establishing meaning.

Differing Terms

However, successful understanding following McNeill's (1991) two-translator approach also requires that one goes beyond the purely linguistic analysis and establishes the significance of the transaction from the other's point of view, establishing the other's personal goals, values and preferences, and the ways in which these are construed within that person's culture. It requires an appreciation that the other party may not simply be disagreeing with one's own way of construing the issue in question but, rather, choosing to think of it in entirely different terms.

For example, the Westerner might describe the meaning of 'managing', and of 'teaching', in terms of Western constructs such as:

'*Autocracy* versus *participation*'
'*Directiveness* versus *avoiding indifference*'
'*Ex-Cathedra teaching* versus *the development of a community of enquiry*'

The Western position would be identified with the right pole of each of these constructs and the Central/Eastern European position with the left pole of each. The person from Central/Eastern Europe might well respond that the constructs he or she prefers to use are entirely different:

'*Wise governance* versus *individualist anarchy and fragmentation*'
'*Specification of required actions* versus *underspecified inaction*'
'*Authoritative statement* versus *having little to offer*'

while identifying his or her own position with the left pole of each.

The process is usually bidirectional. Each participant seeks to establish the other's goals and intentions as a way of illuminating the utterance and capturing all the shades of meaning entailed. Much of that information will be shared, though some will remain private. Sometimes we have no intention of revealing our private values and objectives, and at others we would if we could but we do not, since we cannot quite put them into words ourselves! A construct is a choice among alternatives and independent of the medium in which it is might be expressed. It is possible to experience preferences by means of feelings, intuitions, and indeed unreflective actions—doing one thing rather than another. A construct is not the words in which it is expressed. It is a preference that entails a particular meaning.

It helps if we model this bidirectional exchange of meanings as a negotiative process. Since the point of the exchange is for each party to understand the other, the negotiation of meaning is collaborative. In other words, its purpose is to arrive at a outcome which pleases both parties at minimum costs in terms of concessions of time, effort, and personal or organizational privacy.

In this kind of collaboration, the two parties negotiate common meanings, checking one another's understanding of each other's private terms of understanding, choosing to reveal more, or less, of their personal goals, motives and values in doing so. Doing business across linguistic barriers involves experimentation as much as any other social transaction. One attempts an understanding of the other's position by inference from common observation, and then checks the accuracy of that understanding, by asking the other party directly (always the most informative way, since the reply will automatically be in the other's own terms), or by making inferences from behaviour as both parties engage in further action. Teaching across linguistic barriers is somewhat simpler, in the sense that one engages in an activity which both parties expect to be propositional from the outset, defining the meaning of terms explicitly. But teaching is just as complex in another sense, since there is a process to be discovered, examined and mutually reflected on, to the same extent as there is in a business transaction.

It is assumed throughout that both parties have the opportunity for reciprocity. For every transaction in which one person is the active agent, seeking to construe the other's construing, there can in principle be a corresponding transaction in which the other seeks to construe the first person's construing. If I am teaching you something about the market economy, checking how you are understanding me in the terms suggested by my understanding of your constructs, you may try to explore my constructs, as you seek to understand my material and the assumptions on which it is based.

Transferring Knowledge

In the Western mission to the post-command economies, that kind of reciprocity was rarely achieved. Much of the literature of the 1990s comments on the efforts made by the trainees to understand the trainers' constructs, and the frequent oblivion, on the part of the trainers, that there was a different way of construing the realm of discourse in question. Perhaps this is not surprising, People can engage in role relationships with one another without reciprocity. Kelly's account of sociality presents the leadership role, and the therapist–client role, as situations in which there is an imbalance; in which one person is more successful in understanding the other's construing, or indeed better equipped to do so.

The task of transferring knowledge about the market economy to the post-command economies was construed with that sort of imbalance built in at the outset. It is difficult to offer reciprocity when one takes part in a programme called 'The Know-How Fund', whose purpose is defined as a replacement of failed ideas which led to the collapse of the communist economies, engaging in the role of trainer with trainees whose cultures tend to define the teacher–learner role in a way that gives the trainer maximal authority, initiative and power!

Though the intention of each transfer programme was that it should be designed in collaboration with the Central and Eastern European participants, in the early stages the practical constraints of funding (all Western), time (a matter of weeks to design international programmes with budgets of over £300,000), and reporting (a preponderance of Westerners engaged in monitoring and evaluation) gave maximum initiative to the Western parties, and created a precedent for the later years.

And so a great opportunity for mutual meaning creation was missed. The new meanings which, undoubtedly, were required as replacements for the failings of the command economy were not negotiated on the basis of a reciprocity that would have taken local culture into account through an understanding of its language.

Rather than offering Western solutions to Central and Eastern European problems under the neo-liberal assumption that there is just one best way for a business to be run in a global economy, the opportunity might have been taken to discuss and debate versions which might be newly created, bearing the circumstances, values and history of the local culture in mind. To do that, a reciprocal attempt would be required to understand the ways in which the two languages represent experience. It did not occur. The adjustment of the foreign ideas to local circumstances in order to make them truly local, came later, after the event.

Perhaps there is something about international aid in times of catastrophic change which puts both participants into an expert–client relationship, eschewing mutual meaning creation. Knowledge transfer is limited to a good-willed one-way transmission of one party's meaning into a void. The local parties are left to make local sense of the transaction later when they have had time to draw breath.

CHAPTER 15

Working with Anger

Peter Cummins

Coventry Primary Care Trust, UK

... if we apply the scientist paradigm to man, we someday are going to catch ourselves saying, in the midst of a heated family discussion, that our child's temper tantrum is best understood as a form of scientific inquiry.

(Kelly, 1969e, p. 293)

A DEFINITION OF ANGER

There is relatively little within the personal construct literature written about anger. Two key sources are McCoy's paper 'Reconstruction of Emotion' (1977) and Viney's book *Images of Illness* (1983). There are also relevant papers by Davidson and Reser (1996) and Kirsch and Jordan (2000).

In her paper, McCoy takes up the challenge of emotion within personal construct psychology. In a sense this seminal paper can be taken as a challenge to all personal construct practitioners. McCoy has staked out territory which is immediately recognizable to any practitioner and said 'Here is my version of the definition of these emotions—what do you think!'. She suggests defining anger as 'an awareness of the invalidation which leads to hostile behaviour'. It is an attempt to force events to conform so that the prediction will not be construed as a failure, and the construction will not have been invalidated.

What McCoy is suggesting is that when we are invalidated we have a choice. We can either become anxious (in the Kellyian sense)—the resolution to which may involve radical and difficult core role reconstrual—*or* we may decide that it would be easier to become hostile. McCoy is proposing that anger is the awareness of invalidation and that this invalidation precipitates hostility (1977, p. 119).

McCoy's definition is both puzzling and provoking, and requires some redefinition. The particular difficulty is her insistence that anger and hostility are inseparably entwined. There is no problem in accepting that anger *may* be linked to the awareness of hostility. But is it always so linked? Can a person be angry in a way that is not hostile? It is possible to be angry as a result of invalidation and become anxious; for example, she thinks that she can fight anyone ... she gets beaten up, invalidated . . . angry . . . she may become hostile . . . she had a bad day . . . could have won . . . or she may become anxious . . . and refuse to leave the house at night in case she meets people who she cannot be sure of fighting.

If hostility is not essentially linked to anger perhaps a definition of anger could be used which simply says 'anger is *an* emotional experience of invalidation'. I emphasize the 'an' as anger is only one of a range of possible responses to invalidation. From this it would follow that the level of anger would depend on the level of invalidation. If we can understand what has been invalidated then we can begin to understand the anger. In other words, if we understand anger as an indication of a particular form of construing, then understanding the construing will begin to alter the anger construing process.

An obvious place to start is to find out why the person has developed his anger constructs. Working with people referred with anger problems, I have become more and more aware of the developmental process of developing anger constructs. There is, for instance, a specific developmental sequence which can be summarized as the absence of a parent (usually father) between the age of 8 and 10 or a very abusive parental relationship at about this time. When taking an assessment history from new patients again and again I discovered a familiar tale. For example, John who was abandoned by both parents, taken in reluctantly by an aunt, always told he was an imposition and treated differently from his cousins; Jack who was abandoned by his father aged 8 and was left with a mother who told him that he now had to be the man of the house; Jane who discovered at the age of 10 that she was adopted and that her real mother was in fact her 'older sister'.

Leitner and colleagues (2000) offer a very useful structure which allowed me to understand the developmental process of developing anger constructs. The central theme of Leitner's work is his idea that 'when exposed to trauma the process of meaning making itself can "freeze" around the issues surrounding the trauma'. He goes on to point out that as childhood construing is more simple and concrete one may:

> . . . be less able to tolerate the implications of events that threaten the very nature of one's relationships with parents and other people who can literally hold one's lives in their hands . . . this process of freezing meaning making is more likely to occur around issues of childhood traumas rather than ones that occur later in life. (Leitner et al., 2000, p. 179)

Of particular interest is his development of the idea of self–other constancy: 'without constancy one cannot integrate new experiences of the self and other into a coherent sense of identity'. Leitner goes on to point out that without this constancy I can see you as loving at one point and, when you are angry with me, I see you as evil and hating me. This is a very clear stage in children's development. I chastize a child for his behaviour and the response is an immediate 'you do not love me'. It is critically important to make the distinction 'yes I do love you, it is your behaviour in this situation that I do not like'. As children develop self–other constancy they become able to make this distinction. Without this development, as Leitner and colleagues point out, 'how intimate can a relationship be if when one is sad, angry, bitter or bored, the other's experience of their connection is destroyed?' (Leitner et al., 2000, p. 182).

FAMILY HISTORIES

As will be described later in this chapter, the most effective way to reconstrue anger is within a group setting. For most group members, a family genogram produced within the group revealed that anger had played a large role in their family of origin or, in some cases, of adoption. 'Each family necessarily evolves a unique construct system that structures the family members' perception of their lives and provides a rationale for their actions. It governs their interactions' (Procter, 1996, p. 163).

As described already, there appears to be a constant theme within our clients of early family rejections. That pattern in adults can usefully be construed using Procter's (1985b) idea of family construct systems. Procter shows how systemic bow ties can be used to explore people's interactive construing (see the discussion in Chapter 5, pp. 60–61; also Procter's example in Chapter 17.2, p. 178).

Joan	*John*
Construct: *He does not listen to me*	Construct: *She ignores me*
Action: Stop talking to him	Action: Make her listen

As Procter goes on to show, this framework demonstrates how each action validates, more or less, the other's constructs. Procter suggests that 'we are connected together by a web of invisible loyalties which permeate our choices and actions' (1985b, p. 332). By exploring the generations of a family we usually reveal interesting patterns of similarity and contrast. As Procter (1985b) concludes in his paper: 'We should keep the shared social reality in mind and understand how it works, even if we decide to intervene through only one person' (p. 350).

ANGER AND GENDER

Following on from family interaction comes the question of gender. A recent analysis of the theoretical perspectives regarding the female and male experience of anger concluded that anger as a function of gender has not been adequately tested. It is therefore not clear how women and men differ, if at all, in their experience and expression of anger (Sharkins, 1993).

On a personal note, when I first started working with people referred due to anger problems, the people referred were all male with a history of violence both domestic and in social settings, mainly linked to alcohol. I then began to receive referrals of women who had lost their temper with their children. As child protection issues are often central we may, with permission of the client, provide Social Services with a report about how someone has responded to the group. It is for Social Services to decide if the group treatment has had sufficient effect to allay their fears concerning the safety of the children. We later accepted women who have a history of violent relationships, who often seem to demonstrate Sharkins' comment regarding the lack of difference in the experience of anger between the sexes. However, it is true that the majority of our referrals are male and the majority of referrals for deliberate self-harm are female.

ANGER AND CULTURE

The importance of family construing in the development of anger expression has already been mentioned. It also seems to be true that anger, and often violence, may be culturally construed. In a recent talk on violence, Professor Anthony Clare quoted an experiment looking at the contribution of testosterone to the expression of violence. Five monkeys were allowed to develop a social 'pecking order'. Then number 3 was given a large dose of testosterone. That did indeed make him more aggressive, but only to numbers 4 and 5; he did not try to challenge numbers 1 and 2. Many of our patients express the realization that as they alter their anger pattern 'I will have to change my friends as all our relationships include the expression of anger/violence'. As the person changes it is necessary to see him with his partner as the relationship often struggles to accommodate change. This is, of course, often the case where radical changes in construing are required.

WORKING WITH ANGER GROUPS

Because of the importance of gender, family, the perspective of others and cultural influences, it becomes clear that it is far better to run a therapy group than try to deal with people on an individual basis. The purpose of such groups is nicely summarized by Llewelyn and Dunnett (1987, pp. 251):

> The group provides an opportunity for participants, including the leaders, to explore the implications of their particular construct systems, to examine the implications of specific pre-emptive or constellatory constructions, and to bring to the group results of experiments taking place both inside and outside the group setting.

As I had expressed my difficulties with the phrase *Anger Management* because I did not want my anger 'managed', I call the group the 'Working with Anger Group'. There is no better summary of the aims of 'working with anger groups' than that by Don Bannister (see Chapter 2, p. 24):

> . . . we must facilitate change not by assaulting each other's central beliefs but by helping each other to construct alternatives, beginning with areas of peripheral contradiction. *Thus we may gradually replace a central belief without the need for hostility.* (My italics)

To encourage the construction of alternatives as far as possible, we have run our 'working with anger group' as a mixed group. While at times this has led to tensions—'you are the sort of bastard who beat me up'—it has also forced group members to begin to appreciate the other perspective. In personal construct terms, they are encouraged to develop their capacity to construe from the other's standpoint. When the group has been exclusively male it has been difficult not to have group members stick to a very limited understanding of a female perspective: 'all women are unreasonable and out to get all they can from you'—constellatory construing in personal construct terms.

KEY THEORETICAL CONCEPTS OF CHANGE

The two key personal construct concepts are those of Regnancy and Sociality.

Regnancy and Anger

Kelly defines regnancy as 'a kind of superordinate construct which assigns each of its elements to a category on an all-or-none basis'. For Kelly, 'therapy is concerned with setting up regnant personal constructs to give new freedom and new control to the client who has been caught in the vice-like grip of obsolescent constructs' (1955/1991, p. 204/Vol. 1, p. 241).

Epting (1984) gives the very helpful clarification that 'the regnant construct might be thought of as an express train that runs directly from the superordinate (value-like constructs) down to the constructs that are concerned with everyday activity'. He goes on to point out that 'following this flow of constructs reveals how one's values influence one's behavior' (p. 45). I use the example of travel in this context: 'You can travel from Coventry to Aberdeen by train without stopping or you can stop at every station.' Given that people's construing systems are hierarchically organized, that means that if you irritate me my first reaction may be to get annoyed; that is, I stop at the first station. However, another person's reaction to being irritated may be to knock the other person out. The individual skips all the early stations and proceeds immediately to an extreme solution. That pattern is often seen within the group. For instance, Jim came down the stairs one morning, saw that the table was dusty and reacted by hitting his partner. He presented this behaviour as being incapable of explanation. Anger just came over him; it happened for no reason and he was unable to control it. His ladder is shown in Figure 15.1.

Jim jumps directly from a dusty table to the meaninglessness of life. As Kelly comments, 'this kind of simplified thinking, stemming as it does from ancient logical forms, accounts for a lot of woodenheaded conflict in the world both between persons and within persons' (1955/1991, p. 482/Vol. 1, 356).

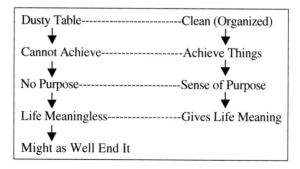

Figure 15.1   Jim's personal construct ladder

HOW MY PARTNER SEES ME	
Her Description of Me	*My Response*
Pig headed Stubborn Want too much Demanding Jealous of my mum	Aren't we all?—We all have opinions I'm standing my ground I'd like to be first It's the situation I'm not jealous, I'm annoyed
MY OVERALL RESPONSE TO MY PARTNER I say that you have not seen my change	

Figure 15.2   How my partner sees me and how I respond

Sociality and Anger

A key task of our approach is to find ways of getting participants to understand the other's perspective. Without exception, participants have been unable to see things as others see them. Male participants have a particular problem construing women. In a group's fourth session we explore this by getting them (a) to describe how their partners would construe them and (b) to produce their own responses to their partners' constructs. Figure 15.2 gives an example of what can be produced.

That exercise was completed with considerable hesitation due to the presence in the group of a female assistant psychologist. There were frequent references to 'nothing personal' with looks at her; they were not attacking her, this was just the way these men thought women are. At the end of the session the group members made such comments as:

'I feel really understood, I will sleep better tonight.'
'I had never seen it from her point of view before.'

THE THERAPY GROUP

The people referred to as the 'Working with Anger Group' are all living within the local community although commonly have a history of prison sentences. The strength of the common themes in the referrals is striking. These include the damage caused to these people's lives (and those of others close to them), a sense that the problem is getting out of control, and the eagerness of the referral agencies to assure me that these clients are highly motivated and worth taking on for treatment.

A real problem in running outpatient groups has been the rate of drop-out. Starting with eight members and ending up with four half-way through the life of the group is a common experience. I was therefore particularly interested in seeing whether I could run such a group in a semi-open format; that is, allowing new people to join the group as and when space became available.

The question that faced me was: 'Can the group members (who have been

THE IMPLICATIONS OF ANGER	
Undesired state Angry	*Desired state* Level-headed, stoned, chilled out, passive, happy, calm, normal
Disadvantages Upsetting people Stress Ill health Guilt Relationship problems	*Advantages* In control Organized Happier Content Better relationships
Advantages Not organized Being powerful One step ahead Able to go some Feel really good Control fear	*Disadvantages* Get nothing done Might be seen as soft More gullible Let things slide Sap Trumpet player for the Salvation Army

Figure 15.3   Example of an ABC inquiry of a group of participants

referred because of a perception/experience of them that their "angry" emotions were out of control), be enabled to reconstrue their anger?' *Or:* 'Can the group work with the idea that anger may be something that the person is unwilling to reconstrue despite the apparent mess it makes of his life?'

That idea seems validated by the second session of the group, which we described as 'looking at the pros and cons'. Within that session the group participants were asked to complete an ABC (Tschudi, 1977) on anger (see also Chapter 4, pp. 54–55). What they produced is shown in Figure 15.3.

As ever in my experience, when this exercise works it is immensely powerful. I really had to laugh at the description of the disadvantages of getting rid of anger. I do not know how well the Salvation Army is known outside Britain. Their bands are a relatively common sight, particularly at Christmas. It is such a powerful image, that without anger you become a trumpet player in a Christian army band! This exercise is one which usually has a major impact on group members.

At this moment it seems clear that the group members see anger as offering the greater possibilities. It protects them from the risk of threat, and as long as they stay angry no change is necessary. At one level of awareness, being an angry person works. It involves having a set of very pre-emptive constructs: either you are angry or you are not.

Anger appears to give people their chief means of anticipation: 'As long as I am angry I can cope with whatever happens to me.' However, as the group progresses the situational dilemmas faced by people with this construing strategy also become clearer.

A member of the group was clear that he got angry because of the unreasonable expectations of his wife. She laid down what he called ground rules; for instance, 'do not bring your friends into my kitchen, take your shoes off before entering the house', and for eighteen years he had resented these rules, complied intermittently with them and suppressed his anger. He was referred to the group with a 'nine-year history of low mood problems with aggression and anger control'. He seems to highlight the 'choice' dilemma:

> Anger as awareness of being put into the position of such a painful choice you have forced me to see that either I am a totally unreasonable man who does not value your opinion or I have to stay having mood problems and nightmares.

This particular client had tried to explain the situation by attributing the problems to his wife's premenstrual tension. I pointed out that it could be that *or* it could be that she tolerated him the other three weeks but was unable to tolerate him the fourth week. As often happens, this simple observation seems to have been a catalyst in getting him to contemplate the development of improved sociality with his partner. Up to this point he seems to have been using what McCoy describes as 'loving hostility':

> Loving hostility is that form of control with a relationship which keeps another individual from maturing. For example, a husband who treats his wife as an incompetent child.

Within the 'working with anger group' we thus decipher each person's construing system, understand that within the family context and go on to understand how the person uses these constructs to survive. From this each group member then begins to work out ways of reconstruing that allow the person to relate to people within their lives without being invalidated.

CONCLUSION

This chapter began from my clinical work and the ideas about anger provoked by McCoy's seminal paper. McCoy points out that anxiety need not culminate in hostility; rather, 'it can impel extension of the system so that construction can be a closer, improved approximation of "raw reality" than at present'. It was not clear to me why that cannot also be true of anger. That is, there is no necessary culmination in hostility as a result of the experience of anger.

My proposed definition of anger as 'an emotional experience of invalidation' falls within this. What I think we see within the group is the replacement of the belief that anger is the only way to keep control, be powerful, control fear, and so forth. A critical part of this is the development of a better attempt to see the world as others see it. This process starts within the group. It facilitates its members in developing the capacity to be aggressive in a Kellyian sense and, in doing so, to replace the central belief about anger. The most important experience within the group has been the clarification of the role that the experience of anger plays for each group member. As Aristotle put it: 'The middle state is praiseworthy—that in virtue of which we are angry with the right people, at the right things, in the right way and so on.' That nicely sums up the experience of working constructively with anger in group settings. A fuller description of this work and the ideas behind it can be found in Cummins (2005).

EVALUATION

Nash (2004) has now evaluated a 10-week program using this framework. Administering mainstream assessment measures: the State–Trait Anger Expression Inventory—2 (STAXI-2; Spielberger, 1999) and the Clinical Outcome in Routine Evaluation (CORE; Evans et al., 2000), she was able to demonstrate the efficacy of the group program.

However, due to real literacy problems, the best evaluation has been verbal. The group has given the following feedback:

- I couldn't believe that there were other people out there who were as angry as I am.
- It is always difficult to understand your anger. I am really surprised that I'm not the only weirdo with a bad temper.
- People with different backgrounds have angry outbursts.
- The group provides a great release of mental tension.
- The first thing I learned was to watch my physical state; if I am tired then I might snap.
- I listen to what you say and then try it out during the week.
- Sometimes the group only stays with me for a few days and then I say f*** it.
- It does last longer as the group goes on and you stay coming to it.
- We learn to step up to the fence and not bite, we are here to learn how to argue and not to lose our temper.
- The best thing I have learned is not to make others pay for my anger.
- Coming to the group has meant that I do not lash out when I get angry; I have learned to get angry but not violent.

CHAPTER 16

An Approach to Post-Traumatic Stress

Kenneth W. Sewell

University of North Texas, USA

> If, then, we are to comprehend what [a man] knows, or what he wants to know, or what he thinks, or feels, or dreads or does, we must understand the system of contradictions within which his possibilities hold their shape and his choices—deliberate or impulsive—are made.
>
> (Kelly, 1969j, p. 115)

The essential feature of Kelly's theory from a post-traumatic stress point of view is found in his Fundamental Postulate. Our psychological processes are channelized by the ways in which we *anticipate* events. Anticipation is thus integrally linked with interpretation and understanding of experience. That emphasis makes personal construct theory particularly useful in conceptualizing and helping those who have experienced some trauma.

Although Kelly focused on the 'personal' side of construing, there is a recognition within personal construct psychology that humans construe in social contexts. Indeed, Kelly's concept of sociality as the role-relationship potential created by persons attempting to anticipate the constructions of others is central to understanding phenomena as diverse as schizophrenia, love and psychotherapy. With the present framework, both of these emphases are incorporated into the understanding of trauma by stipulating that traumatization, although individual in expression, is inherently social insofar as the trauma itself has social components. Furthermore, a traumatized person's attempts to improve symptomatically occur in social context.

UNDERSTANDING REACTIONS TO TRAUMA

More than a decade ago, a personal construct explanatory model of Post-Traumatic Stress Disorder (PTSD) was devised (Sewell & Cromwell, 1990). That model proposes that a person who encounters an extreme experience that cannot be construed in relation to their other life experiences often creates a fragmented trauma-related

The Essential *Practitioner's Handbook of Personal Construct Psychology.* Edited by F. Fransella.
© 2005 John Wiley & Sons, Ltd.

construct subsystem. Thus, a person with PTSD is predicted to be operating, at least sometimes, from within an outlook on life that might have been validated by his traumatic experience, but is not being validated by the rest of his life. Such fragmentation, along with other more esoteric aspects of the model, is said to account for the various symptoms and presentations of PTSD.

The personal construct PTSD model led to further refinements based upon a variety of research findings, for example with Vietnam combat veterans (Sewell et al., 1996; Sewell & Williams, 2001), disaster survivors (Sewell, 1996), sexual assault survivors (Moes & Sewell, 1994) and bereaved persons (Gamino et al., 1998). These particular research studies are not the focus here, but the lessons learned from more than a decade of research and from clinical application of the model are distilled and presented in what follows.

CURRENT CONSTRUCTIONS OF PTSD

Individuals who persist with PTSD seem to view their lives in extreme, negative and relatively unelaborated ways. That is, they tend to become 'stuck' in their construal of experiences around one or two core constructs (such as *good* versus *bad* or *in-control* versus *out-of-control*).

Although there are some difficult-to-assess individual differences in who develops symptoms following a trauma, these differences may have little importance in understanding recovery. It is possible to identify 'risk factors' for PTSD. However, even individuals at low risk can develop PTSD if traumatized at a high level. Perhaps more importantly, once a person develops PTSD, the original risk factors fail to predict the recovery pattern (Sewell, 1996). In other words, once a person has PTSD, it does little good for the treating clinician to focus on what might have made that person vulnerable to the trauma in the first place. The more appropriate therapeutic focal point is how the person is construing and trying to make sense of the traumatizing experience.

The re-adaptation process after developing a post-traumatic stress reaction appears dependent upon elaborating the traumatic experience such that it enters into more varied and hierarchically abstract relations with other life experiences. Elaboration of a trauma is likely to require both the development of new dimensions of meaning as well as some reorganization of how their current constructs relate to each other.

A central focus of this chapter is the important distinction of 'event' versus 'social' elaboration. When a person is traumatized, there is a disruption in at least two different and important areas of construing: event construction and person/social construction. When a person's construing of events is disrupted, the individual's sense of order in the world is disturbed. The result can be catastrophic anticipations and anxiety. When a person's social construing is disturbed, the result is an inability, sometimes leading to an unwillingness, to anticipate and thus effectively participate in social relationships. This impaired ability or unwillingness to relate to other people leads to a sense of social isolation that is independent of the anxiety created by event construal.

In considering what is disrupted in any one person—event construction or social construction—it is crucial to understand that it is almost always *both*. Within this framework, traumas are therefore seen as disrupting a person's construction of experience in both event and social domains. However, the disruption in one of these domains is likely to predominate at any given time in the experience of a person.

These changes in predomination of event versus social disruption imply differences in the optimal role of the therapist as the person recovers. When the disruption of event construing predominates, the therapist can collaborate with the client in combating symptoms, and designing novel behavioural experiments outside of therapy. On the other hand, when social construction disruption is predominating, therapy should be viewed as a controlled microcosm of the client's world in which he or she can be socially related. The therapist's optimal role becomes that of collaborative social problem-solver. In this role, the therapist must invalidate the negative social predictions but persist in valuing the client and offering the self as an available target, rather than retreating from attacks, as most others in the client's environment might. In reference to the client's life story, this role is that of a valued audience member—someone with whom the client *cares* to share her story.

BEST-LAID PLANS

In order to fully understand the invalidation a traumatized person experiences in the social and event domains, a 'planning' metaphor is offered based upon the convention of referring to one's main plan as 'Plan A' and the back-up plan as 'Plan B'. It is important to note that although all plans are forms of anticipation, not all anticipations are plans. Thus, this explanation uses the 'planning' concept in a truly metaphoric manner.

Plan A: How I anticipate the world will work and how I will be humanly connected within it. Plan A is the basis of my ongoing anticipation. In personal construct terms, Plan A is made up of my 'emergent' construct poles.

A non-traumatic example will be carried through the metaphor. As a prelude to the example, I must reluctantly admit that I was an American football player throughout my university years. Suppose that after a game I walk into the football locker room, anticipating a male environment, with lots of testosterone flying about, and with collegial relations. These anticipations are based upon the emergent constructs of *male, testosterone-oriented* and *collegial*.

The level of elaboration of Plan A will determine the likelihood that various happenings will be experienced as validating or invalidating. Trauma is invalidation to the extreme.

> I walk out of the shower in the locker room, and there are women standing around with note pads and pencils. Plan A explodes into vapour.

Plan B: How the world must work and how I would fit into it if Plan A fails. Plan B consists of the implicit poles of Plan A constructions. Implicit poles of constructs are the tools with which invalidation is anticipated.

The level of elaboration (complexity, intricate contingencies, and so forth) of Plan B will determine the likelihood that trauma will result in sustained disruption. This is because trauma causes Plan B to *become* Plan A (the basis of ongoing anticipation). Once Plan B becomes Plan A, psychological energies must be devoted to making the world make sense (be predictable) from this new frame.

> If the implicit poles of my original constructions were *female* (as opposed to *male*), *femininely sexual* (as opposed to *testosterone-oriented*), and *adversarial* (as opposed to *collegial*), the Plan B that gets invoked might lead me to anticipate, even if only briefly, that the women were there to evaluate the bodies of the male athletes (myself included) in order to choose a sexual partner and/or report their findings to others outside the locker room.

Now where is Plan B? A new one must be developed. Due to the energy and attention required to try to make the original Plan B function as a Plan A, the development of a new Plan B can be difficult at best, and neglected at worst. That often leads to the paranoid stance that the new Plan A *must* hold; there simply is no choice. There is no perceived Plan B. That is an expression of a highly simplified (unelaborated) Plan B in which the implicit poles of all constructs are essentially the unitary anticipation that 'I will be out of control' or 'I will cease to exist'. That stance leaves the individual with both symptoms as well as vulnerability to continued invalidation.

> When I see that the women along with some men are interviewing the quarterback about the strategy that was being employed during a crucial part of the game, my new Plan A (old Plan B) is invalidated. If my new Plan B is composed of the single construct pole *I will be overwhelmed with confusion*, I am likely to have a psychological melt-down and run from the locker room naked and screaming. If, however, my new Plan B contains a complex set of contingent possibilities such as *newspaper reporter* (rather than *male* or *female*), *non-sexual* (rather than *masculinely* or *femininely sexual*) and *objective* (rather than *collegial* or *adversarial*), I might be able to get dressed and be only slightly offended that no one is interviewing *me*.

A non-traumatic example was chosen to aid in conceptualizing the Plan A/B metaphor without muddling the explanation with the human pain and suffering involved in the kinds of traumas our clients bring with them. Clearly, a soldier who has seen horrific acts, or a sexual assault survivor who now sees even the most trusted men as potential attackers, may have had the whole of Plan A ripped away in a matter of moments. Plan B cum Plan A—though filled with pain, anxiety and social disconnection—may be the only thread of sensibility in sight. A therapist must assist traumatized clients in elaborating alternative constructions, such that the invalidation experienced daily can be met with positive change rather than relapse. To achieve that end, a model of post-traumatic stress psychotherapy has been developed.

A PERSONAL CONSTRUCT INTEGRATIVE MODEL OF POST-TRAUMATIC STRESS PSYCHOTHERAPY

This model of psychotherapy integrates the descriptive model of post-traumatic stress disorder described above as well as lessons learned from research and clinical application to date. In addition to describing the elements of the process of reconstruction, there is a need to create a mindset or frame for construing a traumatized client from within this theoretical perspective. Toward that end, this section begins with a discussion of the concept of 'metaconstruction' and a metaphorical image of traumatization to exemplify the concept.

Metaconstruction

Metaconstruction is the construal of a construction process. One type of metaconstruction is Kelly's construct of sociality, in which a person construes the construction processes of another. But we also construe and reconstrue our own construction processes. Metaconstruction comprises the sense of self when an individual construes her or his own construction processes at present in relation to her or his own construction processes at various points in the past. That allows the person to build a sense of a future self. In other words, we construct/construe our future construction processes on the basis of past and present processes.

Metaconstruction is the overall process by which individuals constitute themselves, both psychologically and socially. As discussed above, traumas disrupt construing in both the social and the event domains, which affect the self-concept deriving from each type of disruption. Thus, a post-traumatic stress reaction represents a breach in the continuity of metaconstruction—a breach that implies disintegration of the self.

A Reflective Metaphor

Imagine sitting in a barber's chair with a mirror in front and behind. The images of front and back, front and back, front and back . . . repeat until they disappear into infinity. Think of the back image as representing the past, and the front image as representing the future. The chair itself (and your experience of it) is the present. A trauma results when the figure in the chair is different from the image in the back mirror. When this is the case, predicting what will appear on the front mirror from image to image seems mind-boggling at worst, and not conducive to self-definition at best. In this way, any dramatic 'change' can potentially be traumatic.

Thus, a trauma often initiates a construction of the present that seems too incongruous with the past to be seen as emerging from it. Consequently, the lack of continuity between metaconstrued present and past impairs the ability to make a coherent future metaconstruction.

Growth involves elaboration of the present and past metaconstructions of both events and relationships such that they are construed as continuously linked.

Then, the future can be metaconstructed in a non-fragmented, non-constricted fashion.

ELEMENTS OF RECONSTRUCTION

It must be borne in mind that the items discussed here as 'elements of reconstruction' are not to be understood as stages or phases. The elements are discussed in the order that they are likely to emerge in any one therapeutic relationship. For example, it is difficult to engage in effective 'trauma reliving' without first doing a substantial 'life review'. However, it is not the case that a client graduates from one element to the next, never to return to it. Cyclical repetitions of utilizing these elements should be anticipated and validated. The synopses of the elements of the reconstruing process and the case examples provided below are drawn from Sewell and Williams (2002)—see also Sewell (1997) and Sewell and Williams (2001).

Symptom Management

This element can be thought of as the negotiation of present metaconstruction, such as examining what it is like in the barber's chair. The over-riding goal of this reconstruction element is to gain the trust of the client by helping to alleviate some of the presenting distress. In addition to installing the therapist as an important social figure in the client's life, the relief of debilitating anxiety and/or social dysfunction also enables the therapist to 'recruit' the client's energies toward elaborating his experience, as opposed to simply surviving. Any relevant method can be employed in this reconstruction element to find a way to relieve some of the client's pain.

Case Example

Gary had clear memories of sexual abuse as a child but could express only vague complaints upon entering therapy. Early in therapy, Gary started to realize that he would over-eat to protect himself from painful introspection. He and the therapist began assertively distinguishing his emotions from the sensations of physical hunger and satiation. Several symptom management techniques such as scripted self-talk, 'feeling' journals and relaxation training were successfully employed to assist Gary with flashbacks, lack of sleep and anger outbursts. More importantly, however, Gary's successes in collaborating with the therapist to address his pain taught him the process of overt introspection. With this new skill and an important new social role relationship, Gary began his journey of reconstruing with an entrusted therapist.

Life Review

The evocation of past metaconstruction (exploring the rear view mirror) is accomplished via life review. This involves the client sharing her past metaconstruction with the therapist so that the therapist and client share the story of the life upon which the traumatic experience apparently intruded.

Case Example

Michelle was consumed with self-blame for getting in the car with the stranger who later assaulted her. When asked to describe her life before the assault, she reflected on the abandonment by her parents and her street-wise nature at a young age. Although she had become 'tough' as a way to survive her predicament, Michelle also remembered times of great vulnerability—particularly when someone showed signs of caring for her. Reconciling what for Michelle were experienced as opposite self-constructions (*street-smart and tough* versus *vulnerable and needy*) would prove to be a substantial task requisite to re-adjusting after the trauma. The life review helped to identify the elements of her past and the dimensions of her evaluation in need of reconstruction. Moreover, the process recapitulated the content; in other words, Michelle had to risk vulnerability in order to bring the therapist in as audience to her world.

Trauma Reliving

Specific trauma-related metaconstruction is evoked to bring the therapist *into* the trauma (examining how we got in this chair) and allow the experience to be reconstructed together. This element involves psychologically taking the therapist to and through the trauma. The prefix 're-' is never constrained to simple repetition; instead it is open to reformation/transformation. Thus, reliving does not mean 'living it then, the exact same way'; rather reliving requires that the client 'live it now, with my new resources, my new co-narrator, my new audience, toward a new resultant self'. It is in this focus of therapy that the therapist begins to leverage the valued co-narrator and audience status nurtured via symptom management and life review.

Case Example

Every time Tom would begin to approach the details of his traumatic Vietnam combat memories, he would find a reason not to delve deeply into them. He tried simultaneously to glean what he could from therapy, and to protect the therapist from the pain of his experience. In spite of this, Tom would grow frustrated at not being more fully understood by the therapist. Tom was repeatedly encouraged to take the therapist through the story: 'You'll be safe this time; I'll be there with you.' Tom and his therapist went behind enemy lines. Tom and his therapist stayed hidden as the enemy disembarked from a gun-boat and searched among the tall grass, eventually finding several of Tom's comrades. Tom and his therapist listened to the screaming of the soldiers until their screams were punctuated by gunfire. After the gun-boat drifted away, Tom and his therapist arose to find that his partners had been tied to trees and skinned alive before being shot. . . . Now Tom and his therapist could speak the same language. Reconstruction, though by no means an easy task, was now at least possible.

Constructive Bridging

Once the therapist and client are facing the abyss of the client's traumatic experience in a collaborative, joint manner, the therapist can begin juxtapositioning the client's various metaconstructive levels (sketching on the rear view mirror and on the chair . . . that were really sketches all along). The therapist helps the client to lay remembrances alongside introspection, introspection alongside reflection, reflection alongside the sociality with the therapist, and weave stories between these metaconstructive levels that cohere and communicate a viable sense of self. Bridging the temporal and social dimensions of understanding the self in relation to the trauma serves to build a new construct, that is, a new experience of the trauma.

Case Example

Darla was verbally and physically assaulted by a delivery man in her home. She blamed herself for letting the assailant into her home and for not stopping his behaviour. Initially, Darla's sense of her own survival efforts and the sequence in which the trauma occurred were confused and vague. After writing and talking about the trauma, then reading her own writing and processing her previous accounts of the trauma with the therapist, Darla remembered many ways that she had acted to protect herself. Darla was aided in providing links between seemingly inscrutable aspects of her experience: apparently meaningless behaviours on her part, the attack itself, and her survival being highly prized by a caring and empathic therapist. Thus, she was able to reconstrue herself as an active agent in ensuring her safety, rather than as an ineffective and powerless victim.

Intentional Future Metaconstruction

This reconstruction element involves the co-construction of a future for the client (sketching out several front mirrors and trying them on). Often, traumatized clients have no clear sense of the future. With others, the future is seen as presenting only more trauma. Extending the co-creative process of constructive bridging and intentional future metaconstruction involves composing possible future selves.

Case Example

Later in therapy, Gary felt that his depression had lifted and that he had resolved several traumatic incidents from his past, including the early sexual abuse. As termination of therapy was discussed, Gary became anxious and was unsure of a future that did not include the therapist. Gary and his therapist discussed a variety of conceivable challenges, victories and defeats. Then Gary would be asked to write and talk about how he might react to these situations; additional alternative reactions would then be explored in session. By co-constructing his future with the valued therapist, Gary came to see his therapist as an important internalized part of himself and of his future—even after the termination of therapy.

More Constructive Bridging

As intentional future metaconstruction is explored in therapy, new ground for constructive bridging becomes available. These iterative processes continue until the trauma is storied within the client's grand narrative as an important but integrated component of the overall story—one that has influenced but has not single-handedly determined the client's life.

CONCLUDING COMMENTS

Clearly, this presentation of a treatment model for post-traumatic stress lacks the technical precision of a treatment manual or a cognitive-behavioural regimen. As discussed under the 'Symptom Management' section above, there are places within this personal construct model of reconstruction for including such technical interventions. In describing this approach, I make the assumption that any professional psychotherapists reading this either can perform such technical interventions of their own accord or can access instructional resources to lead them through exposure/response prevention methods easily enough. In presenting the model here, I am concerned less with technical instruction and more with attempting to orient the therapist towards helping the 'whole' client. Technical interventions of the sort promulgated by manualized programmes tend to target the clients' *disorders* or *symptoms* as though they exist apart from the person and her or his identity. The theoretical framework presented here, and the broad technical conceptions outlined as 'Reconstruction Elements', are intended to centralize the client and her or his overall (social as well as symptom-based) functioning as the target of psychotherapy.

Nursing

Julie M. Ellis
La Trobe University, Australia
Jacqui Costigan
Late of La Trobe University, Australia
and
Julie Watkinson
Flinders University, Adelaide, Australia

INTRODUCTION

Personal construct psychology provides a framework to guide holistic nursing, nursing education, nursing research and identification of nurses' constructs of themselves, other nurses and other health professionals. Nurse converts to this psychology have shown enthusiasm about the 'goodness of fit' of the approach and its methods with their clinical and research interests, and its potential for a humanistic approach (Costigan, 1985). Personal construct psychology has been recognized as valuable in any situation where the world of the client or patient needs to be explored in order to relate to them in a meaningful way.

However, to date, the range of personal construct applications by nurses to patients and their families, in relation to understanding their constructs of health and illness, diagnosis and treatment, has not been extensive. Obstacles include the lack of attention to this theory in nursing curricula, the nature of nursing work, and difficulties for clinical nurses in collecting data from ill patients.

Still, the usefulness of the personal construct approach has been demonstrated in a variety of aspects of the professional practice of nurses. The majority of nursing research papers using personal construct psychology have been focused on phenomena related to the *nursing role*. Research in this category includes research on *caring*, perceptions of self and others, professional identity, changing role perceptions, experiences in different roles and constructions of *the effective nurse*. There has also been some emphasis on *clinical issues*, often with an overlap between the two. Clinical research has been used in *different fields of nursing*: mental health, drug and alcohol and aged care nursing, as well as nurses' constructions of patients, including the notion of the good or bad patient.

CONSTRUCTIONS OF CARING

While mainstream nursing literature is not replete with constructivist ideas and applications, Morrison and Burnard (1997) included the personal construct approach in research on the nursing role and on interpersonal aspects of nursing practice. Across two studies into nurses' perceptions of *caring* and the *interpersonally skilled nurse,* their findings were consistent in that the most frequently elicited constructs were personal qualities, rather than skills. This held implications for change to nursing curricula that, until then, were primarily based on skill development.

Dyson (1996) developed *themes* from the constructs elicited on caring: consideration and sensitivity, giving of self, work style, motivation, communication and meeting needs, knowledge and learning, individual approach, honesty and sincerity.

Ellis (1992, 1999) investigated ways in which nurses construed *self as a carer* in the context of caring for *older people* living in a nursing home. Personality characteristics (*kind* versus *unkind, giving* versus *selfish, considerate* versus *inconsiderate*) were more frequently used than constructs describing physical caring activities (*meeting needs* versus *frustrated, communicative* versus *reserved*). Personal construct theory notions of developing anticipations, validation and changing anticipations proved to be fruitful in understanding nurses' practice with elderly residents (Ellis, 1997).

In an investigation of nurses' professional identity Ellis-Scheer (2000) showed that, for most of the participants, '*caring*' was indeed an important theme among the constructs but it did not dominate their professional identity. Moreover, students and expert nurses were not homogeneous groups with respect to their professional identity. The majority of the student group did not yet have a clearly defined professional identity. In the expert nurses, two forms of professional identities prevailed: a patient-oriented one and an achievement-oriented one. A rather unsettling result, however, was that one third of the expert nurses were experiencing a conflict about their professional identity that may eventually cause them to leave the profession. This study differed from the majority of studies in that it analysed complex *construction systems of individuals* rather than simply categorizing collections of constructs compiled together from groups of respondents.

NURSES IN DIFFERENT WORKING ENVIRONMENTS

Since the professional role of nurses may vary according to the specific working environment (such as general hospital care, psychiatry, or community care), differences between groups of nurses in construing have been the focus of a number of studies.

Wilson and Retsas (1997) compared the personal constructs that three groups of nurses used to characterize effective nursing within their area of practice. They found that knowledge, technical skills and achievement orientation characterized effective *critical care nurses*, whereas being compassionate, empathetic, ethical and having an holistic approach were valued characteristics of *gerontology nurses*. Nurses in *general acute care* settings showed some similarity to both groups. March and McPherson (1996), also investigating the concept of 'the effective nurse', found that caring and good communication were the most important construct themes.

When comparing the role construct systems of *psychiatric nurses, general nurses* and *social workers*, Rawlinson (1995) found far more variation *within groups* than between them.

Nurses' constructions of their experiences as *intensive care nurses*—using situations as elements—were investigated by Laubach and colleagues (1996), and nurses' constructions of nursing expertise in *accident and emergency nursing* was the focus of the study by Edwards (1998).

NURSING EDUCATION

Some studies used personal construct theory and repertory grid techniques explicitly in both course design and educational research. Watts (1988) studied the effects of shared learning experiences on the attitudes of first-year psychiatric and general nursing students to patients and their nursing care. 'Before and after' repertory grids, together with reflection on and discussion of the findings, have been used as both research and learning tools in studies involving a midwives' refresher course (Diamond & Thompson, 1985) and nursing students' perceptions of their psychiatric practicum (Melrose & Shapiro, 1999).

The majority of studies concerned with nursing training investigated the development of their professional identity, often comparing student and 'expert' nurses (with many years of work experience). According to Heyman and colleagues (1983) nurses' *identification with the medical role* increased as a result of nursing training. They suggested that this is a move of psychological closeness to the role as a caring, supporting, health professional. Howkins and Ewens (1997) investigated the *changing role perceptions* of community nursing students. The majority of the nurses in the study, both when starting and finishing their course, identified 'Self' in a cluster with 'Self as a Community Nurse'. Apparently, these nurses had anticipated themselves as community nurses even before their education in this field of nursing commenced. Crispin (1990) found that both pertinent *events* occurring in the lives of student nurses (such as clinical placements) and *nursing lecturers' constructions* of nursing, influence the student's constructions of nursing. Feelings experienced by *new graduates* were examined by White (1996) who found that these nurses felt connected to the role, satisfied with the role, pressured by the work, and concerned about their skill level and effectiveness. They also had feelings of threat to self in the role as a clinical nurse.

NURSES AND PATIENTS

With nursing being a profession that implies intensive interaction with other, often 'difficult' people, nurses' construing of patients has been an important focus of research.

Some patients are viewed by nurses *less positively* than others (Barnes, 1990). The ideal patients were happy and satisfied and the nurses enjoyed caring for them. The nurses found the 'worst' patients (either overweight or underweight, difficult to feed, fussy or messy) stressful and frustrating to care for. The strategies used by nurses caring for *patients in pain* were focusing on the long-term outcomes for patients rather than on the immediate pain, enabling them to become emotionally distant from the patient and thus helping the patient deal with the pain more effectively. Similar findings were reported by Nagy (1992).

Pollock (1986) used repertory grid elicitation with nurses, patients *and families* as a *basis for collaborative care planning* for patients in the mental health system. Costigan and colleagues (1987) used a personal construct approach to raise student nurses' awareness of *pejorative attitudes towards people who had attempted suicide*. Ellis (1996) identified student nurses' negative and fearful *construing of old age* that appeared to be linked particularly to childhood experiences. This work highlighted the need for nurse educators to provide opportunity for exploration of alternative constructions or ways that student nurses view the aged, in order to avoid harmful consequences of stereotyping on elderly recipients of their care.

Clinton and colleagues (1995) studied *constructions of stress and coping* by nurses who worked in dementia units. The main stressors for these nurses were residents' behaviours, the work they had to undertake and the lack of time in which to do it all. Both adaptive (such as using social supports) and maladaptive (such as withdrawing and being hard towards residents) strategies were used in equal amounts by the nurses.

In the drug and alcohol nursing field, Watkinson (2001) studied *perceptions regarding mood-altering drugs in middle-aged women*, a group with a high incidence of prescribed psychotropic medication use, applying a *constructive alternativism perspective* rather than the traditional conceptualization based on a cost–benefit analysis.

CONCLUDING REMARKS

Despite this body of work, the challenge remains for personal construct psychology to be more effectively integrated into nursing curricula and for nurses to become more aware of the potential benefits of its application to patient care.

One of the reasons for the present situation is probably that the foci of research seem to be rather accidental and not inspired by a systematic research strategy. Furthermore, often the sole connection to personal construct psychology appears to be the application of repertory grids as research tools. Only a few studies use a personal construct *theory* approach. From a methodological point of view, the dominant strategy of data analysis seems to be the analysis of construct content, based on accumulations of constructs collected from groups of respondents. The specific strength of the personal construct approach, the analysis of complex constructions of human individuals, has, as yet, rarely been explored.

Family Therapy

Harry Procter
Taunton, Somerset, UK

Personal construct psychology is ideally suited to making sense of the family and in guiding family therapists in their work. Families may be negotiating their circumstances in a developing and creative way, but when they become bogged down and problems arise, the personal construct approach offers effective help.

Family intervention has broad application—for example, to mental health, disabilities and illness, child protection, marital problems and forensic work. It is applicable across the lifespan from childhood to working with older adults. It may be the therapy of choice in working with *people who are unwilling to speak or have difficulty with communication,* for example those in catatonic states (Procter, 1985b) or with autism (Procter, 2000, 2001).

Personal construct psychology provides a model of the way the family operates (Procter, 1981, 1996). We can see members of families (and other ongoing groups) as Kellyian *scientists* making sense of their lives, and in particular each other, through their personal sets of constructs. Families evolve ways of viewing the world (family construct systems) in which the members hold both shared and idiosyncratic constructs. Each family has a set of constructs which, for example, define gender and generational roles. For example in a family, stepfather might be seen as the *soft one* and mother *strict*. There may be agreement or conflict about how things are seen. Contrasts may be made within the family (he is *soft* compared to her *strictness*) or with an outside figure (he is *soft* compared to grandfather, who is *firm*). The family is an important vehicle through which constructs and values in the wider culture and society, for example about gender roles, are transmitted to the new generation.

Differences in *power* among members may be seen as which member's way of construing things tends to prevail. Some construing may be thereby *suppressed* but continues to exist covertly in an individual or coalition of individual members. The children develop and learn from the way the rest of the family carve up reality but are likely soon to begin to challenge this construing, for example in adolescence.

Problems may exist in an individual member associated with the structure or the content of the way they are construing, as described in other chapters of this hand-

The Essential *Practitioner's Handbook of Personal Construct Psychology.* Edited by F. Fransella.
© 2005 John Wiley & Sons, Ltd.

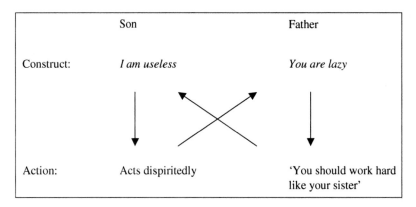

Figure 17.2.1 'Bow-tie' diagram of construing between father and son.

book. However, the family construct approach also emphasizes how problems may be maintained within the interaction patterns among family members. For example, a poor self-concept associated with depression in a young person may be maintained by the father, whose view the young person respects, but who is critical and compares his son unfavourably to his successful older sister. Figure 17.2.1 depicts this pattern between the two of them in the *bow-tie diagram,* so called because of its shape (Procter, 1987). The action resulting from each construct tends to validate the other's construct in a self-maintaining loop or circularity. How other members of the family view this state of affairs and link to this will be crucial. For instance, the mother may support the father or her son, she may help them with their predicament or distance herself, each possible position having very different implications.

The task of the person working with the family is firstly to discover how the family members are making sense of their situation. *Constructive alternativism,* Kelly's basic philosophy, may be explained to the family at the outset, helping them to see different views among them as a *resource.* Families typically rarely have had the opportunity to sit down with someone who will respect all the views held and begin to help them to negotiate some new ways forward. As in individual work, the way they see things is *accepted* in a credulous way, the art here being to do this *simultaneously* with a group of people who may differ sharply.

The therapist listens carefully to what members are saying, understanding the main 'positions' that people take towards issues and noting particular constructs that crop up and the distinctions that they use. Helping each member to spell out their view, and what 'evidence' they use to validate their judgements, begins to help the others listening to get a richer understanding of the person. Often, in families, conflicts rage as members on each side are drawing on different validational evidence to back up the 'rightness' of their view. Parents may be emphasizing the *danger* in their adolescent daughter's escapades. She sees them as *over-intrusive* and *treating her as a much younger girl.* The therapist helps the members to look at the *same episodes* and explore agreements and differences of view. They are encouraged to *put themselves in the shoes* of the other. The therapist may say to the daughter, 'What do you think a mother should do if she is worried about her daughter?' The mother may be asked what her experience was when she was the same age as her daughter. The constructs that people are using have often been carried over from earlier experiences, which are then brought into the discussion. The daughter may not have heard about the story of her mother's adolescence or have strong opinions about how different conditions apply to the two situations.

Techniques may be drawn from personal construct psychotherapy or, for example, Ravenette's approaches with children (Chapter 13, pp. 133–143) or from the various schools of family therapy. Fifteen techniques for working with families are discussed at more length in Procter (2005). Personal construct psychology provides an overarching framework for making sense of what one is doing in therapy, which can then be shared with the family. The personal construct family therapist generally prefers to honour the family's way of construing things rather than imposing his or her own views on the situation. A family situation or genogram constitutes a veritable Rorschach inkblot when it comes to people making elaborate assumptions about what may be happening. We have all grown up in some sort of family or equivalent group and tend to assume what it is like, for example, to be a *middle child* or a *woman who has been cheated on*. Personal construct psychology disciplines us to check: '*Whose* construct are we talking about here?' We *elicit* constructs rather than *supply* them. Of course, if someone is having difficulty expressing themselves or finding a word, we might gingerly suggest a word, but always check with the person that it does justice to their own intended meaning. The therapist may gently begin to invite new ways of construing through questioning and clarifying inconsistencies or alternative views. The therapist is free to share his or her own experiences and ideas with the family, of course, if it is thought that the family can use them. Therapists in any context need always to be aware of their own power in pronouncing what they think is the case.

Many different approaches may be used, the key being to fit the approach to the particular family and the members within it. Kelly provides an ethos of playful and creative therapeutic work in which one is encouraged to be *experimental*. Being playful and humorous is invaluable in family work in encouraging new ways of looking at things and countering the often scary or painful emotion that the family has been experiencing. The family session should as far as possible be a pleasure to attend, especially for young people, with a focus on what interests them and fires their enthusiasm. This helps to put the problematic aspects of life more in perspective, however serious the difficulties may be. This all becomes much more possible given the personal construct axiom that problems, like everything else, lie in the 'eye of the beholder'.

One family therapy technique that fits well with personal construct psychology is the *reflecting team* (Andersen, 1987). An observing team join the family after a while and talk with each other in the family's and therapist's presence about what they have been hearing. They attempt to mirror what the family members are experiencing and to bring the information together in a new and compassionate framework. The team members become a living embodiment of *constructive alternativism* as each of them naturally construes the situation in a unique way. The reflection provides a rich fund of ideas and feelings on which family members are free to draw for inspiration. After the team has reflected, the therapist asks each member for their reactions about what they have heard, allowing the team to revise and elaborate their views.

As Kelly said of individuals, *the family is a form of motion*, and very often the family will return to the next session with some new ideas, or with something having gone slightly better for them.

Repertory grids may be used as part of the therapeutic process and also to evaluate process and outcome in family therapy (Procter, 1985a). A less time-consuming approach involves *qualitative grids* (Procter, 2002) where, for example, the family members write down on a large piece of paper how each sees all the others in the squares of the grid. The names of the members are assigned to the left-hand edge of the grid (as *perceivers*) and the same set of names along the top (how they are *perceived*). Young children may use drawings rather than words. The method helps family members to reflect on the fact that their views are in fact con-structions and not objective reality. Given at the beginning and end of therapy, it provides an informal measure of change. It is particularly useful for children with autism who have a natural difficulty with *sociality* or 'theory of mind' (Procter, 2001) and who find it easier to understand communication presented in *visual form* rather than relying so much on words.

The personal construct approach to working with families, developed in the 1970s, predated other similar theoretical trends that have since become popular in the family therapy field such as *Constructivism* and *Social Constructionism*. These have seldom given Kelly's original writings sufficient acknowledgement and there has been a tendency to 'reinvent the wheel'. They do not have the detailed elaborate theory that personal construct psychology provides—for example, about constructs, construct systems, construing, bipolarity and emotions. The personal construct approach still has the advantage over these often much looser tendencies in pro-viding a systematic psychology with a large research literature together with a long tradition of specific techniques for making sense of human experience, as presented in this handbook. More can be found about the specific applications of personal construct psychology to families in Dallos (1991) and Feixas (1995) as well as this author's various writings referred to above. The implications of the approach applied to the topic of *anger* will be found in Procter and Dallos (2005).

The Metropolitan Police, London: A Personal Account

John Porter
Interactions Ltd, Co. Wicklow, Ireland

In about 1983 personal construct psychology crept into the Metropolitan Police (the Met) quite unnoticed. Let me explain. In 1981–82 serious civil disorder broke out in London and in many other cities of England. These outbreaks were thought to be associated with social deprivation, racial disadvantage, and discrimination and endemic racist behaviours and attitudes among police officers. Of course, since racial prejudice was both a disciplinary and criminal offence, it was doubly difficult to investigate since the rules of justice and evidence precluded any 'factual' or direct approach. No officer could be required to incriminate himself and any investigating officer was likewise required to report any instance of which he had evidence. Once *evidence* was established no further inquiry as to *underlying* reasons was permitted under the Judges Rules. Thus those rules, designed to protect the innocent, created and continue to maintain an environment in which true understanding of the causes of injustice is inhibited.

An oblique approach to the problem was required. Various suggestions appeared in the national press among which was the contention that psychometric or personality testing would enable the detection of racially prejudiced officers (whether already in service or at selection stage). A policy decision was taken at the top level in Scotland Yard. As an officer in the Met at that time, I was asked to set up a 'Psychometric Testing Unit' within the Met's Training School.

If I had known any personal construct psychology at the time, I would have understood better the reception on my arrival. I presented myself in anticipation of the warm welcome and directions to my new office. Had I known about commonality of construing at this point, I might have wondered if anybody had understood

The Essential *Practitioner's Handbook of Personal Construct Psychology.* Edited by F. Fransella.
© 2005 John Wiley & Sons, Ltd.

(a) what I was supposed to do, and (b) what the personal advantage for them was.

Having got over the 'I didn't ask for you', and 'Where am I going to put you?', stages of the welcome, I just about managed to mumble that the Commissioner and Margaret Thatcher wanted the work done. From the office window a huddle of portacabin huts could be seen crouched under the shadow of the main Kings Cross railway line. 'You might find some space in there,' it was suggested. 'Make a plan and draw up a budget.' Problem solved!

So the 'problem' trudged across the field to the huts where he found a commune of enlightened, intelligent people. One or two kindly folk welcomed me and I eventually found an unoccupied section of carpet in a corridor between offices. This was my new home.

I 'stole' a chair and a desk, made a plan and drew up a budget. Now plans and budgets are things that *can* be construed, so before long a thriving 'Unit' of about five people was established.

We embarked on a programme of testing. At the end of 12 months' work and many hundreds of tests, we found that the Force had successfully recruited people with a psychological/personality profile that mirrored . . . the general population! Everybody was randomly normal.

During the time that this work was in progress my colleagues and I embarked on a personal construct psychology course run by the Centre for Personal Construct Psychology in London. After struggling hard with the notions of self-made reality, which contrasted sharply with divine and government-made law, we soon realized that here was a non-judgemental tool which might just give some insights to the 'realities' experienced by officers going about their everyday duties. Perhaps comparisons could be drawn between the 'real' world as seen by different police officers and members of racial minorities and the majority white population.

A study making such a comparison showed that officers who had taken part in race awareness training were more likely to be prejudiced. That rather perverse finding is easy to understand using personal construct theory. Race awareness training elaborated and made officers aware of the different perspectives and lifestyle of recent and first-generation Afro-Caribbean and Asian immigrants. Hence, the construing systems of officers were elaborated with respect to the cultural *differences* (individuality) rather than commonalities between peoples. Officers were thus better equipped by this training to pre-judge the outcomes of encounters with members of racial minorities. During any such encounter episode the officer would of course treat the member of the public as different—thus heightening alienation and laying the ground for increased aggression (actively trying to find out more about each other), and hostility (in the personal construct sense) by denying that here was another bloke just like me. In the context of the race-relations programmes, these findings did not achieve political favour since management did not have the necessary construing to understand them.

However, new avenues for the application of personal construct psychology were opening and these produced rapid and spontaneous change among those who were involved.

During the time of our investigations into racial prejudice, a small number of incidents occurred in which people were shot by armed police officers. Soon the spotlight was on the selection and training processes. A major part of our work was soon devoted to the world of strategic firearms use. Personal construct psychology was used as a diagnostic tool in the following areas:

- Diagnosis of personal qualities required in officers to carry guns in high-risk situations.
- Design of a multi-activity selection centre where officer qualities were assessed on specific behavioural and attitudinal constructs. Success in subsequent training rose from a pass rate of 20% to over 90%, bringing about significant cost and manpower savings as well as selection of a more reliable set of officers.
- Identification of key personal role constructs during stages of operational incidents leading to more realistic and focused training so that officers could better construe the environment, suffer less anxiety and concentrate on operational matters.
- Workshops on stress-coping mechanisms and post-event trauma management, introduction of support rather than straight disciplinary procedures following incidents.

The Research Unit soon became a centre for officers wanting to find out more about themselves and their roles within their jobs. Quite often workshops took place at weekends with officers attending in their own time (sometimes bringing family members). These workshops were mini-personal construct psychology courses with officers learning about eliciting techniques, laddering and pyramiding.

Personal construct psychology sold itself and was soon in even greater demand as the inadequacies of conventional questionnaires, selection, appraisal and management systems became more evident. At the height of activity of the Unit, work was underway in all of the following areas (in addition to the racial prejudice and firearms areas):

- Interviewing techniques
- Training and learning course design and methods
- Management of personnel in high-risk undercover situations
- Annual appraisal/assessment
- Promotion
- Selection
- Stress management

For two years little information was published from our Unit. We had failed to validate the official line that personality and other psychological tests (that is, conventional psychometric instruments) could solve problems of selection, training and behavioural prediction. The recognition of the success and impact of personal construct psychology occurred on a very significant day. It was time to present the results of our work to the Commissioner and his senior staff. As I presented the failure of our attempted validation of conventional psychometric tests compared with the achievements of a personal construct psychology approach, the Commissioner stopped me. 'Are you telling me I was wrong, Mr Porter, (for saying that personality tests would solve the problem)?' The room stiffened. Even more so when

I replied, 'Yes Sir.' 'Thank you,' said Sir Kenneth, smiling. The room relaxed. Personal construct psychology survived.

Since that time much work has been carried out within the personal construct framework in many police forces. Nelarine Cornelius provides two such examples in Chapter 20 (pp. 218–221).

A Sporting Use of Personal Construct Psychology

David Savage

University College of Chester, UK

Sport and exercise is a relatively new field of applied psychology and as such it is still vigorously growing and changing. Recent developments in the field mean that now is a good time for sports and exercise psychologists to consider the use of personal construct theory in their work. It is relevant to what they are trying to do. It can meaningfully inform their professional practice and extend their research options.

Historically, the focus was almost entirely on athletes and the psychological issues relating to their performance and well-being. But recently the focus of interest has widened to encompass issues of professional practice. What psychologists do, how they do it and the theories that guide them are all part of the new focus (e.g. Anderson, 2001). There is a growing awareness that alternative theoretical perspectives need to be explored and traditional approaches to research extended in accordance with the new emphasis of the field. Personal construct psychology is relevant to each of these developments and worthy of inclusion in the growing plurality of sport and exercise psychology. For example, the primary influence on the working partnership between psychologist and client is the guiding theory adopted by the psychologist and the core principles and assumptions that it makes about that partnership.

Change the guiding theory and the working partnership will change accordingly. It has been observed that sport and exercise psychologists have too often implicitly adopted the principle of 'working on' rather than 'working with' the client. This leads to an excessive assumption of psychologist as 'expert' in what the athlete should do and athlete as 'novice'. The principle of 'working with' the athlete leads to some redressing of that balance. A greater emphasis is placed on the psychologist and athlete exploring issues from the athlete's perspective. The expertise of the psychologist now shifts towards being expert at uncovering the athlete's perspective, which is totally congruent with a personal construct way of working with a client. Sports psychologists now choose to approach their athlete in the way that counsellors approach their client.

As an example of the value in uncovering a client's meaning of events, consider how individuals construe exercise (or training). The personal construct *having obligations* at one pole and *can choose* at the other, can be used to appraise an event and give it meaning. One person, for example, who construes an event as having *no specific obligations* might also construe it as *free time* and as *an opportunity*, while another construes it as *wasting time* and *a loss of opportunity*. As the number and type of constructs used by individuals increases, so too do the possible meanings of events. Each person would behave in accordance with his or her personal construction of the event. This individuality of behavioural choice is emphasized as the example is developed further. A person who construes *no obligations* as meaning *free time* and *an opportunity* may, in addition, construe engaging in exercise either as an *exhausting* and *unpleasant* experience or as a *healthy* and *pleasant* one. In the former instance they would be unlikely to choose to exercise. They would choose an alternative activity such as watching television or eating chocolates as that would bring about a more meaningful experience for them. In the latter instance, exercising is construed in a way that gives rise to positive anticipations and the probability that the person would choose to do it.

An implication of the above example is that to move a person from choosing not to exercise to choosing to do so requires a change in the meaning that events have for them. That would occur, for instance, in relation to the reluctant exerciser who is advised to exercise for health reasons and be the joint venture of the psychologist and athlete. Such a venture would involve facilitating athletes' awareness of, reflection on, and alternatives to their personal meaning of events. These are central tasks for the personal construct sports psychologist. The personal meaning of events may typically be explored through eliciting constructs, repertory grids and/or narrative accounts. They can be a powerful means of promoting change in an athlete since the athlete is often unaware of how specific actions come to be chosen and thus can have difficulty in changing them. Meaning needs to be systematically elicited and explored.

A more active intervention on the part of the psychologist could be required for change to occur. Introduction and elaboration of a new construct, such as *long-term benefits* versus *short-term benefits*, may be needed before choosing to exercise becomes a very meaningful option to take.

PERFORMANCE PROFILING

The most established use of a personal construct-based technique in sport psychology is Performance Profiling (Butler, 1996). It is a form of repertory grid that enables a coach or psychologist to uncover an athlete's (or a group of athletes) meaning of their performance. Using their own constructs, a comparison of performance influences can be assessed by comparing 'as I am now' and how the athlete would 'ideally like to be' when performing. That enables areas of the athlete's strengths and weaknesses in relation to performing to be identified and experiences to eliminate the gap devised. The coach may indeed, with this athlete-centred information, be able to spot where new ways to construe performance could be introduced that would be of value to the athlete's development. In one personal athletic consultation, performance profiling was used to enable an athlete to reflect on her sports technique. That, combined with reflection on how the coach viewed 'good' technique, enabled the athlete to become aware of why she was frequently in disagreement and conflict with the coach at training.

A case study with an athlete who had been injured showed both research and intervention uses of personal construct psychology (Savage, 2000). Information was first collected through multiple interview techniques and sessions, and that produced extensive and detailed information which needed to be organized and interpreted. For this purpose, a repertory grid was used which enabled the phases of injury, and what each meant to the client, to be mapped using the client's own constructs. The more abstract representation then enabled the specific information contained in the narrative accounts to be organized without the imposition of the researcher's construing.

BOTH THERAPY AND RESEARCH

As well as richly informing the researcher about the meaning of injury for the athlete, the process gave the athlete a deep insight into the meaning the injury experience held for him. He found that to be therapeutic. The barrier between research and intervention can be blurred and this will often be the case in the future development of sport and exercise psychology. In personal construct work research and practice are often very close together. This theory has relevance in both of these domains whether the focus is on the athlete or the psychologist working with the athlete.

Artificial Intelligence

Jack Adams-Webber

Brock University, Canada

The hybrid field of artificial intelligence (AI) is still an 'open' intellectual frontier which psychologists, together with computer scientists, anthropologists, cognitive biologists, linguists, physicists and philosophers, among others, can explore on a more or less equal footing (Adams-Webber, 1993). All participants in AI research agree that it is potentially useful to construe at least some facets of cognition as involving computation. Computational models of thought processes can be characterized abstractly as based on formal rules that are independent of context. Some advocates of AI adopt a strictly computational approach to understanding all human cognition. Their ultimate goal is to design an abstract machine whose linguistic behaviour is equivalent to that of humans (e.g. Turing, 1950). That objective presupposes that the conceptual bases of all of our linguistic behaviour are amenable to formalization. Others subscribe to the more modest agenda of using computational procedures to model only some aspects of human cognition, for example, 'expertise' in chess or medical diagnosis (see Chapter 8, pp. 87–94).

Proponents of both approaches have developed simulation programs which are models of human cognitive processes in the form of computer software. Such models are essentially theories. The main idea is that the linguistic behaviour of the program should closely approximate that of humans (Simon, 1995). The detailed internal functions of the model are viewed as a potential theoretical explanation of the corresponding human performance when the input–output behaviour of the computer running the program closely resembles that of humans. These computational models can be specified fully in mathematical terms and are unprecedented in the field of psychology with respect to their level of precision and internal consistency.

Kelly's Range Corollary applies to an important problem in the theory of knowledge which has extensive implications throughout the field of AI. That is, the *frame problem* (also called the 'temporal projection problem'). As formulated by Fodor, this is essentially 'the problem of putting a "frame" around a set of beliefs that may need to be revised in the light of specific newly available information' (1983, pp. 112–113). Perhaps the most interesting facet of the frame problem from a psychological perspective is that humans, in contrast to computer programs, rarely suffer from it. As the Dreyfuses note,

> when faced with real world situations, humans need not list in advance all possible relevant features plus rules for determining under what circumstances each feature may become actually relevant, and rules for when these rules are relevant, and so forth. (1986, p. 88)

For example, before picking up the coffee mug on my desk, I do not usually pause to consider whether this action will change its colour, or the location of the desk in my office, or bring down the current government of Canada, or dislodge the earth from its orbit. If designers of computational models of cognition could explain how humans routinely solve the frame problem in their everyday lives they could possibly incorporate formal rules into their models that are consistent with our common-sense intuitions about relevance.

From a Kellyian point of view, the basic issue underlying the frame problem can be understood as essentially one of 'range of convenience' (Adams-Webber, 1989; Ford, 1989). Kelly's Range Corollary stipulates that 'a construct is convenient for the anticipation of a finite range of events only'. It follows that any construct, or by extension, any system or subsystem of interrelated constructs, has a limited range of convenience, which comprises 'all those things to which the user would find its application useful'. According to Kelly, any particular construct may have a somewhat different range of convenience for each person who uses it, or even for the same individual on separate occasions.

A particular construct seldom, if ever, stands alone in our experience. It is typically deployed together with one or more other related constructs in establishing a specific 'context of meaning' for anticipating events. Essentially, in interpreting any event, we categorize it in terms of one or more constructs; and then by reviewing our personal networks of related constructs, we often can derive some predictive inferences or 'hypotheses' about future events. Indeed, this is precisely the operational definition of 'temporal projection' that is entailed in Kelly's Fundamental Postulate: 'A person's processes are psychologically channelized by the ways in which he (or she) anticipates events.'

By definition, only events within the *range of relevance* of a hypothesis can constitute either confirming or disconfirming evidence for that hypothesis (von Wright, 1966). Adams-Webber (1992) has demonstrated that the range of convenience of any construct must necessarily delimit the range of relevance of all possible anticipations (hypotheses) based on that particular construct. In short, Kelly's Range Corollary is an *a priori* formal principle which serves the important logical function of restricting the range of relevance of all empirical hypotheses. It necessarily imposes boundary conditions on the scope ('frame') of a cognitive system, either human or artificial, because the range of relevance of any hypothesis or set of hypotheses is automatically constrained by the ranges of convenience of the constructs used in its formulation.

The Range Corollary also entails the possibility of differentiation of function, not only among constructs, but also systems and subsystems of interrelated constructs in terms of their combined ranges of convenience (Adams-Webber, 1996). By extension, the more functionally differentiated any system or subsystem of constructs, the wider the potential range of relevance ('frame') of hypotheses that can be derived within that system. Kelly's (1969j, pp. 119–120) 'minimax principle' implies that an ideal cognitive system, either human or artificial, would allow the maximum number of differential predictions concerning future events with the minimal number of constructs.

How Can PCP Help Us to Understand People or Help Them to Change?

Part 2: Working With Large Groups of People

CHAPTER 18

Construing Teaching and Teacher Education Worldwide

Maureen Pope
University of Reading, UK

In the foreword to Kelly's chapter 'Social Inheritance', Bannister suggests that: 'the most significant aspect of this early essay is the argument running through it that education should be about personal meaning' (Kelly, 1979, p. 3). It is that emphasis on personal meaning that links Kelly to contemporary constructivist approaches in education. In particular, issues such as the 'perspective of the personal', his focus on relevance and responsibility within the teaching and learning process, his theoretical stance and his recognition and valuing of alternative perspectives, have all had an impact on education. Pope and Denicolo (2001) provide a comprehensive discussion of the ways in which his ideas have been used within education.

A GUIDING METAPHOR

The current vogue for constructivism within education has often failed to consider Kelly's pioneering spirit that enthused many personal construct psychologists to take his lead and explore the educational implications of his work. However, Bruner (1990, p. 163) acknowledged that Kelly's two volumes appearing in 1955, a year before the by-now-standard date for the 'opening of the cognitive revolution', was the first effort to construct a theory of personality from a theory of knowledge. Bruner recognized that Kelly was in the forefront of those concerned with how people make sense of their worlds. Since the 1980s many teacher educators and educational researchers have echoed this viewpoint. Clark (1986, p. 9) suggested that: 'the teacher of 1985 is a constructivist who continually builds, elaborates and tests his or her personal theory of the world . . . we have begun to move away from those . . . mechanical metaphors that guided our earlier work.'

The Essential Practitioner's Handbook of Personal Construct Psychology. Edited by F. Fransella.
© 2005 John Wiley & Sons, Ltd.

Kelly's metaphor of person-as-scientist and, more recently, person-as-story-teller underpinning personal construct psychology have become guiding metaphors for many contemporary educationalists. The 'perspective of the personal' is central. It is explicit in his writings: 'we start with a person. Organisms, lower animals and societies can wait' (see Kelly, 2003, Chapter 1, p. 7).

The importance of personal perspectives has been elaborated by Thomas and Harri-Augstein who argued that, if learning is to be an enriching experience, the meanings that emerge must be personally 'significant in some part of the person's life. The viability of these meanings depends on how richly the individual incorporates them into personal experience' (1985, p. xxiv). Thomas and Harri-Augstein encouraged learners, teachers, teacher trainers and managers in industry to recognize their potential through being able to become self-organized as learners. By *self-organization* they refer to a process by which learners are encouraged to reflect on their own learning process, often with the help of a facilitator. They have pointed out the limitations inherent in previous versions of learning theory that were predicated on experiments in the laboratory (see also Fromm, 2003, Chapter 32).

They argue that construction of personal experience is prior. This process is essentially conversational. 'An awareness of this process demands an awareness of a meta-conversation about learning' (Thomas and Harri-Augstein, 1985, pp. 27–28). Their book shares with the reader the various technologies they have invented which can 'represent personal meaning in ways that enable reflection, review and effective transformation of the quality of human experience and performance'. Learning-to-learn becomes a central task for the learner and the facilitation of this meta-cognition, part of the role of the teacher.

Kelly recognized learning as a personal exploration and saw the teacher's role as helping to design and implement each child's own undertakings. 'To be a fully accredited participant in the experimental enterprise she must gain some sense of what is being seen through the child's eyes' (Kelly, 1970, p. 262). What is relevant to the person is of importance and, for education to be an effective encounter between the teacher and learner, it would be beneficial if each has some awareness of the other's personal constructs.

Bell and Gilbert supported this view in their book on teacher development. They suggested that:

> Kelly's great contribution to constructivism is his assertion that there are no predetermined limits on constructs in terms of the nature and range of their application. The limit to their creation is only set by the imagination of the individual concerned and by the constructs being continually tested. (1996, p. 46)

Constructivist educators, including teacher educators, pay attention to the learner's current ideas and how they change in addition to the structure and sequence of teaching 'received' knowledge.

THE TEACHER'S CHALLENGE

Kelly's theory of knowledge has implications for how the teacher helps the student to actively construe experiences. In viewing our constructions of reality as potentially open to reconstruction, Kelly's stance as a therapist *and* as an educator was to encourage clients/learners to articulate their world views and to recognize these world views as current hypotheses potentially open to invalidation. In this way he hoped the clients/learners would put themselves in the position of opening their minds to potential alternatives, which might serve their cause better. He saw his interest was in helping people to reconstrue their lives so that they need not be the victims of their pasts.

As a direct consequence of his Sociality Corollary, Kelly recognized that learning is a personal exploration and that the teacher must come to some understanding of the experiments, lines of enquiry and personal strategies used by the learner. He saw the teacher's role as helping:

> ... to design and implement each child's own undertakings, as well as to assist in interpreting the outcomes and in devising more cogent behavioural inquiries. But usually she has to begin, as any apprentice begins, by implementing what others have designed; in this case, what her children have initiated.
>
> (Kelly, 1970, p. 262)

Implementing such advice within teacher education poses a challenge, particularly if governmental policies militate against it or such a view runs counter to the teacher's implicit theories of teaching and learning. Teacher educators may wish to encourage conceptual change in the way teaching and learning are promoted. They should remember that the goggles through which others view their worlds might not be easily altered. However, unless the learner's views are articulated, the teacher cannot devise a strategy whereby the learner's model can be put to the test. Kelly noted that change in construing will only take place if people experiment with their own way of seeing things, construe the implications of these experiments and see that it would result in an elaboration of their construing system.

For a personal construct educator, teaching should be based upon a rigorous consideration of alternative theories—those of the students and the teacher as well as 'received wisdom'. There should be a supportive climate for students as they try to articulate their construing by being encouraged to talk about their ideas. Talking about ideas and listening to the conflicting opinions of others and the putting of these ideas to the test is an approach to teaching which is consistent with Kelly's model of 'man the scientist'.

Finding ways to help learners articulate their construing is an important challenge for the teacher that also applies to those involved with teacher education. Within pre- and in-service professional development, teachers are being encouraged to rethink the metaphors they live by (Lakoff & Johnson, 1980). Kelly's guiding metaphor of man the scientist and his philosophy of constructive alternativism imply a view of knowledge and action which suggests that, if practices are to change, teachers need to examine some of 'their fundamental beliefs'. Teachers may find consideration of their current construing threatening, especially if they deduce that change is needed. Constructivist teacher educators see that as a challenge but one that provides potentially empowering experiences for the teacher and the learner. The following examples show that Kelly's challenge to teachers and teacher educators is global.

TEACHER DEVELOPMENT

In an early study of teacher development in Israel, Ben-Peretz (1984, p. 106) advocated participation in 'action research as a process of teacher development'. Curriculum planning exercises were seen as a useful vehicle for such an approach. In discussing her investigation of teacher thinking, Ben-Peretz suggested that assisting teachers to reflect on and become more aware of their construing patterns should be planned as part of a teacher's professional training and development. Denicolo and Pope (1990) agree that action research is potentially an emancipatory approach to staff development and point out a number of assumptions shared by personal construct psychologists and action researchers.

It has been assumed, in action research models, that learning and professional development are enhanced by reflection on and in practice. However, following Kelly's lead, Denicolo and Pope warn of the potential hostility and resistance to change of the individual whose core constructs may be threatened by the consideration of an alternative model which would require too much revision of their current ways of viewing their work. The teacher educator/action researcher needs to be aware of the extreme sensitivity of the reflective material that can be evoked. They must be prepared to give time and support during periods of deconstruction and reconstruction when an individual is confronted with an image or action that he or she may wish to change. That is a fundamental requirement within constructivist approaches to professional teacher education.

In the USA, Clark referred to the fact that, for many, the phrase 'professional development of teachers' contains 'a great deal of negative baggage: it implies a process done to teachers; that teachers need to be forced into developing; that teachers have deficits in knowledge and skills that can be fixed by training; and that teachers are pretty much alike' (1995, p. 124). Constructivist teacher education entails a process akin to the development of learners. The deficit model constrains development and pays insufficient attention to support mechanisms that may be needed during reappraisal.

Diamond, while in Australia, used a staff development approach based on fixed role therapy (see Chapter 11, p. 120) and has conducted research on the constructs of pre- and in-service teachers regarding their role. He found that teachers would give up a viewpoint, even if it were an integral part of them, as long as they had become aware of the more personally meaningful implications of an alternative. As he said: 'if teachers can be helped to "open their eyes", they can see how to choose and fashion their own version of reality' (1985, p. 34). Later, Diamond moved to Canada where, at the time of writing, he continues to develop teacher education strategies based on personal construct psychology. In a subsequent book, Diamond commented that 'teacher education becomes a matter of travelling with different viewpoints and escaping being held prisoner by the fixity of any one perspective' (1991, p. 76). Kelly's voice is apparent here. In both of these works, Diamond provides illuminating examples of how he has worked as a teacher educator using repertory grids and fixed role therapy methods to encourage changes in teachers' construing.

In pre-service teacher education, the formal concepts presented on university and on college courses need to be transformed and assimilated into the particular frame of reference held by the student teacher. From the beginning student teachers, as learners, need to become aware of their implicit theories and continue to explore their developing assumptions, which underlie their teaching behaviour. Drawing extensively from my own work in pre-service education, Boei and his colleagues are concerned with the subjective theories of Dutch student teachers. They suggest that knowledge of these subjective theories would be useful within pre-service and in-service teacher training. Traditionally the task of teacher training in the Netherlands is seen as one of teaching students objective theories that can be put into practice. However, Boei and his colleagues propose that 'to be able to apply the taught objective theories, student teachers must convert them to their idiographic practice' (Boei et al., 1989, p. 175). They used repertory grids to investigate student teachers' construing about 'good' teaching. They first conducted open-ended interviews during which the student teacher's ideas were elicited. When deciding on the elements for the grids, they 'kept as true as possible to the formulations that were made by the student teachers' within the initial interviews (Boei et al., 1989, p. 179). The statements were reformulated in terms of teacher behaviour, for example 'the teacher pays attention to individual children'. In addition to 'teacher behaviour elements' the researchers provided two further elements, 'I as a teacher' and 'I as an ideal teacher'. They identified a number of common constructs used by student teachers. One interesting result was that the difference between 'I as a teacher' and 'I as an ideal teacher' was most marked in terms of the construct *professional activities inside class/school—professional activities outside class/school*. Boei and his colleagues suggest that in their opinion: 'this points to a rather narrow perception of the professional teaching role' (1989, p. 189). They advocated that outside activities should be considered within teacher training to avoid teaching being separated from its ethical, political and social dimensions.

Sendan (1995) saw learning to teach as a complex process of change in student teachers' personal theories during which they develop, test and reconstruct their own hypotheses about teaching. He followed Turkish student teachers throughout their three-year course. His study was concerned with the nature of, and changes in, student teachers' personal theories regarding teaching effectiveness throughout their initial teacher training. Sendan used grids and tape-recorded interviews with each participant. He then classified the various constructs elicited, deriving several categories. Sendan discussed the patterns of change in construing that he observed in his data. Between the first two occasions this was mostly in the area of teacher knowledge and characteristics. There was more focus on constructs concerned with lesson management between the second and third occasions and on lesson management and teacher/pupil relationship between the third and fourth occasion. Sendan (1995, p. 121) saw this as 'indicating a pattern of "deconstruction" of personal theories in the early years of training and "reconstruction" towards the end'.

How Student Teachers View Themselves

In the case studies, Sendan was able to focus on both the change in content and structure of each student teachers' construing. His experience of using the repertory grid technique confirmed his view that student teachers are capable of reflecting on their personal theories and training experiences when given the opportunity and a supportive environment. The student teachers' active involvement in the research process helped them to have a greater consciousness of their personal theories about teaching and their views of themselves as a teacher. This participation also helped them to reflect on various experiences during their period of training. As one student commented, 'I found it extremely useful to articulate my thoughts and feelings about teaching. I now feel more aware of who I am and who I would like to be' (Sendan, 1995, p. 229). Sendan and one of my doctoral students, Saka, have done much to develop a more constructivist approach within Turkish teacher education (Pope & Saka, 1997).

In the UK, Watts and Vaz drew on the work of Paolo Freire and Kelly because they both 'proposed forward-looking theories, the former at the level of the culture of the group and the latter at the psychological level of the individual' (Watts & Vaz, 1997, p. 334). Their research centred on the themes that emerged during conversations with primary teachers of science. These themes were those seen as emotionally significant for them. After the themes were identified they were re-presented to the teachers for further discussion. Watts and Vaz then designed what they referred to as a 'problematizing' programme for teachers' professional development, which drew on the elicited themes for its broad content. In the first session, Watts and Vaz presented the teachers with a number of questions related to recall of episodes of emotional experiences written on individual cards, and teachers were asked to write responses in a designated space. They were also given blank cards to provide any extra elements for discussion. Some cards prompted positive feelings and others prompted episodes associated with negative feelings.

The teachers were asked to select nine from their set of cards, which became the elements in a repertory grid interview. The second and third meetings were devoted to conversations with the teachers about their experience and their beliefs and assumptions about the teaching of science. These discussions began with a reflection on the analysed grid and, according to Watts and Vaz (1997, p. 336), a dialogue with a clearly 'problematizing' tone emerged. The repertory grids allowed the researchers to discuss very specific elements of the teachers' professional knowledge and experience while they were encouraged to justify their personal constructs. Reflection on the grids produced a rich source of generative themes. One example of the many themes which emerged during the course of the conversations concerned the teachers' need to exercise 'didactic restraint, to organize their classrooms for what became known as "hands-off teaching for hands-off learning"'. This theme reflected the teachers' dilemma of hoping to encourage pupils to find out about science for themselves while resisting telling children what to do and transmitting the 'received' view of science. The teachers in Watts and Vaz's study showed clear recognition of the importance of the child constructing their knowledge.

Mair (1989b, p. 5) invited personal construct psychologists to explore a story-telling metaphor and consider 'the stories that they live and that they tell'. Nelson (1993) was interested in teachers as story-tellers and personal meaning using the voice of practising teachers. Nelson sent letters to the entire teaching staff of one school district in the USA asking them to share their stories about meaningful moments in their teaching careers. Fifty-five teachers agreed to contribute stories, which they themselves audiotaped. Nelson, with the help of three independent readers, identified a number of themes from the transcribed tapes. She noted that, even though the stories were self-selected in response to an open invitation, the themes evoked revealed some commonality of perspectives and values. Using teachers' stories with teacher development programmes is a powerful means of helping teachers to reflect on the challenges and rewards of the teaching profession.

Apelgren (2001) also used a story-telling metaphor with Swedish teachers. She asked them to think back on their career in terms of a winding river in which each bend represented an experience that had influenced their direction. Each teacher was then asked to draw this river and write a few words about these critical incidents. The teaching stories that evolved as each teacher discussed the rivers, after they had spent a period alone drawing up their own river, were tape-recorded. The rivers became the agenda for an interview in which the teachers reflected on how they construed teaching.

Apelgren found qualitatively different ways of experiencing language teaching based on the participants' self-perception of the teacher's role and their personal theories of teaching. She identified four themes which, she suggested, were aligned with particular metaphors: *teaching as a mutual affair, teaching as guiding with an invisible hand, teaching as a social activity* and *teaching as being a captain of a ship*. Apelgren called her themes 'orientations' to imply potential fluidity in the teachers' construing. She was able to highlight the complexity of her participants' personal theories on teaching and their views on their own professional development. Apelgren noted that the opportunity to sit down and recollect past experiences with someone else listening was regarded as 'stimulating and satisfying'. As one participant commented:

> It also makes me 'clear my mind' and I have to decide what teaching is about, what goals I have and why I do certain things. Everyday life is so hectic so there is little time to evaluate what you do, what you have done and if you have achieved the goals you set up. (Apelgren, 2001, p. 327)

The expression 'clear my mind' indicates a possibility for the teacher to stop and move behind the actual practice, to reflect and reconstrue. Gaining a perspective means allowing the present to encounter the past, as well as realizing how the past influences teachers' thinking and guides future action. In my own work with teachers I have found similar reactions. One teacher, faced with issues surrounding the inclusion of disabled children within regular classrooms, commented on the importance of teachers confronting their own feelings:

> . . . think PCP could have a great impact in this area as teachers examine their own constructs towards students who have disabilities. If the teacher's perception of the disabled child is negative, then the mainstream experience would be a negative one for the child.

Helping pre- and in-service teachers to consider changing their current practice is not merely a technical process. As one of my teachers put it: 'It is not an easy task this process of being a "scientist" and the ways are very uncharted and at times uncertain. The process seems to require a great deal of emotional energy.'

CONCLUSIONS

Personal and professional change are inextricably linked. An implication of personal construct psychology is that teacher educators should take risks and adopt a reflective and enquiring stance as an example to their students. We must, from time to time, review how we are construing education and the extent to which we understand the position of others with whom we interact. This is a central message of Kelly's work for those striving for a more democratic educational process in schools and in universities and is one that many teacher educators throughout the world now advocate.

CHAPTER 19

Making Sense of the 'Group Mind'

Adrian Robertson

Sunningdale Park, Berkshire, UK

> But how can one spend his whole life, the one and only life that is given us, taking notes on things as they are, without once using his pencil to make a little sketch in the margin depicting things as they might be?
>
> (Kelly, 1978, p. 225)

Personal construct psychology offers a different way of looking at change in organizations from that often encountered in business books. Why? Because it is founded on comprehensive theory and method, yet seeks to encourage each person's creativity and emancipation as part of a broader social reform vision. For practitioners of change in organizations it offers an anchor framework and a springboard for harnessing other approaches. It also transcends the common basic error of making a false distinction between being practical rather than theoretical (Collins, 1998).[1]

PERSONAL CONSTRUCT PSYCHOLOGY: A DIFFERENT VOICE

Kelly proposes that we should look at humankind through the 'perspective of centuries rather than in the flicker of passing moments'. Not only that, but we should also take the view that *all people are scientists.*

The human story is a quest over numerous millennia 'to predict and control the course of events'. That suggests a longer-term view in trying to fathom and design a psychology of personal and social change. Kelly would have us consider that each person is trying to figure out how best to deal with the world as the future races towards him or her.

Kelly developed his ideas in the 1930s and 1940s when the whole enterprise of

---

[1] This text offers a well-argued critique of the lack of theory in management literature.

The Essential Practitioner's Handbook of Personal Construct Psychology. Edited by F. Fransella.
© 2005 John Wiley & Sons, Ltd.

psychology had a certain paucity of vision and imagination. He challenged psychologists to raise their sights and offer an alternative which sets out to uplift the human condition rather than be swept along in a tide of illusory 'scientific' progress. Kelly's criticism could be made for much that nowadays passes as 'change management' or 'organizational development', as a background hum of cynicism seems to be perpetuated rather than the generation of something that could appeal to the higher ethical and community-minded aspirations of a human person.

In Kelly's terms we would view all organizations from way back in time to the modern era as experiments in human progress. Kelly's philosophical starting point is not one of fixing fragments as we muddle along. He challenges us always to work from the big questions: Where are we in the evolution of organizations? What are organizations for—to cage in or liberate the human spirit? What alternatives can we imagine to the kinds of organizations we have now? Should we even care about these issues?

Personal construct psychology is a process of asking the most challenging and adventurous questions and to keep on asking them. This is not a pastime. It is essential to renew and refresh how we view things. It is our humanity—our capacity to free ourselves from the trap of only being able to look at situations in one way.[2]

DESIGNING CHANGE FOR SCIENTISTS

All people are scientists. That is a crucial point for any change practitioner to consider. All people have a wary eye on the future; everyone is trying to make the best guess they can about how things will really turn out, of what can be trusted, what is reliable and well-founded, as well as what is flaky, deceptive and downright hypocritical. Put more formally, each person is deeply immersed in a *psychology of anticipation*.

If everyone is a scientist, how do you deal with them? Kelly's first principle of learning is that if you think someone might have a problem you ask him or her what it is—they might even tell you! If you talk to them, and listen carefully, they might sense that you are a person who respects their scientific status. Moreover, as a scientist yourself, if you are seen as being open to changing your own way of looking at things, they might listen to you, and begin to reflect on their own theories about you. The alternative, sometimes encountered in organizational change and service delivery contexts, is to think *for* other people and do things *to* them. Kelly challenges us to be more generous with the idea of who may or may not be a scientist, and then get down to some practical ways of bringing about positive change.

SUPER-PATTERNS: PRACTICAL WORKING SKILLS

When people try to bring about change in organizations, they are sometimes not very clear or specific about what it is they are trying to change, and what new situ-

---

[2] The author would like to thank Denny Hinkle, one of Kelly's former students, for his memories and insights into Kelly's thinking about social reform.

ation they are trying to bring into being. That may be because there are few available constructs in the business literature to help get beyond vague notions such as 'culture change' or 'working with the soft issues'.

As early as 1930, Kelly addressed himself to issues of 'group mind' and came up with the idea of a 'super-pattern'. That turns out to be a particularly fruitful and strategic perspective which challenges us to be optimistic about the capacity even of lone individuals to be the instigators of significant social change in our workplaces and communities:

> The process of group behaviour is nothing but the behaviour of individual members, although the pattern may be super-individual. In this sense, then, we can say there is a group mind . . . But wait, we should be careful not to jump to conclusions. The group mind is not a separate organism, not a separate process, not a separate will, not a separate force from that of the individual. It is a super-pattern into which the individual sub-patterns fit. . . . The group mind is a situation into which individual tendencies are so combined as to make their effect violently felt by all. (Kelly, 1932)

It is important to link this idea with Kelly's philosophical proposition that personal change is always possible:

> We take the stand that there are always some alternative constructions available to choose among in dealing with the world. No one needs to paint himself into a corner; no one needs to be completely hemmed in by circumstances; no one needs to be the victim of his own biography.
> (Kelly 1955/1991, p. 15/Vol. 1, p. 11)

How do organizations become hemmed in by circumstances? How does each person contribute to the effects 'violently felt by all' in our organizations? In what way do we as individuals contribute to organizations becoming victims of their biographies? We may consider the extent to which underinvestment in British public services such as the railways, the Health Service, the school system, the police, social services, public transport and postal services has arisen because collectively we have painted our life-sustaining social systems into a corner?

A super-pattern is an operational way of getting a window on 'culture'. We can use empirical methods in the form of repertory grids to describe the personal constructs which make up the sub-patterns (see Chapter 6, pp. 67–76). In so doing, we can begin to see culture as a *structure of anticipations*—or predictions about how things will turn out. This is 'mission-critical' for organizational change practitioners because the only thing we can change about other people is their anticipations, their predictions, the outcomes on which they will wager.

HOW CAN WE SEE SUPER-PATTERNS?

How can we find compelling, persuasive and vivid ways of sketching, describing, caricaturing and representing a super-pattern, such that others can see it as well? In particular, how can we show that it has a repeating or replicating quality to it?

How can each individual steel themselves for the uncomfortable moment of seeing their own contribution to a troublesome super-pattern?

The change practitioner who walks through the revolving doors of an organization and encounters a sense of malaise about particular issues may well be on the scent of a troublesome super-pattern. There may have been attempts to change the 'group mind' which have bypassed the most perplexing questions, such as what actually is the super-pattern we are trying to change and how does each person take responsibility for their contribution to it? Such attempts can be called *meandering interventionism*. By working with the idea of super-patterns we can try to get beyond this. Within personal construct psychology it makes sense to talk about *constructive interventions*, and a *constructive interventionist* as a person who seeks to accelerate the capability of individuals and communities and work groups to enhance their experience of everyday living—to transform the super-patterns to which they contribute.

When it first becomes noticeable, a super-pattern is something felt intuitively rather than something that can be spelled out. Our job is to show it as clearly as possible, although in a way that includes, rather than excludes, the people who are involved in it. Super-patterns can be found in the stories people tell, and may be sketched out using flip-chart drawings of systems diagrams in the manner proposed by Senge and colleagues (1994). More formal and mathematically rigorous approaches are also possible, such as Forrester's (1993) work on population dynamics. It is also essential to look at the patterns of open or submerged contention. Mindell's (2000) work on conflict in social fields offers wise counsel about intervening in what may be violently polarized disagreements within super-patterns. Mindell's work supports observations by Collins (1998) that people who plan change in organizations often fail to take sufficient account of the contentious nature of organizational life, and may act with a naïve and false assumption that 'everyone will see the self-evident merits of our view'. What is needed, although often missing, are formal processes and group skills such as *dialogue* (see case study) for working productively with adversarial positions (see Bohm, 1996).

To some extent, seeing super-patterns involves opening our eyes to the unpleasant side of life, and asking if it is humanly possible to construct a better alternative. Psychologically troubling art or literature, such as Dali's warlike *Autumnal Cannibalism*, or Shakespeare's depiction of the self-perpetuating brutality of a military regime in his play, *Coriolanus*, may help to stimulate our super-pattern imagination.

FROM INTENTION TO METHOD

If we are trying to change people's thinking and feeling, it is important that we have a reputable method which is itself scientific, in the sense that its methods are transparent, yet it can modulate cycles of enquiry, creativity, personal experimentation in the real-time of living, and evaluation. Kelly went to great lengths to outline how this could happen in the area of personal change and development. Based on similar principles, Argyris and colleagues (1985) proposed *Action Science* as a way of formulating a more challenging, rigorous and intellectually enquiring approach to intervention in organizations.

When people at work are co-opted onto change programmes they sometimes find the experience threatening. This may well be because the 'change agents' are not treating people as scientists, reinforcing a psychology of anticipation that firmly entrenches itself in wariness and survival politics, even where something more 'wholesome' is proclaimed. This is exactly the kind of conundrum that Argyris has tried to point out in his theory of single- and double-loop learning.

Argyris has spent his career investigating why positive and constructive change at work is sometimes so difficult. He suggests that in our working lives many of us collude in highly skilful self-protection rackets of espousing socially desirable behavioural values, yet at the same time behave in ways that are disingenuous and covertly competitive. Argyris proposes that many of us are stuck in a behavioural loop which he calls Model I (see below).

Model I (*Theory-in-use*)	Model II (*Espoused theory*)
• Strive to be in unilateral control	• Access to valid information
• Seek to win at all times	• Free and informed choice
• Avoid expressing negative feelings	• Internal commitment
• Be rational—keep emotion out of it	

If we are stuck in this loop, then all our attempts at change and reform are destined to be mediocre because we disable ourselves from what Argyris calls double-loop learning. Double-loop learning is the capacity to change our consciousness and reorder our familiar constructs, although for Argyris, that can only take place in a climate of inquiry under-girded by democratic values, where group conversation is the medium for practice.

Single-loop learning traps are identifiable as super-patterns as Kelly defined the term. The root structure of such traps is a *psychological spiral* of anticipation built from the escalating interplay of personal constructs. If people's personal constructs, anticipations or mental models about change are broadly Model I, even though their espoused values are Model II, then change programmes are likely to stoke the embers of cynicism.

Argyris's ideas have a particular focus on management relationships in organizations (with peers or subordinates). They link with Kelly's super-pattern concept, because if Model I is widely followed as a style of reasoning (even if not consciously articulated) then the interventionist may be facing an organization with a preloaded *structure of anticipations*.

From the viewpoint of personal construct psychology, Argyris's distinction between espoused theory and theory-in-use does not tell us whether Model I and Model II are *superordinate* or *subordinate* constructs for any one individual. That is, perhaps, the most difficult challenge for the 'change practitioner', as it is essential to distinguish people's most important preferences from their more worldly pragmatisms. Only a process of careful investigative intervention will enable the interventionist to help individuals confront significant fragmentation between espoused values and theories-in-use, and how their own personal action might be sustaining the most problematic of super-patterns. These issues are illustrated in the following case study.

Addressing 'Real' Issues

Kelly believed that fragmentation between superordinate and subordinate constructs was not necessarily a bad thing. In his view, total consistency is 'an ideal that
could not exist in reality' and a problem occurs only if the 'wagers one lays on the
outcome of life cancel each other out' or do not 'add up'. A constructive interventionist is not in pursuit of perfection, yet where people are creating super-patterns
which damage the capacity of organizations in critical ways, we must find ways to
address the difficult human issues and not side-step them.

Within the investigative methods of both personal construct psychology and
action science, we are trying to make explicit people's deepest values and
consider how these can be lived and enacted in the real world. However, in our
efforts to change a troubled super-pattern, we must first obtain the genuine
consent of those we wish to co-opt. In the rush to reorder things in modern workplaces this essential requirement is easily overlooked. It may be why change initiatives at work are often experienced as coercive and fundamentally fail to engage
individuals.

Change at work is a form of social change. As such, it will inevitably touch upon
people's deepest values (or superordinate constructs). To work with this kind of sensitive psychological material we must be able to design and carry out interventions
where such sensitive material is discussible. The alternative strategy, and common
default approach is, in terms proposed by Argyris, to *bypass* them or render them
undiscussible.

Kelly and Argyris are both concerned with creating laboratories for change—
Kelly in the therapy room and Argyris in reflection and learning groups. In other
words, real life is the practical laboratory for change, and there is a *conversational
core* to initiatives which seeks to change people's thinking and feeling. The key skill
is to design opportunities for people to talk openly and explore different ways of
looking at things and alternative grounds for action. However, in practice doing this
sort of thing in many organizations is extremely difficult.

To get beyond the impasse, it is necessary to foster *effective learning environments*
at work, even in the most uptight organizations. This is a fragile, sensitive and at
times unnerving process which requires personal courage and absolute respect for
other people's rights and dignity if it is to have any chance of success.

It is also important to keep in mind our wider responsibilities to work as
enquiring scientists, so there must also be a concern for understanding what will
constitute effective evidence that our efforts are making a constructive difference.
How do we know that change is occurring? How can we measure changes without
producing meaningless data?

A CASE STUDY: ENGAGING WITH THE LIVED REALITY OF OTHERS

The author carried out the work described in this section in the consultancy wing
of a large British public organization. It seeks to illustrate how the kind of ideas put
forward in this chapter can influence troubled super-patterns through small-scale
interventions which affirm the value of individuals and gently encourage people to

share the challenges of creating something better. 'Big' projects and budgets are not always needed.

As indicated earlier, central to this case study is the assertion that constructive social change starts with group conversation of the kind suggested by David Bohm (as mentioned earlier). If we want to change people's thinking and feeling, to influence their scientific predictions, we need to create places and spaces where people can question their own impermeable or pre-emptive constructs, where they can speak personal truth without being a mouthpiece for rehearsed political positions or 'non-negotiables'.

The background to the work is that the consultancy had failed to recover its outstanding fees by a substantial sum. Difficulties were being experienced in getting some 20 divisional finance managers to produce timely and accurate forecast information. The financial regime was such that divisions inadvertently competed against each other to meet income targets, generating a management system that was fundamentally counter-collaborative. Many people were unhappy and disgruntled, there was much apportioning of blame, and little expectation that things could improve.

People in this system were operating with superordinate constructs (Argyris might say 'master programmes') which were combative and excessively self-protective. Three workshops were set up with the intention of improving collaboration by promoting open-hearted conversation about the key tensions of being a finance manager.

Early on in these workshops people were asked to write down in silence what they wanted to get out of them, and the kind of contributions they wanted other people to make. Silent exercises help people to concentrate and think about what is really important to them. Here are a few of the answers given by participants. They illustrate that people may have been experiencing some fragmentation between their superordinate and subordinate constructs, and desired much more enquiring and authentic communication than is permitted at work:

— 'By being personally open, encourage others to do likewise.'
— 'To be generous with my own listening.'
— 'Really listen to others.'
— 'Surfacing of real issues.'
— 'A willingness to appreciate the stance of others.'
— 'To share the burden of some of the tensions that finance seems to give rise to.'
— 'Help to create a sense of teamwork with finance.'

Each workshop progressed with phases of dialogue and synthesis. Some of the observations and issues that arose during the course of some exceptionally enquiring and reflective conversations were:

— 'There is a them and us culture in the way we handle finance, and it plays out in multiple layers—creating various "thems" and "usses".'
— 'We are not working together.'
— 'We play games.'
— 'Truth isn't justified, nor is honesty.'
— 'We need to work on building trust among ourselves.'

— 'We need to interrupt the trust/games playing cycle in forecasting.'
— 'We need to connect with each other better—build bridges and become tourists in each others' worlds.'

Shortly after these interventions there was a further request for a financial forecast. A full set of responses was collected within days. The Chief Executive of the consultancy commented that 'this is the first time this has happened in living memory'. Participants asked for more sessions, and improvements in the quality of internal finance and other management forums were reported to the author following these interventions.

The more general point here is that evidence in work of this nature may not present itself in forms that can immediately or easily be put on a spreadsheet. It may be simpler, as noted earlier, to invoke Kelly's first law of learning, which in this case, asked people to give oral testimony.

Super-patterns in Action

Each person in the finance system is contributing to a troublesome super-pattern, yet each can play a part in changing it. In the sessions some participants admitted to having deliberately avoided conversation with the finance director, and not responding to e-mail requests for information. As the workshops unfolded, people who had 'taken sides' became more human to each other, and began to develop some understanding of each other's dilemmas and difficulties. In Kelly's terms, they were more willing to see the world through the eyes of their colleagues. Such understanding can be scarce in work relationships, and that prevents people from working together to produce more fundamental solutions.

Taking the systems thinking model of Senge and colleagues (1994), the finance managers are creating an *addiction loop*. That is so, because people are committed to short-term coping strategies which sustain the system at a mediocre level of performance, although it perpetually teeters on the edge of collapse, as happened in this case. This is a classic case of single-loop learning, as no fundamental improvements are possible until the addiction system is modified. Moreover, the addiction system produces side effects such as low-trust relations, job stress and a sense that chronic issues will never be resolved (which further undermine the fundamental solution). A fundamental solution is possible where people can enquire collectively into their own patterns of behaviour, to stand behind their 'official selves' and reflect upon their own contribution to the prevailing super-pattern.

In situations like this, a process of enquiring and compassionate conversation is needed to bring about double-loop learning. A chance may be provided to become aware of the fragmentation between espoused values and covert practice, and for people to modify their anticipations of each other.

The Structure of Super-patterns

The underlying psychological structure of any super-pattern is a *spiral of anticipation*.

> James anticipates what John will do. James also anticipates what John thinks he, James, will do. James further anticipates what John thinks he, James, will do. James further anticipates what John thinks he expects John will do. In addition, James anticipates what John thinks James expects John to predict that James will do. And so on! (Kelly 1955/1991, p. 94/Vol. 1, p. 66)

A spiral of anticipation is the repetition of a way of thinking and reasoning (Balnaves & Caputi, 2000). Single-loop learning is the repetition of a style of thinking and reasoning from which people stuck in the super-pattern it sustains feel they cannot free themselves. International politics is replete with super-patterns. In the absence of true dialogue people may take 'sides' and invent and perpetuate untested attributions and predictions about each other. By way of example, the following quotation has been attributed to Chou En Lai, adviser to Mao Tse Tung, in the 1970s:

> I am sitting here surrounded by my advisers trying to figure out what they may be scheming against us in Moscow and in Washington. In Moscow, they are trying to figure out what Peking and Washington might be scheming against them. And they are doing the same in Washington. But perhaps in reality no one is scheming against anyone. (Cited in Mindell, 1989, p. 133)

As practitioners of change in organizations, rather than trying to figure out what others may be scheming against us, we would do better to employ Kelly's first law of learning, which is, as paraphrased before: if you think someone has a problem ask him, he may tell you what it is.

THE FUTURE OF ORGANIZATIONAL SUPER-PATTERNS

In her novel *Always Coming Home*, Ursula Le Guin (1985) suggests the idea of an 'archaeology of the future', where a distant future civilization critically examines the centuried progress of contemporary humankind. This seems like the kind of imaginative exercise Kelly would encourage, and could be quite revealing and fruitful if the key issue being evaluated is how humans changed and reformed organizational super-patterns over time. Key questions would be: How was power shared? Were differences between people celebrated or censored? Were individual humans treated with dignity or disdain by the prevailing super-patterns? What attempts were made to correct cruelty and suffering, such as that created by international labour supply economics?

How would it be if the future archaeologists discovered that after centuries of conflict humanity evolved super-patterns founded on the base principle that the origin of all compassionate and humane social change is to walk in the shoes of another? Could we imagine in our own lifetimes starting to build a civilization where creating boundless intimacy rather than cynicism between strangers became the first precept of each person's and each organization's foreign policy? Suppose we evolved practical ways of doing this for real in the United Nations, in peace talks between countries and between factions in organizations? How different would politics and international society be? How could we imagine daily life changing for individuals and communities the world over?

As Kelly suggests, if we only observe and do not innovate we are in trouble. It is easy to become a passive victim of the 'group mind' and believe we are stuck in situations that are both intractable and intimidating. Yet as many dictators, tyrants and supremacists have found to their cost, even the most brutally enforced super-pattern can become remarkably fragile when the normally quiescent citizen decides that enough is enough.

Our organizations are the very super-patterns we choose to live in, or design for others to live in—they are the products of our human civilization. The times we live in require people to make constructive interventions for greater mutual under-standing, compassion and sharing of the earth's resources. The place to start is with ourselves and the super-patterns of which we are a part.

CHAPTER 20

Charting Organizational Change

Nelarine Cornelius

Brunel University, Middlesex, UK

> The old ways of looking at things are still so clear, so easily structured, so pal-
> pably available. A bit of confusion, a haunting situation not easily pictured in the
> new light, and click, everything might slip back into place in the old pattern!
>
> (Kelly, 1955/1991, p. 490/Vol. 1, p. 362)

In Chapter 19, Adrian Robertson provides a graphic case illustration of the
'rhetoric–reality' gap that was operating in his organization. He shows how that gap
adversely affected a change programme that looked a sensible way to improve performance. Such 'rhetoric–reality' gaps are common in work-related problems.

Personal construct psychology is an extremely useful framework for making
more visible what lies 'below the surface'. However, the challenge of accessing such
theories-in-use really steps up a gear when change is attempted in areas which are
more deeply personally sensitive to those involved. One such area is tackling workplace equality.

ADDRESSING WORKPLACE INEQUALITY

The most common approaches to tackling workplace inequality have been categorized according to their core principles, and the associated strategy and practices.
However, in spite of the gains made by these traditional approaches, the breadth
and depth of what is going on with regards to workplace inequality 'on the ground'
is often weakly grasped by policy makers.

A good illustration appears in the report commissioned by the United Kingdom
charity, The Runnymede Trust (Sanglin-Grant & Schneider, 2000). In the report on
the policy and practices of Britain's 500 leading companies, the organizations
believed that they were good employers. Indeed, against 'best practice' criteria, the

The Essential *Practitioner's Handbook of Personal Construct Psychology.* Edited by F. Fransella.
© 2005 John Wiley & Sons, Ltd.

companies were *acting* fairly. But the experience of employees was that the organization did not *feel* fair. One factor that is likely to contribute to this yawning gap is the limited information that these companies have gathered on how most effectively to engage with organizational *micro-processes*—the day-to-day factors that operate between individuals and groups 'on the ground'—that contribute both formally and informally to the *experience*. Indeed, equality management practice often primarily promotes compliance rather than learning. The exception is some diversity management approaches, which are more concerned with culture change and organizational learning (see Thomas & Ely, 1996).

CHALLENGES TO TRADITIONAL VIEWS OF INEQUALITY

There are some important ideas that work well in practice as a means of understanding workplace inequality and also challenge more traditional thinking.

Equality of What?

First, it has to be decided exactly what the organization means by equality. The work of the developmental economist Amartya Sen (1992, 1999) and philosopher Martha Nussbaum (1999) have a different but related philosophical framework to most of the more commonplace approaches. Sen, in particular, is critical of many of the popular frames of understanding inequality. He argues that this is because they highlight some specific aspects while masking others and, potentially, allowing these other aspects to remain unchallenged (1992). Sen and Nussbaum have developed an alternative 'capabilities' approach. Their approach asserts that the answer to the question 'equality of what', is 'equality of capabilities', and that what is measured is the degree to which '*one is able to be or do what we have reason to value*'.

Put simply, basic or individual capabilities are the gifts and talents that individuals possess. It is combined with factors such as education, legislation, policies, organizational culture and climate, and so on, that individual capabilities can be readily exercised. Crucially, the implications of Sen and Nussbaum's capabilities theory when applied to work organizations, is that attention should be paid to all 'levels': not just the individual, *or* the group, *or* the organization, *or* the organizational environment, but all of them. Working within one theoretical framework means all information can be cross-referred at all these levels, as discussed in Chapter 3 (pp. 29–38).

These levels are sometimes categorized as the micro-level (individual to group), meso-level (the whole organization) and the macro-level (the organization's external environment): by addressing all of these together, in other words, one would be adopting a metasystemic approach (Gagnon & Cornelius, 2000; Cornelius, 2002; Cornelius & Gagnon, 2004; Rattue & Cornelius, 2002). Sen and Nussbaum argue that as all of these levels are inextricably linked, it would be inappropriate to pick and choose what levels to pay attention to. Processes, systems, structures and events are interconnected, and attention to one level may lead to a lack of attention or indeed, resultant difficulties in another.

Non-decisions

Non-decisions are certain social choices, issues or aspects that, although present, remain largely hidden and, therefore, are never considered (Bachrach & Baratz, 1970). Often related examples include pollution control, parental child sexual abuse or universal suffrage: these issues have remained largely unconsidered for centuries. Non-decisions are present in all social groups, and work organizations are no exceptions, and they are likely to exist 'below the surface' of workplace inequality issues.

The challenge for practitioners is to find ways of unearthing such non-decisions. An important first step is to explore the characteristics of what knowledge is available and how it is captured and shared; in other words, its knowledge structure (see Chapter 3 on knowledge management, pp. 32–33).

What do we 'Know'?

Frank Blackler (1995) has developed a typology of knowledge that captures the array of domains of knowing that operate within an organization; it has been drawn from a range of scientific and social science traditions.

- *Embrained Knowledge.* This depends upon conceptual skills and cognitive ability—Blackler argues that most models of organizational learning are based on this view of knowing.
- *Embodied Knowledge.* This is more action oriented and depends on physical presence, sentient and sensory information, physical cues and gestures.
- *Encultured Knowledge.* This is concerned with achieving shared understandings— these depend heavily on language, are socially constructed and open to negotiation.
- *Embedded Knowledge.* This lies in systematic routines. For example, economic behaviour relates to social and institutional arrangements, and is concerned with the significance of relationships and material resources, such as between technologies, roles, formal procedures and emergent routines.
- *Encoded Knowledge.* This is encoded in books, manuals, codes of practice and communication.

The kind of inequality knowledge captured by many of the organizations in the Runnymede Trust study was embedded and encoded: the above-the-surface knowledge that is more easily measured. The full Blackler typology would suggest that there are many gaps in knowing. Further, Blackler asserts that knowing is mediated, situated, provisional, pragmatic and contested—in other words, dynamic and changing.

Understanding the Characteristics of Transition

In practice, understanding why large-scale change succeeds or fails can be difficult, as there are a number of factors that might potentially interact and lead to the resultant outcomes.

Many organizations have sought to avoid a piecemeal approach through the development of coherent, strategic management. One of the most eminent researchers, Henry Mintzberg (1994), has argued strongly over the years that many accounts of strategic change are often unrepresentative of what actually happens in practice. Mintzberg suggests that the 'ideals' that writers create are too highly structured and overly rational: sanitized accounts of the messiness that really takes place. Such models of deliberate strategies do not reflect the emergent reality of what happens and crucially, such deliberate approaches fail to capture discontinuities that may signal important shifts away from current situations. For Mintzberg, the process of strategy is one of crafting, that reflects the 'below the surface' thinking in his ideas.

> The concept of strategy, as opposed to a planning one, focuses not so much on thinking and reason as on involvement, a feeling of intimacy and harmony with the materials at hand, developed through long experience and commitment. Strategies can form as well as be formulated, and companies can benefit from allowing their strategies to develop gradually through their action and experiences. Emerging strategy fosters learning as the strategy develops; purely deliberate strategy precludes learning once it has been formulated. Managers focusing on strategy need to consider a number of factors ... It is crucial to detect emerging patterns and help them take shape; the manager should know when to change and when to continue. (Mintzberg, 1987, p. 66)

DIFFICULTIES IN THE EVALUATION OF CHANGE

It is not only the common prescriptions for change that fail to get below the surface; this also often applies to the evaluation of change. Take the example of the use of training programmes as a means of facilitating change. One of the most frequently used modes of assessment is the pre-test–post-test format. Put simply, the interventionist assesses what has changed as a result of the training. What is usually being measured with such tests is incremental change in what is assumed to be a stable domain, with constant intervals between measurement points. The change associated with this stable domain is referred to as *alpha change*.

Although such assessment may be sufficient for knowing whether trainees have learned to programme a video recorder, it is woefully inadequate for assessing most forms of attitude and behaviour training-facilitated change. Golnaz Sadri and Peggy Snyder (1995)[1] illustrate this with the example of a participant on a teller training course to improve customer sales, as part of an organization's strategic push to become more marketing- and customer-led. Before the training course, the participant is asked to rate what he thinks is his degree of assertiveness, measured on a scale of '0' for no assertiveness skills to '9' for expert assertiveness skills. He rates himself as '6'.

During the one-week training session, our participant is able to observe others in role-play sessions being more assertive than he is. As a result, he changes his view on what the points on the scale now mean: the scale has now been 'stretched' to take into account all that the participant has observed. Although he did not think

---

[1] See also Vanderberg and Self's work (1993) on changing commitments to organizations by new entrants.

of himself as very assertive before the training, he is clear that he is reasonably assertive now. But after the training, he still rates himself as '6'.

The interventionist might wrongly assume that the training has been ineffective. However, the yardstick by which our participant now measures himself has a new calibration, in other words, *beta change* has taken place, but this is not the change that our trainer is measuring: pre-test–post-test methods commonly measure alpha change only.

There are further subtleties. Imagine that the training also involved the use of video recording of our participant in role-playing exercises, which he can review and discuss. On reflection, what he had thought before the training was assertive behaviour is, in fact, aggression. Our participant redefines and reconceptualizes the construct of assertiveness, as not about aggression. In other words, a *gamma change* has taken place. The post-test score is still a '6'.

Change 'Burnout'

Robert Golembiewski (1986, 1995, 1997), the originator of the terms alpha, beta and gamma change, suggests that, in practice, the three are interlinked. An academic who specializes in organizational change, argues that accessing these below-the-surface beta and gamma changes bedevils not only training interventions but also many types of person-centred change from the micro- to the meta-systemic. Importantly, he argues that a consequence of seeing change at the alpha level only, while failing to capture beta and gamma changes, is 'change burnout'. That can result in a feeling of a lack of personal accomplishment and personal exhaustion for the interventionist, and depersonalization and pessimism for the target individual or groups of the intervention itself.

Kelly and Transition

Golembiewski (1986) has suggested that one of the challenges is evaluating below-the-surface beta and gamma changes, and that a potentially useful method might be the repertory grid (see Chapter 6, for a discussion of repertory grids). The repertory grid by the nature of its design, if skilfully used, is able to capture the changes in superordinate construing that by implication are at the heart of beta and gamma change. For example, a 'good' grid always contains an 'ideal' element, so that any beta or gamma change in the view of what it is to be assertive may be reflected in change in the character, and thus the construing, around the 'ideal'.

However, change and transition were key concerns to Kelly some 50 years before Golembiewski's work. Indeed, the final chapter in his Volume 1 is called 'Dimensions of transition'. The challenge of coping with transition is stated by Kelly in these words:

> Constructs enable a person to hear recurrent themes in the onrushing sound and fury of life. They remain relatively serene and secure while the events above which they rise rumble and churn in continuous turmoil. Yet constructs themselves undergo change. And it is in the transitions from theme to theme that most of life's puzzling problems arise.

... If a person is to embrace the new in his organized system, he needs to have superordinate constructs which are permeable—that is, which admit new elements. Without such permeable superordinate constructs he is limited to a more or less footless shuffling of his old ideas.' (Kelly, 1955/1991, p. 486/Vol. 1, p. 359)

Charting New Routes

From a Kellyian point of view, although interventions have the potential to 'loosen up' construing, there is also the real likelihood of large amounts of energy—on the part of the interventionist, but particularly individuals or target groups—being expended but with little or no impact. The result is running on the spot with no real movement forward: fundamentally, nothing really changes. Kelly also relates how specific processes either help or hinder transition. Diagnosis is clearly important. Kelly devotes a whole chapter to this and argues that:

> a diagnosis system, like a scientific theory, should be fertile as well as neat. . . . A good diagnostic system is a set of coordinate axes with respect to which it is possible to plot behaviour. It makes a great deal of difference, however, whether the axes are designed to catch our fellow men like a fly in a spider's web or are conceived as a series of streets and highways along which he can be encouraged to move in an orderly fashion. . . . The coordinate axes we set up should represent many different lines of movement which are open to him and not a labyrinth of one-way passages from which he can never escape.
> (Kelly, 1955/1991, p. 453/Vol. 1, pp. 335–336)

Therefore challenge for the organizational interventionist using a personal construct psychology approach is to map out the coordinate axes, the coordinates for the meta-system; that is a sufficient mirror of the way in which change is (or is not) occurring. It needs also to capture the interaction between 'hard' and 'soft' factors that are helping or hindering transition.

GETTING STUCK OR GETTING MOVING: CASE EXAMPLES OF TRANSITIONS

The three case examples presented here are illustrative of how workplace inequality may be tackled. The studies have been compiled over different time frames, from a minimum of three years to a maximum of five. In two of the organizations, the work is action research-based, and ongoing. The information that has been used to develop the cases includes interviews, questionnaires, jokes, gossip, repertory grid analysis, observation, action research and the analysis of organizational documents and public documents such as government reports and annual reports. All of these were data mined for constructs and structure.

The case illustrations are based on three large organizations: two United Kingdom police constabularies (A) and (C) and one private telecommunications company (B), all of which have been addressing the issue of workplace inequality. Clearly, the challenges and context of the three organizations are different. The interest here, however, is in how they went about things.

CASE SUMMARIES

Organization A: Stuck in the Past

Organization A has been addressing inequality and discrimination issues for over 20 years. Some progress has been made, but in spite of a number of interventions, major difficulties persist. Although the rhetoric changes, the degree of movement, and social change, remains small. The main impetus for change has typically come from headquarters and central government, and the local divisions of the organization are very much evaluated against 'criteria' and 'rules' set by the former. There have been some strong-willed change champions, but in spite of the rhetoric of change, the reality of creating a critical mass and a 'shared view' has proved elusive. The views of those 'on the ground' are rarely sought explicitly or officially, but there is an awareness of their likely objections to equality action around, for example, reduced opportunities and unfair advantages to 'others'. There is limited likelihood of projecting 'self into the future', seen by Kelly as an important pre-condition for reconstruction. The organization's leadership and key personnel are *'transition aspirant'*, a message not engaged with by many on the ground, and step change has not been achieved.

Broadly speaking, change is at the edges but not at the centre. It remains within the current and long-established paradigm. There is superficial change but the same structure.

This enables small improvements, but no step change in thinking or action. Drawing from Kelly's dimensions of transition, the organization has 'got stuck' through engagement primarily with *peripheral constructs, tightening of superordinate constructs*, and increasing levels of Kellyian *hostility* and *aggression*. Well-worn attitudes towards dealing with the public and minority groups in particular that have failed in the past, and will fail in the future, are clung to tenaciously. The talk in the canteen is about the good work that is done, and any attempts that are made to change this is just about undermining officers who only want to do their job in the way that they 'know' works best: the benefits of change that may accrue are just not seen or acknowledged. So, superordinate constructions are not rigorously challenged or subject to review and thus, reconstruction. The call for changes on the front line are just impositions from their superiors (who have forgotten what it is like at the sharp end) or the government (pen pushers who have no idea). These are *other people's* 'experiments' and 'laboratories', not theirs. So, in the face of such strong and resilient resistance to change, the end result of a wave of initiatives is tinkering at the edges of the real problem. Construing relating to addressing equality remains at a low level of cognitive awareness. Organization A is stuck, strongly resisting change, caught in a Kellyian 'more or less footless shuffling of old ideas'.

Organization B: Steady Progress

Organization B has systematically attempted to get to grips with equality issues over a period of about 18 years. Its sophistication in terms of strategic design and the operational detail is far greater than for either Organization A or C. Clear vision and leadership at the top provided the initial impetus, but there were pushes forward on a number of fronts. A great deal of attention was paid to unearthing the 'below the surface' views, as well as putting into place a range of more 'equality friendly' policies and practices. The new paradigm sought was to some extent 'designed' but getting there has been by a process of 'strategic crafting' in order to continually improve the sophistication of outlook and develop on the basis of new insights and challenges. The transition has been made, but a process of continuous development towards new transitions continues.

Organization B has moved slowly but surely towards a new way of thinking, acting and feeling regarding inequality, and has arrived at and elaborated a new paradigm. Irrespective of the level of seniority or role, people are able to understand what they are striving towards and what needs to change to get there. In Kellyian terms, there are commonly held values about inequality issues: the *'collective self'* is present in visions of the future (*CPC Cycle* involving circumspection, pre-emption and control) and the development of new ideas (*Creativity Cycle*), both key cycles in reconstruing. There is sufficient flexibility for a range of approaches in addressing inequality to be incorporated, but values, superordinate constructs, enable people to make better, more consistent judgements about what might or might not work. Risk taking is seen as legitimate and there are what Kelly calls 'learning laboratories' within which experimentation can take place, such as new personnel procedures, decision-making structures, volunteer networks and initiatives with local communities. This enables the whole organization to move forward in a coherent, but not too rigid, manner. Organization B has found ways of ensuring that it refreshes its views of workplace equality, and is less susceptible to 'getting stuck'. The mechanism is largely a systematic, continuous improvement approach. There is new structure, and different construing.

Organization C: Rapid Movement

Organization C has made a concerted effort to 'step up a gear' from the equality approaches that it had, until six years ago, decided were sufficient. It should be noted that it is in the same line of business as Organization A—it is a police force—but has managed to find a route forward in a sector where making any inroads is often difficult. The impetus for change has been largely internal, and 'root and branch' changes in structure, policy and practice have been undertaken. Also, attention has been paid to revising ethical policy and core values. Senior managers created a clear vision and purpose, but the views of those 'on the ground' are critical influences on both the vision and operational issues. The coordination of effort has been substantial, and what has changed in particular is the attitude towards *risk* in relation to dealing with these issues. The organization has become more risk-tolerant in relation to inequality issues, which is important given the speed with which the organization is progressing and the likelihood of making mistakes.

The organization is driven by the start-up momentum, and is aiming to get as many quick wins in place as quickly as possible. The transition has been rapid. Although the organization has only a partial picture of the future possibilities, it is reflective enough to recognize what it has left behind and what continues to limit its advancement towards its desired future. Enhancing knowledge and learning through training, personnel practices and dialogue and partnerships within the organization and with the community is regarded as core to the change process. Organization C moved with extraordinary speed, on a 'fast track', towards a new paradigm. The necessary catalysts (radical thinking, management of fear of failure, new leadership) were, in part, happened upon by chance but were sufficient to draw the organization's attention to the limitations of its current *modus operandi*. Important changes regarding working practice and human resource policy and practices created shifts towards new construing.

Although the detail of the new paradigm is not as fully formed or understood as for Organization B (much of the construing is covert), it is *sufficient* to inform new ways of thinking, doing and feeling. The new paradigm acts as a rough template for placing clear blue water between the 'new' view and the old one: for projection into a different future. Aspects of the validation of the 'new' paradigm are more felt than reasoned, and the language with which to express the difference is emerging slowly. Changes appear to have taken place to *comprehensive constructs*, and construction shifts that involve CPC and Creativity Cycles and crucially, the CPC Cycle is foreshortened by not circumspecting all the options: which Kelly referred to as *impulsivity*. The process of change has been one of a desire to get below the surface rapidly and an emergent organizational environment that enables fast and continuous learning. New structure and new construing has occurred, but very quickly indeed.

CONCLUSIONS

New patterns and new paradigms are important outcomes of a step change, but the character of the transition between states also merits scrutiny, as it reveals something about the nature and detail of the reconstruction processes and therefore, why and how, for example, new patterns become established. However, it also allows for an assessment of whether an organization is merely at the stage of being 'transition aspirant', irrespective of the amount of time and effort poured into trying to create the shift.

Organizations B and C have both created the step change into new ways of seeing the world, a new paradigm, while A remains stuck in the groove of a long-established paradigm, and in the Kellyian 'labyrinth of one-way passages from which (they) can never escape'. Kelly's constructs of diagnosis and transition are vital parts of the armoury for those choosing to work with personal construct theory in organizations. The case illustrations highlight the power of the theory. Importantly, it is possible to demonstrate that by fitting personal construct theory into a more meta-systemic configuration than it usually is, it still retains the power to reveal things about change in difficult arenas such as workplace inequality that help us to understand success and failure in new ways.

CHAPTER 21

Clarifying Corporate Values: A Case Study

Sean Brophy
Dublin, Ireland

> Science is a system of anticipation: so are values.
> (Kelly, 1959b, p. 6)

The subject of this case study was founded in the first decade of the twentieth century and operated as a family firm committed to a participative management style for 80 years. The third generation of the family decided to float part of the equity of the firm to provide capital for expansion and to bring in professional managers to operate the company. Tension between staff and management and within the Board of Directors soon revealed themselves. These tensions were the inevitable accompaniment of what Chandler (1977) calls the transition from 'family' or 'entrepreneurial capitalism' to 'managerial capitalism' wherein a shift in values takes place and the needs of the family gradually yield to the overarching need to provide an attractive return to capital.

A values task force was established by the Board and in conjunction with the shareholders' values and ethics committee, recommended the use of a personal construct psychology facilitator to clarify the shared values of Board, Management and Staff.

THE PROCESS

After an initial briefing, the facilitator proposed the following process. The objective of the facilitator was to maximize the scope for involvement of important constituencies within the organization in working through the implications of the changed context in which they found themselves and in the search for an agreed set of values to guide them in the future.

(a) Workshops with various staff groups, the senior management and Board members to elicit their values and their assessment of the company's adherence to them.

The Essential Practitioner's Handbook of Personal Construct Psychology. Edited by F. Fransella.
© 2005 John Wiley & Sons, Ltd.

(b) A search for commonality across the groups.
(c) The drafting of a Values' Statement, and a communications' programme to establish the response to it by the three core groups, Staff, Management and Directors.

THE WORKSHOPS

At each workshop the facilitator first sought the groups' understanding of what they meant by 'values'. The responses invariably included words like 'honesty', 'trust', 'doing the right thing' and so on. The facilitator then gave a short introduction to personal construct theory with the emphasis on the person as scientist. Values were described as wagers on the future. George Kelly contrasted the scientists' testing of the truth with that of the moralist and concluded that the difference lay in the time lapse between prediction and ultimate verification. He goes on:

> Values differ from other forms of belief mainly in the dimension of time lapse, the lapse between anticipation and realisation. Science looks for verification to appear as soon as possible; in the cases of values one waits. The scientist is prepared to change his anticipation in the light of tomorrow's outcomes. But values are likely to get changed only when people forget what they were wagering on. While no outcomes ever quite provides a final verification of the anticipations laid for it, we are placed in the position of having to accept in the case of values, conclusions which are much further in advance of their ultimate evidence.'
>
> (Kelly, 1959b, p. 6)

So, values are like a wager. The facilitator moved to get each group to reveal the contexts in which these 'wagers' took place. The firm has been described as an 'open system' (Beckhard & Harris, 1977, p. 58). From this perspective the firm is viewed as having a set of stakeholders, the support of each one being necessary for the firm's survival.

Initially, the stakeholders were identified by the group and usually included the following: customers, suppliers, staff, shareholders, local community, environment and world community.

Each group was asked, 'What must the company do to ensure the long-term support of this particular stakeholder?' They were effectively being asked what they were wagering on, that is, what 'value' they held in relation to this element. The answer provided the preferred pole of a construct. Another question elicited the opposite of this statement. In this way, a number of constructs (or values) were revealed. The facilitator tested the understanding of the group by asking 'Why?' questions to ladder these constructs up to a superordinate to do with *survival* as opposed to *out of business*. Also, he asked 'How?' questions to pyramid downwards to search for examples of particular values in practice (see Chapter 4, pp. 48–54).

When the group had agreed the wording of about 12 values the facilitator listed them and invited the group to write them onto a repertory grid form. The grid in Figure 21.1 is an example of the values of one employee group's values (Task Force). Each group was then asked to rate this grid on a seven-point scale on three elements: (a) 'The company now', (b) 'The minimum standard tolerable' and (c) 'The company as I expect it to be in five years' time'.

Pole	Scale							Contrast	Rank
	1	2	3	4	5	6	7		
1. Respond to the needs of our Customers and Suppliers								Ignoring the needs of our Customers and Suppliers	2
2. Treat people with dignity								Don't recognize their value as a person	1
3. Encourage personal growth								Discourage growth, stagnant	8
4. Treat people fairly								Exploit people for personal gain	3
5. Pay people = or > what could earn elsewhere								Pay people as little as possible and still keep them	9
6. Caring about providing a person's ability to have a job								Not caring	5
7. Holistic approach to meeting employees' work-related needs								Ignores relevant work-related needs	10
8. Attract and give a fair return to investors who share our values								Give as little as have to, to whoever	7
9. Provide an honest flow of good information								Keep them in the dark	5
10. Be a good corporate citizen in the communities in which we operate								Indifferent to the communities and their environment	11
11. Endow future generations with an understanding of the best knowledge we have								Not thinking about them	12
12. Commit to grow and adapt								Stay the way we are	4

Key: ↓ = Average scores
●– – – –● = Range of scores for 'My company now'
◆———◆ = Range of scores for 'The minimum standard'
◄·············► = Range of scores for 'How I expect my company to be in 5 years' time'

Figure 21.1 Sample repertory grid rated by one employee group

The individual ratings were pooled on to three overhead transparencies and the aggregate raw data displayed for the group to appraise and react to. These ratings are represented in the grid as a range of ratings and the average for the group. Finally, to check the relative importance of the constructs, the group was asked to complete a Hinkle's Resistance to Change Grid (Hinkle, 1965). The pooled results were shown as a ranking on the right-hand side of the grid (see Chapter 9, pp. 105–106).

The data yielded a comprehensive picture of the group's construing of the three elements. Comments below are confined to the three most important and three least important constructs in the grid.

The most important construct for this group, No. 2, was *Treat people with dignity*. Here the group saw the company as being quite good on average, with some persons demurring from this viewpoint. Minimum standards were not being adhered to and the situation, on average, was seen as likely to remain the same in five years' time, though some individuals saw it deteriorating.

On the second most important construct, No. 1, the company was seen, moderately, to *Respond to the needs of our customers and suppliers*, though not quite as well as it should. The situation was expected to improve slightly over five years.

The third most important construct, No. 4, *Treat people fairly*, was rated down, indicating some personal anguish. Minimum standards were not being adhered to, though the situation was expected to improve somewhat over five years, but not up to minimum standards.

All told, the data in the grid reveals a picture of some anxiety in the sense that people could not anticipate reaching minimum standards on some important constructs over the next five years. Further, they displayed fear in the sense that their cherished order of priority was going to have to give way to a greater emphasis by management on the right of investors to a fair return, via short-term dividends (construct 8) over the staff's need to have a commitment to develop the company over the long term (construct 12). For people who had worked under a paternalistic regime, characteristic of family capitalism, where dividends are often reinvested in a firm, the transition was mildly threatening. The tension in the values is apparent when we compare the employees' ranking of stakeholders with those of the management team as set out in Table 21.1.

Here we see that there is agreement on the core constructs to do with treating people with dignity (construct 2) and in responding to the needs of customers and suppliers (construct 1). Where the groups parted company, it is interesting that the managers were more concerned with paying people the same as or more than they could get elsewhere than the employees (construct 5). It was as if the employees' security needs (construct 5) were deemed to be subordinate to their needs for growth and a meaningful quality of work life (construct 3). The managers gave joint fourth ranking to the notion of treating people fairly, and the creation of opportu-

Table 21.1 Employees' ranking of importance of constructs compared with that of managers

No.	Stakeholder expectation	Employees' ranking	Managers' ranking
2.	Treat people with dignity	1	1
1.	Respond to the needs of customers/suppliers	2	2
4.	Treat people fairly	3	4
12.	Committed to grow and adapt	4	8
9.	Provide an honest flow of good information	5	11
6.	Caring about a person's ability to have a job	6	4
8.	Attract and give a fair return to investors	7	4
3.	Encourage personal growth	8	7
5.	Staff (fair pay)	9	3
7.	Staff (work related needs)	10	10
10.	Be a good corporate citizen	11	12
11.	Endow future generations	12	9

nities for staff to have a job with a fair return to shareholders. The staff had ranked the shareholders (construct 8) lower down, at 7th place. Herein lay the point of greatest tension with the managers.

A simple reading of the data suggested that the managers were trading off the involvement of staff as innovators and participants in the life of the firm to focus on a better return for shareholders. They were of a mind to satisfy the staff with fair pay and an ethos where a person's dignity was respected. The clash of values was around the employees' freedom to participate in the running of the firm, a tradition that had been built up over decades. Freedom to participate depended on communication, providing an honest flow of good information (construct 9), which was ranked 5th by the employees but ranked 11th by the management. However, the average rating by this staff group on this construct indicated very little change from a moderately good position being anticipated over the next five years.

At each workshop with a particular group, the results of preceding groups were shared to facilitate understanding between groups, culminating in a session with the Board of Directors six months after the commencement of the process. The Board committed itself to reiterating the values of the enterprise in three ways:

1. An elucidation of the basic assumptions underpinning the values.
2. A statement of the values themselves.
3. A formula by which the values would be embedded in the enterprise.

DRAFTING THE CORPORATION'S CODES

The facilitator and the Board Sub-Committee, together with the Human Resources Director, collaborated to draft the following basic premises on which the values were based.

The Values of the Corporation

Most would agree that the value dimension of ethics and morality is an essential characteristic of human existence. Since moral issues transcend economic issues, the starting point for our values is the basic moral premise of respect for the dignity and worth of the human person as an end, and not as a means. We ought to deal with each person in a truthful, honest and just way.

Our greatest dependence is upon our customers. The basic economic rationale for our business is to create value through serving their needs.

Our greatest resource is our employees who create the wealth within our enterprise. Their greatness stems from their strength of character, self-esteem and genius.

We are responsible to the communities in which we work and operate. The decisions we make should be reached in a context that allows the common good to be discovered.

We are responsible to future generations to be wise and careful stewards of their heritage and to provide an endowment of shared values carefully fostered and adapted as our enterprise evolves.

Our final responsibility is towards our investors as trustees of their assets. We ought to make fair profits. We ought to be adaptable, to experiment with new ideas, carry out research, engage in innovative programmes and pay for our mistakes. We ought to invest wisely to grow our enterprise in a planned and orderly way. We ought to create reserves for adverse times. We ought to provide our investors with necessary information to help them to understand and be involved with the enterprise and share in our corporate pride. When we operate according to these values our investors ought to realize a fair return on their investment with security.

The purpose of a business enterprise is to meet society's human and material needs by providing goods and services as efficiently as possible. All business is concerned with human relationships, not only with those who work in the enterprise but also those who provide the financial resources, those who buy its products and services and the wider public whose lives are affected by the business activity.

In a business enterprise the values in use represent the application of knowledge in perspective, i.e. knowledge that these values will lead to a fulfilment of the organization's purpose in the long run. Values therefore cannot be validated immediately, one has to accept conclusions in advance of their ultimate evidence. Immediately this creates the problem of individual world views and competing predictions of what can ensue from which value. It is essential therefore, that any statement of values is rooted in a key assumption concerning the nature of human nature as outlined in the opening paragraph of the Draft Code. This will act as an anchor to restrain competing interpretations of the Corporation's values from diverging too far.

Having underpinned the values with a statement of fundamental assumptions, the Values Task Force, with the facilitator and Human Resources Director, went on to draft the following Values Statement entitled 'The Corporation's Commitment to Value'.

The Corporation's Commitment to Value

We the employees and the shareholders believe that the inherent dignity and worth of the individual are the bedrock of the Corporation's commitment to values. All the other values we cherish flow from and are dependent on this belief.

We freely choose to form partnerships with other stakeholders in mutual pursuit of our common good. Our relationships as stakeholders in the Corporation have significantly deeper meaning than any purely financial transaction.

Our greatest resource is our employees. We place a high value on the continuing development of our participative management system. We expect competent leadership at all levels to foster employee strengths. We are committed to using authority in an affirming way, as a service to those being led and to modelling our values in action. We commit ourselves to creating trust and openness of communication in an ethical workplace. We commit ourselves to providing the Corporation's employees with fair compensation, with job security and with a physically safe environment.

We recognize the reality and truth of each unique person. The well-being of the corporation and our commitment to the individual both require that each employee, and every stakeholder, have the opportunity to grow and to develop our human capabilities within our relationship to the Corporation. We hold ourselves as individuals, accountable for our values and our actions.

We have a responsibility to be stewards of our resources, the physical environment, our immediate and our global communities, as well as our families. We are committed to dealing ethically and honestly with our stakeholders and with the larger community.

We have both financial and ethical responsibilities to our investors as trustees of their assets and as guardians of these shared values. We are committed to giving them both a fair return on investment and the necessary information to help them understand our goals and share our corporate pride.

We are responsible to future generations of stakeholders. We will provide a legacy of shared values that we carefully foster and adapt as our enterprise evolves, and an inheritance of a viable and profitable Corporation.

We are, therefore, committed to making decisions with a long-term perspective. We commit to research products and processes, to adapt to the changing markets and world, to experiment with new ideas in the social structure and management system of the Corporation, to create reserves to carry us during adverse economic times or the necessary failures of risk-taking. We commit ourselves as a partnership of stakeholders, customer, employees, investors, suppliers, communities, to the planned growth which marks a living and successful system.

FINALIZING THE DRAFT CODE OF VALUES AND EMBEDDING THEM IN USE

The facilitator was satisfied that the Draft Code, summarized above, represented a true synthesis of the views of the people who attended the various workshops. It was desirable that those participants had an opportunity to give the Values Task Force their observations on the Draft Code before it was finalised with the management team and Board. A process of consultation was designed and implemented by the Values Task Force members themselves.

The Corporation's Employees Council also reviewed the draft code of values. In the event not much modification was required to the code itself. Some questions regarding the sequence of values arose. A few people found the prospect of living up to these values a little daunting and sought a dilution of the language. The facilitator advised the Task Force to resist these attempts and encourage those concerned to rise to the challenge and experience personal growth in the process.

IMPLEMENTING AND SUSTAINING THE CODE OF VALUES IN PRACTICE

Values are an integral part of the culture of the Corporation. Culture basically serves two purposes for an organization, to integrate people, that is, to cooperate, to be productive, to grow as individuals, and help them to adapt to the world outsides—that is, to respond to customers and so forth. Thus, these values represented the organization's knowledge, or prediction, that their use will serve these two fundamental purposes. To do this, the values had to be reflected in the norms of behaviour and sustained by the customs, practices and institutions within the firm. New people joining the firm (recruits or because of acquisitions) would have to be socialized into adopting these values through appropriate induction, behaviour modelling and reinforcement.

In the final analysis, organizations protect the integrity of their culture by disengaging people who flagrantly violate their values. Thus, the process of implementing values had to be eclectic and ongoing. A useful way to address this issue was to consider a number of 'levers' for applying pressure to have the values used. Those could include, *inter alia:*

1. ***Induction and orientation process***
   — A written history of the firm, an explanation of the Values Statement, and a code of conduct based on the values provided to all new employees.
2. ***Personnel policies***
   The following have criteria related to the values:
   — Promotion, appraisal, equity, grievance process, benefits.
3. ***Reinforcement***
   — Creation of 'Heroes', through history, anecdotes, stories, newsletters, awards, rites, ceremonies, competitions.
   — Use of slogans, symbols, language in speeches, promotional material directed at various interest groups, official reports.
4. ***Technology/structure***
   — Work designed to maximize the scope for self-determination.
   — Appropriate decentralization.
5. ***Management style***
   — Behaviour modelling of the values through visible observance by management of the code of conduct appended to the values statement, especially when responding to critical incidents like a breach of values in a case where a staff member is being disciplined or an issue of job redundancy.
6. ***Training***
   — Values awareness training to refresh and renew the living out of the values.
   — Self-development to promote personal growth.
   — Training in personal construing of self and others to facilitate mutual respect and understanding.
   — Management effectiveness training, based on practices derived from values.
   — Quality management training to affirm the company's commitment to value.
7. ***Information and decision processes***
   — Information used to foster a sense of participation and inclusion in the running of the company.
   — Quality and Customer Service Information Systems.
   — Application of values during strategic planning and goal-setting processes.
8. ***Values audit***
   — Benchmark study of perceptions of values in use.
   — Regular, e.g. annual/biennial, audit to evaluate change occurrence or required.

These initiatives spanned a range of norms within the firm, yet, creative people inside the organization could add to them. Culture is merely a root metaphor for the organization itself. Values are the deepest discussible aspect of culture, therefore, every aspect of the organization is ultimately connectable to its values and can be used for initiatives to promote their use.

'MEANING' FROM VALUES STATEMENT

The test of a Values Statement is to ask the question 'Why?' one or more times after each value. The answers from individuals should converge rapidly onto the fundamental superordinate assumptions regarding the nature of human beings, of reality and truth, of morality and of cooperative pursuit of the common good. Similarly, the question 'How?' after each value should reveal the many possibilities for action which reflect the reality of the various individuals who subscribe to them (see pyramiding in Chapter 4, p. 54 in this volume). This process of questioning reveals the Values Statement as a dynamic, living document at once rooted in firm assumptions and also capable of being construed, manifest (and monitored) in explicit language, behaviour and institutions.

OUTCOME

The facilitator reframed his role in the process from being catalyst, leaving the internal Values Task Force to complete the draft Values Statement. It was approved by the Board of Directors three months later. Finally, the Values Statement was shared with all employees in small groups where discussion on its working out was encouraged. The dilemmas around participation and providing a fair shareholder return were discussed and people were helped to come to terms with new realities.

The collective struggle to create a Values Statement was in itself an indication of the authenticity of these values. With the sharing with staff of the Board approved statement, 'The Corporation's Commitment to Value', this chapter was closed and the Corporation moved into the next phase, living the values and monitoring progress.

Personal construct psychology was useful as a theoretical framework in this intervention in several ways. First, its use engendered a great empathy between the facilitator and the various groups he interacted with. That had the effect of legitimizing and engendering trust in the authenticity of the process and confidence in the direction that the facilitator was charting for the organization. Further, the hierarchical character of construing systems inherent in personal construct theory made it easy to transfer this concept to the elucidation and embedding of values at the three levels of the organization's culture, assumptions, values and code of conduct, as set out in Schein (1985).

Where Might Personal Construct Psychology Be Going Now?

CHAPTER 22

Personal Construct Psychotherapy and the Constructivist Horizon

Robert A. Neimeyer
University of Memphis, USA

and

Scott A. Baldwin
University of Memphis, USA

> Personal construct psychotherapy is a way of getting on with the human enterprise.
>
> (Kelly, 1969i, p. 221)

What is personal construct therapy, and how has it evolved across time? As if to set the stage for an answer to this question, Kelly continues the above quotation as follows:

> (psychotherapy) may embody and mobilize all of the techniques . . . that man has yet devised. Certainly there is no one psychotherapeutic technique and no one kind of interpersonal compatibility between psychotherapy and client. . . . Hence one may find a personal construct psychotherapist employing a huge variety of procedures—not helter skelter, but always as part of a plan for helping himself and his client get on with the job of human exploration and checking out the appropriateness of the constructions they have devised for placing upon the world around them. (1969i, pp. 221–222)

Considered closely, that original definition of psychotherapy emphasizes several features that are relevant to the evolution of personal construct therapy over the half-century of its development. Kelly viewed his therapy as simply an accelerated form of personal development; it has more to do with facilitating the essentially human 'effort after meaning' and experimenting with new social actions than with an arcane set of procedures for diagnosing and curing 'psychopathology'. Such therapy is technically eclectic, evolving to embrace all manner of techniques and procedures,

The Essential *Practitioner's Handbook of Personal Construct Psychology.* Edited by F. Fransella.
© 2005 John Wiley & Sons, Ltd.

whose variety is limited only by the imaginations of the therapist and client—and perhaps implicitly, by the historical and cultural framework that shapes and constrains their efforts. Despite this methodological openness, personal construct therapy maintains a certain level of conceptual consistency, carefully coordinating its change strategies in the light of a responsive reading of the client's unique efforts to engage life constructively.

This chapter discusses some of the ways in which contemporary personal construct therapists have extended Kelly's ideas to address a broader range of problems and generate an expanding repertory of interventions, while still exemplifying a recognizable therapeutic stance. We will therefore begin by considering the intellectual *zeitgeist* that has informed many of the developments in personal construct therapy, and note the major themes that define the stance of the therapist, before reviewing a representative sampling of recent developments in this clinical perspective.

THE CONSTRUCTIVIST HORIZON

In many respects, Kelly's vision of psychotherapy, although iconoclastic in the 1950s, proved to be a prophetic preface to the psychology of the next millennium. Sharpening existential themes in psychology that emphasized human agency and choice, Kelly nonetheless embedded the individual in a social world, emphasizing the identity-defining nature of *core roles* that the person constructs with reference to others. To a far greater extent than most psychologists of his day, Kelly offered an image of persons as authors of their own biographies, but in a way that acknowledged their anchoring in the social realm.

As psychotherapy grew beyond the psychoanalytic and behavioural orthodoxies that dominated the field in mid-century, other theorists began to elaborate similar constructivist ideas, sometimes consciously borrowing from Kelly, and sometimes appropriating these concepts from broader discourses. The result, by the early 1990s, was a loose confederation of constructivist psychotherapies joined by their resistance to more authoritative, objectivistic approaches that emphasized the therapist's power, and that viewed intervention as improving the client's 'reality contact' through challenging clients' 'irrational thinking' and training them in approved 'social skills' (Neimeyer, 1995). Instead, constructivist therapists focused on the way in which clients construct a model of self and world in the context of close attachment relationships (Guidano, 1991), articulate and symbolize their own internal complexity in experiential therapy (Greenberg et al., 1993), and maintain 'symptoms' that are coherent with their unconscious 'emotional truths' about life (Ecker & Hulley, 1996). Meanwhile, family therapy was being revolutionized by a wave of social constructionism, which focused on how problems are created and dispelled in the way they are formulated in language (Efran et al., 1990; see also Procter in Chapter 17.2, pp. 177–180). The result was a broad coalition of approaches sharing a 'family resemblance' with personal construct therapy, while moving the field in new directions (Neimeyer & Bridges, 2003; Neimeyer & Mahoney, 1995; Neimeyer & Raskin, 2000). (See also Chiari & Nuzzo, 2003, on constructivism and constructionism, pp. 41–50.)

THE NARRATIVE APPROACH

One of these directions has been the *narrative trend*, the idea that human lives can be viewed as 'stories' that are formulated, told, and enacted on a social stage (Polkinghorne, 1988). In keeping with the postmodern Kellyian view that our identities are constructed rather than simply discovered, narrative theorists address the processes by which people can perform 'preferred' stories of who they are, or alternatively, live lives 'colonized' by a 'dominant narrative' that defines their identity only in terms of problems (White & Epston, 1990). Like the pre-emptive construing that Kelly cautioned could define someone as 'nothing but' a depressive, anorexic, borderline, or some other diagnostic category, dominant narratives can marginalize and obscure the person's resources and positive features.

Accordingly, narrative therapists draw attention to moments that clients resist the call of problem-saturated identities, and instead act in ways that are more self-nurturing and affirming of their relationships to others. Therapy then turns towards building an alternative story of who one is, by anchoring it in 'dependable strengths' the client has exemplified in the past (Forster, 1991), projecting the story into an anticipated future, and recruiting an audience of receptive others who will affirm the positive potentials being enacted in present relationships (Neimeyer, 2000; Neimeyer & Stewart, 2000).

As constructivist, social constructionist and narrative discourses have permeated the helping professions (see Chiari & Nuzzo, 2003, Chapter 4), personal construct theorists have found further inspiration in these trends, using them to extend their own distinctive contributions to clinical conceptualization and intervention. Before reviewing these developments, however, we will address a few remarks to the stance of contemporary personal construct therapists, insofar as it is in the context of the therapeutic relationship that clients are encouraged to articulate, test and revise those constructions on the basis of which they live.

THE STANCE OF THE THERAPIST

Perhaps one of the most unsatisfying aspects of many traditional psychological theories is that they do not provide a way to understand the theorizing of the theorist—most theories lack reflexivity (see Chapter 4, pp. 43–44). Dunnett and Miyaguchi (1993) point out: 'Like young children who forget to include themselves when counting the number of people in a room, psychologists have consistently failed to include themselves as humans to which psychological theories need to also apply' (p. 19). Kelly and subsequent constructivist theorists attempt to address this shortcoming in psychotherapy by providing an account of not only the client's behaviour, but also the therapist's, and stressing that a credulous, unassuming attitude on the part of the therapist is the foundation of any healthy therapeutic relationship. This credulous stance creates an accepting environment, in which clients need not feel defensive about their experience, but instead are free to 'try on' new constructs and meanings without the fear of judgement or rejection. With a clearer understanding of the problem at hand, the client and therapist can work together to develop potential solutions to the problem.

CLINICAL CONCEPTUALIZATIONS

Although personal construct theory has been applied to a vast range of clinical problems (see Winter, 2003, Chapter 19, and Chapter 9, pp. 95–106), we will concentrate on two—substance abuse and grief and loss—that convey some of the breadth and novelty of this clinical perspective.

Substance Abuse

The ways in which reflexivity, a credulous approach, and creativity are manifested in the clinical context can be illustrated by looking at how substance abuse problems are understood within a constructivist framework. According to many substance abuse experts, addiction is a disease. The disease process begins with one drink of alcohol or one dose of heroin in a genetically vulnerable person, whereupon the abuser progressively loses control, and experiences physical addiction, social and occupational problems, medical complications and, in the worst case, death.

In contrast to this traditional framework, constructivist theorists view substance abuse not as the necessary consequence of a disease process, but as a method of constructing or preserving meaning in a social environment (Burrell, 2002). For example, consider the story that Burrell and Jaffe (1999) relate about Steve, a young man struggling with cocaine addiction. Steve stated that his cocaine use was pointless and it led him to waste both time and money. Nevertheless, when viewed from a constructivist point of view, his abuse was not pointless. For example, 'Steve reported that when he wasn't focusing on cocaine, he usually thought about very disturbing and experientially "overwhelming" aspects of his past and current life (divorce, despair about the future, etc.). He felt like he was "living someone else's life" and "lost"' (p. 53). Cocaine became a way for Steve to avoid the feelings of being overwhelmed and lost—wasting money was preferable to facing these existential challenges.

If therapists view substance abuse problems in a constructivist light, a credulous attitude to the client's problem and a creative implementation of interventions is required. Addicts actively create meaning through the use of chemical substances, meaning which is highly personal and often idiosyncratic. Moreover, when problems are deeply ingrained, maintaining them can become a purposeful activity that protects the client's core identity—even if this identity is problematic (Klion & Pfenninger, 1997). Because of the personal and identity-defining nature of the problem, therapists must adopt a credulous attitude to discover its significance to the client. In the case of substance abuse, pat interventions would stifle the exploration of the deep meanings of addiction. Suppose Steve had just been told that he was an addict because he had an addictive disease and protocol interventions had been used. Perhaps Steve would have reduced his cocaine use, but he might never have confronted his existential problems, for they never would have even been considered. His addiction would have forever remained pointless and without meaning. But the creative therapist could, together with the client, create highly personal solutions to the problem. One such intervention is the tendency of narrative therapists to 'externalize' the problem, by regarding cocaine as an intruder into Steve's life, one that beguiles him into regarding the drug as a comforting friend, while insidiously destroying his sense of self and relationships with others. Once the effects of 'cocaine's behaviour' are clearly recognized, they can be resisted, and a less drug-saturated identity can be constructed and socially validated by others (Winslade & Smith, 1997).

Grief and Loss

In traditional psychological theories, mourning is understood as a process of 'letting go' of a loved one who has died, and grieving is depicted as a stage-like process of adapting to this harsh emotional reality. Prolonged signs of grief such as enduring sadness and longing are in this view considered symptoms to be medically managed or eliminated with the goal of fostering recovery, resolution or 'moving on'. In contrast, the overarching proposition animating constructivist work in this area is that *grieving is a process of reaffirming or reconstructing a world of meaning that has been challenged by loss* (Neimeyer, 2002b). Issues of meaning-making in the wake of loss had of course received some attention in earlier work on bereavement (Marris, 1974), but for the most part this had been a side note to a psychiatric preoccupation with acute symptomatology of grieving construed in largely pathological terms. But by the 1990s a new breed of grief researchers began to attend to the ruptured assumptive world of the bereaved person, the cognitive processes by which the bereaved cope with loss, and the post-traumatic growth displayed by many of those who suffer adversity. Likewise, scholars began to take a second look at time-worn assumptions about the need to 'withdraw emotional energy' from the one who had died, in order to 'reinvest' it elsewhere. Instead, thinkers were beginning to focus on the potentially sustaining continuing bonds the bereaved construct to the deceased, and the active processes by which they strive to 'relearn the world' in the wake of loss (Neimeyer, 2001a).

An initial constructivist contribution to this reorientation took place at the juncture of grief theory and personal construct theory, conceptualizing loss in terms of the traumatic assault on the survivor's world of meaning (Neimeyer & Stewart, 1996). The guiding metaphor in this work was the *self-narrative*, defined as the life story one both enacts and expresses that gives a sense of coherence to one's identity over time. In this view, traumatic loss disrupts the continuity of the narrative construction of self, dislodging the individual from a sense of who he or she is (Neimeyer, 2000, 2005). For example, the struggle to incorporate traumatic events within one's self-narrative can leave one with a fragmented sense of autobiographical continuity through time, much as a previously naïve conscript into the war in Iraq might survive horrific experiences of combat that his fellow infantrymen did not, only to find it impossible to build a bridge between the person he once was and the person he has become. Traumatic losses can introduce sharp experiential discrepancies into the survivor's self-narrative, while at the same time challenging the individual's capacity to include the traumatic events into the pre-existing construct system. Adaptations of repertory grid technique (see Chapter 6, pp. 67–76), which prompt the traumatized person to compare and contrast 'chapters' of her life (for example, 'me as a young mother', 'me as a widow') on important life themes (for example, *secure* versus '*at sea*') have proved illuminating both in grief counselling (Neimeyer et al., 2000) and in more formal research efforts.

Although grid technique can aid in the articulation of meaning systems disrupted by loss, broader narrative methods also can provide a valuable glimpse of how people accommodate death in their life stories. For example, Neimeyer and his colleagues[1] (Neimeyer, 2001b) invited hundreds of bereaved people to respond to probing questions regarding (a) the *sense* they had made of their loss experience, (b) any form of unexpected *benefit* or life lesson the experience had brought them, and (c) and progressive or regressive shifts they had noticed in their sense of personal *identity* in the wake of the loss. They found that bereavement is accompanied by a painful but profound growth for many people, who reported that the experience made them appreciate the brevity of life (19%), or left them more sensitive and open to others (15%). However, these positive forms of meaning reconstruction were by no means assured, as others emphasized how their losses left them sadder and more fearful (12%), or made it harder for them to be close to others (6%). Thus, attention to the meanings people place upon their bereavement experience, as opposed to a pre-emptive focus on presumably universal grief symptoms, highlights the remarkable individuality in how people respond to loss, in ways that leave some resilient, and others as candidates for psychotherapeutic help.

One of the strengths of a constructivist approach to loss is its encouragement of imaginative practices—biographical, interview-based, reflective, metaphoric, poetic and narrative—that help bereaved people take perspective on their losses and weave them into the fabric of their lives (Neimeyer, 2001b, 2002a). Some of these consist of straightforward adaptations of personal construct techniques, such as 'loss characterizations' that invite survivors to ponder in writing who they are 'in light of their loss,' through a modification of Kelly's self-characterization technique described in Chapter 5 (pp. 59–60) and Butt (2003, Chapter 38). Others involve creative exercises to foster greater reflexivity through writing about the 'life imprint' of the lost loved one on the bereaved person's own life or the videotaping of storytelling with a seriously ill family member prior to her or his death.

One unanticipated offshoot of this work has been the discovery by other clinicians and helping professionals that a constructivist and narrative approach provides a more coherent and useful framework for their best practices (for example, the creation of meaningful rituals; transformative procedures for restoring a sense of community in the wake of violation or loss) than did traditional theories (Neimeyer & Tschudi, 2003). Such reports are highly affirming as, in the words of an insightful participant in one recent meaning reconstruction workshop, 'we as bereavement professionals finally have a chance to put our practice into theory'.

---

[1] This work has been pursued over the last few years in conjunction with James Gillies, Heather Hardison and Scott Baldwin, who are currently studying the relationship between intensified grieving and such factors as the bereaved person's continuing bond to the deceased, and meaning-making processes in their accounts of loss.

PSYCHOTHERAPEUTIC FORMATS AND PROCEDURES

Apart from the interventions linked to particular presenting problems such as substance abuse or traumatic loss, personal construct theorists have also devised a wide range of procedures that can be flexibly applied to a great range of clinical issues. To supplement coverage of individual and family therapy in other chapters, we will look at innovations in group work that trace their roots directly to personal construct theory.

Interpersonal Transaction Group

First introduced by Landfield (1979) as a means of exploring socialization processes in small groups, the Interpersonal Transaction or IT format has proved to be a flexible and powerful approach to brief therapy. The distinctive structure of IT groups is grounded in Kelly's Sociality Corollary, 'with its emphasis upon "construing the construction processes of the other" as a prerequisite for enacting meaningful social roles' (Neimeyer, 1988, p. 181). IT groups use what are termed rotating dyads, in which group members engage in a series of one-on-one interactions with other group members to converse about topics agreed upon in advance as relevant to the group's problems (for example, 'ways people understand and misunderstand me', 'positive and negative things about getting close to others'). The intimate context of disclosure, in combination with the 'bipolar' phrasing of the discussion topics, encourages a permissive exploration of similarities and differences among group members. In this way, IT groups provide psychotherapists with a 'happy medium' between the sometimes threatening atmosphere of process-oriented groups and the rigid, impersonal style of psycho-educational groups. The primary aim of the IT group is in harmony with other constructivist therapies, 'since [the group] emphasizes the elaboration of a broader range of social construing without first having to invalidate the client's existing constructions' (Neimeyer, 1988, p. 182).

IT groups consist of six to twelve members and meet in a room large enough to allow for the rearranging of chairs for the dyads. The group members begin the session by discussing an assigned topic with each member of the group (rotating dyads) for about five minutes. Leaders are encouraged to set guidelines for these discussions, encouraging members to listen carefully to each other and allow their disclosures to evolve or deepen across their successive encounters. Following the dyadic phase, the members reconvene to discuss their experiences in the dyads, aided by the therapist's 'bridging questions' to help them integrate personal observations into the plenary group format, for example: 'What did you learn that most surprised you?', 'Whose experience did you most identify with, and why?' The length of this phase varies from 15 minutes to one hour depending on the purpose of the group. Often the groups end in a ritual of integration, sharing food and drinks while members casually interact (Neimeyer, 1988).

Empirical studies of IT groups have suggested that they have beneficial effects, particularly for such clients as incest survivors, who have grappled with issues related to threat and betrayal in close relationships (Alexander et al., 1991). There are several potential reasons for the success of the IT group that relate to its distinctive format and structure. Because all group members participate equally in the dyads, there tends to be even group participation, high levels of group cohesion, and the development of heightened empathy for other group members. Participants experience themselves not simply as disturbed and distressed patients, but also as healthy, supportive listeners. The most important advantage of the IT group could lie in its adaptability, as therapists can 'tweak' the structure of the dyad interactions to address special problems (Neimeyer, 1988). For example, therapists can participate in the rotating dyads to provide more individual attention to needy group members, or gradually 'fade out' dyadic interactions in longer-term groups once high cohesion among members is attained (see Neimeyer, 1988, p. 188, for more suggestions).

Multiple Self-Awareness Groups

Like IT groups, Multiple Self-Awareness groups (Sewell et al., 1998) have a decidedly constructivist orientation and, perhaps, an even more postmodern flavour. The structure of the group revolves around its conception of the self. Most psychologists would conceptualize a healthy self 'as a dominant single entity in control of all aspects of psychological functioning' (Sewell et al., 1998, p. 60). The constructivist theorist, however, tends to take an alternative view, contending that identity is better conceptualized as a 'community of selves' (Mair, 1977) than as a fully coherent and essential 'I'. That is, various partial identities are organized as distinctive subsystems of constructs associated with different self-roles. This 'decentralized' view might seem strange or even pathological to some, but this is likely to be a reflection of how dominant is the accepted view of a unified self.

The aim of Multiple Self-Awareness groups is to provide a stage on which group members can explore the role of these multiple selves in their interpersonal relationships. After the group members have an understanding of the concept of multiple selves, time is spent eliciting each participant's different identity characteristics, such as shy or incompetent, and creating character names for each of these partial identities, such as Mr Wallflower or Little Man. The group members are then assigned to write 'autobiographies' for each of these characters. This writing exercise facilitates an understanding of the role each self has played or continues to play in the group members' lives. Next, the group leader helps to construct a scenario in which each member plays a role, perhaps a fictional joint outing on which they must all decide, or the allocation of responsibilities for running a make-believe business.

The catch is that each member must select one of his or her characters to take part in the collective enactment. This exercise provides a powerful method by which group members can understand the ways in which their selected role (that is, the character they play—Mr Wallflower) influences their interactions with others. Following this exercise, participants process the results, achieving greater clarity about the intrapersonal and interpersonal dynamics that shape their relational styles.

A second group format that encourages the performance of multiple aspects of the self is therapeutic enactment or TE, a special form of psychodrama pioneered by Westwood and his colleagues (2002) to promote the healing of psychological traumas associated with military combat, sexual assault, complicated bereavement and histories of abuse. In this innovative format, the therapist or facilitator meets with the client or 'lead' to develop a rough script of a series of critical scenes that represent focal points in his or her traumatic narrative. Later, in the enactment phase, the facilitator and lead recruit members of the group to perform the parts of significant antagonists and support figures from his or her life, including aspects of the lead's self (such as a younger self or the self that copes defensively or effectively with the unfolding events). Likewise, a designated group member selected by the lead acts as a 'double' for his or her present self, stepping in to the performance at important junctures so that the lead can stand back and gain perspective on what he or she experienced, and later 'de-role' and process it with the validation of the entire group of performers and witnesses. A detailed example of this intervention with a young man who had been abused by his father is provided by Neimeyer and Arvay (2004), who interpret it in light of narrative theory.

RETROSPECT AND PROSPECT

Working in a distinctively postmodern *zeitgeist*, present-day personal construct theorists have extended the boundaries of Kelly's original vision, while also drawing inspiration from other constructivist, social constructionist, and narrative perspectives that share some of its iconoclastic premises. In this brief chapter we have tried to suggest the vitality of this perspective by surveying some of the ongoing contributions of personal construct theorists to the conceptualization of human problems, as well as to their treatment.

CHAPTER 23

New Avenues to Explore and Questions to Ask

Fay Fransella

University of Hertfordshire, UK

> To construe is to invent, pure and simple. As far as discovery is concerned, all
> that one ever discovers is whether or not the predictions, to which his inventions
> have led him, actually pan out.
>
> (Kelly, 1959b, p. 9)

In Chapter 17.1–17.5 five authors have given their accounts of the development of
their work in areas not so far covered in this volume. Here we can look at some
other applications of personal construct psychology in very diverse areas that have
still to become well established. One point to be noted is that by no means are all
these areas being explored by psychologists. For instance, here we have musicians,
literary critics and historians describing the advantages of using a personal construct
framework for their work.

THE WORLD OF MUSIC

One of the few accounts of Kelly's ideas being applied to the world of music comes
from Kelly himself in his description of the Construction Corollary. Every time we
hear a piece of music with which we are familiar, it may have changed key, changed
rhythm or volume, but we still recognize the melody. Construing is about prediction and anticipation and a piece of music can only be recognized by our being able
to predict those notes that are about to follow.

An early study by Davies (1976) provides a fascinating account of how brass and
string players in a orchestra construed each other. For instance, string players saw
brass players, among other things, as less intelligent, liking the limelight and as being
the clowns of the orchestra. Brass players saw string players as like a flock of sheep,
oversensitive and seeming to think they were 'God's gift to music'. Eric Button
(1988) talks about his own experience as someone who always wanted to study
music and how our construing processes relate to our understanding of music. He

points out that music is all about movement—'music is always going somewhere'. He also talks of its predictability. As he says, we would soon get bored if our music were entirely predictable. Catherine Butler has spent many years working with music students. Among other things, she has isolated some of the factors that may lead to music students failing during their studies. She found that those failing suffered both internal and external stresses. For instance, their parents tended not to play instruments or sing, they saw their peers as competitors, as well as having high levels of performance anxiety. Successful students, on the other hand, only experienced one kind of stress. They had good self-esteem and enjoyed the excitement of performing, seeing it as a challenge to be met (Butler, 1995). Ben-Peretz and Kalekin-Fishman (1988) discuss how the construing of music might be related to sociocultural constructs. Blowers and Bacon-Shone (1994) looked at methods for detecting perceptual differences in jazz. All these authors give us a glimpse at how easily personal construct theory can be used to gain a greater understanding of why, for many people, music is an essential part of life. There is enough interest in the construing of music to suggest that this could burst into life at any time.

LITERARY CRITICISM

John Lee is a literary critic who has made a study of the difficulties literary critics have had over the years in dealing with what he terms 'interiority'. They have a problem construing the inner nature of a literary character. Lee has looked at this issue in his book *Shakespeare's 'Hamlet' and the Controversies of Self* (2000). He says (2002) that his work started in response to the influential movement within recent literary criticism that sees individuals, whether in plays or in life, being little more than the products of their cultures. Such a movement, to those outside literary criticism, may well look rather out-of-date, particularly if one has constructivist sympathies. However, within literary criticism it proved very successful, in part because the modern vocabulary of 'interiority' tended not to exist before 1650, but more importantly because previous critics had themselves talked in very vague terms about how the inner worlds of dramatic characters are constituted.

When the relative importance of Shakespeare was being debated in the late seventeenth and eighteenth centuries, his promoters and detractors both chose his ability (for the detractors an inability) to create lifelike 'characters' as their proof. The promoters won out, and Shakespeare was installed as the national poet, but this was as much a theatrical and political victory as an argumentative one. Few critics talked convincingly about what it was in Shakespeare's *dramatis personae* that gave them lifelike personalities. Later attempts, often reliant on Freud, talked about this lifelikeness coming from the 'gaps' between—for example, what 'characters' said and what they did. The psychological depth of the character was then seen to be the measure of the complexity of contradictory elements that the critic needed to bridge. Such depth was easy to portray as a critics' fiction, and this was exactly the point of attack chosen by some recent literary critics; they allege that what Hamlet possessed was not a series of meaningful gaps, but rather, simple absences or, as one critic put it: 'At the centre of Hamlet, in the interior of his mystery, there is, in short, nothing.'

Lee makes a very interesting case for the importance of using personal construct psychology as a framework for literary critics to use for understanding the characters in literature. He says: 'Kelly's approach—in its humanist and constructivist aspects—lends itself to an account of the literally literary aspects of personality and of change' (Lee, 2000, p. 175).

In a sense, one might say that Kelly was, himself, something of a literary critic. He talks at length towards the end of his second volume about Hamlet in relation to the CPC (decision-making) and the Creativity Cycle. He sees these cycles as different in that the CPC Cycle involves the personal commitment to action at the end of the cycle, whereas no such personal commitment is involved in the Creativity Cycle.

Kelly then discusses the cycles that Hamlet was involved with in his soliloquy: 'To be or not to be?' In Kelly's view, Hamlet was involved in both cycles during that soliloquy, neither of which he was able to complete. First there is loose construing about his relationships with men and women:

> ... vaguely conscientious with respect to his father, vaguely incestuous with respect to his mother, and vaguely illusive with respect to Ophelia. His creative mind had contrived the notion of having a play presented which would dramatize, in some way involving his uncle, what he is not quite able to put into explicit terms. (Kelly, 1955/1991, p. 1061/Vol. 2, p. 351)

Having been through this loosening phase of the Creativity Cycle, Hamlet moves to the CPC Cycle. His words: 'To be or not to be' have pre-empted the issue. He has decided that this is the crux of the matter. He must now make the decision. 'He must fling himself to the one side of this slot or to the other; he must live or die—it is as simple as that.' But it does not end there and he moves into the Creativity Cycle again and then the CPC Cycle once more—and so on. Lee states that:

> Kelly's approach ... gives to man a radical degree of agency. One can free oneself from old constructs and enslave oneself to new constructs again and again. This is the process seen being repeatedly attempted in the soliloquies. ... At the same time, he gives us reasons why literature should create so powerfully and so well the effect of personality; since literature may be, like personality, an argued, philosophical representation of the world. (Lee, 2000, p. 183)

In fact, Kelly makes his admiration for Shakespeare's writings clear in his acknowledgements in Volume 1. He says '... and, of course, that distinguished and insightful colleague of all personal-construct theorists, Mr. William Shakespeare' (1955/1991, p. xii/Vol. 1, p. xiii).

CONSTRUING HISTORICAL DECISIONS

Why were great decisions of history made the way they were? Historians badly want to know, but they are balked by lack of evidence and denial of access to the long-dead players.

It is not possible for a historian to elicit from documents the personal constructs of, say, past policy-makers in the way a personal construct psychologist can from direct contact with the living. However, it has proved extremely useful to approach the problem from a Kellyian perspective. According to David Gillard (2002), we can assume that foreign policy consists of the construing by a small number of identifiable individuals of the behaviour of their counterparts in other states. This they do through identifying their opponents' personal constructs and trying to change or reinforce them by a wide choice of methods, which can range from intimate discussion to total war.

The challenge to the historian lies in the number of policy-holders involved in the voluminous but patchy records of their attempts to modify the construing of their own colleagues before a policy could be agreed and implemented. Gillard's forthcoming book analyses these data during the six months after the Munich crisis. His data come from tracing, on a day-to-day basis, the changes in thinking of a handful of individual policy-makers, in this case key British Cabinet ministers, Foreign Office officials and Service chiefs.

Historically, he finds this. Neville Chamberlain, the British Prime Minister's announcement in 1939 that if Germany attacked Poland, Britain would go to Poland's aid has always been a matter for controversy. Obviously it did Poland no good, as Hitler swiftly overran that nation, and it landed Britain in a war for which its armed forces were not yet ready. Britain had just reneged on a guarantee over Czechoslovakia, so why did Chamberlain expect Hitler to believe in a new guarantee a few weeks later?

A small group of some 20 people in Britain were the policy-makers construing the international situation at the time, and in a position to determine peace or war. Central to their task was the need to interpret the behaviour of Hitler, to anticipate what his moves might be, and to decide the means to deter him from threatening the security of Britain or its allies.

By diplomacy and propaganda those policy-makers relied on their own construing of Hitler's personal constructs in their bid to change them—and those of his subjects. Hitler, of course, was doing the same kind of thing. Both sides got it wrong.

It is Gillard's view that of all the possible approaches to the problems of international history, the theory of personal constructs comes closest to being scientific. He is about to finish a book on the whole subject with the proposed title of *Why Guarantee Poland?*

A PROBLEM OF 'TIME'

Time

Kelly's whole theory is permeated with references to and the importance of the dimension of time. He states that '... the meaning of an event—that is to say, the meaning we ascribe to it—is anchored in its antecedents and its consequents. Thus meaning displays itself to us mainly in the dimension of time' (Kelly, 2003, p. 4). In his first chapter in Volume 1, he says:

> Man ultimately seeks to anticipate real events.... Anticipation is not merely carried on for its own sake; it is carried on so that future reality may be better

represented. It is the future which tantalizes (us), not the past. . . . Always (we)
reach out to the future through the window of the present.

(Kelly, 1955/1991, p. 49/Vol. 1, 34)

With this knowledge of the importance Kelly put upon the dimension of time, it was
most interesting to view a British Broadcasting Corporation programme televised
in 1999 in which two physicists discussed 'The flow of time'. They said that physics
has a problem because it cannot account for the passage of time. They concluded
that ultimately this sense of temporal flow must be attributed to poorly understood
features of human perception. They agreed that 'human consciousness probably has
the secret as to how and why we think of time as going by'. Did Kelly understand
this dilemma in physics in the early 1950s, or before? Did he see that it was psychology that would be able to solve the problem of physics? Did he wonder what
new questions would arise if physics and psychology were to work together? He
says:

> If man, as the psychologist is to see him, exists primarily in the dimensions of
> time and only secondarily in the dimensions of space, then the terms which we
> erect for understanding him ought to take primary account of this view. If we
> want to know why man does what he does, then the terms of our whys should
> extend themselves in time rather than in space; they should be events rather than
> things in the present. He stands firmly astride the chasm that separates the two
> universes. He, and only he, can bring them into harmony with each other.
>
> (Kelly, 1969b, p. 86)

KELLY'S ALTERNATIVE FUNDAMENTAL POSTULATE

> 'There's no use trying,' said Alice: 'one can't believe impossible things.' 'I dare
> say you haven't had much practice,' said the Queen . . . 'Why sometimes, I've
> believed as many as six impossible things before breakfast.'
>
> (Lewis Carroll, 1865, *Alice in Wonderland*)

We now enter the realm of loose construing if not fantasy. As this is a trail I have
been following for many years, I shall finish this book by recounting my personal
pursuit of the answer to the question 'Where does construing start?'

In the first chapter in this book, Kelly says his theory is about 'the person' and
that 'organisms, lower animals, and societies can wait'. But for how much longer?
Throughout this book, authors have provided support for Kelly's adamant convic-
tion that the distinction between mind and body is not useful. We are a construing
process, a form of motion. In his 1955 volumes Kelly suggests that the idea of
non-verbal constructs may, indeed, embrace such things as digestive or glandular
secretions.

In 1966, I went to the United States of America on a lecture tour and talked with
George Kelly and his students at Brandeis University. He gave me copies of many
of his unpublished papers, some of which were published later. Browsing through
those, I came across his *Alternative* Fundamental Postulate. His 1955 Fundamental
Postulate states that: *A person's processes are psychologically channelized by the
ways in which he anticipates events.* His *Alternative*, biological Fundamental Postu-

late states that: *It is the nature of life to be channelized by the ways events are antic-ipated* (Kelly, 1980, p. 29). He goes on to say: 'This is a more venturesome postulate than the one from which the psychology of personal constructs was launched. But from it may spring some additional ideas about the whole of psychology.' Like the Queen in *Alice in Wonderland*, Kelly liked to think the impossible and then see where that might lead. So, as an exercise in loose construing, where might the idea lead that it is the nature of life or living matter to be channelized by the ways in which events are anticipated? Kelly argued against our talking across disciplines, such as physiological psychology, but it would seem here that the study of such inter-actions may be necessary. He did, after all, say: 'The notion of construing . . . may even be used within borderland areas of the realm of physiology' (Kelly, 1955/1991, p. 51/Vol. 1, p. 36).

There are two words in that Alternative Postulate which need exploring. One is the absence of the word 'processes'. Defining the word in his 1955 Postulate he says:

> Instead of postulating an inert substance, a step which would inevitably lead to the necessity for establishing . . . the existence of some sort of mental energy, the subject of psychology is assumed at the outset to be a process. . . . For our pur-poses, the person is not an object which is temporarily in a moving state but is himself a form of motion. (Kelly, 1955/1991, p. 48/Vol. 1, p. 33)

Since that is his view of living matter, there is no need for the word 'processes' in his Alternative Fundamental Postulate. The other word in both postulates is 'chan-nelized'. He defines this for the first postulate as:

> We conceive a person's processes as operating through a network of pathways rather than as fluttering about in a vast emptiness. The network is flexible and is frequently modified, but it is structured and it both facilitates and restricts a person's range of action. (Kelly, 1955/1991, p. 49/Vol. 1, p. 34)

If the word 'person's' is removed, we have a Fundamental Postulate that can be applied well beyond the human being.

I was personally very taken with that idea, and for years in various talks and the occasional paper, I slipped in the problem of deciding when construing starts. I would argue that there is no problem about the foetus construing. So, what about the sperm? If construing is all about predicting and then behaving in relation to those predictions, why not think about plants predicting where the best nutriments may be and then 'behaving' by sending their roots in that direction. I suggested that perhaps one has to go back as far as living matter to find where construing starts. Perhaps it is living matter itself that is in the anticipation business. I cannot say that psychologists got wildly excited by that idea! But in the past few years, things seem to be changing.

Psychoneuroimmunology

One link in the chain of events I followed in relation to Kelly's Alternative Funda-mental Postulate was attending a British Psychological Society branch scientific meeting in Cornwall in November 2001. I attended in spite of its user-unfriendly title of 'psychoneuroimmunology'. Not really my sort of thing, I thought. How wrong I was! Here I heard psychologists all saying that there is no boundary between mind and body—that there is empirical research to show that they are totally interconnected. Here I heard Marianne Morris talk about the use of guided imagery with patients with cancer or who are HIV positive. Of course, personal construct psychologists have considered the problem of cancer before now (for example, Nuzzo & Chiari, 2001, and Kenny, 1987). But here were people providing neuroscientific research evidence of the bidirectional connection between the physical and the psychological. John Gruzelier demonstrated how the immune function can be enhanced by self-hypnosis. The research that excited me the most was that of Marcel Ebrecht showing how cells of the immune system 'deal with' damage to the skin. He had a slide showing a 'killer cell' and described how that cell 'hangs on' to something until it can 'see' a way to go to the aid of that damaged skin. Would Kelly see this as construing? *It is the nature* of the immune system *to be channelized by the ways events are anticipated.*

The Construing of Plants

Well, at long last I do not feel I have to 'slip in' the idea about plants construing. Professor Trewavas at the Institute of Cell and Moleculor Biology, University of Edinburgh, is one of the world's leading researchers into the sensory abilities of plants. He says:

> The problem is that plants don't move and that leads to the supposition that movement is essential to intelligence—and thus the word of contempt—vegetable. However, if one replaces growth for *movement* then intelligent behaviour there is. . . . The best known example of assessment and decision making comes from Cuscuta—a parasitical plant. This plant touches a potential host and is able to assess whether it is worth parasitising many days before it gains nutriments from the host. Also the investment in resources to produce parasitical structures is directly related to the resources the parasite will eventually achieve many days later. (Personal communication, 2002; see also Trewavas, 1999)

There was an article entitled 'Not just a pretty face' in the magazine *New Scientist* on 27 July, 2002, all about Trewavas's ideas. The problem people have is that he uses the word 'intelligence' for the behaviour of plants, and Trewavas is reported as saying that he uses it because it starts controversy, which will be 'all the better for our understanding'. Perhaps 'construe' would be a more acceptable word. After all: *It is the nature* of plants *to be channelized by the ways events are anticipated.*

A SELF-REGULATING EARTH

I do not expect many people care too much about being able to 'understand' the behaviour of plants, but there is more to Kelly's *Alternative Fundamental Postulate* than that. Soon after reading that plants may be seen to construe, I came across

James Lovelock's autobiography *Homage to Gaia* (2000). Here an eminent chemist-cum-medical doctor-cum-biologist explains how he devised the theory he called Gaia (Greek goddess of the earth). The earth is a self-regulating system—just like the human being. In effect, Lovelock sees the surface of the earth as being more like a living organism than a machine. It maintains conditions in which life can exist.

Lovelock used the growth of daisies as an example of what he was talking about. It goes something like this. We know the sun is increasing in heat over the centuries, but the Earth does not heat up accordingly. His 'Daisy World' is an earth covered with daisies orbiting a star. When the star was young it was cool and dark daisies covered the Earth and made it warmer by absorbing sunlight. As the star warmed up and got older, lighter daisies flourished and they reflected the star's heat and so cooled the earth down. It was an example that got him into a lot of trouble in the scientific world. But he and his colleagues have produced much evidence to support his theory.

Mary Midgley, a philosopher, calls Gaia 'the next big idea'. Like Kelly, she says that it is Cartesian dualism that has held back our thinking. 'Our moral, psychological and political ideas have all been armed against holism' (2001, p. 11).

Very fanciful, but is it more so that the 'behaviour' of the parasite plant? I, personally, believe that Kelly would be intrigued to know how others are seeing plants, the immune system and even the earth itself as 'construing' entities. Lovelock considers that there should be much more 'biodiversity' in science. That is, too much of science is divided into compartments such as biology, geology, chemistry and so forth. He says we need to combine biology with environmental sciences to be able to deal with the interaction he and others see as so important. That is what Kelly seems to be suggesting with his Alternative Fundamental Postulate. Dualism disappears completely, we are a construing system. One other point arises from Lovelock's ideas. If we were to conclude that there was something in his theory that is, indeed, relevant to construing, then perhaps we have a theory which would subsume personal construct theory itself. After all: *It is the nature of* the earth *to be channelized by the ways events are anticipated.*

AND SO, WHAT NOW?

A last quotation from George A. Kelly:

> . . . what we know as the body of science, (is) in itself, an amazing display.
>   But this is not the most exciting part of the story that history has to tell us.
> . . . Infinitely more exciting is what potentiality these audacious feats suggest is locked up in the unrealized future of man. While the man of yesterday was develping a physicalistic science that tested itself by experiments and its ability to predict their outcomes, he was, without intending to do so, stating the basic postulates of a psychology for the man of tomorrow. Slowly he demonstrated not merely that events could be predicted, but, what was vastly more important, that he was a predictor. It was not only that hypotheses could be generated, experiments controlled, anticipations checked against realizations, and theories revised, but that he—man—was a hypothesizer, an experimenter, an anticipator, a critical observer, and an artful composer of new systems of thought. What he did, physically, portrayed what he was, psychologically. (Kelly, 1980, p. 23)

Theoretical Definitions

Kelly starts his Volume 2, which gives psychotherapy as an example of his theory 'at work', with definitions of his theoretical terms. After the Fundamental Postulate, which is 'the basic assumption upon which all else hinges', he details the eleven corollaries that elaborate it. He says: 'These, also, are assumptive in nature, and they lay the groundwork for most of what follows' (Kelly, 1955/1991, pp. 561–565/Vol. 2, pp. 4–8).

FUNDAMENTAL POSTULATE AND COROLLARIES

Fundamental Postulate: A person's processes are psychologically channelized by the ways in which he anticipates events.

Construction Corollary: A person anticipates events by construing their replications.

Individuality Corollary: Persons differ from each other in their constructions of events.

Organization Corollary: Each person characteristically evolves for his convenience in anticipating events, a construction system embracing ordinal relationships between constructs.

Dichotomy Corollary: A person's construction system is composed of a finite number of dichotomous constructs.

Choice Corollary: A person chooses for himself that alternative in a dichotomized construct through which he anticipates the greater possibility for extension and definition of his system.

Range Corollary: A construct is convenient for the anticipation of a finite range of events only.

Experience Corollary: A person's construction system varies as he successively construes the replication of events.

Modulation Corollary: The variation in a person's construction system is limited by the permeability of the constructs within whose ranges of convenience the variants lie.

Fragmentation Corollary: A person may successively employ a variety of construction subsystems which are inferentially incompatible with each other.

Commonality Corollary: To the extent that one person employs a construction of experience which is similar to that employed by another, his processes are psychologically similar to those of the other person (altered according to Kelly's footnote in Chapter 1, 2003).

Sociality Corollary: To the extent that one person construes the construction processes of another he may play a role in a social process involving the other person.

FORMAL ASPECTS OF CONSTRUCTS

Range of Convenience: A construct's range of convenience comprises all those things to which the user would find its application useful.

Focus of Convenience: A construct's focus of convenience comprises those particular things to which the user would find its application maximally useful. These are the elements upon which the construct is likely to have been formed originally.

Elements: The things or events which are abstracted by a person's use of a construct are called elements. In some systems these are called objects.

Context: The context of a construct comprises those elements among which the user ordinarily discriminates by means of the construct. It is somewhat more restricted than the range of convenience, since it refers to the circumstances in which the construct emerges for practical use, and not necessarily to all the circumstances in which a person might eventually use the construct. It is somewhat more extensive than the focus of convenience, since the construct may often appear in circumstances where its application is not optimal.

Pole: Each construct discriminates between two poles, one at each end of its dichotomy. The elements abstracted are like each other at each pole with respect to the construct and are unlike the elements at the other pole.

Contrast: The relationship between the two poles of a construct is one of contrast.

Likeness End: When referring specifically to elements at one pole of a construct, one may use the term 'likeness end' to designate that pole.

Contrast End: When referring specifically to elements at one pole of a construct, one may use the term 'contrast end' to designate the opposite pole.

Emergence: The emergent pole of a construct is that one which embraces most of the immediately perceived context.

Implicitness: The implicit pole of a construct is that one which embraces contrasting context. It contrasts with the emergent pole. Frequently the person has no available symbol or name for it; it is symbolized only implicitly by the emergent term.

Symbol: An element in the context of a construct which represents not only itself but also the construct by which it is abstracted by the user is called the construct's symbol.

Permeability: A construct is permeable if it admits newly perceived elements to its context. It is impermeable if it rejects elements on the basis of their newness.

CONSTRUCTS CLASSIFIED ACCORDING TO THE NATURE OF THEIR CONTROL OVER THEIR ELEMENTS

Pre-emptive Construct: A construct which pre-empts its elements for membership in its own realm exclusively is called a pre-emptive construct. This is the 'nothing but' type of construction. 'If this is a torpedo it is nothing but a torpedo.'

Constellatory Construct: A construct which fixes the other realm memberships of its elements is called a constellatory construct. This is stereotyped thinking.

Propositional Construct: A construct which carries no implications regarding the other realm memberships of its elements is a propositional construct. This is uncontaminated construction.

GENERAL DIAGNOSTIC CONSTRUCTS

Preverbal Construct: A preverbal construct is one which continues to be used, even though it has no consistent word symbol. It may or may not have been devised before the client had command of speech symbolism.

Submergence: The submerged pole of a construct is the one which is less available for application to events.

Suspension: A suspended element is one which is omitted from the context of a construct as a result of revision of the client's construct system.

Level of Cognitive Awareness: The level of cognitive awareness ranges from high to low. A high-level construct is one which is readily expressed in socially effective symbols; whose alternatives are both readily accessible; which falls well within the range of convenience of the client's major constructions; and which is not suspended by its superordinating constructs.

Dilation: This occurs when a person broadens his or her perceptual field in order to reorganize it on a more comprehensive level. It does not, in itself, include the comprehensive reconstruction of those elements.

Constriction: Constriction occurs when a person narrows his or her perceptual field in order to minimize apparent incompatibilities.

Comprehensive Constructs: These are constructs that subsume a wide variety of events.

Incidental Constructs: These are constructs that subsume a narrow variety of events.

Superordinate Constructs: These are constructs that include others as one or more of the elements in their context.

Subordinate Constructs: These are constructs that are included as elements in the context of others.

Regnant Constructs: These are kinds of superordinate construct which assign each of their elements to a category on an all-or-none basis, as in classical logic. They tend to be non-abstractive.

Core Constructs: These are constructs that govern a person's maintenance processes.

Peripheral Constructs: These are constructs that can be altered without serious modification of the core structure.

Tight Constructs: These are constructs that lead to unvarying predictions.

Loose Constructs: These are constructs that lead to varying predictions, but retain their identity.

CONSTRUCTS RELATING TO TRANSITION

Threat: This is the awareness of an imminent comprehensive change in one's core structures.

Fear: This is the awareness of an imminent incidental change in one's core structures.

Anxiety: This is the awareness that the events with which one is confronted lie mostly outside the range of convenience of one's construct system.

Guilt: This is the awareness of dislodgement of the self from one's core role structure.

Aggressiveness: This is the active elaboration of one's perceptual field.

Hostility: This is the continued effort to extort validational evidence in favour of a type of social prediction which has already been recognized as a failure.

C–P–C Cycle: This cycle is a sequence of construction involving, in succession, circumspection, pre-emption, and control, and leading to a choice precipitating the person into a particular situation. (Later, Kelly suggested that 'control' be changed to 'choice'.)

Impulsivity: This is a characteristic foreshortening of the C–P–C Cycle.

Creativity Cycle: This is a cycle which starts with loosened construction and terminates with tightened and validated construction.

Some Basic Books on Personal Construct Psychology

General

Don Bannister and Fay Fransella (ebook) *Inquiring Man* (3rd edn). See address in Appendix 3, p. 261.

Vivien Burr and Trevor Butt (1992) *Invitation to Personal Construct Psychology*. London: Whurr Publications (also in Chinese).

Peter Cummins (2005) *Working with Anger*. Chichester: John Wiley & Sons.

Peggy Dalton and Gavin Dunnett (1992) *A Psychology for Living*. Chichester: John Wiley & Sons.

Fay Fransella (1995) *George Kelly*. London: Sage Publications (also in Chinese).

Fay Fransella (Ed.) (2004) *International Handbook of Personal Construct Psychology*. Chichester: John Wiley & Sons.

Fay Fransella, Richard Bell and Don Bannister (2004). *A Manual for Repertory Grid Technique* (2nd edn). Chichester: John Wiley & Sons.

George A. Kelly (1955/1991) *The Psychology of Personal Constructs*, Volumes 1 and 2. London: Routledge.

Robert A. Neimeyer and Greg J. Neimeyer (Eds) *Advances in Personal Construct Psychology: New Directions and Perspectives*, Volume 5. New York: Praeger.

Dorothy Rowe (2002) *Friends and Enemies*. London: Harper Collins.

Jörn W. Scheer and Kenneth W. Sewell (Eds) (2005) *Creative Construing: Personal Constructions in the Arts*. Giessen: Psychogogical-Verlag.

Bill Warren (1998) *Philosophical Dimensions of Personal Construct Psychology*. London: Routledge.

Counselling, Psychotherapy and Clinical Practice

Michael Bender (2003) *Explorations in Dementia: Theoretical and Research Studies into the Experience of Remediable and Enduring Cognitive Losses*. London: Jessica Kingsley Publishers.

Geoffrey Blowers and Kieron O'Connor (1996) *Personal Construct Psychology in the Clinical Context*. Ottawa: University of Ottawa Press.

Fay Fransella and Peggy Dalton (2000) *Personal Construct Counselling in Action* (2nd edn). London: Sage Publications.

Robert A. Neimeyer (Ed.) (2001) *Meaning Reconstruction and the Experience of Loss*. Washington, DC: American Psychological Association.

Robert A. Neimeyer (2002) *Lessons of Loss: A Guide to Coping* (2nd edn). New York: Brunner Routledge.

Robert A. Neimeyer and Jonathan Raskin (Eds) (2000) *Constructions of Disorder: Meaning-*

Making Frameworks for Psychotherapy. Washington, DC: American Psychological Association.

Jonathan Raskin and Sarah Bridges (Eds) (2002) *Studies in Meaning: Exploring Constructivist Psychology*. New York: Pace University Press.

Jonathan Raskin and Sarah Bridges (Eds) (2004) *Studies in Meaning 2: Bridging the Personal and Social in Constructivist Psychology*. New York: Pace University Press.

Dorothy Rowe (2002) *Beyond Fear* (2nd edn). London: Harper Collins.

Dorothy Rowe (2003) *Depression: The Way Out of Your Prison* (3rd edn). London: Routledge.

Linda Viney (1996) *Personal Construct Therapy: A Handbook*. Norwood: Ablex Publishing Corporation.

David Winter (1992) *Personal Construct Psychology in Clinical Practice*. London: Routledge.

David Winter and Linda Viney (Eds) (2005) *Personal Construct Psychotherapy: Advances in Theory, Practice and Research*. London: Whurr.

Working with Children

Richard Butler and David Green (1998) *The Child Within: The Exploration of Personal Construct Theory with Young People*. Oxford: Butterworth-Heinemann.

Tom Ravenette (1999) *Personal Construct Theory in Educational Psychology: A Practitioner's View*. London: Whurr Publications.

Culture and Society

Gabriele Chiari and Maria Laura Nuzzo (Eds) (2003) *Pychological Constructivism and the Social World*. Milan: Franco Angeli.

Jim Horley (Ed.) (2004) *Personal Construct Perspectives on Forensic Psychology*. London: Brunner-Routledge.

Julia Houston (1998) *Making Sense with Offenders: Personal Constructs, Therapy and Change*. Chichester: John Wiley & Sons.

Devorah Kalekin-Fishman and Beverly Walker (Eds) (1996) *The Construction of Group Realities: Culture, Society and Personal Construct Theory*. Malabar: Krieger.

Education

Pamela Denicolo and Maureen Pope (2001) *Transformative Professional Practice: Personal Construct Approaches to Education and Research*. London: Whurr Publications.

Maureen Pope and Pamela Denicolo (2001) *Transformative Education: Personal Construct Approaches to Practice and Research*. London: Whurr Publications.

The Family

Rudi Dallos (1994) *Family Belief Systems, Therapy and Change*. Milton Keynes: Open University Press.

Repertory Grids

Fay Fransella, Richard Bell and Don Bannister (2004) *A Manual for Repertory Grid Technique* (2nd edn). Chichester: John Wiley & Sons.

Devi Jankowicz (2003) *The Easy Guide to Repertory Grids*. Chichester: John Wiley & Sons.

There is also the *Journal of Constructivist Psychology*, published quarterly, and available from Taylor & Francis on e-mail: *online@tandfpa.com*.

SOME COURSES

Distance Learning

This is a six-modular programme on personal construct psychology and its method offered by The Centre for Personal Construct Psychology in the UK. The first two modules are combined into an Intermediate certificated course. These two modules provide a secure grounding in the basics of personal construct theory, its philosophy, its methods of assessment and some interpersonal skills. As far as possible, practical work focuses on the context within which the student works.

The grounding achieved in the first two modules is built upon in Advanced distance learning modules III, IV, V and VI. Each module covers four calendar months. The Advanced course includes monthly seminars, normally held in London. Special arrangements are made for those unable to attend the London seminars on a regular basis.

The personal work focuses on the individual needs of each participant, e.g. research work, work in organizations, clinical work or work with children.

A Diploma in the Applications of PCP in a specific area is offered by the Centre for Personal Construct Psychology, UK.

Full details of all modules from:

Professor Fay Fransella, The Sail Loft, Mulberry Quay, Falmouth TR11 3HD, UK

Tel: 01326 314 871; Fax: 01326 212 085; E-mail: *Ffransella@aol.com*

Training in Personal Construct Psychotherapy and Counselling

This is offered by *PCP Education and Training Limited*. Information can be obtained from Peggy Dalton, e-mail: *daltonpcp@talk21.com*.

Internet Resources for Personal Construct Psychology

Brian R. Gaines

There is a wide range of resources supporting researchers and practitioners in personal construct psychology available through the Internet. These include mailing lists, calls for contributions to journals and conferences, journal contents, publication archives and repertory grid elicitation and analysis programs.

The Internet and World Wide Web are dynamic resources subject to frequent change. The notes below are not intended to be exhaustive but rather to provide links to reasonably stable starting points from which to explore the support for personal construct psychology available through the Internet.

WEB SITES WITH LINKS TO PCP RESOURCES

The following sites provide links to many other sites, and are a good starting point from which to explore PCP Internet resources. Some of the major resources are listed under categories below.

The PCP Info Site: http://www.pcp-net.de/

Personal Construct Psychology: http://repgrid.com/pcp/

George A. Kelly: http://www.oikos.org/kelen.htm

MAILING LISTS

The first mailing list below has been operating since 1994 and is fully archived on the web. It was instigated to provide mutual support among researchers and practitioners, and welcomes newcomers with questions about PCP.

List for discussion of *Personal Construct Psychology*: http://www.jiscmail.ac.uk/lists/pcp.htm

List for discussion of *Computer-based Tool Usage* in personal construct psychology: http://www.jiscmail.ac.uk/lists/pcptools.html

Each site provides facilities for joining and leaving the associated mailing list, together with access to archives of past mailings.

SOCIETIES AND MAJOR CENTRES

The first three societies listed each organize regional conferences and jointly coordinate the biennial PCP Congresses.

Australasian Personal Construct Group: http://www.pcp-net.org/aus/

Constructivist Psychology Network (formerly North American Personal Construct Network): http://www2.newpaltz.edu/~raskinj/CPN.html

European Personal Construct association: http://www.pcp-net.org/epca/

German PCP Group: http://www.pcp-net.de/dppk/

Italian Constructivist Psychology and Psychotherapy Group: http://www.aippc.it/

PCP Education and Training Limited: http://www.pcpet.org.uk/

The Centre for Personal Construct Psychology: http://centrepcp.co.uk/

JOURNALS

Many journals, including psychology, education, management and computing, carry articles relating to personal construct psychology and their contents are available on the web through the publisher sites. The journals listed below specialize in the discipline.

Journal of Constructivist Psychology (formerly International Journal of Personal Construct Psychology): http://www.tandf.co.uk/journals/titles/10720537.asp

Personal Construct Theory and Practice: http://www.pcp-net.org/journal/

SOFTWARE AND SERVICES

There are a number of well-supported repertory grid elicitation and analysis programs. The major ones are listed below in alphabetical order, and others are listed at 'The PCP Info Site' cited above. The primary analysis techniques for single grids are Slater's (1977) *Ingrid* for principal components analysis and Shaw's (1980) *Focus* for hierarchical clustering, and it is noted which packages offer these, together with their other main features.

Enquire Within for Windows manages the repertory grid elicitation process using a range of techniques and uses *Focus* matching and clustering for feedback: http://www.enquirewithin.co.nz/

GRIDCOR for Windows provides various analyses including *Focus* and correspondence analysis: http://www.terapiacognitiva.net/record/gridcor.htm

GridLab for Windows is a simple version of *Ingrid*: http://www.charite.de/psycosomatik/pages/forschung/groups/gridlab/

GRIDSTAT (Bell, 1998) for Windows contains all of the major forms of analyses for a single grid, GRIDSCAL (Bell, 1999) supports the analysis of multiple grids, and IMPSTAT (Bell, 2003) produces bipolar implication grid statistics. The programs can be downloaded free from the Wiley website by those who have purchased a copy of the second edition of *A Manual for Repertory Grid Technique* (2004, Fransella, Bell & Bannister): http://www.wiley.co.uk/fransella/

GridSuite for Macintosh and Windows supports elicitation, *Ingrid* and *Focus* analyses, and comparison of grids based on the same elements:

http://www.uni-stuttgart.de/pae/gridsuite/index.php

Idiogrid for Windows provides *Ingrid* and a number of other univariate and bivariate statistics and measures: http://www.idiogrid.com/

Rep IV (RepGrid, SocioGrids, WebGrid & RepNet) for Macintosh and Windows supports conversational elicitation, *Focus*, *Ingrid*, comparison of grids with common elements or constructs, web-based elicitation and analysis, and is user-extensible through scripting. A simplified personal version of RepGrid can be downloaded free: http://repgrid.com/RepIV/

WebGrid for web browsers provides some of the elicitation and analyses capabilities of Rep IV as a freely available service on the web: http://repgrid.com/WebGrid/

OTHER RESOURCES

The following sites provide access to the literature and concepts of personal construct psychology.

Lists of chapters in virtually all the PCP edited books: http://centrepcp.co.uk/

PCP References Database: http://www.oikos.org/biblen.htm

Searchable PCP References Database: http://www.psyc.uow.edu.au/pcp/citedb/

Internet Encyclopaedia of Personal Construct Psychology:

http://www.pcp-net.org/encyclopaedia/

Research papers by Boose, Bradshaw, Gaines and Shaw: http://repgrid.com/reports/

Chapters from *Business Applications of the Repertory Grid* by Stewart: http://www.enquirewithin.co.nz/BUS_APP/business.htm

eBook *Inquiring Man* (3rd edition by Bannister and Fransella): http://www.ebookstore.tandf.co.uk/html/index.asp

The 'Fransella PCP Collection' at the University Hertfordshire contains copies of all Kelly's unpublished manuscripts plus most PCP books and other PCP materials. Photocopies of some items can be obtained from Fay Fransella (email: Ffransella@aol.com), and the contents of the Collection can be seen at the University of Hertfordshire website: http://www.voyager.herts.ac.uk

References

Adams-Webber, J.R. (1970) Elicited versus provided constructs in repertory grid technique: a review. *British Journal of Medical Psychology*, **43**, 349–354.

Adams-Webber, J.R. (1989) Kelly's pragmatic constructivism. *Canadian Psychology*, **30**, 190–193.

Adams-Webber, J.R. (1990) Some fundamental asymmetries in the structure of personal constructs. In G.J. Neimeyer & R.A. Neimeyer (Eds) *Advances in Personal Construct Psychology*. Greenwich, CT: JAI Press.

Adams-Webber, J.R. (1992) Construct asymmetry and the range of relevance of personal anticipations. *European Journal of Social Psychology*, **22**, 465–481.

Adams-Webber, J.R. (1993) The robot's designer's dilemma. *American Journal of Psychology*, **106**, 300–303.

Adams-Webber, J.R. (1996) Personal construct theory. In R. Corsini & A.J. Auerbach (Eds) *Encyclopedia of Psychology*. New York: John Wiley & Sons.

Adams-Webber, J.R. (1997) Positive-negative asymmetry in the evaluation of familiar versus unfamiliar persons and objects. *Journal of Constructivist Psychology*, **10**, 139–152.

Adams-Webber, J.R. (1998) Differentiation and sociality in terms of elicited and provided constructs. *Psychological Science*, **9**, 499–501.

Adams-Webber, J.R. (2003) Research in personal construct psychology. In F. Fransella (Ed.) *International Handbook of Personal Construct Psychology*. Chichester, UK: John Wiley & Sons.

Alexander, P.C., Neimeyer, R.A. & Follette, V.M. (1991) Group therapy for women sexually abused as children: a controlled study and investigation of individual differences. *Journal of Interpersonal Violence*, **6**, 219–231.

Alexander, P.C., Neimeyer, R.A., Follette, V.M., Moore, M.K. & Harter, S. (1989) A comparison of group treatments of women sexually abused as children. *Journal of Consulting and Clinical Psychology*, **57**, 479–483.

Alford, J., Cairney, C., Higgs, R., Honsowetz, M., Huynh, V., Jines, A., Keates, D. & Skelton, C. (2000) Real rewards from artificial intelligence. *InTech*, 52–55.

Andersen, T. (1987) The reflecting team. *Family Process*, **26**, 415–428.

Anderson, J.R. (1983) *The Architecture of Cognition*. Cambridge, MA: Harvard University Press.

Anderson, M.B. (Ed.) (2001) *Doing Sport Psychology*. Champaign, IL: Human Kinetics.

Apelgren, B.M. (2001) *Foreign Language Teachers' Voices: Personal Theories and Experiences of Change in Teaching English as a Foreign Language in Sweden*. Gothenburg: University of Gothenburg Press.

Applegate, J.L., Kline, S.L. & Delia, J.G. (1991) Alternative measures of cognitive complexity as predictors of communication performance. *International Journal of Personal Construct Psychology*, **4**, 193–213.

Argyris, C., Puttnam D. & McClain Smith, D. (1985) *Action Science*. San Francisco: Jossey-Bass.

Armstrong, T. & Eden, C. (1979) An exploration of occupational role: an exercise in team building. *Personnel Review*, **8**, 20–23.

Bachrach, P. & Baraty, M. (1970) *Power and Poverty*. New York: Oxford University Press.

Balnaves, M. & Caputi, P. (2000) A theory of social action: why personal construct psychology needs a superpattern corollary. *Journal of Constructivist Psychology*, **13**, 117–134.

Bannister, D. (1960) Conceptual structure in thought-disordered schizophrenics. *Journal of Mental Science*, **106**, 1230–1249.

Bannister, D. (1963) The genesis of schizophrenic thought disorder: a serial invalidation hypothesis. *British Journal of Psychiatry*, **109**, 680–686.

Bannister, D. (1965) The genesis of schizophrenic thought disorder: re-test of the serial invalidation hypothesis. *British Journal of Psychiatry*, **111**, 377–382.

Bannister, D. (1966a) A new theory of personality. In B. Foss (Ed.) *New Horizons in Psychology*. Harmondsworth: Penguin.

Bannister, D. (1966b) Psychology as an exercise in paradox. *Bulletin of the British Psychological Society*, **19**, 21–26.

Bannister, D. (1975) Personal construct theory psychotherapy. In D. Bannister (Ed.) *Issues and Approaches in the Psychological Therapies*. London: John Wiley & Sons.

Bannister, D. (1985) Foreword in N. Beail (Ed.) *Repertory Grid Technique and Personal Constructs: Applications in Clinical and Education Settings*. Cambridge, MA: Brookline Books.

Bannister, D. (2003) Kelly versus clockwork psychology. In F. Fransella (Ed.) *International Handbook of Personal Construct Psychology*. Chichester, UK: John Wiley & Sons.

Bannister, D., Adams-Webber, J.R., Penn, W.I. & Radley, P.L. (1975) Reversing the process of thought disorder: a serial validation experiment. *British Journal of Social and Clinical Psychology*, **14**, 169–180.

Bannister, D. & Fransella, F. (1967) *Grid Test of Schizophrenic Thought Disorder*. Barnstaple: Psychological Test Publications.

Bannister, D. & Fransella, F. (1986) *Inquiring Man* (3rd edition). London: Routledge.

Bannister, D., Fransella, F. & Agnew, J. (1971) Characteristics and validity of the Grid Test of Thought Disorder. *British Journal of Social and Clinical Psychology*, **10**, 144–151.

Bannister, D. & Mair, J.M.M. (1968) *The Evaluation of Personal Constructs*. London: Academic Press.

Bannister, D. & Salmon, P. (1966) Schizophrenic thought disorder: specific or diffuse? *British Journal of Medical Psychology*, **39**, 215–219.

Barnes, K.E. (1990) An examination of nurses' feelings about patients with specific feeding needs. *Journal of Advanced Nursing*, **15**, 703–711.

Beail, N. & Parker, C. (1991) Group fixed role therapy: a clinical application. *International Journal of Personal Construct Psychology*, **4**, 85–96.

Beaver, R. (1996) *Educational Psychology Casework*. London: Jessica Kingsley Publications.

Beckhard, R. & Harris, R. (1977) *Organisation Transitions: Managing Complex Change*. Reading, MA: Addison-Wesley.

Bell, B. & Gilbert, J. (1996) *Teacher Development: A Model from Science Education*. London: Falmer Press.

Bell, R.C. (1988) Theory-appropriate analysis of repertory grid data. *International Journal of Personal Construct Psychology*, **1**, 101–118.

Bell, R.C. (1990a) Analytic issues in the use of the repertory grid technique. In G.J. Neimeyer & R.A. Neimeyer (Eds) *Advances in Personal Construct Psychology*, Volume 1. New York: JAI Press.

Bell, R.C. (1990b) Repertory grids as mental tests: implications of test theories for grids. *International Journal of Personal Construct Psychology*, **3**, 91–103.

Bell, R.C. (1994) *Using SPSS to Analyse Repertory Grid Data*. Unpublished report, School of Behavioural Science, University of Melbourne, Australia.

Bell, R.C. (1998) *GRIDSTAT: A Program for Analysing the Data of a Repertory Grid*. [Computer software] Melbourne: Author.

Bell, R.C. (1999) *GRIDSCAL: A Program for Analysing the Data of Multiple Repertory Grids*. [Computer software] Melbourne: Author.

Bell, R.C. (2000a) On testing the commonality of constructs in supplied grids. *Journal of Constructivist Psychology*, **13**, 303–311.

Bell, R.C. (2000b) Why do statistics with repertory grids? In J. Scheer (Ed.) *The Person in Society: Challenges to a Constructivist Theory*. Giessen, Germany: Psychosozial-Verlag.

Bell, R.C. (2001) Some new measures of the dispersion of dependency in a situation-resource grid. *Journal of Constructivist Psychology*, **14**, 303–311.

Bell, R.C. (2003) *IMPSTAT: A Program for Analysing the Data of an Implications Grid.* [Computer Software] Melbourne: Author.

Bell, R.C. & Keen, T.R. (1981) A statistical aid for the grid administrator. In M.L.G. Shaw (Ed.) *Recent Advances in Personal Construct Technology.* London: Academic Press.

Bell, R.C., Vince, J. & Costigan, J. (2002) Which vary more in repertory grid data: constructs or elements? *Journal of Constructivist Psychology,* **15,** 305–312.

Ben-Peretz, M. (1984) Kelly's theory of personal constructs as a paradigm for investigating teacher thinking. In R. Halkes & J.K. Olson (Eds) *Teacher Thinking: A New Perspective on Persisting Problems in Education.* Lisse: Swets & Zeitlinger.

Ben-Peretz, M. & Kalekin-Fishman, D. (1988) Applying PCP to constructs related to music. In F. Fransella & L. Thomas (Eds) *Experimenting with Personal Construct Psychology.* London: Routledge.

Bieri, J. (1955) Cognitive complexity–simplicity and predictive behavior. *Journal of Abnormal and Social Psychology,* **51,** 263–286.

Bivens, A.J., Neimeyer, R.A., Kirchberg, T.M. & Moore, M.K. (1994) Death concern and religious belief among gays and bisexuals of variable proximity to AIDS. *Omega,* **30,** 105–120.

Blackler, F. (1995) Knowledge, work and organisations: an overview and interpretation. *Organisational Studies,* **16,** 1021–1046.

Blowers, G.H. & Bacon-Shone, J. (1994) On detecting the differences in jazz: a reassessment of comparative methods of measuring perceptual veridicality. *Empirical Studies of the Arts,* **12,** 41–58.

Boei, F., Corporaal, A. & Wim, H. (1989) Describing teacher cognitions with the rep grid. In J. Lowyck & C.M. Clark (Eds) *Teacher Thinking and Professional Action.* Leuven: Leuven University Press.

Bohart, A.C., OHara, M. & Leitner, L.M. (1998) Empirically violated treatments: disenfranchisement of humanistic and other psychotherapies. *Psychotherapy Research,* **8,** 141–157.

Bohm, D. (1996) *On Dialogue.* London: Routledge.

Bonarius, J.C.J. (1965) Research in the personal construct theory of George A. Kelly: role construct repertory test and basic theory. In B.A. Maher (Ed.) *Progress in Experimental Personality Research,* Volume 2. New York: Academic Press.

Boose, J.H. (1984) Personal construct theory and the transfer of human expertise. In *Proceedings AAAI-84.* California: American Association for Artificial Intelligence, pp. 27–33.

Boose, J.H. (1986) *Expertise Transfer for Expert Systems.* Amsterdam: Elsevier.

Botella, L. (2000) Personal construct psychology, constructivism, and psychotherapy research. In J.W. Scheer (Ed.) *The Person in Society: Challenges to a Constructivist Theory.* Giessen, Germany: Psychosozial-Verlag.

Botella, L. & Feixas, G. (1992–1993) The autobiographical group: a tool for the reconstruction of past life experience with the aged. *International Journal of Aging and Human Development,* **36,** 303–319.

Bright, J.C. (1985) *A pack of lies.* Unpublished dissertation. London: Centre for Personal Construct Psychology, UK.

Brophy, S. (2002) *Organisation development interventions using PCP.* Paper read at the 6th Conference of the European Personal Construct Association, Florence, Italy.

Brophy, S. & Epting, F.R. (1996) Mentoring employees: a role for personal construct psychology. In B.M. Walker, J. Costigan, L.L. Viney & B. Warren (Eds) *Personal Construct Theory: Psychology for the Future.* Carlton, South Victoria: The Australian Psychological Society.

Brown, R.W. (1958) Is a boulder sweet or sour? *Contemporary Psychology,* **3,** 113–115.

Bruner, J.S. (1956) A cognitive theory of personality. *Contemporary Psychology,* **1,** 355–358.

Bruner, J.S. (1990) *Acts of Meaning.* Cambridge, MA: Harvard University Press.

Bugental, J.F.T. (1964) Investigations into the self-concept: instructions for the Who-Are-You method. *Psychological Reports,* **15,** 634–650.

Burrell, M.J. (2002) Deconstructing and reconstructing substance use and 'addictions'. In R.A. Neimeyer & G.J. Neimeyer (Eds) *Advances in Personal Construct Psychology,* Volume 5. New York: Praeger.

Burrell, M.J. & Jaffe, A.J. (1999) Personal meaning, drug use, and addiction: an evolutionary constructivist perspective. *Journal of Constructivist Psychology,* **12,** 41–63.

Butler, C. (1995) Investigating the effects of stress on the success and failure of music conservatory students. In *Medical Problems of Performing Artists*. Philadelphia, PA: Hanley & Belfus.

Butler, R.J. (1996) *Performance Profiling*. National Coaching Foundation. Leeds, England: Coachwise.

Butler, R.J. (2001) *The Self Image Profiles: Manual*. London: The Psychological Corporation.

Butler, R.J. & Green, D. (1998) *The Child Within: The Exploration of Personal Construct Theory with Young People*. Oxford: Butterworth-Heinemann.

Butt, T. (1995) Ordinal relationships between constructs. *Journal of Constructivist Psychology*, **8**, 227–836.

Butt, T. (2003) The phenomenological context of personal construct psychology. In F. Fransella (Ed.) *International Handbook of Personal Construct Psychology*. Chichester, UK: John Wiley & Sons.

Butt, T., Burr, V. & Epting, F.R. (1997a) Core construing: self-discovery or self- invention? In G.J. Neimeyer & R.A. Neimeyer (Eds) *Advances in Personal Construct Psychology*, Volume 4. Greenwich, CT: JAI Press.

Butt, T., Burr, V. & Bell, R. (1997b) Fragmentation and the sense of self. *Constructivism in the Human Sciences*, **2**, 12–29.

Button, E.J. (1980) *Construing and clinical outcome in anorexia nervosa*. Unpublished PhD thesis, University of London.

Button, E.J. (1987) Construing people or weight? An eating disorders group. In R.A. and G.J. Neimeyer (Eds) *Personal Construct Therapy Casebook*. New York: Springer.

Button, E.J. (1988) Music and personal constructs. In F. Fransella & L. Thomas (Eds) *Experimenting with Personal Construct Psychology*. London: Routledge.

Button, E.J. (1993) *Eating Disorders: Personal Construct Therapy and Change*. Chichester, UK: John Wiley & Sons.

Caputi, P., Breiger, R. & Pattison, P. (1990) Analyzing implications grids using hierarchical models. *International Journal of Personal Construct Psychology*, **3**, 77–90.

Caputi, P. & Keynes, N. (2001) A note on the stability of structural measures based on repertory grids. *Journal of Constructivist Psychology*, **14**, 51–55.

Caputi, P. & Reddy, P. (1999) A comparison of triadic and dyadic methods of personal construct elicitation. *Journal of Constructivist Psychology*, **12**, 253–264.

Chandler, A.D. Jr (1977) *The Visible Hand: The Managerial Revolution in American Business*. Cambridge, MA: Harvard University Press.

Chiari, G., Mancini, F., Nicolo, F. & Nuzzo, M.L. (1990) Hierarchical organization of personal construct systems in terms of the range of convenience. *International Journal of Personal Construct Psychology*, **3**, 281–311.

Chiari, G. & Nuzzo, M.L. (2003) Kelly's philosophy of constructive alternativism. In F. Fransella (Ed.) *International Handbook of Personal Construct Psychology*. Chichester, UK: John Wiley & Sons.

Clancey, W.J. (1989) Viewing knowledge bases as qualitative models. *IEEE Expert*, **4**, 9–23.

Clapp, R. & Cornelius, N. (2002) *New views on equality action in organisations*. Paper read at the 6th Congress of the European Personal Construct Association, Florence, Italy.

Clark, C.M. (1986) Ten years of conceptual development in research on teacher thinking. In M. Ben-Peretz, R. Bromme & R. Halkes (Eds) *Advances in Research on Teacher Thinking*. Lisse, Netherlands: Swets & Zeitlinger.

Clark, C.M. (1995) *Thoughtful Teaching*. London: Cassell.

Clinton, M., Moyle, W., Weir, D. & Edwards, H. (1995) Perceptions of stressors and reported coping strategies in nurses caring for residents with Alzheimer's disease in a dementia unit. *Australian and New Zealand Journal of Mental Health Nursing*, **4**, 5–13.

Coish, B.J. (1990) *A personal construct theory of bulimia*. Unpublished PhD thesis, La Trobe University, Australia.

Collins, D. (1998) *Organizational Change: Sociological Perspectives*. London: Routledge.

Cornelius, N. (Ed.) (2002) *Building Workplace Equality: Ethics, Diversity and Inclusion*. London: Thomson.

Cornelius, N. & Gagnon, S. (2004) Still bearing the mark of Cain? Ethics, diversity and inequality measurement. *Business Ethics: A European Review*, **13**, 27–40.

Cortazzi, D. & Root, S. (1975) *Illuminative Incident Analysis*. London: McGraw-Hill.

Costigan, J. (1985) Personal construct psychology: a theoretical and methodological framework for nursing research. *The Australian Journal of Advanced Nursing*, **2**, 15–23.

Costigan, J., Closs, B. & Eustace, P. (2000) Laddering: theoretical and methodological contingencies—some order and a little chaos. In J.W. Scheer (Ed.) *The Person in Society: Challenges to a Constructivist Theory*. Giessen, Germany: Psychosozial-Verlag.

Costigan, J., Humphrey, J. & Murphy, C. (1987) Attempted suicide: a personal construct psychology exploration. *The Australian Journal of Advanced Nursing*, **4**, 39–50.

Crispin, W.M. (1990) *The personal myths, mysteries and metaphors of student nurses as they adapt to the educational process*. Paper presented at the 4th National Nursing Education Conference, Melbourne.

Cummins, P. (2005) *Working with Anger*. Chichester, UK: John Wiley & Sons.

Dallos, R. (1991) *Family Belief Systems, Therapy and Change: A Constructional Approach*. Milton Keynes: Open University Press.

Davidson, G. & Reser, J. (1996) Construing and constructs: personal and cultural? In B.M. Walker, J. Costigan, L.L. Viney & B. Warren (Eds) *Personal Construct Theory: A Psychology for the Future*. Australian Psychological Society Imprint Book.

Davies, J. (1976) Orchestral discord. *New Society*, 8 January, pp. 46–47.

Dempsey, D.J. & Neimeyer, R.A. (1995) Organization of personal knowledge: convergent validation of implications grids and repertory grids as measures of system structure. *Journal of Constructivist Psychology*, **8**, 251–261.

Denicolo, P.M. & Pope, M.L. (1990) Adults learning–teacher thinking. In C. Day, M.L. Pope & P.M. Denicolo (Eds) *Insight into Teachers' Thinking and Practice*. London: Falmer Press.

Denicolo, P.M. & Pope, M.L. (2001) *Transformative Professional Practice: Personal Construct Approaches to Education and Research*. London: Whurr Publishers.

Diamond, C.P.T. (1985) Fixed role treatment: enacting alternative scenarios. *Australian Journal of Education*, **29**, 161–173.

Diamond, C.P.T. (1991) *Teacher Education as Transformation*. Milton Keynes: Open University Press.

Diamond, P. & Thompson, M. (1985) Using personal construct theory to assess a midwives' refresher course. *The Australian Journal of Advanced Nursing*, **2**, 24–35.

DiLollo, A., Neimeyer, R.A. & Manning, W.H. (2001) A personal construct psychology view of relapse: indications for a narrative therapy component to stuttering treatment. *Journal of Fluency Disorders*, **26**, 1–24.

Dreyfus, H.L. & Dreyfus, S.E. (1986) *Mind Over Machine: The Power of Human Intuition and Expertise in the Era of the Computer*. New York: Free Press.

Dunn, W.N., Cahill, A.G., Dukes, M.J. & Ginsberg, A. (1986) The policy grid: a cognitive methodology for assessing policy dynamics. In W.N. Dunn (Ed.) *Policy Analysis: Perspectives, Concepts, and Methods*. New York: JAI Press.

Dunnett, N.G.M. & Miyaguchi, R. (1993) Reflexivity in theory and practice. In L.M. Leitner & N.G.M. Dunnett (Eds) *Critical Issues in Personal Construct Psychotherapy*. Malabar, FL: Krieger.

Dyson, J. (1996) Nurses' conceptualizations of caring attitudes and behaviours. *Journal of Advanced Nursing*, **23**, 1263–1269.

Ecker, B. & Hulley, L. (1996) *Depth-Oriented Brief Therapy*. San Francisco: Jossey Bass.

Edwards, B. (1998) A & E nurses' constructs on the nature of nursing expertise: a repertory grid technique. *Accident and Emergency Nursing*, **6**, 18–23.

Efran, J.S., Lukens, M.D. & Lukens, R.J. (1990) *Language, Structure, and Change*. New York: Norton.

Ellis, J. (1992) *A personal construct approach to perceptions of care: The registered nurse and the elderly nursing home resident*. Unpublished masters dissertation.

Ellis, J. (1996) He was big and old and frightening: nursing students constructs' of older people. In B.M. Walker, J. Costigan, L.L. Viney & W. Warren (Eds) *Personal Construct Theory: A Psychology for the Future*. Melbourne: Australian Psychological Society.

Ellis, J. (1997) Nurses' anticipations of caring for elderly patients. In P.M. Denicolo & M.L. Pope (Eds) *Sharing Understanding and Practice*. Farnborough: EPCA Publications.

Ellis, J. (1999) Nursing care of older people: a personal construct theory perspective. *Journal of Advanced Nursing*, **29**, 160–168.

Ellis-Scheer, J. (2000) *The professional identity of nurses: An empirical investigation of personal constructions using the repertory grid technique*. Unpublished doctoral dissertation.

Epting, F.R. (1984) *Personal Construct Counseling and Psychotherapy*. Chichester: John Wiley & Sons.

Epting, F.R. & Nazario, A.Jr. (1987) Designing a fixed role therapy: issues, techniques, and modifications. In R.A. Neimeyer & G.J. Neimeyer (Eds) *Personal Construct Therapy Casebook*. New York: Springer.

Epting, F.R., Prichard, S., Wiggins, S.C., Leonard, J.A. & Beagle, J.W. (1992) Assessment of the first factor and related measures of construct differentiation. *International Journal of Personal Construct Psychology*, **5**, 77–94.

Epting, F.R., Probert, J.S. & Pittman, S.D. (1993) Alternative strategies for construct elicitation: experimenting with experience. *International Journal of Personal Construct Psychology*, **6**, 79–98.

Epting, F.R. & Suchman, D.I. (1999) The therapist's use of self and personal experience. In A.C. Richards & T. Schumrum (Eds) *Invitations to Dialogue: The Legacy of Sidney M. Jourard*. Dubuque, IA: Kendall/Hunt.

Evans, C., Mellor-Clark, J., Margison, F., Barkham, M., Audin, K., Connell, J., & McGrath, G. (2000) CORE–Clinical Outcomes in Routine Evaluation. *Journal of Mental Health*, **9**(3), 247–255.

Evesham, M. & Fransella, F. (1985) Stuttering relapse: the effects of a combined speech and psychological reconstruction program. *British Journal of Disorders of Communication*, **20**, 237–248.

Feigenbaum, E.A. (1980) Knowledge engineering: the applied side of artificial intelligence. STAN-CS-80–812, Department of Computer Science, Stanford University.

Feigenbaum, E.A., Buchanan, B.G. & Lederberg, J. (1971) On generality and problem solving: a case study using the DENDRAL program. In D. Michie (Eds) *Machine Intelligence 6*. Edinburgh: Edinburgh University Press.

Feixas, G. (1995) Personal constructs in systemic practice. In R.A. Neimeyer & M. Mahoney (Eds) *Constructivism in Psychotherapy*. Washington, DC: American Psychological Association.

Feixas, G., Geldschläger, H. & Neimeyer, R.A. (2002) Content analysis of personal constructs. *Journal of Constructivist Psychology*, **15**, 1–9.

Feixas, G., Moliner, J.L., Montes, J.N., Mari, M.T. & Neimeyer, R.A. (1992) The stability of structural measures derived from repertory grids. *International Journal of Personal Construct Psychology*, **5**, 25–39.

Fisher & Brown (1989) *Getting Together: Building a Relationship That Gets to Yes*. London: Business Books.

Fisher, R. & Ury, W. (1991) *Getting to Yes: Negotiating Agreement Without Giving In* (2nd edition). London: Penguin.

Flavell, J.H. (1963) *The Developmental Psychology of Jean Piaget*. Princeton: Van Nostrand.

Fleck, J. (1982) Development and establishment in artificial intelligence. In N. Elias, H. Martins & R. Whitley (Eds) *Scientific Establishments and Hierarchies*. Holland: D. Reidel.

Fodor, J. (1983) *The Modularity of Mind*. Cambridge, MA: MIT Press.

Ford, K.M. (1989) A constructivist view of the frame problem in artificial intelligence. *Canadian Psychology*, **30**, 188–190.

Ford, K.M., Bradshaw, J.M., Adams-Webber, J.R. & Agnew, N.M. (1993) Knowledge acquisition as a constructive modeling activity. *International Journal of Intelligent Systems*, **8**, 9–32.

Forrester, J. (1993) Systems dynamics and the lessons of 35 years. In K.B. De Greene (Ed.) *A Systems-Based Approach to Policy Making*. Boston: Kluwer Academic Publishers.

Forster, J.R. (1991) Facilitating positive changes in self-constructions. *International Journal of Personal Construct Psychology*, **4**, 281–292.

Foster, H. & Viney, L.L. (2005) Personal construct workshops for women experiencing menopause: reconstruction and validation of non-verbal, preverbal and verbal construing. In D.A. Winter & L.L. Viney (Eds) *Personal Construct Psychotherapy: Advances in Theory, Practice and Research*. London: Whurr.

Fransella, F. (1970) Stuttering, not a symptom but a way of life. *British Journal of Communication Disorders*, **5**, 22.

Fransella, F. (1972) *Personal Change and Reconstruction*. London: Academic Press.

Fransella, F. (1981) Nature babbling to herself. In H. Bonarius, R. Holland & S. Rosenburg (Eds) *Personal Construct Psychology: Recent Advances in Theory and Practice*. London: Macmillan.

Fransella, F. (1983) What sort of scientist is the person-as-scientist? In J.R. Adams-Webber & J.C. Mancuso (Eds) *Applications of Personal Construct Theory*. Ontario: Academic Press.

Fransella, F. (1988) The ideographic research unit of the Centre for Personal Construct Psychology. In F. Fransella & L. Thomas (Eds) *Experimenting with Personal Construct Psychology*. London: Routledge.

Fransella, F. (1993) The construct of resistance in psychotherapy. In L.M. Leitner & N.G.M. Dunnett (Eds) *Critical Issues in Personal Construct Psychotherapy*. Malabar, FL: Krieger.

Fransella, F. (1995) *George Kelly*. London: Sage Publications.

Fransella, F. (2000) George Kelly and mathematics. In J.W. Scheer (Ed.) *The Person in Society: Challenges to a Constructivist Theory*. Giessen, Germany: Psychosozial-Verlag.

Fransella, F. & Bannister, D. (1977) *A Manual for Repertory Grid Technique*. London: Academic Press.

Fransella, F., Bell, R. & Bannister, D. (2004) *A Manual for Repertory and Technique* (2nd edn). Chichester: John Wiley & Sons, Ltd.

Frisbie, L., Vanasek, F. & Dingman, H. (1967) The self and the ideal self: methodological study of pedophiles. *Psychological Reports*, **20**, 699–706.

Fromm, F. (2003) Learning and diagnosis of learning results. In F. Fransella (Ed.) *International Handbook of Personal Construct Psychology*. Chichester, UK: John Wiley & Sons.

Gagnon, S. & Cornelius, N. (2000) Re-examining workplace inequality: the capabilities approach. *Human Resource Management Journal*, **10**, 68–87.

Gaines, B.R. & Shaw, M.L.G. (1980) New directions in the analysis and interactive elicitation of personal construct systems. *International Journal Man–Machine Studies*, **13**, 81–116.

Gaines, B.R. & Shaw, M.L.G. (1993) Basing knowledge acquisition tools in personal construct psychology. *Knowledge Engineering Review*, **8**, 49–85.

Gaines, B.R. & Shaw, M.L.G. (1997) Knowledge acquisition, modeling and inference through the World Wide Web. *International Journal of Human–Computer Studies*, **46**, 729–759.

Galsworthy, P. (1997) Pan-company marketing at British Airways 1983–1994. *Marketing Council Case Study*.

Gamino, L.A., Sewell, K.W., Easterling, L.W. & Stirman, L. (1998) Scott & White grief study: an empirical test of predictors of intensified mourning. *Death Studies*, **22**, 333–355.

Gardner, R.A. (1971) *The Mutual-Story-Telling Technique*. New York: Science House.

Gillard, D. (2002) Personal communication.

Golembiewski, R.T. (1986) Contours in social change: elemental graphics and a surrogate variable for gamma change. *Academy of Management Review*, **11**, 550–567.

Golembiewski, R.T. (1995) *Managing Diversity in Organizations*. Tuscaloosa, AL: University of Alabama Press.

Golembiewski, R.T. (1997) Flight plan acknowledged: but definite restrictions apply; and more direct routes may exist. *Academy of Management Review*, **22**, 16–19.

Greenberg, L., Elliott, R. & Rice, L. (1993) *Facilitating Emotional Change*. New York: Guilford.

Guidano, V.F. (1991) *The Self in Process*. New York: Guilford Press.

Gutt, E.A. (2000) *Translation and Relevance: Cognition and Context*. Manchester: St Jerome.

Hagans, C.L., Neimeyer, G.J. & Goodholm, C.R. (2000) The effect of elicitation methods on personal construct differentiation and valence. *Journal of Constructivist Psychology*, **13**, 155–173.

Harter, S.L. & Neimeyer, R.A. (1995) Long-term effects of child sexual abuse: toward a constructivist theory of trauma and its treatment. In R.A. Neimeyer & G.J. Neimeyer (Eds) *Advances in Personal Construct Psychology*, Volume 3. Greenwich, CT: JAI Press.

Hartmann, A. (1992) Element comparisons in repertory grid technique: results and consequences of a Monte Carlo study. *International Journal of Personal Construct Psychology*, **5**, 41–56.

Haugli, L., Steen, E., Nygard, R. & Finset, A. (2001) Learning to have less pain—is it possible? A one-year follow-up study of the effects of a personal construct group learning programme on patients with chronic musculoskeletal pain. *Patient Education and Counseling*, **45**, 111–118.

Hay, J. (1995) *Transformational Mentoring*. Maidenhead: McGraw-Hill.

Hayes-Roth, F. (1984) The industrialization of knowledge engineering. In W. Reitman (Ed.) *Artificial Intelligence Applications for Business*. Norwood, NJ: Ablex.

Hayes-Roth, F., Waterman, D.A. & Lenat, D.B. (1983) *Building Expert Systems*. Reading, MA: Addison-Wesley.

Heyman, R., Shaw, M.P. & Harding, J. (1983) A personal construct theory approach to the socialization of nursing trainees in two British general hospitals. *Journal of Advanced Nursing*, **8**, 59–67.

Hinkle, D.N. (1965) *The change of personal constructs from the viewpoint of a theory of implications*. Unpublished PhD thesis, Columbus, OH: Ohio State University.

Hinkle, D.N. (1970) The game of personal constructs. In D. Bannister (Ed.) *Perspectives in Personal Construct Theory*. London: Academic Press.

Hirst, W. (1988) *The Making of Cognitive Science*. Cambridge, UK: Cambridge University Press.

Horley, J. & Francoeur, A. (2003) Personal construct group therapy with domestic abusers: a program rationale and preliminary results. Paper presented at 15th International Congress of Personal Construct Psychology, Huddersfield, UK.

Howkins, E. & Ewens, A. (1997) Community nurses' perceptions of self in role. In P. Denicolo & M. Pope (Eds) *Sharing Understanding and Practice*. Farnborough: EPCA Publications.

Hoy, R.M. (1973) The meaning of alcoholism for alcoholics: a repertory grid study. *British Journal of Social and Clinical Psychology*, **12**, 98–99.

Humphreys, C.L., Dutile, R. & Leitner, L. (2001) *Empirical support for experiential personal construct therapy: A common 'factor analysis'*. Paper presented at the 14th International Congress of Personal Construct Psychology, Wollongong, Australia.

Ishmael, A. (1999) *Harassment: Bullying and Violence at Work*. London: The Industrial Society.

Jackson, D.N. & Paunonen, S.V. (1981) Personality structure and assessment. *Annual Review of Psychology*, **31**, 503–551.

Jackson, S. (1992) A PCT therapy group for adolescents. In P. Maitland and D. Brennan (Eds) *Personal Construct Theory Deviancy and Social Work*. London: Inner London Probation Service/Centre for Personal Construct Psychology.

James, W. (1884) Essay 'What is an Emotion?' See W. James (1890) The emotions. In *The Principles of Psychology*, Volume 2. New York: Dover Publications.

Jankowicz, A.D. (1994) The new journey to Jerusalem: mission and meaning in the managerial crusade to Eastern Europe. *Organization Studies*, **15**, 479–507.

Jankowicz, A.D. (1999) Planting a paradigm in Central Europe: do we graft, or must we breed the rootstock anew? *Management Learning*, **30**, 281–299.

Jankowicz, A.D. (2001) Why does subjectivity make us nervous? Making the tacit explicit. *Journal of Intellectual Capital*, **2**, 61–73.

Jankowicz, D. (2003) *The Easy Guide to Repertory Grids*. Chichester, UK: John Wiley & Sons.

Jones, H. (1993) The core process interview. *EPCA Newsletter*, **2**, 19–20.

Jones, H.G. (1971) In search of an ideographic psychology. *Bulletin of the British Psychological Society*, **24**, 279–290.

Jones, R.E. (1961) Identification in terms of personal constructs: reconciling a paradox in theory. *Journal of Consulting Psychology*, **25**, 276.

Kalekin-Fishman, D. (2003) Social relations in the modern world. In F. Fransella (Ed.) *International Handbook of Personal Construct Psychology*. Chichester, UK: John Wiley & Sons.

Karst, T.O. & Trexler, L.D. (1970) Initial study using fixed role and rational-emotive therapy in treating speaking anxiety. *Journal of Consulting and Clinical Psychology*, **34**, 360–366.

Keen, T.R. & Bell, R.C. (1981) One thing leads to another: a new approach to elicitation in the Repertory Grid Technique. In M.L.G. Shaw (Ed.) *Recent Advances in Personal Construct Technology*. London: Academic Press.

Kelly, G.A. (1924) The sincere motive *The Messenger of Peace*. Indiana: Peace Association of Friends of America. Copy in Fransella PCP Collection, University of Hertfordshire, UK.

Kelly, G.A. (1932) *Understandable psychology*. Unpublished manuscript, Chapter 20. Copy in Fransella PCP Collection, University of Hertfordshire, UK.

Kelly, G.A. (c. 1954) *Knowledge: discovery or invention?* Unpublished manuscript. Copy in Fransella PCP Collection, University of Hertfordshire, UK.

Kelly, G.A. (1955/1991) *The Psychology of Personal Constructs*. Volumes 1 and 2. First published by Norton, 1955, then by Routledge in collaboration with the Centre for Personal Construct Psychology, 1991.

Kelly, G.A. (1959a) *The function of interpretation*. Unpublished manuscripts of three talks. Falmouth: Fransella.

Kelly, G.A. (1959b) *Values, Knowledge and Social Control*. Symposium of the American Psychological Association, Cincinnati (1989) Falmouth: Fransella.

Kelly, G.A. (1962) Europe's matrix of decision. In R.M. Jones (Ed.) *Nebraska Symposium on Motivation*. University of Nebraska Press, Lincoln, Nebraska. Reprinted in D. Kalekin-Fishman & B.M. Walker (Eds) (1996) *The Construction of Group Realities*. Malabar, FL: Krieger.

Kelly, G.A. (1963) Aldous: the personable computer. In Tomkins, S.S. & Messick, S. (Eds) *Computer Simulation of Personality*. New York: John Wiley & Sons.

Kelly, G.A. (1966a) *Experimental dependency*. Unpublished unfinished manuscript, Brandeis University. Copy of manuscript in Fransella PCP Collection, University of Hertfordshire, UK.

Kelly, G.A. (1966b) Unpublished audio-taped interview with Fay Fransella.

Kelly, G.A. (1969a) Humanistic methodology in psychological research. In B. Maher (Ed.) *Clinical Psychology and Personality: The Selected Papers of George Kelly*. New York: John Wiley & Sons.

Kelly, G.A. (1969b) Man's construction of his alternatives. In B. Maher (Ed.) *Clinical Psychology and Personality: The Selected Papers of George Kelly*. New York: John Wiley & Sons.

Kelly, G.A. (1969c) Sin and psychotherapy. In B. Maher (Ed.) *Clinical Psychology and Personality: The Selected Papers of George Kelly*. New York: John Wiley & Sons.

Kelly, G.A. (1969d) The language of hypothesis: man's psychological instrument. In B. Maher (Ed.) *Clinical Psychology and Personality: The Selected Papers of George Kelly*. New York: John Wiley & Sons.

Kelly, G.A. (1969e) The role of classification in personality theory. In B. Maher (Ed.) *Clinical Psychology and Personality: The Selected Papers of George Kelly*. New York: John Wiley & Sons.

Kelly, G.A. (1969f) A mathematical approach to psychology. In B. Maher (Ed.) *Clinical Psychology and Personality: The Selected Papers of George Kelly*. New York: John Wiley & Sons.

Kelly, G.A. (1969g) In whom confide: on whom depend for what? In B. Maher (Ed.) *Clinical Psychology and Personality: The Selected Papers of George Kelly*. New York: John Wiley & Sons.

Kelly, G.A. (1969h) Ontological acceleration. In B. Maher (Ed.) *Clinical Psychology and Personality: The Selected Papers of George Kelly*. New York: John Wiley & Sons.

Kelly, G.A. (1969i) The psychotherapeutic relationship. In B. Maher (Ed.) *Clinical Psychology and Personality: The Selected Papers of George Kelly*. New York: John Wiley & Sons.

Kelly, G.A. (1969j) The strategy of psychological research. In B. Maher (Ed.) *Clinical Psy-*

chology and Personality: The Selected Papers of George Kelly. New York: John Wiley & Sons.

Kelly, G.A. (1969k) The autobiography of a theory. In B. Maher, *Clinical Psychology and Personality: The Selected Papers of George Kelly*. New York: John Wiley & Sons.

Kelly, G.A. (1969l) Hostility. In B. Maher (Ed.) *Clinical Psychology and Personality: The Selected Papers of George Kelly*. New York: John Wiley & Sons.

Kelly, G.A. (1970) Behaviour as an experiment. In D. Bannister (Ed.) *Perspectives in Personal Construct Theory*. London: Academic Press.

Kelly, G.A. (1977) The psychology of the unknown. In D. Bannister (Ed.) *New Perspectives in Personal Construct Theory*. London: Academic Press.

Kelly, G.A. (1978) Confusion and the clock. In F. Fransella (Ed.) *Personal Construct Psychology 1977*. London: Academic Press.

Kelly, G.A. (1979) Social inheritance. In P. Stringer & D. Bannister (Eds) *Constructs of Sociality in Individuality*. London: Academic Press.

Kelly, G.A. (1980) A psychology of the optimal man. In A.W. Landfield & L.M. Leitner (Eds) *Personal Construct Psychology: Psychotherapy and Personality*. New York: John Wiley & Sons.

Kelly, G.A. (1996) Europe's matrix of decision. In D. Kalekin-Fishman & B. Walker (Eds) *The Construction of Group Realities: Culture, Society and Personal Construct Psychology*. Malabar, FL: Krieger.

Kelly, G.A. (2003) A brief introduction to personal construct theory. In F. Fransella (Ed.) *International Handbook of Personal Construct Psychology*. Chichester, UK: John Wiley & Sons.

Kelly, G.A. with Warnock, G.W. (1935) *Inductive trigonometry*. Unpublished book manuscript.

Kenny, V. (1987) Family somatics: a personal construct approach to cancer. In R.A. Neimeyer & G.J. Neimeyer (Eds) *Personal Construct Therapy Casebook*. New York: Springer.

Kim, J. (1993) *Supervenience and Mind: Selected Philosophical Essays*. Cambridge: Cambridge University Press.

Kirchberg, T.M., Neimeyer, R.A. & James, R.K. (1998) Beginning counselors' death concerns and empathic responses to client situations involving death and grief. *Death Studies*, **22**, 99–120.

Kirsch, H. & Jordan, J. (2000) Emotions and personal constructs. In J.W. Scheer (Ed.) *The Person in Society: Challenges to a Constructivist Theory*. Giessen, Germany: Psychosozial-Verlag.

Klion, R.E. & Pfenninger, D.T. (1997) Personal construct psychotherapy of addictions. *Journal of Substance Abuse Treatment*, **14**, 37–43.

Krieger, S.R., Epting, F.R. & Leitner, L.M. (1974) Personal constructs, threat, and attitudes toward death. *Omega*, **5**, 299–310.

Kroonenberg, P.M. (1985) Three-mode principal components: analysis of semantic differential data: the case of a triple personality. *Applied Psychological Measurement*, **9**, 83–94.

Krosnick, J.A. (1999) Survey research. *Annual Review of Psychology*, **50**, 537–567.

Lakoff, G. & Johnson, M. (1980) *Metaphors We Live By*. Chicago: University of Chicago Press.

Landfield, A.W. (1971) *Personal Construct Systems in Psychotherapy*. Chicago: Rand-McNally.

Landfield, A.W. (1977) Interpretive man: the enlarged self-image. In J.K. Cole & A.W. Landfield (Eds) *Nebraska Symposium on Motivation 1976: Personal Construct Psychology*. Lincoln, NE: University of Nebraska Press.

Landfield, A.W. (1979) Exploring socialisation through the Interpersonal Transaction Group. In P. Stringer & D. Bannister (Eds) *Constructs of Sociality and Individuality*. London: Academic Press.

Landfield, A.W. & Cannell, J.E. (1988) Ways of assessing functionally independent construction, meaningfulness, and construction in hierarchy. In J.C. Mancuso & M.L.G. Shaw (Eds) *Cognition and Personal Structure: Computer Access and Analysis*. New York: Praeger.

Landfield, A.W. & Schmittdiel, C. (1983) The interpersonal transaction group: evolving measurements in the pursuit of theory. In J. Adams-Webber & J. Mancuso (Eds) *Applications of Personal Construct Psychology*. Toronto: Academic Press.

Lane, L.G. & Viney, L.L. (2001a) *When the unreal becomes real: an evaluation of personal construct group psychotherapy with survivors of breast cancer.* Paper presented at the 14th International Congress of Personal Construct Psychology, Wollongong, Australia.

Lane, L.G. & Viney, L.L. (2001b) *Role relationships and the restoration of coherence in the stories of women diagnosed with breast cancer: a group intervention.* Paper presented at the 14th International Congress of Personal Construct Psychology, Wollongong, Australia.

Lane, L.G. & Viney, L.L. (2005) Personal construct group work with women with breast cancer: role relationships and support. In D.A. Winter & L.L. Viney (Eds) *Personal Construct Psychotherapy: Advances in Theory, Practice and Research.* London: Whurr.

Laubach, W., Brown, C.E. & Lenard, J.M. (1996) Nurses and physicians evaluate their intensive care experiences. *Heart and Lung: The Journal of Acute and Critical Care*, **25**, 475–482.

Lawlor, M. & Cochran, L. (1981) Does invalidation produce loose construing? *British Journal of Medical Psychology*, **54**, 41–50.

Le Guin, U. (1985) *Always Coming Home*. New York: Harper & Row.

Leach, C. (1981) Direct analysis of a repertory grid. In M.L.G. Shaw (Ed.) *Recent Advances in Personal Construct Technology*. London: Academic Press.

Leach, C., Freshwater, K., Aldridge, J. & Sunderland, J. (2001) Analysis of repertory grids in clinical practice. *British Journal of Clinical Psychology*, **40**, 225–248.

Lee, J. (2000) *Shakespeare's 'Hamlet' and the Controversies of Self*. Oxford: Oxford University Press.

Lee, J. (2002) Personal communication.

Leitner, L.M. & Epting, F.R. (2001) Constructivist approaches to therapy. In K.J. Schneider, J.F.T. Bugental & J.F. Pierson (Eds) *The Handbook of Humanistic Psychology: Leading Edges in Theory, Research, and Practice*. Thousand Oaks, CA: Sage Publications.

Leitner, L.M., Faidley, A.J. & Celentana, M.A. (2000) Diagnosing human meaning making: an experiential constructivist approach. In R.A. Neimeyer & J.D. Raskin (Eds) *Construction of Disorders: Meaning Making Frameworks for Psychotherapy*. Washington, DC: American Psychological Association.

Leitner, L.M. & Thomas, J. (2003) Experiential personal construct psychotherapy. In F. Fransella (Ed.) *International Handbook of Personal Construct Psychology*. Chichester, UK: John Wiley & Sons.

Levy, L.H. & Dugan, R.D. (1956) Personal constructs and predictive behaviour. *Journal of Consulting Psychology*, **53**, 54–58.

Lighthill, J. (1973) Artificial intelligence: a general survey. In *Artificial Intelligence: A Paper Symposium*. UK: Science Research Council.

Lira, F.T., Nay, W.R., McCullough, J.P. & Etkin, W. (1975) Relative effects of modeling and role playing in the treatment of avoidance behaviors. *Journal of Consulting and Clinical Psychology*, **43**, 608–618.

Llewelyn, S. & Dunnett, G. (1987) The use of personal construct theory in groups. In R.A. Neimeyer & G.J. Neimeyer (Eds) *Personal Construct Theory Casebook*. New York: Springer.

Lohaus, A. (1986) Standardizations in methods of data collection; adverse effects on reliability? *Australian Psychologist*, **21**, 241–251.

Lovelock, J. (2000) *Homage to Gaia: The Life of an Independent Scientist*. Oxford: Oxford University Press.

Lovenfosse, M. & Viney, L.L. (1999) Understanding and helping mothers of children with 'special needs' using personal construct group work. *Community Mental Health Journal*, **35**, 431–442.

Mackay, D. (1975) *Clinical Psychology: Theory and Therapy*. London: Methuen.

Mackay, N. (1992) Identification, reflection, and correlation: problems in the bases of repertory grid measures. *International Journal of Personal Construct Psychology*, **5**, 57–75.

Magna Books (1993) *Naïve Painting. Book of 30 Postcards*. Wigston: Magna Books.

Mair, J.M.M. (1970) Psychological problems and cigarette smoking. *Journal of Psychosomatic Research*, **14**, 277–283.

Mair, J.M.M. (1972) Personal communication.

Mair, M. (1977) The community of self. In D. Bannister (Ed.) *New Perspectives in Personal Construct Theory*. London: Academic Press.

Mair, M. (1985) The long quest to know. In F. Epting & A.W. Landfield (Eds) *Anticipating Personal Construct Theory*. Lincoln, NE: University of Nebraska Press.

Mair, M. (1988) Psychology as story telling. *International Journal of Personal Construct Psychology*, **1**, 125–137.

Mair, M. (1989a) *Between Psychology and Psychotherapy: A Poetics of Experience*. London: Routledge.

Mair, M. (1989b) Kelly, Bannister, and a story-telling psychology. *International Journal of Personal Construct Psychology*, **2**, 1–14.

Makhlouf-Norris, F. & Jones, H.G. (1971) Conceptual distance indices as measures of alienation in obsessional neurosis. *Psychological Medicine*, **1**, 381–387.

Mancuso, J.C. (2003) Children's development of personal constructs. In F. Fransella (Ed.) *International Handbook of Personal Construct Psychology*. Chichester, UK: John Wiley & Sons.

Mancuso, J.C. & Hunter, K.V. (1985a) Constructivist assumptions in the person theories of G.A. Kelly and Jean Piaget *http://www.capital.net/mancusolpiagkely.html*.

Mancuso, J.C. & Hunter, K.V. (1985b) Assunti construttivisti nelli teorie di G.A. Kelly e J. Piaget. In F. Mancini & A. Semerari (Eds) *La Psychologia dei Construtti Personali: Saggi Sulla Teoria di G.A. Kelly*. Milano: Franco Angeli Libri.

Manning, W. (2004) Constructing an Atlantic crossing for stuttering treatment. Paper given at the North Atlantic Personal Construct Network Conference, Memphis, USA.

March, P.L. & McPherson, A. (1996) The important attributes of a nurse from the perspective of qualified and student nurses. *Journal of Advanced Nursing*, **24**, 810–816.

Marris, P. (1974) *Loss and Change*. London: Routledge.

Mascolo, M.F., Craig-Bray, L. & Neimeyer, R.A. (1997) The construction of meaning and action in development and psychotherapy: an epigenetic systems approach. In G.J. Neimeyer & R.A. Neimeyer (Eds) *Advances in Personal Construct Psychology*, Volume 4. Greenwich, CN: JAI Press.

McCarthy, J., Minsky, M.L., Rochester, N. & Shannon, C.E. (1955) *A Proposal for the Dartmouth Summer Research Project on Artificial Intelligence*. Dartmouth College. *http://www-formal.stanford.edu/jmc/history/dartmouth/dartmouth.html*.

McCoy, M.M. (1977) A reconstruction of emotion. In D. Bannister (Ed.) *New Perspectives in Personal Construct Theory*. London: Academic Press.

McFayden, M. & Foulds, G.A. (1972) Comparison of provided and elicited grid content in the grid test of schizophrenic thought disorder. *British Journal of Psychiatry*, **121**, 53–57.

McNeill, I. (1991) The reality of doing business in Poland. *The Intelligent Enterprise*, **1**, 9–16.

McPherson, F.M., Blackburn, I.M., Draffan, J.W. & McFadyan, M. (1973) A further study of the Grid Test of Thought Disorder. *British Journal of Social and Clinical Psychology*, **12**, 420–427.

McWilliams, S.A. (2003) Belief, attachment and awareness. In F. Fransella (Ed.) *International Handbook of Personal Construct Psychology*. Chichester, UK: John Wiley & Sons.

Melrose, S. & Shapiro, B. (1999) Students' perceptions of their psychiatric mental health clinical nursing experience: a personal construct theory exploration. *Journal of Advanced Nursing*, **30**, 1451–1458.

Mendoza, O. (1985) The exchange grid. In N. Beail (Ed.) *Repertory Grid Technique and Personal Constructs: Applications in Clinical and Educational Settings*. London: Croom Helm.

Michie, D. (Ed.) (1979) *Expert Systems in the Micro Electronic Age*. Edinburgh: Edinburgh University Press.

Midgley, M. (2001) *Gaia: The Next Big Idea*. London: Demos.

Mindell, A. (1989) *The Year I: Global Process Work*. Harmondsworth: Penguin Books.

Mindell, A. (2000) *The Leader as Martial Artist: Techniques and Strategies for Resolving Conflict and Creating Community*. San Francisco: Harper.

Mintzberg, H. (1987) Crafting strategy. *Harvard Business Review*, **65**, 66–76.

Mintzberg, H. (1994) Re-thinking strategic planning. Part 1: pitfalls and fallacies. *Long Range Planning*, **27**, 12–22.

Mischel, W. (1980). George Kelly's appreciation of psychology: a personal tribute. In M.J. Mahoney (Ed.) *Psychotherapy Process: Current Issues and Future Directions*. New York: Plenum Press.

Mitsos, S.B. (1958) Representative elements in the role construct technique. *Journal of Consulting Psychology*, **22**, 311–313.

Moes, A.J. & Sewell, K.W. (1994) *Post Traumatic Stress Disorder: a symposium on constructivist findings of combat, disaster, and rape survivors. III. Repertory grid and rape trauma.* Presented at the 6th North American Conference on Personal Construct Psychology, Indianapolis, IN.

Morris, J.B. (1977) Appendix I. The prediction and measurement of change in a psychotherapy group using the repertory grid. In F. Fransella & D. Bannister (Eds) *A Manual for Repertory Grid Technique*. London: Academic Press.

Morrison, P. & Burnard, P. (1997) *Caring and Communicating*. Basingstoke & London: Macmillan.

Nagy, S. (1992) *Nurses' constructions of pain*. Paper presented at the 6th Australian Personal Construct Psychology Conference, Sydney.

Nash, D. (2005) Evaluating the anger programme. In P. Cummins (Ed.) *Working with Anger*. Chichester: John Wiley & Sons.

Neimeyer, G.J. (1993) *Constructivist Assessment: A Casebook*. Newbury Park, CA: Sage Publications.

Neimeyer, G.J. (2002) Towards reflexive scrutiny in repertory grid methodology. *Journal of Constructivist Psychology*, **15**, 89–94.

Neimeyer, G.J. & Hagans, C.L. (2002) More madness in our method? The effects of repertory grid variation on construct differentiation. *Journal of Constructivist Psychology*, **15**, 139–160.

Neimeyer, R.A. (1985a) Problems and prospects in personal construct theory. In D. Bannister (Ed.) *Issues and Approaches in Personal Construct Theory* (pp. 143–171). London: Academic Press.

Neimeyer, R.A. (1985b) Personal constructs in clinical practice. In P.C. Kendall (Ed.) *Advances in Cognitive Behavioral Research and Therapy*. San Diego, CA: Academic Press.

Neimeyer, R.A. (1985c) *The Development of Personal Construct Psychology*. Lincoln: University of Nebraska Press.

Neimeyer, R.A. (1988) Clinical guidelines for conducting Interpersonal Transaction groups. *International Journal of Personal Construct Psychology*, **1**, 181–190.

Neimeyer, R.A. (1993) Constructivist approaches to the measurement of meaning. In G.J. Neimeyer (Ed.) *Constructivist Assessment: A Casebook*. London: Sage Publications.

Neimeyer, R.A. (1994) The Threat Index and related methods. In R.A. Neimeyer (Ed.) *Death Anxiety Handbook*. New York: Taylor & Francis.

Neimeyer, R.A. (1995) Constructivist psychotherapies: features, foundations, and future directions. In R.A. Neimeyer & M.J. Mahoney (Eds) *Constructivism in Psychotherapy*. Washington, DC: American Psychological Association.

Neimeyer, R.A. (2000) Narrative disruptions in the construction of self. In R.A. Neimeyer & J.D. Raskin (Ed.) *Constructions of Disorder: Meaning Making Frameworks for Psychotherapy*. Washington, DC: American Psychological Association.

Neimeyer, R.A. (Ed.) (2001a) *Meaning Reconstruction and the Experience of Loss*. Washington, DC: American Psychological Association.

Neimeyer, R.A. (2001b) Reauthoring life narratives: grief therapy as meaning reconstruction. *Israel Journal of Psychiatry*, **38**, 171–183.

Neimeyer, R.A. (2002a) *Lessons of Loss: A Guide to Coping* (2nd edition). New York: Brunner-Routledge.

Neimeyer, R.A. (2002b) Deconstructing 9/11: a constructivist perspective. *The Humanistic Psychologist*, **30**, 293–305.

Neimeyer, R.A. (2005) Widowhood, grief and the quest for meaning: a narrative perspective on reliance. In D. Carr, R.M. Nesse, & C.B. Wortman (Eds) *Late Life Widowhood in the United States*. New York: Springer.

Neimeyer, R.A., Anderson, A. & Stockton, L. (2001) Snakes versus ladders: a validation of laddering as a technique as a measure of hierarchical structure. *Journal of Constructivist Psychology*, **14**, 85–106.

Neimeyer, R.A. & Arvay, M.J. (2004) Performing the self: therapeutic enactment and the narrative integration of traumatic loss. In H. Hermans & G. Dimaggio (Eds) *The Dialogical Self in Psychotherapy* (pp. 173–189). New York: Brunner-Routledge.

Neimeyer, R.A. & Bridges, S. (2003) Postmodern approaches to psychotherapy. In A. Gurman & S. Messer (Eds) *Essential Psychotherapies* (2nd edn) (pp. 272–316). New York: Guilford.

Neimeyer, R.A. & Chapman, K.M. (1980) Self/ideal discrepancy and fear of death: the test of an existential hypothesis. *Omega*, **11**, 233–240.

Neimeyer, R.A. & Dingemans, P. (1980) Death orientation in the suicide intervention worker. *Omega*, **11**, 15–23.

Neimeyer, R.A. & Epting, F.R. (1992) Measuring personal meanings of death: 20 years of research using the Threat Index. In R.A. Neimeyer & G.J. Neimeyer (Eds) *Advances in Personal Construct Psychology*. Volume 2. Greenwich, CT: JAI Press.

Neimeyer, R.A., Heath, A.E. & Strauss, J. (1985) Personal reconstruction during group cognitive therapy for depression. In F. Epting & A.W. Landfield (Eds) *Anticipating Personal Construct Psychology*. Lincoln, NE: University of Nebraska Press.

Neimeyer, R.A. & Jackson, T.T. (1997) George A. Kelly and the development of personal construct theory. In W. Bringmann, H. Lück, R. Miller & C. Early (Eds) *A Pictorial History of Psychology*. Carol Stream, IL: Quintessence.

Neimeyer, R.A., Keesee, N.J. & Fortner, B.V. (2000) Loss and meaning reconstruction: propositions and procedures. In R. Malkinson, S. Rubin & E. Wiztum (Eds) *Traumatic and Non-Traumatic Loss and Bereavement*. Madison, CT: Psychosocial Press.

Neimeyer, R.A. & Mahoney, M.J. (Eds) (1995) *Constructivism in Psychotherapy*. Washington, DC: American Psychological Association.

Neimeyer, R.A. & Neimeyer, G.J. (Eds) (1987) *Personal Construct Therapy Casebook*. New York: Springer.

Neimeyer, R.A. & Raskin, J.D. (Eds) (2000) *Constructions of Disorder: Meaning-Making Frameworks for Psychotherapy*. Washington, DC: American Psychological Association.

Neimeyer, R.A. & Stewart, A.E. (1996) Trauma, healing, and the narrative emplotment of loss. *Families in Society*, **77**, 360–375.

Neimeyer, R.A. & Stewart, A.E. (2000) Constructivist and narrative psychotherapies. In C.R. Snyder & R.E. Ingram (Eds) *Handbook of Psychological Change*. New York: John Wiley & Sons.

Neimeyer, R.A. & Tschudi, F. (2003) Community and coherence: Narrative contributions to a psychology of conflict and loss. In G. Fireman, T. McVay & O. Flanagan (Eds) *Narrative and Consciousness: Literature, Psychology, and the Brain*. New York: Oxford.

Nelson, M.H. (1993) Teachers' stories: an analysis of the themes. In C. Day, J. Calderhead & P.M. Denicolo (Eds) *Research on Teacher Thinking: Understanding Professional Development*. London: Falmer Press.

Nisbett, R.E. & Wilson, T.D. (1977) Telling more than we can know: verbal reports on mental processes. *Psychological Review*, **84**, 231–259.

Norris, H. & Makhlouf-Norris, F. (1976) The measurement of self identity. In P. Slater (Ed.) *The Measurement of Intrapersonal Space by Grid Technique*, Volume 1. *Explorations of Intrapersonal Space*. London: John Wiley & Sons.

Nussbaum, M. (1999) Women and equality: the capabilities approach. *International Labour Review*, **138**, 227–245.

Nuzzo, M.L. & Chiari, G. (2001) *The personal construction of cancer: A constructivist framework for exploring malignancies*. Paper read at the 7th International Congress on Personal Construct Psychology, Memphis, TN.

Osborne, R. & Gilbert, J. (1980) A technique for exploring students' views of the world. *Physics Education*, **15**, 376–379.

Parry, G. & Richardson, A. (1996) *NHS Psychotherapy Services in England: Review of Strategic Policy*. London: NHS Executive.

Peck, D. & Whitlow, D.D. (1975) *Approaches to Personality Theory*. London: Methuen.

Pekkola, D. & Cummins, P. (2005) Evaluating the anger program. In P. Cummins (Ed.) *Working with Anger*. Chichester, UK: John Wiley & Sons.

Polkinghorne, D.E. (1988) *Narrative Knowing and Human Sciences*. Albany, NY: State University of New York.

Pollock, L. (1986) An introduction to the use of repertory grid technique as a research method and clinical tool for psychiatric nurses. *Journal of Advanced Nursing*, **11**, 439–445.

Pope, M.L. & Denicolo, P.M. (1986) Intuitive theories—a researcher's dilemma: some methodological implications. *British Educational Research Journal*, **12**, 153–165.

Pope, M.L. & Denicolo, P.M. (2001) *Transformative Education: Personal Construct Approaches to Practice and Research*. London: Whurr Publications.

Pope, M.L. & Saka, R. (1997) The learning of English as a foreign language: a personal constructivist approach. In P.M. Denicolo & M.L. Pope (Eds) *Sharing Understanding and Practice*. Farnborough: EPCA Publications.

Procter, H.G. (1981) Family construct psychology: an approach to understanding and treating families. In S. Walrond-Skinner (Ed.) *Developments in Family Therapy*. London: Routledge.

Procter, H.G. (1985a) Repertory grids in family therapy and research. In N. Beail (Ed.) *Repertory Grid Technique and Personal Constructs: Applications in Clinical and Educational Settings*. Beckenham: Croom Helm.

Procter, H.G. (1985b) A construct approach to family therapy and systems intervention. In E. Button (Ed.) *Personal Construct Theory and Mental Health*. Beckenham: Croom Helm.

Procter, H.G. (1987) Change in the family construct system. In G.J. Neimeyer and R.A. Neimeyer (Eds) *Personal Construct Therapy Casebook*. New York: Springer.

Procter, H.G. (1996) The family construct system. In D. Kalekin-Fishman & B. Walker (Eds) *The Construction of Group Realities: Culture, Society and Personal Construct Psychology*. Malabar, FL: Krieger.

Procter, H.G. (2000) Autism and family therapy: a personal construct approach. In S. Powell (Ed.) *Helping Children with Autism to Learn*. London: David Fulton.

Procter, H.G. (2001) Personal construct psychology and autism. *Journal of Constructivist Psychology*, **14**, 107–126.

Procter, H.G. (2002) Constructs of individuals and relationships. *Context*, **59**, 11–12.

Procter, H.G. (2005) Techniques of personal construct family therapy. In D.A. Winter & L.L. Viney (Eds) *Personal Construct Psychotherapy: Advances in Theory, Practice and Research*. London: Whurr.

Procter, H.G. & Dallos, R. (2005) Making me angry—the constructions of anger. In P. Cummins (Ed.) *Working with Anger: A Constructivist Approach*. London: Whurr.

Raskin, J.D. & Epting, F.R. (1995) Constructivism and psychotherapy: transitive diagnosis as humanistic assessment. *Methods: A Journal for Human Science* (Annual Edition), pp. 3–27.

Raskin, N.J. & Rogers, C.R. (1989) Person-centered therapy. In R. Corsini & C. Wedding (Eds) *Current Psychotherapies* (4th edition). Ithaca, IL: F.E. Peacock.

Rattue, R. & Cornelius, N. (2002) The emotional labour of police work. *Soundings: Journal of Politics and Culture*, **20**, 190–201.

Ravenette, A.T. (1968) *Three methods of grid analysis*. Unpublished manuscript.

Ravenette, A.T. (1997) Open letter to the psychologists in training at Southampton University. In G. Daniel (Ed.) *Tom Ravenette: Personal Construct Theory and the Practice of an Educational Psychologist*. Farnborough: EPCA Publications.

Ravenette, A.T. (1999) *Personal Construct Theory in Educational Psychology: A Practitioner's View*. London: Whurr Publications.

Rawlinson, J. (1995) Some reflections on the use of repertory grid technique in studies of nurses and social workers. *Journal of Advanced Nursing*, **21**, 334–339.

Reed, N.B. (2000) *Personal construct psychology and knowledge management in organisations*. Unpublished dissertation, Centre for Personal Construct Psychology, UK.

Rogers, C.R. (1956) Intellectualized psychotherapy. *Contemporary Psychology*, **1**, 335–358.

Roth, A. & Fonagy, P. (1996) *What Works for Whom? A Critical Review of Psychotherapy Research*. New York: Guilford.

Ryle, A. & Lunghi, M. (1970) The dyad grid: a modification of repertory grid technique. *British Journal of Psychiatry*, **117**, 323–327.

Sadri, G. & Snyder, P.J. (1995) Methodological issues in assessing training effectiveness. *Journal of Managerial Psychology*, **10**, 30–32.

Salmon, P. (2003) A psychology for teachers. In F. Fransella (Ed.) *International Handbook of Personal Construct Psychology*. Chichester, UK: John Wiley & Sons.

Sanglin-Grant, S. & Schneider, R. (2000) *Moving On Up? Racial Equality and the Corporate Agenda*. London: Runnymede Trust.

Savage, D.J. (2000) Telling the story finding the plot. In J. Fisher & N. Cornelius (Eds) *Challenging the Boundaries: A PCP Perspective for the New Millennium*. Lostock Hall, UK: EPCA Publications.

Scheer, J. (2003) Cross-cultural construing. In F. Fransella (Ed.) *International Handbook of Personal Construct Psychology*. Chichester, UK: John Wiley & Sons.

Schein, E.H. (1985) *Organisational Culture and Leadership*. San Francisco: Jossey-Bass.

Schoeneich, F. & Klapp, B.F. (1998) Standardization of interelement distances in repertory grid technique and its consequences for psychological interpretation of self-identity plots: an empirical study. *Journal of Constructivist Psychology*, **11**, 49–58.

Sen, A. (1992) *Inequality Re-examined*. Cambridge, MA: Harvard University Press.

Sen, A. (1999) *Development as Freedom*. Oxford: Oxford University Press.

Sendan, F.C. (1995) *Patterns of development in EFL student teachers' personal theories: A constructivist approach*. Unpublished PhD thesis, University of Reading, UK.

Senge P., Kleiner, A., Roberts, C., Ross, R. & Smith, B. (1994) *The Fifth Discipline Fieldbook*. London: Nicholas Brealey.

Sewell, K.W. (1996) Constructional risk factors for a post-traumatic stress response following a mass murder. *Journal of Constructivist Psychology*, **9**, 97–107.

Sewell, K.W. (1997) Post-traumatic stress: towards a constructivist model of psychotherapy. In R.A. Neimeyer & G.J. Neimeyer (Eds) *Advances in Personal Construct Psychology*, Volume 4. Greenwich, CT: JAI Press.

Sewell, K.W., Baldwin, C.L. & Moes, A.J. (1998) The multiple self awareness group. *Journal of Constructivist Psychology*, **11**, 59–78.

Sewell, K.W. & Cromwell, R.L. (1990) *A personal constructs model of Post-Traumatic Stress Disorder*. Presented at the North American Personal Construct Psychology Conference, San Antonio, Texas.

Sewell, K.W., Cromwell, R.L., Farrell-Higgins, J., Palmer, R., Ohlde, C. & Patterson, T.W. (1996) Hierarchical elaboration in the conceptual structures of Vietnam combat veterans. *Journal of Constructivist Psychology*, **9**, 79–96.

Sewell, K.W. & Ovaert, L.B. (1997) Group treatment of posttraumatic stress in incarcerated adolescents: structural and narrative impacts on the permeability of self-construction. Paper presented at the 12th International Congress of Personal Construct Psychology, Seattle.

Sewell, K.W. & Williams, A.M. (2001) Construing stress: a constructivist therapeutic approach to posttraumatic stress reactions. In R.A. Neimeyer (Ed.) *Meaning Reconstruction and the Experience of Loss*. Washington, DC: American Psychological Association.

Sewell, K.W. & Williams, A.M. (2002) Broken narratives: trauma, metaconstructive gaps, and the audience of psychotherapy. *Journal of Constructivist Psychology*, **15**, 205–218.

Sharkins, B.S. (1993) Anger and gender: theory, research and implications. *Journal of Counselling and Development*, **71**, 386–389.

Shaw, M.L.G. (1980) *On Becoming a Personal Scientist: Interactive Computer Elicitation of Personal Models of The World*. London: Academic Press.

Shaw, M.L.G. & Gaines, B.R. (1981) Recent advances in the analysis of a repertory grid. *British Journal of Medical Psychology*, **54**, 307–318.

Shaw, M.L.G. & Gaines, B.R. (1983) A computer aid to knowledge engineering. In *Proceedings of British Computer Society Conference on Expert Systems*. Cambridge: British Computer Society.

Shaw, M.L. & McKnight, C. (1981) *Think Again*. Englewood Cliffs, NJ: Prentice-Hall.

Shaw, M.L. & Thomas, L.F. (1978) FOCUS on education: an interactive computer system for the development and analysis of repertory grids. *International Journal of Man–Machine Studies*, **10**, 139–173.

Sheehan, M.J. (1985) A personal construct study of depression. *British Journal of Medical Psychology*, **58**, 119–128.

Shortliffe, E.H. (1976) *Computer-Based Medical Consultations: MYCIN*. New York: Elsevier.

Simon, H.A. (1995) The information-processing theory of mind. *American Psychologist*, **50**, 507–508.

Skinner, B.F. (1948) *Walden Two*. New York: Macmillan.

Slater, P. (1964) *The Principal Components of a Repertory Grid*. London: Vincent Andrew.

Slater, P. (1976) *The Measurement of Intrapersonal Space by Grid Technique*, Volume 1. *Explorations of Intrapersonal Space*. London: John Wiley & Sons.

Slater, P. (1977) *The Measurement of Intrapersonal Space by Grid Technique*, Volume 2. *Dimensions of Intrapersonal Space*. London: John Wiley & Sons.

Soffer, J. (1993) Jean Piaget and George Kelly: towards a stronger constructivism. *International Journal of Personal Construct Psychology*, **6**, 59–77.

Soldz, S. & Soldz, E. (1989) A difficulty with the functionally independent construction measure of cognitive differentiation. *International Journal of Personal Construct Psychology*, **2**, 315–322.

Spielberger, C.D. (1999) STAXI 2; state-trait anger expression inventory; Psychological Assessment Resources, Odessa, Florida.

Steen, E. & Hauli, L. (2001) From pain to self awareness: a qualitative analysis of the significance of group participation for persons with chronic musculoskolotal pain. *Patient Education and Counseling*, **42**, 35–46.

Stewart, T. & Birdsall, M. (2001) A review of the contribution of personal construct psychology to stammering therapy. *Journal of Constructivist Psychology*, **14**, 215–226.

Strauss, B.M. & Kachele, H. (1998) The writing on the wall: comments on the current discussion about empirically validated treatments in Germany. *Psychotherapy Research*, **8**, 158–170.

Sulejewicz, A. (Ed.) (1994) MBA, czyli Jak Kształcić Menedżerów (The MBA, or How to Develop Managers). Warsaw: Fundusz Współpracy (The Cooperation Fund).

Thomas, D.A. & Ely, R.J. (1996) Making differences matter: a new paradigm for managing diversity. *Harvard Business Review*, 79–80.

Thomas, L.F. & Harri-Augstein, S. (1985) *Self Organised Learning: Foundations of a Conversational Science of Psychology*. London: Routledge & Kegan Paul.

Trewavas, A. (1999) How plants learn. *Proceedings of the National Academy of Science, U.S.A.*, **96**, 4216–4218.

Truneckova, D. & Viney, L.L. (1997) *Assessing the effectiveness of personal construct group work with problematic adolescents*. Paper presented at the 12th International Congress of Personal Construct Psychology, Seattle, WA, USA.

Truneckova, D. & Viney, L.L. (2001) *Can personal construct group work be an effective intervention with troubled adolescents?* Paper presented at the 14th International Congress of Personal Construct Psychology, Wollongong, Australia.

Truneckova, D. & Viney, L.L. (2005) Personal construct group work with troubled adolescents: unhelpful and helpful forces. In D.A. Winter & L.L. Viney (Eds) *Personal Construct Psychotherapy: Advances in Theory, Practice and Research*. London: Whurr.

Tschudi F. (1977) Loaded and honest questions: a construct theory view of symptoms and therapy. In D. Bannister (Ed.) *New Perspectives in Personal Construct Theory*. London: Academic Press.

Turing, A.M. (1950) Computing machinery and intelligence. *Mind*, **59**, 433–460. Unpublished B.A. (honours) thesis, Guelph: University of Guelph.

Vaihinger, H. (1924) *The Philosophy of 'as if': A System of the Theoretical, Practical and Religious Fictions of Mankind* (C.K. Ogden, Trans.). London: Routledge & Kegan Paul.

Vanderberg, R.J. & Self, R.M. (1993) Assessing newcomers' changing commitments to the organization during the first 6 months of work. *Journal of Applied Psychology*, **78**, 557–569.

Viney, L. (1983) *Images of Illness*. Malabar, FL: Krieger.

Viney, L.L. (1986) *The Development and Evaluation of Short Term Psychotherapy Programs for the Elderly: Report to the Australian Institute of Health*. Unpublished MS, University of Wollongong, Australia.

Viney, L.L. (1993) Listening to what my clients and I say: content analysis categories and scales. In G.J. Neimeyer (Ed.) *Constructivist Assessment: A Casebook*. London: Sage Publications.

Viney, L.L. (1994) Sequences of emotional distress expressed by clients and acknowledged by therapists: are they associated more with some therapists than others? *British Journal of Clinical Psychology*, **33**, 469–481.

Viney, L.L. (1998) Should we use personal construct therapy? A paradigm for outcomes evaluation. *Psychotherapy*, **35**, 366–380.

Viney, L.L., Benjamin, Y.N. & Preston, C. (1989) An evaluation of personal construct therapy for the elderly. *British Journal of Medical Psychology*, **62**, 35–41.

Viney, L.L., Clarke, A.M., Bunn, T.A. & Benjamin, Y.N. (1985a) Crisis intervention counseling: An evaluation of long-term and short-term effects. *Journal of Counseling Psychology*, **32**, 29–39.

Viney, L.L., Clarke, A.M., Bunn, T.A. & Benjamin, Y.N. (1985b) The effect of a hospital-based counseling service on the physical recovery of surgical and medical patients. *General Hospital Psychiatry*, **7**, 294–301.

Viney, L.L., Clarke, A.M., Bunn, T.A. & Teoh, H.Y. (1985c) Crisis intervention counseling in a general hospital: development and multi-faceted evaluation of a health service. *Australian Studies in Health Care Administration*, **5**.

Viney, L.L., Clarke, A.M., Bunn, T.A. & Benjamin, Y.N. (1985d) An evaluation of three crisis intervention programs for general hospital patients. *British Journal of Medical Psychology*, **58**, 75–86.

Viney, L.L. & Henry, R.M. (2002) Evaluating personal construct dynamic group work with adolescent offenders and nonoffenders. In R.A. Neimeyer & G.J. Neimeyer (Eds) *Advances in Personal Construct Psychology: New Directions and Perspectives*. Westport, CT: Praeger.

Viney, L.L., Metcalfe, C. & Winter, D.A. (2005) The effectiveness of personal construct psychotherapy: a systematic review and meta-analysis. In D.A. Winter & L.L. Viney (Eds) *Personal Construct Psychotherapy: Advances in Theory, Practice and Research*. London: Whurr.

Viney, L.L., Rudd, M.G., Grenyer, B.F.S. & Tych, A.M. (1995b) *Content Analysis Scales of Psychosocial Maturity (CASPM) Scoring Manual*. Wollongong: University of Wollongong.

Viney, L.L., Truneckova, D., Weekes, P. & Oades, L. (1997) Personal construct group work with school-based adolescents: reduction of risk-taking. *Journal of Constructivist Psychology*, **10**, 167–186.

Viney, L.L., Walker, B. & Crooks, L. (1995a) Anxiety in community-based AIDS caregivers before and after counseling. *Journal of Clinical Psychology*, **51**, 274–279.

von Wright, G.H. (1966) The paradoxes of confirmation. In J. Hintikaa & P. Suppes (Eds) *Aspects of Inductive Logic*. Amsterdam: North Holland.

Walker, B.M. (1992) Values and Kelly's theory: becoming a good scientist. *International Journal of Personal Construct Psychology*, **5**, 257–266.

Walker, B.M. (1993) Looking for a 'whole Mama': personal construct theory and dependency. In L.M. Leitner & N.G.M. Dunnett (Eds) *Critical Issues in Personal Construct Therapy*. Malabar, FL: Krieger.

Walker, B.M. (1997) Shaking the kaleidoscope: dispersion of dependency and its relationships. In G. Neimeyer & R.A. Neimeyer (Eds) *Advances in Personal Construct Psychology*, Volume 4. Greenwich, CN: JAI Press.

Walker, B.M. (2002) Nonvalidation vs. (in)validation: implications for theory and practice. In J.D. Raskin & S.K. Bridges (Eds) *Studies in Meaning: Exploring Constructivist Psychology*. New York: Pace University.

Walker, B.M., Oades, L.G., Caputi, P., Stevens, C.D. & Crittenden, N. (2000) Going beyond the scientist metaphor: from validation to experience cycles. In J.W. Scheer (Ed.) *The Person in Society: Challenges to a Constructivist Theory*. Giessen, Germany: Psychosozial-Verlag.

Walker, B.M., Ramsay, F.L. & Bell, R.C. (1988) Dispersed and undispersed dependency. *International Journal of Personal Construct Psychology*, **1**, 63–80.

Warren, B. (1990) Psychoanalysis and personal construct theory: an exploration. *Journal of Psychology*, **124**, 449–464.

Warren, B. (2003) Pragmatism and religion: Dewey's twin influences? In F. Fransella (Ed.) *International Handbook of Personal Construct Psychology*. Chichester, UK: John Wiley & Sons.

Watkinson, J. (2001) *Painting by numbers*. Abstracts of the 14th International Personal Construct Psychology Conference. *Australian Journal of Psychology*, **53**, *2001 Supplement: Combined Abstracts of 2001 Australian Patterns, Conferences*, W. Noble (Ed.), p. 107.

Watson, S. & Winter, D.A. (2005) A process and outcome study of personal construct, cognitive and psychodynamic therapies in a National Health Service setting. In D.A. Winter & L.L. Viney (Eds) *Personal Construct Psychotherapy: Advances in Theory, Practice and Research*. London: Whurr.

Watts, M. (1988) *Shared Learning*. London: Scutari Press.

Watts, M. & Vaz, A. (1997) Freire meets Vaz: using constructs to generate themes in education. In P.M. Denicolo & M.L. Pope (Eds) *Sharing, Understanding and Practice*. Farnborough: EPCA Publications.

Watzlawick, P., Beavin, J. & Jackson, D. (1967) *The Pragmatics of Human Communication: A Study of Interactional Patterns, Pathologies and Paradoxes*. New York: Norton.

Weihs, K.D. (2004) George Kelly at Friends University: the Quaker Influence on Personal Construct Psychology. MA thesis, State University of New York at New Paltz.

Wertheim, E.H., Weiss, K.R. & Coish, B.J. (1988) Evaluation of a structured group therapy program for bulimics. In S. Abraham & D. Llewellyn-Jones (Eds) *Eating Disorders and Disordered Eating*. Melbourne: Astor.

Westwood, M.J., Black, T.G. & McLean, H.B. (2002) A re-entry program for peacekeeping soldiers. *Canadian Journal of Counselling*, **36**, 221–232.

White, A. (1996) A theoretical framework created from a repertory grid analysis of graduate nurses in relation to the feelings they experience in clinical practice. *Journal of Advanced Nursing*, **24**, 144–150.

White, M. & Epston, D. (1990) *Narrative Means to Therapeutic Ends*. New York: Norton.

Williams, E. (1971) The effect of varying the elements in the Bannister–Fransella grid test of schizophrenic thought disorder. *British Journal of Psychiatry*, **119**, 207–212.

Wilson, J. & Retsas, A. (1997) Personal constructs of nursing practice: a comparative analysis of three groups of Australian nurses. *International Journal of Nursing Studies*, **34**, 63–71.

Winslade, J. & Smith, L. (1997) Countering alcoholic narratives. In G. Monk, J. Winslade, J. Crockett & E. Epston (Eds) *Narrative Therapy in Practice*. San Francisco: Jossey-Bass.

Winter, D.A. (1992) *Personal Construct Psychology in Clinical Practice: Theory, Research and Applications*. London: Routledge.

Winter, D. (1997) Personal construct theory perspectives on group psychotherapy. In P. Denicolo & M. Pope (Eds) *Sharing Understanding and Practice*. Farnborough: EPCA Publications.

Winter, D. (2000) Can personal construct theory succeed in competition with other therapies? In J.W. Scheer (Ed.) *The Person in Society: Challenges to a Constructivist Theory*. Giessen, Germany: Psychosozial-Verlag.

Winter, D.A. (2003) Psychological disorder as imbalance. In F. Fransella (Ed.) *International Handbook of Personal Construct Psychology*. Chichester, UK: John Wiley & Sons.

Winter, D., Bhandari, S., Metcalfe, C., Riley, T., Sireling, L., Watson, S. & Lutwyche, G. (2000) Deliberate and undeliberated self-harm: theoretical basis and evaluation of a personal construct psychotherapy intervention. In J.W. Scheer (Ed.) *The Person in Society: Challenges to a Constructivist Theory*. Giessen, Germany: Psychosozial-Verlag.

Winter, D., Gournay, K. & Metcalfe, C. (1999) An investigation of the effectiveness of a personal construct psychotherapy intervention. In J.M. Fisher & D.J. Savage (Eds) *Beyond Experimentation into Meaning*. Farnborough: EPCA Publications.

Winter, D.A., Gournay, K., Metcalfe, C. & Rossotti, N. (2005) Expanding agoraphobics' horizons: an investigation of the effectiveness of a personal construct psychotherapy intervention. *Journal of Constructivist Psychology* (in press).

Winter, D., Tschudi, F. & Gilbert, N. (2001) *Psychotherapists' theoretical orientations as elaborative choices: a study of personal styles, epistemological preferences, and construing*. Paper presented at the 14th International Congress of Personal Construct Psychology, Wollongong, Australia.

Winter, D.A. & Watson, S. (1999) Personal construct psychotherapy and the cognitive therapies: different in theory but can they be differentiated in practice? *Journal of Constructivist Psychology*, **12**, 1–22.

Winter, D.A., Watson, S., Gillman-Smith, I., Gilbert, N. & Acton, T. (2003) Border crossing: a personal construct therapy approach for clients with a diagnosis of borderline personality disorder. In G. Chiari & M.L. Nuzzo (Eds) *Psychological Constructivism and the Social World*. Milan: FrancoAngeli.

Wittgenstein, L. (1953) *Philosophical Investigations*. Oxford: Blackwell.

Wright, P. (1974) *The Language of British Industry*. London: Macmillan.

Young, E. (1989) On the naming of the rose: interests and multiple meanings as elements of organizational culture. *Organization Studies*, **10**, 187–206.

Index

CPSIA information can be obtained at www.ICGtesting.com
Printed in the USA
LVOW050332161111

255129LV00003B/4/P

9 780470 013236